Incredible Era

THE LIFE AND TIMES OF
WARREN GAMALIEL HARDING

by SAMUEL HOPKINS ADAMS

Capricorn Books   New York

CAPRICORN BOOKS EDITION 1964

SECOND IMPRESSION

Printed in the United States of America

★

Preface

Around no other President of the United States has there been cast such a smoke screen of obscuration as that which beclouds the personality of Warren G. Harding. This is largely defensive. Before posthumous scandal had touched him, his widow collected and burned the great bulk of his correspondence. What little remains, outside of scattered specimens, is segregated in the archives of the Harding Memorial Association which has denied access to it, alike to general reading and to individual research. How far efforts at concealment have been carried in the past may be judged by the fact that one published book on the subject of Harding was secretly suppressed by Government authorities, acting without any warrant of legality.

Because of the scarcity of original and authoritative documents, it has been necessary to rely upon hearsay — that is, word-of-mouth testimony — for some important phases of the Harding record. In many cases this has been obtained under pledge of secrecy as to the source. Particularly is this true of the long-perpetuated, though factually unauthenticated, rumor of mixed blood in the Harding line. Gossip is not, *per se*, history. But gossip, however lacking in proof, which affects the life and inferentially the character and acts of an individual, becomes an integral part of his biography, material which a biographer cannot overlook.

Formal biographies of Harding are so exclusively eulogistic as to be negligible. They are frankly and honestly 'glory-stories,' written either by personal friends or for political effect. In the matter of direct testimony, which figures so largely in this book, I have included, with such differentiation as seemed appropriate, witnesses whose comparable reputation for veracity ranges all the way from George Washington to Ananias. Accuracy of quotation I can guarantee, but not reliability of the testator. The reader is cautioned to weigh the evidence with due regard to source.

Much of the hitherto unpublished matter has been given to me by newspapermen. If they, as a class, appear to have been called to the witness stand with disproportionate frequency, the fact represents my considered judgment that, on the whole, their evidence is the most dependable. Politicians, as witnesses, are liable to personal or partisan bias. Writers of autobiographies, in so far as they are the chief factors in the action which they portray, palliate, embellish, or conceal. The reporter has nothing to conceal, and to embellish fact is a violation of his code. Furthermore, the expert political commentator is a highly qualified specialist. The history which he turns out from day to day suffers from necessary haste. The history which forms the running scroll of his professional experience is, in my opinion, as free from error as any medium.

So many of my informants prefer to remain anonymous that it would be invidious to acknowledge individually my wide obligation for assistance. To one contributor, however, I must record a special debt. Doctor H. F. Alderfer, of Pennsylvania State College, has spent five years of research on Harding and his contemporaries. Not only have I made extensive use of his thesis, *The Personality and Politics of Warren G. Harding*, but through his courtesy I have had access to his notes and the benefit of his investigations and of his advice. Historians and research workers, interested in the Harding period, will find the Alderfer thesis invaluable. It is available in the Syracuse University Library, Syracuse, New York, and in the New York City Public Library.

WIDE WATERS
AUBURN, N.Y., *Sept.* 8, 1939

⋆

Contents

Contents

I. Genesis of a Journalist

THREE young men sat in Reilly's Beefsteak Palace on Main Street, discussing their unpromising outlook. The year was 1884; the place, Marion, Ohio. The young men's names were Sickel, Warwick, and Harding. All were temporarily jobless.

The youngest of the trio, a stalwart lad with an engaging smile, was trying to argue the others into buying a bankrupt local daily. There was money in a paper properly handled, he insisted. The town was growing. It was the best little town in Ohio and he guessed that made it the best little town in the United States if not in the world. Look at the new enterprises starting up! Where was there any richer farmland than Marion County, any farmers with more money to spend or readier to spend it? Hadn't they heard that the railroad was putting on a couple of new trains? Why, by next summer, the way things were moving there would be five thousand up-and-coming, full-blooded American hustlers in Marion. Nothing could stop it. And an enterprising daily was bound to grow with the growing population.

Sickel, the moneyed man by virtue of a recent legacy of a few hundred dollars, knew nothing of newspapers. Warwick had been a casual reporter on local sheets. Harding was the enthusiast. He had played around with type since, when a boy of six, he had the run of a country weekly of which his father had become half owner. He could, he assured his companions, rustle news, solicit ads, stick type, make up forms, put the paper to bed, and wash up rollers. Also he professed his competency as reporter, editor, business and advertising manager, and staff of a job-printing outfit on the side.

The bankrupt *Star* could be released from the sheriff's hands for three hundred dollars and the assumption of the mortgage. It was a sure thing; couldn't miss. He discoursed upon the prospect with a voluble optimism; he was striving to talk himself into a desperately needed job.

Sickel and Warwick listened amiably. They were used to the younger man's fervor and liked it. As for backing it with real money, that was another matter. Better wait until after election, anyway. Compelled to be content with this, Harding left to attend a Blaine and Logan Republican Club rally. He was an ardent devotee of the Plumed Knight.

Discussing the project, the other two were favorably inclined. They knew that Harding was popular. They knew, too, that he was capable of leadership, and that he had some knack of management. He played substitute first base on the local ball nine with some success and handled its finances with more. But his really brilliant achievement was the Citizens' Cornet Band. Warwick, himself a virtuoso on the big brass, knew all about that.

Inheriting a musical ear from his father who had been a short-term fifer in the Civil War, young Warren had turned to brass, and after dallying with the trombone and the bass, settled down to the alto horn. Melodic aptitude, combined with a natural *esprit de corps*, pushed him rapidly forward in the local organization. He became manager, in which capacity he ran the band deep into debt by purchasing a full outfit of snappy uniforms on credit, with a view to entering some of the musical competitions then so popular at county fairs.

Small towns of the eighties were full of musical talent. Any competent performer, no matter what his status, from priest to barkeep, was welcome if he would faithfully attend rehearsals. A song of the era runs:

> Our butcher played the big bass drum,
> And Father used to say
> The tuba was a sporting man,
> But, Lordy! he could play.

They made stirring music, the pick of those last-century bandsters, now, alas! extinct. Finesse was not their forte; the *nuances* of expression were not for them. But they played with a virile blare and bang, and their rhythm was something to quicken the torpid blood.

The Marion aggregation must have been good. Wearing the new and unpaid-for uniforms, it entered the State Band Festival at Findlay. Heavy competition was there from Cleveland, Cincinnati, Columbus, Dayton, Toledo, and smaller places. Beside their splendor of scarlet-and-gold, blue-and-silver, the modest trappings of the Marionites paled. Discouraged but determined, they blew and thumped their bravest, with a complimentary response from the crowds. So hopeless were they of a place that they dispersed before the awards were announced. Third prize to the Citizens' Cornet Band of Marion! [1]

Two hundred dollars. Enough to pay off the debt and leave a balance in the bank. Young Warren Harding came back to Marion, a hero for a day. A sad sequel awaited him. Scandal spattered the knightly plumes of his idol, James G. Blaine, and the bandsman must play a melancholy but conscientious alto at the Democratic jubilee over the victory of Grover Cleveland.

The record commended Harding to Warwick and Sickel as a prospective success. On the professional side, however, experience hardly justified the young man's pretensions. Besides his very juvenile career as a printer's devil, he had for a

[1] Willis Fletcher Johnson: *The Life of Warren G. Harding.*

brief period been reporter and utility man on Colonel James
H. Vaughn's local Democratic weekly; this was the sum-total
of his claim to being an all-round newspaperman. It looked
like a good deal of a gamble. But they were sports. They
held another powwow and told the young promoter that they
would come in if he could furnish his share of the cash.

But could he? He had been making pocket money — no
more — out of his percentage of the band earnings, and these,
with winter approaching, would decrease to the vanishing
point. He applied to his former employer. For some obscure
reason, perhaps a saturnine sense of humor, Vaughn loaned
him the cash to set up a rival publication.

On November 26, 1884, an announcement with a touch of
defiance appeared at the masthead of the reissued daily.[1]

WE HAVE PURCHASED THE STAR
AND WE WILL STAY
The Star Publishing Company

Life was beginning at nineteen for Warren Gamaliel
Harding. He had found his appointed place.

2

Little was known of the Hardings when they arrived in
Marion. They took an old house in a shabby locality. The
father, Doctor George Tryon Harding, practiced homoeopathy
on a small and unprofitable scale. The mother was more successful in her humbler calling of midwife. There were eight
children, three of whom were girls. Warren was the eldest.

Older people from the farm country around Blooming
Grove and Caledonia, whence the family came, remembered
more or less explicitly some sort of social detriment attaching

[1] Joe Mitchell Chapple: *The Life and Times of Our After-War President.*

to the Hardings. Phoebe Dickerson's people, rural brick-layers and carpenters, had protested angrily when she insisted on marrying young George, home from the wars and become a casual farmer with a bent for veterinary work. From animals his interest expanded to humans; he 'read and rode' with a country physician, which means that he had access to a few medical books and was privileged to drive Doctor McCune on his wide rounds, hold his instruments while he operated, and listen to him prescribe. This was a typical medical education of the day. He concluded it with a few terms at the Cleveland Homoeopathic College, where he got his diploma in 1873. Warren was eight years old when the father came back home.

Hoss-tradin' was Doctor Harding's relaxation. Any and every sort of exchange is included in this elastic term. He swapped himself into a half-ownership of the *Caledonia Argus*, a somewhat hypothetical weekly, which appeared when it had the funds. Here the boy received the inoculation of printer's ink which was to remain insistent in his blood all his life.

The record of Warren's early years is singularly sterile. There are no letters, no documents, no diaries, few family ana. His own reminiscences of his childhood are scanty, one might almost say grudging. If Heaven lay about him in his infancy, he appears to have preserved few and not specially felicitous memories of the celestial environment. In no wise does his boyhood pattern conform to the accepted blueprint for success. He manifested neither industry nor ambition. When a corn-husking job was offered at the special rate of four bits a day — well above the regular pay for a boy, because his family were in need of the money [1] — he quit in the first hour. He hated chores, but would consider odd jobs if the money was good and the labor light. Because his gentle and pious mother had hopes of his becoming a preacher, he was sent, when fourteen, to near-by Iberia and entered in an

[1] Affidavit of Montgomery Lindsay, the employing farmer.

institution which overrated its academic status in terming itself the Ohio Central College. It has long since passed from existence, leaving no traceable record of distinction other than that of having been the alma mater of a President.

There he edited the school annual, practiced on the alto horn, and dabbled in school oratory. 'Glib, but not always easy to understand,' is the opinion of a perspicuous and prophetic schoolmate. Another acquaintance of those days recalls that he was interested in political personages and could rattle off the names of governors, congressmen, and other high officials.

For lack of any special bent, he naturally took up school-teaching on graduation. Thirty dollars a month was good pay, with room and board at four dollars a week and other necessaries in proportion. But the young alumnus could not stand the strain. 'It was the hardest job I ever had,' he says in painful retrospect. One term was the limit of his endurance.

The uneasy fortunes of the family having led them to Marion, the ex-pedagogue followed, and tried reading law. He had no aptitude for Blackstone. But he had to do something. Being supported by his hard-pressed parents was both a distasteful and an exiguous way of life. There must be, in a town like Marion, other expedients for a young fellow who had a knack of getting along with people. He surveyed the field.

Bond-selling had not yet developed into a major industry for the otherwise unemployed. Its predecessor was insurance. No special training was required. The regimen was not arduous. He could circulate among the folks, which was much to his liking. It was worth a trial.

At the outset he enjoyed a smile of fortune. His bid on a new $30,000 hotel, testimony to Marion's growth, prevailed. But fortune's smile was a trick, a come-on, a cruel joke.

For there had been error in the rate quoted, and though the fault was not his, he was mulcted of his commissions of $110, more money than he had ever before seen at one time. Insurance, he clearly perceived, was not his predestined calling. He resigned.[1]

There remained the newspaper business. His boyhood chores as devil of the *Caledonia Argus* qualified him, in his own mind, for the vacant job on the *Mirror*. Again his tenure was short. As to why, there are two versions. His employer says that the tyro spent too much time at Republican headquarters in unproductive political talk. The reporter claimed that loyalty to a Blaine and Logan campaign hat which he had bought with his first earnings caused his ouster. There were no hard feelings on either side. Once more he was jobless and nearly penniless.

So handicapped, his venture into ownership of a paper might seem the height of temerity. Sound instinct inspired it. If he was anything — and this still remained to be proven — he was a newspaperman. That was his bent, his destiny. He was always happy and mostly successful when he followed it. The gravest error of his life was quitting the editorial sanctum for the White House.

Legends always cluster about a President's youth. The usual efflorescence of them is to be found in the affectionate biographies compiled by his admirers. In so far as they deal with the subject's juvenile years, they are of doubtful authenticity and almost total insignificance. One episode, however, derives from an unimpeachable source, Warren G. Harding himself. He recounted it, half-humorously, half-ruefully deprecating his own easy-going acquiescences, in an off-the-record talk at a National Press Club dinner. His father said to him one day:

'Warren, it's a good thing you wasn't born a gal.'

'Why?' asked the youth.

[1] Joe Mitchell Chapple: *The Life and Times of Our After-War President.*

'Because you'd be in the family way all the time,' returned the blunt-spoken doctor. 'You can't say No.' [1]

In his maturing days, young Warren was a cheerful and attractive personality. Tall, well-proportioned, a little slouchy in posture, a little slack of muscle, he was, despite the handlebar moustache of the period, a strikingly handsome specimen, with his large, liquid, friendly eyes, expansive forehead, fine, straight nose between rather prominent cheekbones, pleasantly moulded chin, and a mouth prone to smile. The countenance was the index to his character. He wanted to be everybody's friend.

He was the type of small-town playboy. He liked to shoot pool and he loved the poker table, at which he was formidable. He would lay a small bet on anything. He was just expert enough to hold down first base on the local nine. His speech was the heedless jargon of his youth and his kind; there came instinctively to his lips those four-letter words which our modern novelists strive so conscientiously to popularize, though they had not yet attained the dignity of print. When he wanted a drink, he took it, but was no 'lush.' Without religious principles or romantic attachments to deter him — he seems not to have 'gone with' any special girl — he pursued the casual lecheries of the unattached. Loose he certainly was, by strict standards; he was not vicious or dissolute.

His associations were not of the highest. Lines were drawn with some severity in Marion. Socially the Harding family might be classed as nondescript. They did not, in the prim phrase of the period, 'mingle with the best people.' Warren probably thought little or nothing about social status.

Natural simplicity and freedom from self-consciousness would preserve him from any burdensome consideration of exclusion, although there is one instance of his feeling hurt

[1] Harding's off-the-record speech at a National Press Club banquet in Washington, 1922.

at being left out of a broadly inclusive wedding list. His club was the skating rink, his social center, the drugstore. He was just one of the town boys.

3

A local commentator describes the *Star*, at the time of its transfer, as 'wholly destitute of either circulation or reputation.' Two competitors were already in the field, the Democratic *Mirror* and George Crawford's *Independent*, organ of the locally dominant Republicans. Both were weeklies. There was no more demand in Marion for a daily than there was for a Mahometan mosque. The *Star's* survival is a minor miracle.

It was an evening paper; the subscription price, ten cents a week. Conditions in the plant were desperate. Repairs were needed on the press. The type was old and battered. Supplies were low. Interest on the mortgage must be paid. Combined, the bank credits of the partners summed up to zero. Print-paper, that prime essential of publication, could be had only for cash. The early issues testify eloquently to these difficulties. They are a melancholy product.

Nevertheless, the *Star* was on the street, a four-page daily, made up of local items, exchanges, and a thin spatter of advertisements.[1] Having had a little newspaper experience, Warwick acted as general newsman. Harding helped him, and lent a hand in the pressroom where two printers had been hired, mainly on faith and promises. On the side, he hustled for advertising, tried to boost circulation, and performed the duties of purchasing agent when there was any money in the till.

Politically the paper announced itself as independent. That, in itself, seems enough to have doomed it in an environment which took its politics as passionately as Ohio.

[1] Scattering copies of early issues are preserved in the *Star* office.

But the young editor knew what he was doing. His policy was to make friends in both parties and enemies in neither.

Sickel played small part in the operations. His money was in the venture but not his heart. He soon dropped out, by what composition does not appear, though he may have accepted notes from his associates in lieu of the cash which they did not possess. Warwick stayed for several years, but finally left, after a difference of opinion over that new-fangled jimcrack, a telephone. Always the experimentalist, Harding pointed out that it would not only facilitate the gathering of news, but would also impress advertisers. To Warwick's conservative objection that the budget could not stand it, he retorted that here was one accessory that could be had on credit. As neither would give in, Warwick left.

Harding was now the whole editorial and business staff. However others might falter, he was there to carry out the masthead boast, 'AND WE WILL STAY.' Hiring extra help for the pressroom, he continued to bring forth his thin little issue, scant of news and starved for advertising. When down to his last dollar, he could always go for a loan to his mother, who kept a little private hoard. In the office poker game on payday, after the paper had been put to bed, he would frequently win back a fair proportion of what he had dispensed in wages.

From the outset he was scheming for a slice of official cake. To get it, he started a weekly edition. This was the corollary to his 'independent' daily. County-seat newspapers were nourished largely on paid official matter. There were county, township, and town advertising; election notices, tax delinquencies, calls for contract bids, and the like. Though Marion was Republican, the county was reliably Democratic. Ohio's established practice was to distribute this patronage between the leading — or the favored — mediums representing each major party. Professing independence, the daily issue was out of the running for these juicy plums. But this would not apply to an avowedly party weekly. The goodwill, which the youthful editor had been building up by judicious flattery of the party leaders on both sides, was due to show returns. The *Marion Weekly Star* proclaimed itself Republican to the backbone, and, as such, boldly bid for a share of the hand-outs. The *Mirror* observed this maneuver without alarm. As sole Democratic mouthpiece, it was assured of its cut. Not so with the *Independent*. Violently partisan in the universal fashion, Crawford had inevitably stirred up hard feelings among the Democratic politicians who controlled the county purse-strings, a hostility which the insinuating editor of the *Star* proceeded to capitalize. The *Independent* impeached his party loyalty. 'Republican for revenue only,' it raged. Accusations of trickery, treachery, and venality bristled in its pages.

It is undeniable that the intrusive weekly's Republicanism was a one-way partisanship. It supported the Republicans while tactfully refraining from denunciation of the Democrats, a policy of appeasement impracticable for its rival. If not treason, this was at least heresy. But it worked. By such soft impeachments, the *Star* commended itself to the friendly enemy and began to cut in on its rival's emoluments. The procedure displays Harding as already a capable strategist for a legitimate political profit.

War was declared. Ohio journalism of the eighties did not deal exclusively in sweetness and light. Expressions of editorial opinion were bound by no limitations other than those of the dictionary. Between rival publishers the law of libel was a dead letter. A product of his day and calling, Editor Harding, once started, could sling as strong a mixture of ink and mud as the next man. The initial charge that he was a 'Republican for revenue only' he could afford to ignore. That was light political persiflage. But the *Independent* was just getting under way. It began to call names under the guise of political controversy. In retaliation Editor Harding rolled up his sleeves and gave a sample of what he could do along those lines.

> This Crawford, who works the temperance and pious racket for church support while his inebriate associate caters to saloon patronage ... foams at the mouth whenever his sordid mind grasps anything done without his counsel; he rolls his eyes and straight evolves from his inner consciousness a double-twisted, unadulterated, canvas-back lie that would make the devil blush. His sordid soul is gangrened with jealousy. This sour, disgruntled, and disappointed old ass gets frenzied at the prospect of a successful rival and must vent the feelings of his miserable soul by lying about those he cannot browbeat or cajole. ... His acquaintance is tottering him; [*sic*] he only remains an imbecile whose fits will make him a paralytic, then his way of spitting venom will end.[1]

(One of Harding's admiring biographers, S. E. Cuneo, thus compliments him upon his editorial principles: 'One of these, which he early adopted and from which he never deviated, was that of a never-failing courtesy to his competitors. No unkind, unseemly reference to his contemporary publishers ever appeared in his columns.')

Thereafter epithets hurtled through the once placid air of Marion. 'Sneaking whelp,' 'low-down pup,' 'lying thief,' 'low hound,' were countered by 'skunk,' 'dirty subject,' 'Mephetis Americana' [*sic*], 'filthy mess,' and 'lying dog.'

(Harding's father, in proud reminiscence of those days, says: 'You can read the *Marion Star* for the thirty-odd years that Warren has owned it, without finding a vilification of anybody in any issue.')

An out-of-town contemporary printed a reflection upon General Grant, and the editor of the *Star* turned the vials of wrath upon him as 'a cowardly, sneaking copperhead in Van Wert County.'

[1] *Marion Star*, April 7, 1886.

Genesis of a Journalist

('He never descended to personalities,' says his biographer, Willis Fletcher Johnson.)

Between the three Marion papers amenities continued for years, in fact, until Crawford and his *Independent* were driven from the field.[1] Here is his matured and considered purview of the *Star*, which may be considered as expert opinion with due allowance for bias:

> That odorous sheet is filled with accounts of every family quarrel its editor can get hold of. Every scandal is aired with particularity. Gossip of the meanest kind finds a place in its columns. The sanctity of the Sabbath is sneered at and the religious sentiment of the country is defied and scorned in its nasty columns. And yet people will read the dirty bantling and allow their children to read it, and when their children go to the bad, they whine and cry over the natural result of allowing their children to read moral filth.[2]

The animus is patent: 'the dirty bantling' was cutting into Brother Crawford's circulation as well as threatening his advertising revenue. Also, there is a clear intimation that the Harding publication tended to the 'yellow' side. Later the *Independent* waxed superior and dignified.

> We do not care to bandy filthy, lying epithets with the moral leper who edits the *Star*. His heart, mind, blood, and flesh form a mass of corruption.... Some of the best men in the city have been assailed by him in the coarsest and most brutal manner. When called to account personally, he whines about his illness as if that were the fault of others. In politics he shows the real 'yaller dog' that he is unless he can have his own way.[3]

Harding retorted with a blast in which 'lickspittle organ,' 'parasite,' 'flopper,' and 'protozone' [*sic!*] shone with verbal luster.

(At the same time he was holding up his *Star* as a model

[1] In 1896.
[2] *Marion Independent*, September 1, 1893.
[3] *Marion Independent*, October 12, 1894.

of what he termed 'inoffensivism.' And long after, he was to gaze sentimentally back upon that period with the kindly haze of memory softening the harsh asperities of fact, and declare: 'I have never once allowed my paper to make manifest a suggestion of revenge in my own heart, and if there is one thing that contributed most to my modest success as a publisher, it is because the paper was always on a higher plane than getting even.')

Reprisals more forceful than those of type were a natural consequence of this type of journalism. Harding once threatened to 'mop up the street' with Crawford.[1] Some person or persons unidentified did mop up the *Star* office, as the *Mirror* thus chronicles:

> The little unpleasantness in the *Star* sanctuary yesterday with its incidental thumps, broken chairs, cuts, bruises, and bloody noses ought to have been avoided. It was the result of offensive personalities indulged in by the *Star* that might well have been omitted. That kind of newspaper work don't pay. It lowers the standard of journalism, and besides, it's unsafe.[2]

As a rule Vaughn was mildly patronizing toward the young man whom he had helped to start in journalism. He thus attempts to allay with some cold drops of modesty the skipping spirit of his youthful competitor.

> Brother Harding is a nice young man and we like him — and he is smart, too — but he is not consistent. Yes, we like him — and he is smart, too — most too smart. He talks so much about 'newspaper ethics' and makes such nice distinctions between 'journalists' and 'newspapermen' that we are bewildered at times — but, as we said before we like him — we do for a fact. All he needs is to tone down the estimate he puts on himself. Not too much, of course, because he is a smart young man and his abilities should not be underestimated, even by himself.[3]

[1] Thomas H. Russell: *The Illustrious Life and Work of Warren G. Harding.*
[2] *Marion Mirror*, October 10, 1894.
[3] *Marion Mirror*, October 17, 1894.

But Vaughn could hit below the belt, too. He printed a vicious little paragraph with a reference to 'the woolly head of Doctor George T. Harding,' a sneer not to be misinterpreted in a locality where there was so much rumor as to the Harding lineage. The report still persists in Marion that the physician, accompanied by his son and a shot-gun, visited the *Mirror* office and demanded a retraction, which was contemptuously refused. Lacking the wisdom to ignore the taunt, Harding printed a rather silly retort:

> The *Mirror* grows amusing on the subject of wool. The suspicion is abroad that Colonel Vaughn has been chased by a vicious ram in one of his boyhood days.

Mr. Walter F. Brown, afterward Postmaster General in President Hoover's cabinet, who knew the Ohio of those days as well as anyone, states that, in one form or another, the rumor of negro blood was gratuitously resurrected every time that Harding ran for office.

One advantage which the young man might reasonably have expected from his paper was an improvement in social status. It was the local tradition that newspaper representatives should be invited to all important festivities. Notwithstanding, Harding was conspicuously omitted from the guest-list of a large wedding. Stung, he published only a petty 'stickfull' instead of the spread to which an event of such social significance was entitled. The unhappy reaction taught him a lesson in ethics to which he bore testimony years afterward, with admirable equanimity.

> The little notice of the wedding was so remarked about that there came to me the inevitable remorse, that I concluded never after that, in the newspaper which I was connected with, should the news in any manner be appraised by the prejudice of the editor and the paper.[1]

Though the saline injection of political money kept the *Star* alive, the paper did not yet greatly prosper. But its

[1] Willis Fletcher Johnson: *The Life of Warren G. Harding.*

youthful publisher had another string to his bow. To make a living out of circulation alone was manifestly impossible in a town of four or five thousand and on a basis of a dime a week. Harding proceeded to create an opportunity to which his competitors had been blind.

Like kissing, advertising goes by favor. A merchant, a manufacturer, a railroad, or a hotel gave an occasional grudging advertisement to a publisher as a sort of petty nuisance philanthropy; it was accepted with gratitude as a benefice. There was no idea of mutual benefit.

Harding advanced a theory; to wit, that newsprint could sell goods. He did not invent the slogan, 'It Pays to Advertise,' but he pioneered it in Marion.

'Run an ad in the *Star*,' he told the local shops, 'and you'll boost your sales.'

They did not believe him. Out of goodwill they might buy a little space now and then, but as for steady display, that would be a waste of money. It was all right for big stores in big cities, maybe, but nobody had ever done it in Marion.

'All right,' said the solicitor. 'If your business doesn't show an increase you needn't pay for the ad.'

Fortunately for his thesis, there had developed a keen rivalry between several drygoods establishments competing for the town and farm trade. One merchant agreed to try a series of announcements in the *Star*. Results seemed to bear out the Harding theory. With this as argument, the publisher warned the other establishments that unless they followed suit, they would fall behind in the rush of business. As a matter of fact, trade was improving normally since the town was growing and drawing to itself a larger patronage from an expanding area; but certainly the Harding experiment did no harm and probably accelerated the pace in some degree.

For once, a pioneer reaped the benefit of his resourceful-

ness. The *Star* acquired a steady if small clientèle of advertisers. Soon the other newspapers seized upon the notion
and divided the patronage with the original booster. It
was too late to save the *Independent*, however. Crawford
was on the down grade; he eventually gave up the fight and
moved away. Harding did not get rich on his enterprise,
but he did keep the sheriff from the door.

Little was done, however, in the way of building circulation. Five hundred copies per day was probably the early
maximum.[1] The ten-cent subscribers came to the office and
picked up their copies, or went without. There were no
deliveries and no street sales. Nothing indicates that the
publisher's ingenuity had conceived the advanced notion of
increasing circulation as a basis of raising advertising rates.
However, the mere continued existence of the paper is a
tribute to the courage and enthusiasm, and in some degree,
to the luck of the editor-publisher.

Not until the superior executive brain of a shrewd and
forceful woman supplemented Harding's journalistic efforts
did the *Star* move toward established success.

[1] The paper claimed 700.

★

II. The Rising Star

FLORENCE KLING was born to small-town wealth, position, and privilege. Her father, a Pennsylvania Mennonite, had started in the hardware business in Marion, made a killing on a deal in nails at the time of the Civil War, branched into real estate and banking, and became the local magnate. He was a pattern of a self-made egoist, narrow, oppositious, arrogant, a generous public benefactor, but neither kindly nor tolerant in personal relationships.

With his only daughter he did not get along. They were too similar in self-will and obstinacy. He wished that she had been a boy, although he already had two sons. Quite early she developed a positive individuality. Amos Kling did not approve of it. He expected from her obedience and conformity. As he got neither, they clashed. The town's finest mansion housed a discordant family.

Nevertheless, he did his duty by her. She had good though not fashionable schooling, topped off by a course in the Cincinnati Conservatory of Music. As she grew to womanhood no flattery could call her pretty. But there was a certain vigor of personality about her, a frank appetite for living which gave her emphasis. Back in Marion, after her musical education was finished, she set herself to contriving what satisfaction she might in the state to which it had pleased Heaven to call her.

Chafing in the stiff, stodgy, sect-conscious society of her circle, she went a little beyond the strait limitations of being a perfect lady. In the contemporary phrase, she was 'a mite wild.' This must not be construed in terms of moral turpitude. It meant no more than that she frequented the skating rink, sometimes went out with boys who would not have been welcomed in the Kling household, and had been known to ignore the 11 P.M. deadline. More than once she was locked out, in the best stern-parent tradition, and had to find lodging with some girl friend.

One admirer, at least, she did have in her own class. Henry De Wolfe was some years her senior and equally an addict to the spell of the roller skate. Though the De Wolfes were almost as rich as the Klings and came from an older Ohio stock, Pete, as he was called, was a detrimental. He was more than a bit of a sport. He drank too much — eventually he drank himself to death — and his associates were dissolute. His reputation was worse than, for example, Warren Harding's, though his position was far superior. Father Kling declared an embargo against the suitor. The result was logical; Florence married Pete. She was then nineteen years old.

Marriage did not reform the rounder. He continued to be a festive wastrel. Two years after the wedding a new roller-skating palace was financed in Galion by a group with whom he had been running and the managership was offered to him.[1] It appealed to his sporting instincts. He left Marion, taking with him his wife and their year-old son. A small house was found and furnished and she settled in while he was putting the finishing touches to a gala program for the formal opening of the rink on Christmas Eve.

---

[1] For the Galion episode I am indebted to a contemporary of Florence Kling De Wolfe.

Two days before the date he vanished, leaving his family without money, coal, or food. Too proud to appeal to strangers for help in her humiliating dilemma, the young wife saw no other course than to go home. When the evening train came in, she was waiting at the station. Fortunately the conductor was an old hand who knew the Klings. Railroading was then operated on a more human basis than it is today. A conductor was lord of his train. It was his recognized right to furnish free passage to anyone he considered entitled to it. Would he carry Mrs. De Wolfe back to Marion? Certainly. He guessed Amos Kling's daughter was good for the amount. All aboard!

It was midnight when she arrived in Marion. The weather was rough and cold. Florence did not go to the paternal mansion. It may be that her father's ostracism against her for making a marriage which he disapproved was still operative. Or perhaps she remembered that eleven o'clock deadline. Not far from the station stood a vacant and dismantled house, the property of friends. She managed to get into it. There she spent the night, with the baby wrapped in her woollen skirt against the chill. Not exactly a Christmas idyll, but it shows the stuff of which Florence Kling was made.

In the morning she went, not to her own family or her husband's, but to friends. On her behalf they appealed to Amos Kling. He set his jaw and refused to help. It was all in the standardized melodrama manner as prescribed for stern and unrelenting fathers. One can almost hear the formula, 'She has made her bed; now let her lie on it.' Simon De Wolfe, father of the errant Pete, was of gentler susceptibilities. He guaranteed her grocery bill and other necessities. Some of her old associates rallied to her. Lodgings were found. A girl of her church circle [1] took the baby to care for until she

---

[1] She married George Van Fleet, who later became managing editor of the *Star*, it is said through Mrs. Harding's favor.

could get on her feet. A piano was loaned and Florence De Wolfe with quiet courage started in giving music lessons. Within a short time she was able to maintain herself, and reclaim her child.

By what mutual concessions she and her father drew together again may only be surmised. Public opinion doubtless had some influence in loosening the rivets of his stiff neck. Then, too, he may well have been impressed by the manifestation of his daughter's ability to provide for herself. In any case, they made it up and she went back to her home to become again the richest-man-in-town's daughter.

Florence never returned to De Wolfe. Indeed, there is no indication that he wished her to, though his family made some feeble efforts to patch things up. Incurably idle and rootless, Pete would prefer the freedom of the bars to any marital tie. In the course of time there was a divorce and he went West. So passed the husband out of Florence's life. A few years later and before her second marriage, Pete died.[1]

Marriage had not greatly changed Florence. Her liking for the bright lights was not lessened. She began to 'play around' again to an extent which her father considered unseemly. In his opinion, a married daughter, living under his roof, was entitled to no more licence than a maiden. Florence differed. The old quarrel was resumed.

She could not have been specially attractive to men at this period. Otherwise, how account for the fact that, with her advantages of family and prospective wealth, she remained for ten years unmarried? When her intentions toward Warren Harding crystallized, ill-disposed Marionites used to say that it was she that was marrying him, not he that was marrying her.

[1] Amos Kling adopted the boy, his grandson, and had his name changed to Marshall Kling. He lived in Marion until his death at the age of thirty-five.

Small and compact though the town was, it is improbable that there was any acquaintanceship between the two in earlier days. Five years' disparity of age would have operated against it; Florence was a married woman when Warren was still a fledgling schoolboy. Their circles did not intersect. The church, with its sociables and oyster festivals, which was so potent a factor in amalgamating sets, would not have helped in this case, since the young man had no religious affiliations. An unauthenticated legend has it that, shopping with a friend, young Mrs. De Wolfe was attracted by the stalwart physique and good looks of a man standing on a street corner.

'Who is that handsome young fellow?' she inquired.

'Warren Harding of the *Star*.'

'Do you know him? I'd like to meet him.'

'He doesn't come to our house,' said the other girl dubiously. 'But maybe I could get word to him to be at the Baptist supper Wednesday.'

And so it came about.

Another version, which has at least equal elements of likelihood, attributes their meeting to the easy environment of the skating rink. Soon it was noised abroad, 'Warren Harding and Flossie De Wolfe are going together.'

Amos Kling raged. The other entanglement had been bad enough; this was a thousand times worse in his angry eyes. Persuasion would not serve with the infatuated and headstrong widow. Kling met his future son-in-law in the Court House. In a tirade of profanity, interspersed with corrosive references to the Harding heredity, he threatened to blow the young man's head off if it ever appeared on his premises.[1]

To make matters worse for the young couple, the issue

---

[1] Dr. H. F. Alderfer refers to this encounter in his thesis 'The Personality and Politics of Warren G. Harding.' It was told to me in slighly varying forms by several old Marion residents.

flared into print. Some years earlier Harding had used his columns, with deplorable taste, as the implement of a gross practical joke upon Colonel Vaughn. Through a pretext he lured the rather straitlaced editor of the *Mirror* to a disreputable roadhouse, staged a fake raid, and derided his victim's discomfiture in next day's paper. The offence rankled and continued to rankle as long as Vaughn lived.[1]

He took a bitter revenge. His *Mirror* published a full-page article at the time when people's tongues were busy with gossip of Harding and Flossie Kling De Wolfe, circumstantially alleging that the Harding family were of mixed blood and that they had always been regarded and treated as negroes in and around Blooming Grove.

That issue has vanished from the face of the earth. A contemporary tells me that it was 'smothered'; that very few copies got into circulation. He believes that Amos Kling either wrote or inspired the article. But this seems improbable, since Kling's journalistic associations were with the *Independent*, which he helped to finance. Before Harding's death, Vaughn told Doctor Alderfer that the last copy extant was in his safe, that he had refused five thousand dollars for it, and that his will provided for its destruction, unread. He is dead and the newspaper has been destroyed.

Assuming that Kling may have had a part in the publication, with the purpose of breaking off the match between the young people, the attempt was nevertheless futile. The couple continued to go about together, though with precautions against paternal violence. They were married on July 8, 1891, and went to live in a modest house on pleasant Mount Vernon Avenue. Only Harding's family and a few intimates were present. One of the witnesses was Bartholomew Tristram, an old friend of Amos Kling. Meeting him on the street shortly afterward, Kling cursed him and formally repudiated the friendship. For seven years he

[1] Vaughn complained to Dr. Alderfer of it in 1920.

refused to speak to his daughter on the street; for twice that period he persecuted his son-in-law with every political and business resource at his command. It was fifteen years after the marriage when he first set foot in the Hardings' house. Florence Harding changed her church affiliations, dropped out of her old circle, and settled down to being a struggling editor's wife.

Why did Harding, handsome, magnetic, virile, marry a widow several years his senior, lacking in beauty and charm? No old resident with whom I have talked believes that he was in love with her. Perhaps her prospective fortune — she had no money at the time — influenced him, though there is no other evidence of a mercenary side to his character. Socially the alliance might have been expected to prove advantageous, but Harding, as a young man, was little concerned with such considerations. Possibly the element of revenge might have been a factor. As a love-match it was decidedly unilateral. She was thirty-one; her husband, twenty-six.

Chance first made a business woman of Florence Harding, though her innate capacity would probably have manifested itself sooner or later. Notwithstanding his brisk vigor and impressive physique, Harding's health was not of the best. Shortly after their marriage he exhibited disturbing symptoms. The seat of the trouble seemed to be digestive, affecting his nerves and his spirits. For some reason he did not consult his father, but, after dosing himself with several varieties of promising nostrums, fell into the hands of a quack. Discovering this, Doctor Harding got after him, gave him a thorough going-over, tossed out his fake medicines, put him on a diet, and soon had him as good as or better than new. If not of the loftiest professional standing, the ex-veterinary was probably a good, common-sense diagnostician and clinician.

Easing up at the office was part of the healing regimen.

About this time the staff member who was supposed to look after circulation left. Mrs. Harding was already discontented with the business methods of the office. More than once she had complained to her husband about them. Now she visited the plant and verified her misgivings from the books.

'I went down there,' she told an interviewer, 'intending to help out for a few days and remained fourteen years.'

One of her first improvements was the organization of a force of delivery boys. She trained them and disciplined them into an efficient unit. There is an office legend to the effect that one recalcitrant urchin was turned up and spanked.

'Many of the boys,' she recalled with pleasure, 'grew up to be splendid young men.' [1]

The most distinguished of her acolytes writes me:

Mrs. Harding in those days ran the show. She was a woman of very narrow mentality and range of interest or understanding, but of strong will and, within a certain area, of genuine kindliness. She got along well with newsboys of all sorts and kinds, in whom she took a genuine interest. It was her energy and business sense which made the *Star*. She was, for years, pretty nearly the whole show on the business side; — advertising manager, circulation manager and what have you. Even when the paper was strong enough for her to get help, she kept a close eye on those to whom she delegated various tasks.

Her husband was the front. He was, as you know, very affable; very much of a joiner and personally popular. He was a fine small-town or city booster and wrote editorials telling how Marion, Ohio, had more miles of Berea sandstone sidewalks than any town of its size in the United States. Nay, he ventured to say, in the whole world. This was his best line.

In the days of my youth, Mrs. Harding and his tailor had not discovered how well Warren could be dressed up. He used to loaf around his office in shirtsleeves and, if memory serves me, very often with a chaw of tobacco in his mouth. He was

[1] Joe Mitchell Chapple: *Life and Times of Our After-War President.*

always personally more popular than his wife, but I am quite sure that most folks up to the end of the nineteenth century who lived in Marion, would have told you that it was she who was the real driving power in the success that the Marion *Star* was unquestionably making in its community.

My ex-newsboy correspondent is Norman Thomas. Though his socialism was strongly antipathetic to the Harding orthodoxy, both husband and wife retained a warm regard for him, and he was a welcome guest at the White House. Loyalty to early friends was an abiding quality in both of them.

It was inherent in Florence Harding's nature to wish to boss everything. Often she prevailed by sheer force of character and capacity. Some of the staff thought her too domineering. Her husband, half-jocularly, called her 'Duchess.'

Sweetness and light automatically halo the personality of the First Lady of the Land. Since the aura is retroactive, it confuses the picture for the biographer. Accurate portrayal of character is difficult enough in all conscience, without having it complicated by the prismatic distortions of the hero-worshippers who color the records with their hundred per cent encomiums. 'Loved by all with whom she came in contact.' 'A sweet, domestic influence.' 'The most sought-after girl of her set.' 'Universal popularity.' 'The idol of the office.' 'A gentle, loving companion.' All the old, familiar garlands bedeck the portraits of the editor's helpmeet. Creditable though they may be to the kind intentions of the flatterers, they give a false idea of the subject.

Florence Kling Harding was in many respects an admirable character. She was a woman of firm principle, of clear purpose, and of essentially decent standards, possessed of a high heart, a shrewd brain, and a rigid will. But the softer side of womanhood was not hers. An arid home life and the bitter disillusionment of her first marriage account in part for this. It is clear that she was not affectionate by nature, nor did she inspire affection. Her feeling for Harding was one of fierce and ambitious possessiveness.

Like her father, she was autocratic. The office force of the *Star* respected her professionally. They appreciated her value to the paper. They never loved her as they did her husband. City-room legends of him all centre on some kindly or helpful act, some expansive expression of fellowship. The typical memento of her is the omission of the usual four-bit or a dollar raise all around, in one of the early years when she was asserting herself in the management. With Harding she had attended a banquet in Columbus, celebratory of his election to the lieutenant-governorship. 'You men needn't look for a raise this time,' she informed the staff, gathered about to welcome and congratulate them when they returned. 'That little show cost us thirteen hundred dollars.' [1]

A more tactful approach might have taken the sting out of the disappointment. Tact was not her strong point, nor did she ever acquire it.

As between husband and wife, hers was definitely the stronger spirit. She was more highly energized, more industrious, more ambitious, and more farseeing. Even when she became a semi-invalid, that pressing vitality of hers persisted. Without her Warren Harding would have been content to cultivate his popularity and enjoy a moderate measure of advancement. But she must capitalize on his capabilities, goad him to efforts and aims which, left to himself, he would never have pursued. At times she had her doubts of him, distrusted his capacity, feared that he would not measure up to the requirements and responsibilities that increased with his amazing rise. But these misgivings she stifled. Of herself I think she never had any doubts. She implicitly believed the professional seers and crystal-

[1] Statement of a member of the staff.

gazers who assured her that she carried a Star of Destiny on her brow.

With prosperity the newspaper had taken new quarters. It was now suitably housed on the principal business street. The editorial and news department occupied part of the second floor. Across from it, the windows of a divided room displayed in gold lettering the professional legend of George T. Harding, M.D. The ageing doctor was travelling in the wake of his son's success. One of the early staff of the *Star*, then a young reporter, gives me this description of the medical quarters:

'Doc Harding's place was a hoorah's nest. There was dust over everything, including a couple of coats on the windows. A few books and medical supply catalogues gave a professional touch, but they were as likely to be lying on the chairs or even on the floor as in their proper place. I remember there was a shabby, sagging sofa in the inside office where he held his consultations. The old boy would often bed down on that for the night, with his long overcoat thrown over him. I don't think he ever had much of a practice: mostly old people, and farmers and their families who stopped in from their Saturday marketing. He was slow and kind and patient. He could look wise. With his experience I expect he was plenty competent to handle most of the cases that came his way. But he didn't strike my youthful eyes as very antiseptic.'

None with whom I have talked recalls that Warren Harding paid much attention to his father, though they were always on friendly terms. It was his mother to whom his unstinted affection was given. Every Sunday he brought to her what was elegantly termed in those days a floral offering. If he was out of town over a week-end, someone in the office was commissioned to see that the bouquet reached her. He liked to drop in and talk things over with her in the course of his daily rounds. Of his relations with his sisters and brother there is practically no record. Harding family letters are scarcer than hen's teeth.

The *Star* office was a clubby establishment. Fairly regular to the hour the boss would come in, take off coat and hat and hang them on their appointed peg.

'Good morning, boys.'

'Good morning, W. G.'

He shook hands all around. This was ritual. His next move was to approach George Hinds.

'Can you spare a cut off your plug, old man?'

'Sure, W. G.'

The tobacco was handed over and Harding, cutting off a generous section, stowed it in his cheek. He was now ready for the day's work.

'What's on the hook today?'

Van Fleet, his managing editor, told him.

'Guess I'd better go out and take a look around.'

Invariably he would pick up an item or two of news; sometimes an idea or a suggestion for an editorial. Then back to the desk to turn in his daily stint. For inspiration he could look to the walls of his sanctum which were liberally equipped with pictures of his schoolday heroes; Napoleon, 'that god of little minds,' and Alexander Hamilton, his model of style; also the idols of his political admiration, James G. Blaine and Joseph B. Foraker, one already smirched, the other to be tainted with the proof of corruption.

Harding was always more the printer and publisher than the editor. Writing editorials was a chore. He was far happier on the streets, in the city hall or the court house, where he could mix, hear gossip, be part of the intimate, busy life of the town he loved. Personal contacts were his fad. Callers were welcome at the *Star* office. All sorts of people made a habit of dropping in; businessmen, politicians, farmers from the outlying districts, visitors with axes to grind, hard-luck hopefuls — for all of them the editor had a pleasant word and smile. He had more than that for the unfortunate. At Christmas, he would fill his pockets with bills, three or four hundred dollars, go out and, with what secrecy he could manage, distribute them where they were most needed.

Among his regular visitors was a girl, hardly more than a child. Nan Britton, daughter of a local physician, was a pretty, full-bosomed, physically and emotionally precocious schoolgirl, intelligent and well-liked by her fellows. The little sheaf of school items which she brought in as often as she could were a pretext for having a word with the handsome and suave editor. With all the fervency of her palpitant and susceptible twelve years, she was infatuated with a man thirty years her senior.

Judging by editorial product, Warren Harding was an indifferently equipped journalist. His writings are conventional and parochial to the verge of banality. When he deliberately spread himself, he was worse than his normal. Early he developed that false eloquence, that love of the sonorous, that employment of words without a just understanding of their significance which was to pain his friends and rejoice his critics in a larger sphere. The word 'sloppy' fairly describes his style. William Allen White, greatest of American country journalists, remarks of Editor Harding that he had 'never written a line that has been quoted beyond the confines of his state.' [1]

Partisanship inspired all his political output. This was natural and proper to the standards of the age. The *Star* was now professedly a Republican organ. 'A newspaper first and editorially Republican to the backbone' was its editor's own prescription for it. His partisanship was wholly genuine. In fact, it was his form of patriotism. The fervor which, had he been religiously inclined, might have been directed to the church, informed his attitude toward the

[1] William Allen White: *Masks in a Pageant.*

party of his inheritance and his choice. He might and later did turn his Republicanism to his own profit along recognized lines, but it was none the less heartfelt for that, and he was never a Republican for profit only.

As the paper grew in influence, standing, and respect, its editor modified its violence. Examples of blackguardism in print have been cited to show how far Warren Harding would go when unfairly goaded. Such philippics were gradually toned down; became less frequent, eventually all but disappeared. In his final days as an editor it was only political incitement that could rouse him to the old habit of calling names. Other personalities he eschewed.

Internally the *Star* was a happy office. In thirty-five years, Harding never discharged a man or reduced a wage. His is said to have been the first daily in the Middle West to initiate profit-sharing through distribution of stock among the employees. Although in political principle he tended to be anti-labor where he judged it expedient, he encouraged his men to form a union and when their treasurer departed with the funds, made up the deficit out of his own pocket.[1] The loyalty and affection which his staff manifested toward him were the reflex of his own feeling for the *Star*. While it was still a problem child, his ex-partner, Jack Warwick, offered to get him a good job on a Cleveland paper. He replied:

'I am going to stick to the *Star* and to Marion.'

Later, when Senator Foraker wanted to buy an important Columbus paper and put his supporter in charge, he met a polite but decisive declination.[2]

Upon discarding his old methods of vituperative journalism, Harding posted a set of rules which he headed, 'The Creed of the Marion Star':[3]

[1] H. F. Alderfer: notes.
[2] Statement of George B. Christian, Jr., Secretary to President Harding.
[3] Thomas H. Russell: *The Illustrious Life and Work of Warren G. Harding.*

Remember there are two sides to every question. Get them
both.

Be truthful. Get the facts.

Mistakes are inevitable, but strive for accuracy. I would
rather have one story exactly right than a hundred half wrong.

Be decent, be fair, be generous.

Boost, don't knock.

There is good in everybody. Bring out the good and never
needlessly hurt the feelings of anybody.

In reporting a political gathering, give the facts. Tell the
story as it is, not as you would like to have it. Treat all parties
alike. If there is any politics to be played, we will play it in
the editorial columns.

Treat all religious matters reverently.

If it can possibly be avoided never bring ignominy to an
innocent man or child in telling the misdeeds or misfortune of
a relative.

Don't wait to be asked, but do it without asking, and, above
all, never let a dirty word or a suggestive story get into type.

I want this paper to be conducted so that it can go into any
home without destroying the innocence of children.

No newspaper could quite live up to that prospectus. The
Star did not. In its ethical attitude toward news, it was no
better and no worse than its contemporaries.

In his searching analysis of the *Star's* editorial content,
Doctor Alderfer writes of its editor that

he gave very little attention to the issues of the day. Very few
of his editorials in this period dealt with the subjects upon
which people were debating. Now and then he would quote
the comment of one of the leading Republican journals and
endorse it. But when he, himself, made any excursion into
the field of tariff, regulation of railroads, or money, the result
was conventional, naïve, and superficial.... There is no evidence that he read or studied any subject well. He had no pet
theories of government or economics.[1]

Ethical scruples were not permitted to hamper unduly the
business side. Competition for the public printing had

[1] H. F. Alderfer: notes.

become so stiff that it threatened profits. Harding entered into a private arrangement with the other Marion County publishers. One man was delegated to make the low bid for the contract, the others all bidding higher. The low figure was set so high that all the supposedly competitive bidders divided up a nice profit on the deal. Harding told William Allen White, with placid self-satisfaction over his own shrewdness, that this plan was successfully carried through year after year. That secret and collusive bidding was a form of graft on the public funds did not trouble his mind. Presumably that view did not occur to him.

It is important to have a rounded view of Warren G. Harding in his current phase as the controlling mind of the *Star*, for here he crystallizes intellectually. Further than this he will not go along his chosen line of thought and endeavor. He will take on political coloration, but he remains essentially the small-town editor, to whom the responsibilities of high office are always a little alien, more than a little burdensome and bewildering. His paper will continue to expand; to improve its position in revenues and influence. But its editor, *qua* editor, will not develop. In thought, attitude, and ambition he will remain a newspaperman of small calibre, an integer of a closely centripetal community. He was that when he entered the White House. He wistfully hoped to be that again when his term of service was over.

Left to his own devices and purposes, Harding would have made the *Star* his career. Politics appealed to him as a pleasant bypath. Always he yearned for the smell of printer's ink and the rhythm of the roaring presses. With his aptitude for conciliating men, for composing differences, for being serviceable along many lines, he might logically have developed into a local boss. Analysis of his character suggests that he would have been a benevolent one; personally honest, charitably blind to the petty graft of others as long as it did no harm and helped party solidarity, intent upon giving his community the kind of government that its sterling business leaders wished, since that would be his conception of good government; and unfailingly docile to the plans of bigger bosses in state or nation.

He would have stuck to Marion. For he loved the city, as he watched and helped it develop to that status from a country town. Treat him as shabbily as it might, exclude him for long from its 'best circles,' his stubborn loyalty gave him strength — or weakness — to support its slurs and win a wholesouled loyalty in return.

III. *An Ohio Group*

Once in his life Harding hit upon *le mot juste;* the completely appropriate term. He told Mark Sullivan that he liked to go out into the country and 'bloviate.' That word describes with onomatopoetic felicity the cheerful and windy expressiveness of the Harding oratory. It was 'bloviation' that led him into politics.

It began with his being sent by the Marion Republican Committee as guide to a routine speaker, assigned to a small village near-by. For lack of a local chairman, the young editor undertook to introduce the speaker of the evening. To his gratification he found it easy and agreeable. His fine presence, lush flow of verbiage, and partisan passion made a hit. The heady wine of applause incited him to further forensics. He had made a discovery about himself. 'I really think I know how to deliver a good speech' was his fond boast in after-years.[1]

The committee was glad to use him as an orator, but he was pitchforked into his first candidacy. In the nineties, Marion County was so irreclaimably Democratic that the Republicans often let the offices go by default. This did not appeal to Harding's hundred per cent Republicanism and he

[1] Mark Sullivan: *Our Times*, vol. VI.

said so in meeting. When his arch-enemy, George Crawford, suggested endorsement of the opposition candidate for county auditor, Harding objected. Crawford caught him up. Let him take the nomination himself.

'I'll do it,' said Harding. 'I'll make the run.'

There was no chance of his winning. Nevertheless he made the best canvass in his power. Not only was he soundly beaten by the Democrat, but he suffered the embarrassment of running sixty votes behind his ticket. Amos Kling, his father-in-law, and Crawford, Kling's ally, had knifed him. His commentary in the *Star* is characteristically good-humored.[1]

> It is easy to explain Guthrie's majority. He had an easy mark for an opponent.

Though he could not win for himself, he could help others to victory. He became a regular of the speaking corps. No record is preserved in print of his early spellbinding, not even in the columns of the *Star*. (Editor Harding did not consider Orator Harding as news.) But from local reminiscence, one gathers that he went in heavily for patriotism, the superiority over other and less-favored localities of the grand old State of Ohio, the supreme contribution of the Grand Old Party to our national civilization, and the debt owed by the country to the Grand Army of the Republic, then a potent and cohesive element at the polls. The young editor could wave the bloody shirt with the best of them. He could flatter local pride. He could crack a joke and win a laugh. He never let an audience down.

On one of these political excursions he met Harry M. Daugherty at a crossroads rally in Richwood. Accounts of the fateful encounter vary. Presumably Mr. Daugherty's own recollection is reliable.[2]

[1] *Marion Star*, November 10, 1892.
[2] Harry M. Daugherty: *The Inside Story of the Harding Tragedy*.

An Ohio Group

Observing an unknown young man washing his boots at the school pump, Daugherty was struck with his statesmanlike aspect. (He neglects to mention whether the stranger's oratory bore out the impression.) They struck up an acquaintanceship. Daugherty liked the younger man's suavity and friendliness. Ohio politicians think in terms of the Presidency. It flashed into Daugherty's mind that this man (then about thirty-five) looked like a President. He was possible material. The more seasoned politician expressed a hope of meeting the other again. He kept that image in mind.

It is in order to consider Harry Micajah Daugherty. He was born of Scotch-Irish-American stock in Washington Court House, a comfortable town of southern Ohio, and was five years senior to the man he was to project into the White House. Young Harry's childhood was something of a struggle. His father died when he was quite young, leaving another son besides himself. At school age Harry took a job in a grocery to help out the meagre family exchequer. He managed to get his schooling, completed high school, and took a law course, without the usual previous college training, at the University of Michigan, graduating with his LL.B. in 1881. Returning to his home, he opened an office, picked up a bit of practice, and three years later married Lucy Walker, the traditional 'prettiest girl in town' whom all future celebrities marry. It was a happy marriage. Scandals of various kinds beat about Harry Daugherty's unbowed head in the course of a long life, but none that impugned his devotion as a husband.

Daugherty was self-destined to politics. His start was election to the council. From that he was promoted to be prosecuting attorney of Fayette County. In 1889 he was elected to the lower house of the legislature and re-elected for a second term, running to 1894. Then and there his career terminated in so far as suffrage of the people is concerned. He was that anomaly of American politics, a voteless but powerful political factor. Daniel Webster is the most notable example in our history.

Two terms in the legislature sufficed to give him a foothold. He became part of the smooth-running machine. He knew the ropes. He had something valuable to dicker with, and his natural market was the corporation lobby. One of those 'vanity books,' [1] which trade upon the naïve self-esteem of the great and near-great through flattering write-ups, portrays him walking down the street between a little trolley car and a little telephone instrument, each clinging trustfully to a protective hand. That tells the story of his legal usefulness. 'See Harry Daugherty' was standard advice to utilities counsel with legislative problems. Daugherty and Todd (later Daugherty, Todd and Rarey) had for clients the American Tobacco Company, Armour and Company, the American Gas and Electric Company, the Western Union Telegraph Company, and the Ohio State Telephone Company.

Professional success did not satisfy Daugherty's ambitions. He hankered for the honors of office. Herein is found a singular contrast to the man whom he pushed to the top of the ladder. Harding cared little for office; he preferred to remain in the background and enjoy life. But Daugherty, perhaps the ablest tactician of his day, found the direction of the battle insufficient. He wanted to carry the banner. This desire was doomed to frustration. *Vox populi* was not for him. He simply was not a vote-getter. In the current word of the time, he could not have been elected dog-catcher in a ward full of cats.

A member of the opposition who knew him in the heyday of his Columbus operations says of him:

> Harry Daugherty was what we used to call a fringe politician. He was the fly on the rim of the wheel. You'd always find him outside, looking in. When a good office was to be

[1] *Clubmen of Columbus in Caricature.* Roycroft Press.

filled, Harry would always be among those mentioned — he'd
see to that — and that let him out. He kept himself surrounded by we-men, but they couldn't deliver the vote.[1]

The series of disappointments and defeats is long, though
intermittent. In 1895 he was an unsuccessful candidate for
attorney general of the state. Two years later he was in the
field for the gubernatorial nomination, but finished among
the also-rans. He twice tried for Congress and missed. Competing with Myron Herrick for the United States senatorship in 1916, when he particularly hoped to become the colleague of his protégé, Harding, in 'the most exclusive club in
the world,' he carried but three counties out of eighty-eight.
That re-election to the legislature in 1893 was his last little
popular triumph. As a final stroke of pure irony, the jeering
fates thwarted his attempt to get himself chosen delegate-at-
large to the Republican Convention of 1920; so he had to go
as a private citizen. This time, however, he had the last
laugh on the fates, since he completely stole the show with
the nomination of his dark-horse candidate.

A caustic contemporary once remarked of him that the
only victory he could consistently depend upon was re-election to the Order of the Tin Can. And a witty writer in the
New York Times, reviewing his career, likens him to a disillusioned prizefighter who, punch-drunk from many knock-
outs, decides that his future lies in management.

Harding became his meal ticket.

More than any other factor, the implacable enmity of
Robert F. Wolfe, millionaire shoe-man and owner of the *Ohio
State Journal* and the *Columbus Dispatch* obstructed the path
of Daugherty's ambitions. In Harding's opinion, gloomily
expressed to a friend, it was impossible for Harry Daugherty
to get anywhere in Ohio over Bob Wolfe's opposition. There
was a curious impersonality in the mutual hostility. On

[1] Interview with Harry F. Busey of Columbus, by the writer.

Daugherty's part it did not extend to the newspapers which so consistently sided against him. Often he would make editorial suggestions to them for the conduct of a current campaign, many of which were adopted. He was as available to interviewers from the Wolfe newspapers as from more friendly dailies. At the close of the talk he would perhaps say: 'When you see that old son-of-a-bitch, Bob Wolfe, tell him he can —— — ——.

Meeting the gentleman whom he had invited to this osculatory ceremonial the same day, he would greet him with a casual pleasantry. A drink might follow. They would part on easy terms. That was Harry Daugherty. Ruthless in politics, he harbored no personal bitterness. Or, if he did secrete rancor, he would not permit himself to exhibit it. This may have been insensitivity; it may have been a set policy; but, in view of other angles of his personality, it argues a certain largeness of character. He could always see the other fellow's point of view, even when most adverse to himself.

Evil report beset him early and pursued him throughout his active life. In the Foraker-Sherman contest for the senatorial nomination in 1892, the *Columbus Post* charged that Daugherty, then in the legislature, had been influenced by 'seven crisp five-hundred-dollar bills' to switch his vote. After a grand jury had found no cause for action, the accused man demanded a full investigation by his peers. A House committee heard the charges. Daugherty denied everything. The evidence against him was flimsy in the extreme. The committee exonerated him, and properly.[1]

Shortly thereafter, the *Post* suspended publication, throwing its staff out on the street with arrears of salary unpaid and practically penniless. Out of his own pocket — and with a wry remark that there were no 'crisp five-hundred-dollar bills' in the disbursement — the object of the *Post*'s strictures

[1] *New York Times*, March 2, 1924.

distributed eighteen hundred dollars among the hard-pressed staff, brought suit for what was owing them, recovered the amounts, and made no charge for the legal service. Is it to be wondered at that Harry M. Daugherty made friends who were steadfast to him through good cause and ill?

Other and more searching inquiries were to harass him. Skilled prosecutors and hostile committees were to call him to account, and put both his reputation and his freedom in jeopardy. Partners and associates of his enterprises were disgraced, convicted, disbarred, driven to suicide. Harry M. Daugherty confronted every charge, accepted every challenge, and won out, though at some cost to his good name. Only at the bar of public opinion was he convicted. His career ended in dismissal from the high office which he had conducted in a steadily thickening cloud of scandal.

No just estimate of Daugherty can fail to give him credit for courage, capacity, loyalty, keen comprehension of the psychological elements of his own special brand of politics, and consistency in the pursuit of his principles, such as they were. With his mental equipment he might have been an able lawyer. His tastes did not lie in that direction. First, last, and all the time he was the political manipulator, the adroit fixer.

Personally he was a likable fellow, direct and robustious. He made no pretence to culture. He was ready in profanity, by no means chary of 'rough talk,' and he had an oblique and sometimes subtle wit which was likely to puzzle and exasperate the slower-minded of his associates. Nobody could face him down; not the domineering Mark Hanna, nor the powerful boss Penrose, nor the President of the United States who, indeed, never tried. He could take orders. But for one that he took, he issued ten. He was for himself and his friends all the time with open and unashamed directness. A dangerous enemy, a more dangerous friend.

Another resident of Washington Court House who was to

bulk large in Warren Harding's career was Jesse W. Smith.[1]
He was a few years younger than Harry Daugherty, whose
faithful vassal he became. The Smiths were more important
folk than the Daughertys. They enjoyed much the same
status in their community that the Klings did in Marion.
They were the local 'biggies,' proprietors of the department
store, owners of the finest business block.

A sketch of the youth in a local publication [2] thus pictures
him:

> Jesse Smith is tall in stature and pigeon-toed in walk. The
> most prominent feature of Jesse is his senatorial swing and his
> flipflops in language. He is a great sport, takes in all the shows,
> and is a ladies' man in general.

With no more than a high-school education, young Smith
went into the family trade. He was a merchant, *con amore*.
He had a passion for texture and color; he loved fabrics and
the sheen of silk. Women consulted him on the cut of a skirt
or the choice of a shade. If a poll had been taken on the
snappiest dresser in town, Jesse would have had no competition. In his last appearance in public before he blew out his
troubled brains, he was 'a symphony in gray and lavender.'

Artistry was not the only quality which he brought to the
family enterprise. He was a keen businessman. He improved
and extended the trade which his father had established until
it provided a tidy income, though nothing to be compared to
the returns from his operations in the broader field of political
graft.

Jesse had his personal peculiarities. Otherwise than in
sartorial splendor he was unattractive to the eye. His face
was pulpy, his heavy lips everted; he spluttered in speech,
particularly when he was struggling with some important

---

[1] For the data on the Smiths and their local environment, the writer is indebted
to Aileen Hess Harper (Mrs. Robert S.) of Columbus, whose childhood was spent
in Washington Court House.

[2] *The Washington Court House Cyclone and Record Republican*, May 14, 1890.

word of which he did not quite grasp the meaning. He was timorous as a rabbit, afraid to be in a room or apartment alone after nightfall. Tears came easy to him; he could blubber like a child over a slight or a disappointment, especially when he had been drinking. He never went in for athletics, being flabby and indolent of physique. Shooting was the popular pastime for the youth of the place; not for Jesse. He was mortally afraid of firearms.

It was his fond pride to be known as Harry Daugherty's confidant and pal. People liked him with a sort of amused tolerance. One flaw of character is to be noted. Jesse had no moral sense.

How Daugherty first found Jesse of use is a matter of speculation. Jesse was not interested in politics *per se*. His angle was the profits. Roxy Stinson, his short-term wife, said that 'Jess was Harry Daugherty's bumper.' Asked by a Senate committee to define the term, she replied, 'Intimate friend.' A bumper he was in a more literal sense, in that when the pair got to Washington he stood between the Attorney General and the horde of office-seekers and favor-hunters that besieged the official doors.

At first, one may assume, the older and stronger character was flattered by the affectionate subservience of the liege-man. As time passed, Jesse proved his ability to translate loyalty into usefulness. He became indispensable. He was private secretary, major-domo, political henchman, financial manager, household paymaster, and personal agent all in one. He became known as Daugherty's closest friend. They lived together from the time of their arrival in Washington, first in a small house provided by Edward B. McLean, newspaper publisher, multimillionaire, and playboy; then in a luxurious Wardman Park Hotel housekeeping suite. Mrs. Daugherty was at this time a hopeless invalid. When Jesse went away on a visit, his housemate would write, complaining of loneliness, urging a prompt return. Jesse, wiring to him, signed

himself in playful mood, 'Your little friend, Jesse.' No inferences of an abnormal phase to the friendship are to be drawn.
Both men were thoroughly masculine.

They were partners in a 'fishing club' on Deer Creek, fifteen miles from home, where some of the week-end activities
were far from piscatorial. To this advantageously remote
spot politicians with private business to transact paid quiet
visits. Daugherty's banker brother, Mally S., and his law
partner, John Todd, were other members.

Here is a close-up view of Jesse W. Smith in his heyday,
as he appeared when playing his rôle of Home Town Boy
Makes Good:

> He would come home to Washington Court House, stand on
> a corner, and pose with the happy naïveté of a high-school
> athlete. Jesse never grew up. He loved money, position, and
> above all, publicity.

He never ran for office or sought appointment. The
rough-and-tumble of politics was not for his otiose spirit. He
adored the social side of the Great Game, the flag-decked
platform where he could find a seat among the mighty, the
presidential junkets on which he was permitted to go as
utility man, the Washington parties, ranging from the smoky
revelries of the Little Green House on K Street to the politico-
fashionable menagerie conducted by the Ned McLeans in
their huge downtown mansion. Also his innocent vanity was
flattered by the respect, amounting to veneration, which he
inspired in the souls of the bootleggers, privilege-buyers, and
other outlaws who paid him court and cash. To them he was
one of the major powers behind the throne. Jesse took no
pains to disabuse them. He may even have shared their
opinion.

If Jesse had never met and fallen instantaneously in love
with a tall, statuesque, handsome red-head of nineteen, the
recorded history of the Harding Administration might have
been less complete. For, though hers was no more than a

subsidiary rôle in the sordid drama, her revelations did much to open up the whole scandal and furnish the clues which, followed up, wrecked so many reputations.

Roxy Stinson, afterward Smith, and a little later again Stinson, came to Washington Court House with her mother who inaugurated an ambitiously styled Conservatory of Music on the second floor of the Smith block. Jesse, then over thirty, was the town catch. But not to Miss Roxy. She accepted his attentions, drove with him, attended the infrequent shows which played the town in his company, and that was all. Leaving him disconsolate, she went to Europe to study — she had a good voice and some aptitude for the piano — and did not return until she was nearly twenty-four. Her faithful Jesse was waiting. She married him.

Washington Court House disapproved. Not that there was anything against the girl. But she and her mother did not quite 'belong.' Given an eligible bachelor, worth more than one hundred thousand dollars, amiable, dandified, and a leader in the 'best set,' there was bound to be hard feeling when he married an outsider.

Chief among the mourners was Mrs. Smith, senior. From all report she was a determined, interfering, and lachrymose individual. 'The wedding was featured by the tears of Mrs. Smith,' wrote a guest. Mrs. Smith continued to weep until, within a year and a half, the marriage dissolved in the brine of her lamentations. Extreme cruelty was the allegation. Locally this was regarded as a mixture of joke and libel. Jesse Smith was incapable of cruelty toward anyone, least of all toward his adored Roxy. Credit for the rupture went to the mother-in-law; Jesse had always been something of a mamma's boy.

But was it a rupture? For a time the grass widow lived elsewhere. She returned and the town began lifting eyebrows and comparing notes. Never was there a queerer aftermath to divorce. Roxy joined her mother in the quarters above the

Smith emporium. There followed a repetition of the early days of the courtship. Long rides, shows, flowers, candy, attentions. 'What's going on here?' local society asked itself in an access of shock to its complacent conventionality. All the earmarks of 'keeping company' were in evidence. Or was it more than that? The church people undertook to cold-shoulder the ex-wife. It failed to influence her behavior. Miss Roxy Stinson-Smith-Stinson was an independent soul.

At the height of his career, when the rich graft was pouring in upon him from scores of sources, Jesse would still make time to run out to Washington Court House every few weeks. There was a business alliance between the divorced couple. Roxy was privy to his deals. He sent her stocks and bonds, the proceeds of his corrupt operations, with instructions as to their disposal. 'She knows enough,' one of the Ohio gang is supposed to have remarked uneasily, 'to hang us all.'

Roxy did not like Harry Daugherty. The feeling was reciprocal.

Unsuspecting of the ambitions of Harry Daugherty, igno-rant of the existence of Jesse Smith and Roxy Stinson, Hard-ing contentedly pushed the fortunes of the *Star*. The paper was growing with the rapid growth of Marion. No longer was the city dependent chiefly upon the output of the prosperous agricultural region to which it was focal. Manufactures began to come in. Always a booster, never a knocker, in pursuance of its code, the *Star* commended itself to the ex-panding enterprises. They gave it their advertising. Some of them did more; they bound the rising young editor to their interests by gifts. It is said that he got ten thousand dollars in stock from a farm implement company, for no other ascertainable consideration than the presumptive favor of the *Star*'s columns.[1] By his own admission he accepted stock in a local brewery. When, in opposition to his candidature, the

[1] H. F. Alderfer: *The Personality and Politics of Warren G. Harding:* statement of old Marion resident.

Drys brought this up against him, his defence was that it was a gift. Apparently no doubts obtruded upon his candid mind as to the propriety of a newspaper proprietor accepting such a benefit. That sort of thing was not banned in the Creed of the *Marion Star*.

Inevitably the paper conformed more and more closely to the safe and sane proprieties. Gone were the days of epithet and vituperation. Orthodoxy was the keynote of the editor's policy. Consciously or sub-consciously, he attempted to represent and express the mass mind, the opinions, desires, and prejudices of the average reader of the *Star*. His creed was that the People are always right — though he wavered when later they voted against him. Whatever was the proper thing to do and say, he did and said with wholesouled conviction which sometimes verged upon the ludicrous, because of its consistently high pitch. Though he had not yet invented the hybrid term 'normalcy,' he was following that ideal. Because Prohibition was considered freakish, he poked fun at the Prohibitionists. 'Mugwump' was a term of hilarious derision to his pen. Women who were active in public affairs he jeered at because they 'want to wear pants and make the night hideous.' He advocated 'cold lead' for that naïvely impotent rathskeller anarchist, Herr Most. He invoked specific damnation upon 'the colored voter who will vote against the party that proved his savior.' He called down the cyclonic destruction of Heaven upon the Mormons to uproot them from the earth. He denounced organized labor, not for its sins, but because it organized. His standard of humor was set by the gags of the variety shows, and his test of the unpopular (and therefore indefensible) was what he believed that the most and best people opposed. Always and everywhere the *Star* would be found on the side of the angels and against the man-eating shark.

The paper prospered. The Hardings were among the first people in town to own an automobile. Soon they were able to take a yearly vacation in the South. From a purely material viewpoint Florence Harding's change of status had justified itself. But socially she still felt the disfavor of her father's conservative circle. Amos Kling's implacable hatred of the man his daughter had married found vent in political hostility. This was a serious matter, for Harding had now reached the point of considering himself due for practical recognition of the *Star's* labors in the faith. Shut off from hopes of city office by the barricade of the Kling faction, from county office by the stable Democratic majority, he could look only to the legislature.

The Thirteenth District, of which Marion County was a part, normally voted Republican. Harding went out for the state senate.

By the closest of calls and only through the exercise of a strategy which would have been creditable to one of larger experience, Harding escaped defeat in this, his initial venture of any importance. First, one of the bosses who had promised support — or so the hopeful candidate interpreted his attitude — double-crossed him and himself came out for the office. Nevertheless, Harding had a majority of a scant one in the convention. The chairman was for him. The Rules and Credentials Committee was controlled by his opponents. The importance of this lay in the fact of a contest over the delegates from one ward. Whichever faction won it would name the candidate. Knowing that the committee's majority report, conventionally presented first, would be adverse, Harding gave his followers directions to vote it down. But the canny committee chairman put in the minority report first, and before the confusion cleared, Harding's adherents had voted down their own delegation. Only swift action would save the day. Orders were hurriedly distributed: 'Vote No on the next report.' Thus the majority report was rejected. Both delegations were out. The contest was a tie; no decision. Objection was raised that this was illegal. Harding's partisan in the chair ruled it in order. The editor's nomination went through by the narrowest of margins.[1]

'See you later in Columbus,' Harry Daugherty had said to the young orator at Richwood who looked so like a potential President.

The prophecy was justified. Harding was elected, and in 1901 assumed his first office.

[1] *World's Work*, September, 1920; 'Harding,' by George McAdam.

★

IV. Political Induction

THE Marion editor went to Columbus, bought himself a frock coat and silk hat and became a statesman. Mrs. Harding stayed at home and ran the paper. It was a propitious time for the entry into the state senate of an ambitious Republican neophyte. His party held a comfortable working majority of nine in a total of thirty-one. Only seven of the senators had served previously. The new member suffered no disadvantage of inexperience, and in political capacity he outranked most of his fellows.

Ohio at the time was run by two powerful bosses, Mark Hanna in Cleveland, Joseph B. Foraker in Cincinnati, whose lieutenant was the notorious George B. Cox. Frederick C. Howe, just entering politics, says that the state was managed like a private demesne.[1] A legislator found his course conveniently mapped out for him. He must first decide to which overlord he would attach his fortunes. After that, all he had to do was obey orders.

Harding had a pretty talent for ingratiation. Men liked him on sight; so did women. He had the instinct for making friends, the ability to use them, and the propensity to serve

[1] Frederick C. Howe: *Confessions of a Reformer.*

them. He made no enemies because he deserved none. A reporter at that time covering the Capitol says of him:

> It was not long before Harding was the most popular man in the legislature. He had the inestimable gift of never forgetting a man's face or name. He was a regular he-man in the sign-manual of those days, a great poker-player, and not at all averse to putting a foot on the brass rail.[1]

Shortly his gifts commended the new senator to the favor of the powers. His remarkable knack of conciliating opposition and of reconciling men who held different opinions was oil for the party machinery. Harry Daugherty was at his elbow, ready to give him the benefit of his experience in the quieter arts of politics. Governor Nash found words of warm praise for his willingness and usefulness.

> There may be abler men in the Senate than Harding, but when I want things done I go to him.

A shrewd, first-hand observer and commentator on contemporaneous Ohio politics says of him:

> He would do almost anything in the name of party regularity and do it with the rectitude of a religious zealot.[2]

Harding's own recipe for such manipulative success as he consistently achieved is, in itself, a diagram of the man as politician:

> We all know the town meeting, if not by experience, by hearsay. Now, if I had a program that I wanted to have adopted by a town meeting, I should go to the three or four most influential men in my community. I should talk it out with them. I should make concessions to them until I had got them to agree with me. And then I should go into the town meeting, feeling perfectly confident that my plan would go through. Well, it's the same in the nation as in the town meeting, or in the whole world if you will. I should always go first to the three or four leading men.[3]

[1] *World's Work*, September, 1920; 'Harding,' by George McAdam.
[2] Frederick C. Howe: *Confessions of a Reformer*.
[3] Clinton W. Gilbert: *Mirrors of Washington*.

Viewed from the angle of constructive accomplishment the Harding legislative record is insignificant. Of fifteen bills sponsored by him, fourteen have a local or personal slant. They were put forward to get something done for his town, his friends, or himself. Once, however, he flirted dangerously with the siren Reform.

City control was an open scandal in those days for corruption and graft. George B. Cox ruled Cincinnati on those principles. A measure had been formulated to restore some degree of self-government to the cities, to render the officials more directly responsible and responsive to the will of the citizens. Harding sponsored it, amidst the acclaim of progressive newspapers and civic organizations. In recognition of his services he was made chairman of the Committee of the Whole on the bill, which had already passed the lower house.

Was his course an earnest of his future intentions, a challenge to the bosses? At first it appeared in that light. The fact that they afterward manifested no ill-will toward him suggests an alternative theory, that he was being permitted to further the measure as a build-up for his standing with the general public. This could do no harm since there was no intention of permitting the bill to become a law. The corporations and their ready agents saw to that. They issued their ukase. The bill was called up in the legislature for reconsideration. Harding had his orders. 'You be good now and say nothing.' He lost interest in that particular legislation. It died. The next session another municipal bill of vitally different import was submitted. This one gave the city looters everything they wanted. It assured their hold on the machinery. Consistent enemies though they were, always at each other's throats in the fight for domination of the Republican Party in the state, Hanna of Cleveland and Foraker of Cincinnati got together on this. Harding voted for it. He had seen the light. Reform wouldn't do. The Party couldn't use it.

'He washed his hands of the affair and beat a hasty and diplomatic retreat.' [1]

He was not, however, altogether happy about it. It was apropos of this and similar exigencies that he sighed one day to a newspaper friend,[2] holding his right hand to his forehead in a characteristic pose of discouragement: 'Pretty raw, some of these bills. I don't like 'em. But what can I do? The Organization wants 'em.'

He was already recognizing a higher arbiter than his conscience. Whatever the Organization wanted must be for the ultimate good. Not for him 'to choose, to see his path.' The kindly light of Party would lead him on and he would piously follow.

There is one other instance of his standing out against his superiors. A bill for the extension of local option had the approval of the machine. On its introduction in the senate the galleries were manned — or womanned — by the massed forces of the W.C.T.U., supported by allied Dry champions, holding out reprisal at the polls as vengeance upon those who espoused the cause of the Demon Rum. For Senator Harding it may well have been a case of choosing the lesser of two threats, the voting power of the Drys as compared with the disfavor of the bosses. Which was the more to be feared?

He voted No, thereby making capital with the White-Ribboners. This is the more striking in that by political bent and certainly by personal predilection and habit, he was a libertarian; and it was the more commendable in that he was the owner of brewery stock. Yet Harry Daugherty, a Dry only from expediency, sharply objected to his protégé training with 'that gang of Wets and saloonkeepers down in Cincinnati.'

How well appreciated his services during his first term were is testified to by his re-election. It was against the rules. No

---

[1] H. F. Alderfer: *The Personality and Politics of Warren G. Harding.*
[2] Jacob A. Meckstroth of the *Ohio State Journal.*

state senator, according to the procedure of the Thirteenth District, could succeed himself. But the harmonizing and pacifying Harding influence was needed at Columbus. Orders were issued. A regulation which had stood for more than half a century was rescinded.[1] The Marion man was renominated by acclamation and re-elected by an increased majority, though his home county still went against him.

He could well afford the luxury of office-holding now. The paper was coming along nicely. George Van Fleet, a competent newspaper man, looked after the editorial functions. Mrs. Harding could be trusted to run the business mechanism. She was better fitted for such details than her husband had ever been. Taking advantage of his absence, his local enemies launched an attack hopefully calculated to eliminate him from the journalistic field.

One of Harding's vulnerable points was his propensity for plunging. From the early days, he would order supplies and equipment and trust to luck or Providence to meet the bills. The expanding *Star* involved expanded loans. The paper is said to have had notes out with the local bankers to the extent of twenty thousand dollars. These were bought up by J. F. McNeal, a Republican associated with the Kling faction, hence a political enemy of Harding. The senator hurried back from Columbus, hustled about among his friends, raised the money, and saved his imperilled newspaper.[2]

So far as readers of the *Star* were apprised, State Senator Harding might almost as well not have been in politics at all. This did not please his ambitious helpmeet. She said to Van Fleet, the managing editor:

'George, how is it we never have anything in the paper about Warren Harding?'

'Orders from the boss.'

[1] *Marion Star*, July 8, 1901.
[2] H. F. Alderfer: *The Personality and Politics of Warren G. Harding.*

'Well, just now I am boss. Forget that old order. I'll take the responsibility.'

Thereafter the owner received a reasonable, though never a disproportionate share of notice in his own paper.[1]

Honors increased in his second term. He was chosen floor leader. There were strong men in the state senate that term, stronger than the man who rose far beyond any of them: Atlee Pomerene, afterward United States Senator and a nemesis of the Harding Administration; Nicholas B. Longworth, future Speaker of the House of Representatives; and Myron T. Herrick, on his way to the governorship and the United States Senate. Nevertheless, Harding was an outstanding if not precisely a dominant figure. Not only had he found official preferment, but he was put forward as spokesman for the party when graceful adjustments were to be made or delicate compromises engineered. Definitely committed to Foraker, Cox, and the down-state faction, he contrived to maintain pleasant relations with the Hanna contingent, partly through the good offices of his friend, Harry Daugherty. Not the Republican side alone, but the Democratic members liked him and were generous to applaud the flights of his ever-ready eloquence.

Popularity was his stock-in-trade. Who could help but like a fellow-member so smooth, amenable, deft at playing the game, and assiduous in doing small favors for adherent or opponent? He was rich in eulogy, sparing in denunciation. The blackguardism of his earlier editorial days was suppressed. Flowers he loved to throw; never mud. He liked people. He was genuinely a humanitarian. With Terence he might have said, had he ever heard of Terence, 'I am a man. Nothing that is human is outside my interest.'

To the hand of his superiors in the party he was a fit tool. No prickly principles hampered him. Theories of good government, of public service, those stumbling-blocks to party

[1] Statement of staff member to the writer.

progress, were not permitted to interfere with his carrying
out of orders, after his one lesson with the ill-fated Municipal
Corporations Bill. He would not repeat that mistake. He
was safe. He would stand without hitching. Withal, he kept
a clean name. He worked with and for the corruptionists. He
served their ends. But there was no talk of dirty money
sticking to his fingers. That Harding at any time in his long
rise was deliberately and consciously venal, no man who
knew him well believes. Many influences, not all of them
worthy, could sway him. Money was not among them.

Conciliation was sorely needed in his party. As an impar-
tial observer remarked, the Republicans battled with each
other more savagely than they ever fought the Democrats.
Hanna and Dick were pitted against Foraker and Cox. It
was Cleveland *vs.* Cincinnati. 'Politics in Ohio is the tale of
two cities,' wrote Lincoln Steffens.[1] Although Mark Hanna,
king-maker to McKinley, was one of the most powerful single
figures in the United States, he was not undisputed boss of
his own domain. No one man in Ohio was. It was a divided
empire, with a shifting battle for control in progress. Impatient, intolerant, tyrannical, Hanna was usually ruthless
in his attitude toward those who would not accept his orders.
Young Harding was an exception.

'I suppose you want to be President some day,' he growled
out. 'Every Ohio youngster does. Well, you better keep
closer in touch with us fellows up in Cleveland and not train
so exclusively with those damn trouble-makers down in
Cincinnati.'[2]

In every respect except party usefulness Harding's second
term was as sterile of achievement as his first. Considered as
educational preparation for the United States Senate and the
Presidency, the experience would appear inadequate. It
measured up to the requirements of Harding's ambition. He

[1] Lincoln Steffens: *The Shame of the Cities.*
[2] Joe Mitchell Chapple: *Warren G. Harding, The Man.*

closed his legislative course with these assets: a wide acquaintance and popularity, the easy name of a good fellow and a boon companion; the reputation of being at call for unquestioning service as a party handy-man, and a thorough working knowledge of the legislative wires and who was at the controlling end of each one. It is an interesting and significant comparison that, while his overt and official power was probably less than the undercover influence of Harry M. Daugherty, his reputation was better. He played a more open game of politics.

Active as he was on the rostrum, Harding found time to further his outside prospects. The senate was very much to his liking. He wanted to stay there. Re-election was out of the question. Something like *force majeure* had been necessary to override tradition and give him a second term. To extend it to a third would be too much. His only possible method of maintaining his membership would be to come back as presiding officer. He proposed to stand for the lieutenant-governorship.

For services rendered he was solid with Foraker and Cox. Would they back him for the desired office? They would. Whether they could put him over against the Hanna opposition was a question. For the moment, the Cincinnati ring was in the ascendant. Foraker, the corruptionist, had allied himself in the presidential free-for-all with Roosevelt, the reformer. Into such incongruous bedfellowship do the exigencies of politics lure sheep and goat. Beaten in this field, for he was bitterly opposed to any party or person bearing the taint of reform, Hanna was solaced by having his man, Myron T. Herrick, named for governor. On the principle of alternation it was now the turn of the Cincinnatians. Cox demanded the second place on the ticket for Harding, and he became the nominee of the convention.

Herrick, Harding, and Harmony was the slogan of 1903. To its ringing measure the Republicans marched into office.

Harding still lost his home county, but he ran ahead of his ticket. The opposition to him at home was waning in proportion to his success outside.

There is little to be recorded of him as presiding officer of the senate. Nowhere did he leave any discernible impress upon legislation through the influence which he unquestionably could have exercised. More than ever he was the genial, suave, smiling conciliator, adjuster, compromiser; all things to all men, and, as far as might be, both parties. On the Democratic side he was as warmly liked as on the Republican. When his term was over, it left no dregs of rancor or ill-will. This is a tribute to amiability. Whether it be an unqualified testimonial to capacity for more important office is open to question.

The high mark of his Columbus career was forensic rather than legislative. The 1904 state convention was seething with intra-party hatreds and rivalries. All the big guns were loaded to kill: Hanna, Foraker, Cox, Herrick, Dick. Lieutenant Governor Harding was put on the programme to soothe the angry passions of the contestants with the lullaby of his eloquence. Sometimes it happens in the theatrical business that the winsome juvenile steals the show from the star performers. That is what occurred here. Harding's speech carried everything before it. So persuasive were his impartially distributed encomiums that he drew fervid and unanimous cheers alike for Foraker and Cox, Herrick and Hanna. Said the *Cleveland Plain Dealer*: [1]

> The man who stepped into the breach today was Lieutenant Governor Harding. To him had been set the difficult task of 'bundling' into one united package of 'harmony,' Dick, Foraker, Herrick, and Cox.
>
> The skilful and most successful accomplishment of the task earned a genuine triumph for the speaker. By the use of a rare flow of words the lieutenant governor for the moment made the delegates believe that the word 'harmony' had been writ-

[1] May 19, 1904.

ten with indelible ink. Roused from a condition of lethargy produced by the previous monotony of the convention, the delegates vociferously cheered the name of each one of the men who will constitute the Republican 'Big Four,' and at the end poured forth approval on Harding himself. If the enthusiasm this afternoon is any criterion, Lieutenant Governor Harding is destined to figure in an increasing extent in the future counsels of the party.

Oratory is a flame that feeds itself. It warmed the Harding eloquence, when he came to mention Boss Cox, to a degree of fulsome characterization which was to re-echo with unfortunate effect upon his own future. Thus did he attest his allegiance: [1]

> And next I want to name a great big, manly, modest but grand marshal of an invincible division of the grand old Republican army of Ohio. Modest, I say, but a man of ability, trusted in advice, just in judgment. We yield him our deference and devotion, George B. Cox. (Cheers.)

Ohio was not squeamish. But to have Cox, the saloonkeeper slum-boss of the Cincinnati council, the man who was notoriously living on a millionaire scale without visible funds to justify it, made the subject of such dithyrambic glorification, however well it might be received in the white-hot glow of the convention enthusiasm, produced a chillier reaction when reported throughout the state. Harding did not come to full realization of it, however, until years later. Just now he was on the top of the wave.

He let it subside beneath him. Why? Walter F. Brown, who was deep in Ohio politics of the day, believes that he foresaw Republican defeat.[2] That he could have had a renomination for the asking is certain. He did not ask. Everything would seem to draw him back to Columbus. He had had the best time of his life there, though happier days were to come. His election had been specially celebrated by

[1] *Cleveland Plain Dealer*, October 1, 1910.

[2] Statement to the writer.

the banquet which he apparently tendered to himself at an expense painful to the thrifty instincts of his life. Nothing else could have succeeded for him in Marion like his success at the capital. He was fast attaining the honor of being the Most Prominent Citizen. If he now turned his back on the arena, it might mean his elimination from the fighting ranks of t. e party. The actor who retires from that stage is so swiftly forgotten. Indeed, Frederick C. Howe, who noticed him pottering about Columbus the next year, relegates him to the position of 'an inconspicuous editor in Marion, O.,' while noting that he was 'often about the State House.'[1]

One wonders why. Was he lobbying? He could hardly have been building up his fences, since his decision to withdraw from public life was deliberate. Was it an instance of farsighted acumen? Did he sense the growing popular discontent with the machine, the spreading resentment against the encroaching corporations and their tools personified picturesquely in Tom L. Johnson, the reformed millionaire traction magnate who gave Cleveland an example of honest government as mayor and who used to tell his audiences: 'The public utility corporations are a bunch of grafters and thieves. I ought to know. I was one of 'em.' Was a prevision of the fact that coming reform meant trouble for the old-liners the basis for a strategic retreat on Harding's part? One must doubt it. Shrewd though he was in manipulative politics, he was not endowed with the gift of weighing probabilities with a judicial mind. Always his loyalty to the party would incline him to believe that others would be equally steadfast and that 'the grand old Republican army of Ohio' would remain invincible.

Periodically throughout his upward progress, Harding suffered from accesses of pessimism, of self-distrust, of defeatism, probably connected with the abuse to which he had been subjected by Amos Kling and others, and against which he

[1] Frederick C. Howe: *Confessions of a Reformer.*

had no defence. It may be that he now believed himself to have risen as high as he could go. Another theory is that the music of his presses, turning out ever larger editions of a prospering Marion *Star*, sounded an imperative call to his journalistic instincts. It must not be forgotten that first, last, and all the time, Warren G. Harding thought of himself as a newspaperman. Other matters were on the side.

★

V. 'W. G.,' Leading Citizen

Harding came back to a changed Marion, a city increasing in friendliness and mollifying in hostilities. Even the unhappy family rift was in process of being patched up. Amos Kling and his group had vainly tried to block the way to the lieutenant governorship. Before the election, Kling declared publicly that he hoped to God he would never live to see a negro governor of Ohio.[1] In his bitterness he went so far as to give an interview to a Pittsburgh reporter, but if it was ever published it has vanished from the records and memory of men.

This was the final splatter of his venom. At long last the hardboiled father-in-law gave up a losing fight. Harding's invincible equanimity under persecution, his resolute refusal to retaliate, his restraint and fairmindedness won out. The bitter occasion of Amos Kling's split with him had been publicized with all the force and fury which the magnate's autocratic spirit could summon. The circumstances of the reconciliation are unknown. For some years Kling had been more or less grudgingly recognizing his daughter on the street. Now he visited her at her home. The son-in-law had been ready at any time to shake hands and be friends. He ac-

[1] Statement by a former Marion reporter to the writer.

cepted the old man's surrender — for it was hardly less than that — with the same smiling self-control in which he had armored himself against the slings and arrows of his outrageous vilification.

Evil report, once set in motion, is not easy to overtake. Others perpetuated the abuse which Kling now abandoned. A new paper, the *Marion County Democrat*, was started by a father and son named Thatcher who had no known cause of enmity against Harding. An old resident writes me:

> Ned [Thatcher] was a heavy drinker and would hesitate at nothing. Being a fairly capable chalk-plate artist, he made a silhouette, in solid black, of Harding, explaining to his readers in a caption that, because of the color of the subject, he could not present the features. The Hardings threatened to kill Thatcher for this, but they were not fighting men and the threats were idle.

Florence Harding, it is said, assumed an attitude toward her father stiffer than that of her amiable and forgiving husband. Amos Kling was welcome in her house whenever he might choose to come. Also she would go to his, but only accompanied by her husband. Her natural resentment was not too readily overcome. As between husband and father, she left no doubt as to where her fealty lay.

From a reluctant admiration for his son-in-law's achievements, Kling passed to a real liking for the man. There may be instances where man, woman, or child succeeded in maintaining a hatred against Warren G. Harding permanently; I have been unable to discover any. Kling, however, thought that there should be an end to political activity. Presumably[1] he feared that the apparition of mixed blood, which he himself had raised, would rise to haunt the candidate's path if he pushed further forward, as indeed it did. I have talked with contemporaries who believe that Kling's persuasions were a decisive factor in Harding's temporary eclipse; with

[1] H. F. Alderfer: notes.

one old resident who, through no first-hand evidence, insists that the father-in-law made this a condition of the treaty of family peace.

Once more, then, the country editor is contentedly back on the job.

It is a Saturday evening in Marion. Country folk, flocking in for their weekly shopping, crowd the streets. A fine figure of a man stands on the corner near the *Star* office. He is distinctly, almost nobly handsome, with stalwart frame, nattily clad, a high forehead, direct, light-blue eyes, a well-modelled nose, a strong jaw, and a healthy color. There is an effect of vigor, of virility about him. Nowhere in that countenance would a physiognomist find anything symptomatic of the man's innate weakness and softness of fibre, though possibly in his carriage, for he slouches a little as he moves. True, the face is slightly asymmetrical, but that is no indication for a criminologist, being only the outward and visible evidence of an inward and comforting cut of tobacco, snugly tucked away in the pouch of the cheek. Warren G. Harding is holding his little, informal court, before climbing up to the office to help put the paper to bed.

'Evening, W. G.'

'Hello, John. How you doing?'

'All right, W. G. You're looking fine.'

'Never felt better in my life. Hello, Steve.'

'Well, well, W. G.! Glad to see you back.'

'Glad to see *you*, boy. Hear you got measles at your house. Hope everything's coming along all right.'

'Hi, W. G.! Be at the ball game tomorrow?'

'Sure. Sure. Wouldn't miss it.'

'Wouldn't hardly be legal without you.'

The town band marches past. Someone says, 'They sure miss W. G.'s old alto horn.'

The great man beams with unaffected pleasure. 'I'd like to be back in there,' he admits. 'The old wind is still pretty good.'

'Hello, W. G.' This is a farmer. 'They tell you what happened out at my house?'

'You betcha, Thurlow! Congratulations to you and the missus. Triplets, huh? Some lad! There'll be a piece in the paper tomorrow.'

A woman advances on him. 'We're holding our festival out at the Grove Wednesday. A few words from Governor Harding would be appreciated.'

'Count on me, Mrs. Johnson.'

'Hey, W. G. Who's goin' to cop the pennant this year?'

'Well, I wouldn't be sure this early, but I might make you a little bet on our boys.'

A man sidles up to him to whisper, 'About that road contract, W. G.'

'Yes, yes. All right. I'll see what I can do.'

Someone imparts information. 'I hear a new bank's going to be started. Think that's a good idea?'

'Well, I dunno. Maybe we've got enough banks to handle the money. Still, we're a growing community.'

'Anybody touch you yet for tickets to the benefit, W. G.?'

'Have they! But I'm still in the market. Gimme a pair. We all have to help out in a good cause.'

'I'd like your advice, W. G.' The man leans confidentially to the other's ear.

Harding nods seriously. 'Yes; yes. I think so.... Well, I'd maybe go a little slow there.... Not just yet. I'll think it over.'

'What d'you think of Tom's chances for the election, W. G.?'

'Good. Good. Why wouldn't they be? He's a Republican, ain't he?' His laugh was infectious.

To one and all he was 'W. G.' For everyone he had a pleasant word; often a wise one; his counsel was widely sought. He was lavish of encouragement, sparing of negation. If he could not support a project, he would seldom directly oppose it. 'Boost, don't knock.' His system was to ease the promoter down, leave him with a pleasant feeling. Genial was the word for Harding.

A visiting politician, witness to one of these sidewalk receptions, commented:

'They don't do much in this town without your say-so, do they, Harding?'

'Well, I tell 'em the best I know,' was the reply.

After these conferences, admiring comment would follow his receding form.

'Just plain folksy.' 'Common as an old shoe.' 'You don't see *him* putting on any lugs.' 'There may be slicker politicians, but old W. G.'s the man for my money.' 'Listen! We'll see him in Washington yet.'

It was inevitable that he should be a joiner. He is said to have belonged to more organizations than any other Marionite of his day; the Elks, Red Men, Hoo Hoos, Oddfellows, Moose, and all local and civic groups. Every new association meant additional friends and supporters. Here a curious contradiction appears. Despite his universal popularity, the most frequent testimonial to the esteem which a public man enjoys is strangely lacking: few children of the period were named for him. One wonders why.

No newspaper, however mild in method, can escape treading upon local toes. Such an instance was the indirect occasion of an editorial which is cited by Harding's admirers as the high mark of his journalistic achievement. To a member of the editorial staff of the *Star* under Harding I am indebted for the following data on the two dogs who preceded the famous Laddie Boy of the White House:

> Mr. Harding and his wife were great lovers of animals, especially dogs and horses. She was an expert horsewoman. The first dog, Jumbo, introduced into the *Star* office had a very spectacular entrance. He was a big, tawny Newfoundland sleigh dog, having the proportions of a mastiff. Lewis Gunn, a

giant shopworker, had threatened to thrash Harding in his office because of an article concerning a spite fence erected by Gunn. Following this, Jumbo was put on the job of preserving order. His size was a guarantee of peace. Harding loved Jumbo, and Jum, as he was called, loved Harding. In those days political and personal animosities were plentiful in the Harding life and not much trouble was taken to conceal them. Jumbo did his service nicely until the dog poisoner got him. Harding knew that the man who poisoned Jumbo would have preferred him as the victim, but the dog suffered for his master. The thought hurt the man and Jumbo's death was not soon forgotten.

Next Hub came to the office and he got the place in Harding's heart vacated by Jumbo. Years passed and the lovable Hub fell to the dog poisoner and Harding was wounded again by the thought that the beast once more had suffered for the master. Under great stress and emotion, Mr. Harding poured out his heart in his editorial.

Editor Harding wrote:

Edgewood Hub in the register as a mark of his breeding, but to us just Hub, a little Boston terrier, whose sentient eye mirrored the fidelity and devotion of his loyal heart. The veterinary said he was poisoned; perhaps he was — his mute sufferings suggested it. One is reluctant to believe that a human being that claims man's estate could be so hateful a coward as to ruthlessly torture and kill a trusting victim, made defenceless through his confidence in the human master, but there are such. One honest look from Hub's trusting eyes were worth a hundred lying greetings from such inhuman beings, though they wore the habiliment of men.[1]

It is an amiable little effort, genuine in emotion and therefore with a quality of its own. But it is hardly likely to find its way into the textbooks as a paragon of newspaper style. A hundred other small contemporaries could furnish items of equal virtuosity.

Politically the paper was cashing in on its party virtue. Out of office by his own choice, Editor Harding was at no

[1] The *Star*, March 11, 1913.

time out of politics. It was the era of reform in national Republicanism, with Theodore Roosevelt as standard-bearer. With little enthusiasm for the 'new nationalism' or any such slogan of an idealism suspect to his brand of political thought, Harding nevertheless supported T. R. as long as he remained regular. But his real fervor centred in Ohio.

Perturbing murmurs against the old-time rule were making themselves heard in the state. Mark Hanna's political heirs — he had died in 1904 — the practical Charles F. Dick and the affluent and affable Myron T. Herrick, had been obliged to make concessions in Cleveland. Foraker and Cox were still dominant in Cincinnati, though even there Reform had reared its ugly head. The *Star* stuck to Foraker. Its editor was making speeches in support of him, bolstering the local machines, exalting the standpat gospel in the party councils.

True to nothing but his own corrupt machinations, Foraker split away from Roosevelt, after helping to elect him, and when that belligerent President undertook to name his own successor in the White House ('They'll take Taft or they'll get me') announced himself as a candidate for 1908. The Republican State Committee endorsed Taft. Foraker's long-time confederate, Boss Cox, deserted him. The powerful Ohio Republican League came out for Foraker in a set of defiant resolutions, extolling him for his opposition in the Senate to the Roosevelt measures, and proceeding:

> Entertaining these views, we send him greeting and assure him, as he returns to his labors at Washington, that he has our unqualified confidence and esteem, and we not only pledge him our loyal support for his re-election to the Senate, but we further declare that he is our choice as the Republican candidate for President of the United States in 1908.[1]

An unequivocal commitment, surely. Its author was ex-Lieutenant Governor Warren G. Harding.

[1] Joseph Benson Foraker: *Notes of a Busy Life*, vol. II.

But a swing around the political circle aroused in the keen observer's mind the uneasy suspicion that he was in the wrong boat, and that the boat was sinking. Harding emulated the proverbial and sagacious rat; he got off in time. There was nothing furtive in his *volte-face*. On the contrary, he spread it, leaded, across a double column of his editorial space, headed, 'Foraker is Defeated and Ohio is for Taft.'

> This is not a bandwagon climb; it is the calm recording of the trend in Ohio politics. The bandwagon is full, anyway. The contest for Presidential preference is at an end.... Senator Foraker may keep up a semblance of a fight for district delegates, but it will make no difference.... Licked is the laconic way to put it, and in political honor his followers are prisoners of war and will have to be good.... When politicians play the game of politics, they must play gamely, regardless of the umpire.[1]

Doctor Alderfer remarks wonderingly that 'this is the man who somehow achieved a great reputation for personal and political loyalty. The truth of the matter is that Harding was loyal to only one thing and that was the strongest political factor on which he could lean for support.'

This is perhaps a little too harsh. True, Harding was in matters of principle inherently shifty, an opportunist and a time-server. That is because principles meant little to him; he had small comprehension of them. But people meant much. So far as I know, his treachery to Foraker, which the latter only mildly resented, is unique in his career as a personal betrayal.

Harding's defection not only cost the candidate his state's support in the convention, which is of small importance since he had no chance of the nomination in any case, but it resulted in his being supplanted as Senator by the supposedly Progressive Burton.

The pay-off for the editor's switch came in 1909. Boss Cox,

[1] The *Star*, January 22, 1908.

now the Number 1 man of Southern Ohio Republicanism, had put off the temporary misfit of reform and was fighting to prevent the naming of Nicholas B. Longworth for governor. To beat Longworth, he picked Harding. Except by the Foraker faction, the nomination was well received. The platform was standpat.

Platforms do not necessarily determine issues. The Democrats, who had put up Judson Harmon, chose the ground on which they preferred to fight. They made bossism the issue. And George B. Cox was the vulnerable spot in the Republican line-up.

Cox seems to have bragged ill-advisedly that he engineered the choice of Harding. The opposition dug up Harding's old encomium of the boss in all its fulsome gush of 'deference and devotion.' The opposing candidate devised an unpleasant method of digging a dictionary out of his pocket and reading the definitions of the two words. Had Mr. Harding anything to add to them?

'I have no quarrel with the political leaders of the great cities, no denunciations to offer, and no renunciations to make,' was the best that the Republican candidate could do.[1]

His feelings, always oversensitive for one in the rough-and-tumble of the arena, were ravaged by a *Cleveland Plain Dealer* cartoon depicting him as the innocent young greenhorn from the country, upon whose arm hangs an obvious painted-lady, Boss Cox, to the horror of Mother G.O.P., who, with uplifted hands of scandal, exclaims, 'Warren! where *did* you get that?'

Macchiavellian enough to realize that his support would hurt the candidate more than it would help him, by alienating the already lukewarm liberals, Foraker cunningly denounced their leader, James B. Garfield, for ignoring Harding in his speeches. The annoyed committee gave Foraker his choice of behaving himself or keeping off the stump. Censorship,

[1] *Plain Dealer*, September 24, 1910.

particularly of the intra-party variety, did not commend itself to the man who had gloried in the sobriquet of Fire Alarm for so long. He pointed out that nobody had ever put a muffler on him yet, and if the committee thought they could do it, now was as good a time as any other to try.

Callously he continued to distribute his monkey-wrenches where they would do the most harm. He was not the only storm centre. Cox talked plaintively of vote-juggling — Cox, Boss Cox! Dick insisted that he was not getting proper support from the organization. Daugherty, still prickly with the itch for office, threatened to give him a battle for the senatorial nomination. Grumblings from several cities over local corruption and boss-tyranny made themselves heard. All of which helped the candidate not at all.

What could that sweet singer of harmony do in a situation full of discords? There is a note of lamentation, of foreboding in some of his campaign speeches:

> Right here and now I appeal for a brotherhood of all Republicans. All we have to do is to chain down hysterical old women that at present are ranting about in the field of American politics. I want all kinds of Republicans to get under the banner this year. I want the Taft Republicans, Roosevelt Republicans, Burton Republicans, Dick Republicans, Foraker Republicans, Garfield Republicans, and Cox Republicans.[1]

He was doing his desperate, ineffectual best to play both sides, to straddle every difficult fence, to keep in the good graces of one and all.

Harry M. Daugherty managed his campaign, how well or ill cannot be estimated, since so many other factors entered into the odds against him. As Republican state chairman, Daugherty was striving to hold Ohio in line for Taft. His methods were rough; he needlessly antagonized people, with the result that he was forced out of the state chairmanship. His failure militated against Harding's chances.

[1] *Plain Dealer*, September 21, 1910.

Meantime the candidate was straddling issues as they presented themselves. His conception of political progress was to make no enemies. In times of comparative peace, this may serve. But cry peace as he might, there was no peace. It was internecine war between the Republican factions. Naturally he was for the standpat creed of the platform. But the reform element, which had proved its strength by electing a senator in Foraker's place, must be placated. Consider this adventure on the tightrope.

> I have no objection to an insurgent [he must have swallowed hard when he said it], though I couldn't be one myself. I have no objection to a progressive Republican, because one must be a Republican to be progressive.[1]

Inevitably the liquor question thrust itself upon his unwilling attention. Where did he stand on it? (Why must they bring that up!) He executed the time-honored side-step:

> The temperance question is legislative rather than executive, and is not to transcend all other important issues in this campaign. My legislative record is written in the journals of two general assemblies. I couldn't change that record if I would. I stand for enforcement of the law and would not be worthy of your suffrages if I did not.[2]

Roosevelt came to Ohio late in the fight and gave Harding a negligent and perfunctory pat on the back, which could not have helped much.[3] It amounted to a watery endorsement of Harding because he was not Harmon. There was not and never could be any sympathy between the fiery and aggressive Roosevelt and the timorous Laodicean Harding. The man who is eternally saying, right or wrong, 'Let's fight it out,' can have nothing in common with the man who pleads, 'Can't we get together on this?'

[1] *Plain Dealer*, September 24, 1910.

[2] *Plain Dealer*, October 19, 1910.

[3] 'Mr. Harding is sure to do for you the things that Governor Harmon will not do for you.' — *Plain Dealer*, November 6, 1910, reporting Roosevelt's speech.

If Harding did not know by this time that his case was desperate, he was about the only man in the state who did not. He is reported to have intimated that he had been made a scapegoat to beat Longworth and that he would give a hundred thousand dollars to be out of his predicament.

The figure was a portent. He was beaten by just about that many votes. Several of his fellow candidates on the ticket made a better showing than he did. It was his first taste of defeat. (The early campaign for county Auditor, it will be remembered, was no more than a joke.) He took it hard. Lamenting to one of his editorial staff the morning after the crash that he would never again try to get anywhere in Ohio, he said bitterly: 'These things will happen as long as Tom, Dick, and Harry have the right to vote.'

Not for anything in the world would he have given utterance to so impolitic a sentiment in public. Goaded by the exasperation of defeat, he spoke his inner thought. Unconsciously, perhaps, but none the less surely, he was following the Hamiltonian creed of selective suffrage. In a properly constituted democracy, property-holders alone should have the privilege of voting. He was now a man of property. The rabble had beaten him. There was no virtue in Tom, Dick, or Harry.

Though he had decided (not irrevocably) to abandon hope of office, there were honorific rewards in store for him. He was chosen to present Taft's name for the Presidential nomination in 1912. It was the most welcome honor ever accorded him. Not even his own nomination for the highest office, he afterward declared, gave him so great a thrill.[1]

Taft was the logical candidate to succeed himself. But Roosevelt, who had forced him upon the party in 1908, now turned against him. T. R. charged that his successor had betrayed progressivism. The fact is that the President had revolted against the effort of the ex-President to dictate his

[1] Speech, New York City, May 23, 1921.

course. The most disastrous split in the history of Republicanism followed.

Blind to the omens, Harding went to the convention full of confidence. Taft belonged to his clan. He was an Ohioan and a regular. The nominating speech opened most auspiciously. He had the great audience with him. Then he made a tactical slip. In the midst of his eloquence, with a third of the way still to go, he uttered the name of Taft, inadvertently, of course, for he was too experienced thus to spoil his climax deliberately. Uprose the assemblage in wild, uncontrollable enthusiasm, and the rest of the speech was lost in the flood of acclaim. The unhappy orator had to sit down with a good part of his oratory still pent up within him.

Nevertheless he was a success. The Ohio leaders marked him for preferment.

Still assured that all was well, the editor returned to his desk to help elect the candidate. Then Theodore Roosevelt spurred into the fray, a wildcat mounted on a bull moose.

No mediaeval saint, seeing his shrine profaned, could have suffered a more burning sense of outrage than Warren G. Harding. All the old venom gathered and festered at his pen's end. The insurgent leader was excommunicated in every issue of the *Star*. He was worse than Aaron Burr. He was another Benedict Arnold. He was 'utterly without conscience and truth, and the greatest faker of all time.' His running mate, Hiram Johnson, was 'not only a faker, but a blackguard.' (One recalls Biographer Willis Johnson's testimonial to Editor Harding, that he 'never descended to personalities.') To 'stand at Armageddon and battle for the Lord' was the hypocrisy and heresy of the damned. The Bull Moosers were outcastes, traitors, beyond the pale.

The cataclysm which overwhelmed Taft in the worst defeat on record was a body blow to his Ohio supporter. Thoroughly disillusioned, Harding was confirmed in his determination to quit a pursuit so fruitless for the faithful.

Harding may have honestly thought that he was through with politics. Mrs. Harding had other ideas. Her ambitions were not to be chilled by a setback which her resolute spirit regarded as no more than temporary. While the editor was back at his desk, she was keeping a watchful eye on developments. There were rumors that Senator Burton was tired of Washington and would not seek re-election at the close of his term. A member of the *Star* staff said to Mrs. Harding:

'What's the matter with W. G. pointing for the Senate?'

Her face lighted up. 'Do you think he could get it?'

'Why not? The Republicans are getting together. He's got a lot of friends.'

The 'Duchess' sighed. 'It costs such a lot of money to live in Washington.'

'Oh, it isn't so expensive. And the paper isn't doing badly.'

'If he was only a corporation lawyer and could pick up a lot of business on the side,' she continued after a ruminative pause, 'I'd say yes. But he couldn't do anything there. No; I don't know as we can afford it yet.'

Was there an emphasis on the final word? The other party to the dialogue thought so.

Party differences in the state had been pretty well forgotten in the salutary shock afforded by Wilson's victory. It was Harry Daugherty's idea that a man of Harding's stamp would have a good chance for the senatorship. Senator Burton was said to be weary of Washington. Daugherty was growing in power. The other leaders offered no considerable opposition. But the prospective candidate himself was the unreckonable factor.

When the time was ripe, Daugherty made a trip to Marion. Comfortable and secure at his desk, secure in his prestige and local power, the editor of the *Star* was in no mood to exchange these tangibles for the dubious struggles of the political arena. He had every reason to be content with the progress of the paper. It was being quoted, not widely but in frequent exchange columns of the lesser Ohio press. It was making money. Its influence in the party councils was strong and growing stronger. Mention has already been made of the pleasant fact that new enterprises, coming to settle in Marion, 'chipped in' for the paper's goodwill and support, with slices of stock.

Why should a man with these advantages give them up and offer himself as a target for the shafts of the unappreciative and ungrateful? Harding was still sore over his bad beating for the governorship. Harry Daugherty could have pointed out that he himself had taken worse beatings without letting it impair his fighting spirit. Fighting spirit was not the editor's forte. He knew when he was beaten. (Sometimes he knew that he was beaten when he wasn't.)

Difficult to discourage, Daugherty went back to the quest, not once but several times. Harding vacillated. It was his nature to. Some of their fellow-citizens believe that Mrs. Harding now allied herself with the state leader, that she was gazing longingly from afar upon the fabled glories of Washington. Possibly that might account for the fact that, as the pressure became heavier, Harding packed up and ran away to Florida for a vacation. The pursuer was not to be thrown off the trail. He followed. Legend puts these words in his mouth:

'I found him sunning himself like a turtle on a log and pushed him off into the water.' [1]

It was not true that Senator Burton was willing to quit his job. But he had proved a peculiar sort of Progressive. Elected as a reform candidate, he had voted almost one hundred per cent with Nelson W. Aldrich, arch-standpatter of the Republican Party. Furthermore, the Cuyahoga County (Cleveland) leaders were incensed at him for ignoring their heavily voted endorsement of Theodore Roosevelt and supporting Taft. With not oversubtle strategy, the Ohio bosses

[1] Mark Sullivan: *Our Times*, vol. VI.

pointed out to him that his renomination would be an affront to the liberal wing and would endanger party success. Loyalty demanded that he sacrifice himself in favor of some candidate with Progressive leanings, who could unite all elements. When he found who was picked to supplant him, though ordinarily a man of kind temper, he exploded profanely against 'that goddamned, honeyfugling pussyfoot, Warren Harding.'

The direct primary was in force for its first trial in Ohio. Foraker was in the field again, seeking the bubble Vindication. The letters between him and John D. Archbold, published in the Hearst newspapers, had proved that he was in the secret pay of the Standard Oil Company while Senator. The scandal had cost him his seat. Now, with the singular ratiocination of the politician besmirched, he sought to go before the electorate and be washed whiter than snow by their votes. As a parallel to this curious procedure, one might conceive the case of an unmarried girl who, after having a baby, should appeal to a Sunday school class of her peers for a certificate of maidenhood.

It is a commentary on the political standards of the day and place that Foraker was still a formidable contestant.

The two men were on friendly terms, despite Harding's earlier abandonment of his benefactor in the Taft campaign. He now went to see the Cincinnati man, to persuade him that he had no chance, to induce him to quit a hopeless battle. For if Foraker was removed, Harding might expect to get the formal backing of the organization. Without that he was still dubious of his prospects. In vain did he tell the Fire Alarm that the leaders did not want him and the voters would be against him. Foraker was no quitter. He could boast many friends and a power of oratory far superior in fire and force to Harding's. This was his last chance. In spite of hell and high water he would run. There was a third entry in the field, Ralph Cole from the northwest part of the state.

Harding went into the contest with a sinking heart. New methods were called for in this untried field of the direct primary. The glory of the Republican Party would not serve as topic, because he was campaigning against other Republicans. He must give reasons why Warren G. Harding was the man for the people's votes, and his brand of oratory did not lend itself happily to the theme. His typical bursts of magnificent verbiage, applied to himself, would have been just a little ridiculous. Harding was not without a saving sense of humor. And he was not a vain man. He complained to Daugherty:

'Harry, it's awful.'

'What's awful?'

'This stumping the country and howling for myself.'

Not being thin-skinned himself, the older politician could not see it. 'Who would you howl for? Foraker?'

'I'm discouraged and disgusted. I'm going home and go to bed.'[1]

If he did, his sponsor and his wife got him out again. He continued to 'howl for myself' as best he could. Had he stayed in bed, he would probably have been defeated. Foraker, for all that the leaders thought him out of the running, proved no mean antagonist. Indeed, but for the presence of a third man in the field, he might well have come out the victor. The final count was

> Harding.... 88,540
> Foraker.... 76,870
> Cole....... 52,237

Against him the Democrats put up Timothy S. Hogan. There was a third candidate, A. L. Garfield, carrying the banner of a small force of irreconcilable Progressives. With

[1] Harry M. Daugherty: *The Inside Story of the Harding Tragedy.*

that impending split in the ranks, the prospects for the Republican standard-bearer did not seem bright. But he was lucky in having Hogan for an opponent. As attorney general under Governor Judson Harmon, Hogan had relentlessly prosecuted those election frauds which had come to be accepted as standard procedure in Ohio. There was not a county where he had not put or tried to put prominent workers in jail. Malcontents of both parties ganged up on him. Moreover, he was a Roman Catholic, which militated against him in the rural districts. A popular Democrat might have had a chance, though the tide was now setting in the other direction. Harding was victorious by the impressive plurality of about 75,000. He ran far ahead of the gubernatorial candidate, Frank B. Willis. That the Cleveland machine was loyal in support is proved by his carrying Cuyahoga County. For the first time his home county, Marion, supposed to be staunchly Democratic, gave him a rousing testimonial of nearly three votes to one for his opponent. Garfield was a weak also-ran everywhere.

It was regarded as an endorsement of the old-line and supposedly discredited control. The *Cleveland Plain Dealer*, which always gave Harding credit for unimpeachable personal character, did not see him measuring up to his new duties. It judged him by the yardstick of his campaign utterances, and, on that basis, stigmatized him as 'Spokesman of the Past.' [1]

> A speech by Mr. Harding knows neither time nor circumstance. It would have been as applicable at the time of Benjamin Harrison or James G. Blaine as to that of Theodore Roosevelt and Woodrow Wilson. It has not the slightest relation to current problems.... No one need doubt his sincerity, for he himself is a relic of the good old days which assuredly were good to the Republican beneficiaries. Time and conditions change, but not Harding.

[1] October 18, 1914.

Time and conditions continued to change. Warren Harding remained stationary. On the national stage he is still the country editor, translated but not transformed. Hence it is not unfair to measure him by the yardstick of his editorial product and standard.

Someone has said that the newspaper which does not educate its owner is a failure. From available evidences, the *Marion Star* was neither the product of, nor an incentive to, an educated mind. It is difficult to identify in its style and content any cultural or literary influence, even of the simplest; any trace of the Bible, Shakespeare, the classics, the English poets, *Alice*, the *Congressional Record*, Mother Goose, the *World Almanac*, or George Ade. It is sterile alike of allusion or quotation. The exception is a semi-occasional and dimly suggested Hamiltonian touch, but that is evident more in matter than in manner.

The fact is that Warren G. Harding was and remained an unread man. Books did not enter into his scheme of life in any important sense. The magic and the music were alien to him. He cannot fairly be called illiterate, although some of his verbiage, when he strives to attain the impressive, furnishes a sad example of the grandiloquently inept. We shall find it later in his speeches. He was aware of it and sensitive to criticism on the point. No; he was not illiterate. But he was unliterate. Or perhaps pseudo-literate would be the juster characterization.

A representative of the *Bookman*,[1] sent to Marion to get an interview from the candidate on his literary tastes and choice, had a terrible time of it. Between the lines of his pathetic and dogged struggle to dig out something available for print, it becomes obvious that Harding had no literary views and was too honest to pretend that he had. The best the visitor could do was to fill his space with the distinction that Senator Harding preferred history and biography to

[1] October, 1920.

fiction or drama, that he admired Alexander Hamilton (whose successor he was to find in Andrew Mellon), and had gathered quite a library of Hamiltoniana; that he admired Maurice Hewlett and considered 'The Passing of the Third Floor Back' the most enjoyable play he had ever seen (here shows his emotional humanism), though he conscientiously approved Shakespeare also.

This is the man who, with hardly discernible increase in intellectual equipment, little broadened by experience, little enriched by travel, little affected in standards, loyalties, and creed, is to transport his unstable principles, his rigid partisanship, his unchastened verbosity, his dim ignorance of the greater world's issues, problems, and thought to the stage of national effort.

★

VI. The Goodly Fellowship
of the Senate

Sunny days now dawned for Warren G. Harding. The senatorship answered his every ambition, every hope. Had he been permitted to retain this status, following election with re-election, with his beloved *Marion Star* to retire to eventually, he would have been as fortunate and blessed an Ohioan as ever rose above his capacities or expectations and this biography would never have been written. Nor any other on the subject. There would have been nothing to write about. Warren G. Harding would have lived and died, unnoted, leaving just another group of entries as just another senator in the forgotten pages of that mausoleum of petty and perishable glories, the *Congressional Record*.

If a mere recorder may gratify himself with a personal satisfaction, I should like to testify to a definite pleasure in viewing those six coming years of happiness. They must have more than compensated for the exacerbations of his early struggle upward, and even for the disillusionment and disaster that shadowed the closing scenes of his life. Not yet was he in the grip of those compulsions which were to lift him with the force of a wave beneath an unseaworthy ship.

Or, if he were, he did not realize it. Nor, I think, did the forces themselves. For all his self-ascribed gift of prophecy, Harry Daugherty could hardly at this time have regarded his exceedingly dark horse as anything better than a thousand-to-one shot.

It was, on the whole, a disorganized Senate into which the commonplace Senator made his genial entry in 1915. The war was raging in Europe. The Democrats, in complete congressional control, were looking to Woodrow Wilson for leadership in a crisis which nobody understood and everybody feared. There was little for the Republicans to do other than to follow the time-honored policy of criticism and obstruction, except in matters affecting the national safety, where partisanship gave way to patriotism.

As a freshman on the minority side, Harding could 'coast.' Abstention from marked activity was an easy and safe rôle. Nothing more was required of him. Seldom was he required to make up his mind or assert his position with distasteful positiveness. Follow-my-leader was his rule of conduct. He played safe with his party. That was one of the Senates which Lynn Haines, in his *Searchlight on Congress*, calls 'indefensibly political.' Ascribing to it 'the playing of politics for the Senate's sake,' he writes:

> Its whole atmosphere has become partisanly and personally political. It has descended from the plane of intellectual combat to the level of election deal and dicker. Pork is king.... Never, we believe, has there been so little mental and moral strength as in the present body.

This is a recurrent plaint of all political critics. Unremarkable though the average of quality was, there were still men of the courage and progressive breadth of La Follette the elder, of the convictions and fervor of Norris, of the intellect and influence of Penrose, of the studious and conscientious industry of Smoot, of the experience and force of Borah, not to mention such others as Kenyon, Walsh, and Clark.

Not among the strong men did the neophyte from Ohio seek his cronies. With unerring instinct he picked the congenial second- and third-raters, including some of the 'wrong uns.' There was no harm in most of them. They were good fellows. Harding was a good fellow. All good fellows together in that House of Fellowship, the United States Senate. Nevertheless from the angle of political ethics, such members as Penrose of Pennsylvania, Fall of New Mexico, and Brandegee of Connecticut can hardly be regarded as the safest guides to a neophyte's footsteps.

George B. Christian, Jr., President Harding's devoted secretary and friend, once surprised the writer by saying of his chief: 'He had no taste for politics. Never had.'

'But he liked to be a Senator, didn't he?'

Mr. Christian made a shrewd distinction. 'No: he didn't like being a Senator. He liked being in the Senate.'

Although the loyal Mr. Christian would not admit it, Harding was not a useful Senator. He disliked routine. Letter-writing was irksome to him. Soon his constituents of his own party took to routing their business through his Democratic colleague, Atlee Pomerene, to save time.[1] Senator Harding was too likely to be otherwise occupied when wanted.

In this he was not distinctive. Devotion to the public interest weighed lightly upon many of his associates. The Solons played a lot of golf and a lot of poker. They patronized liberally the ball park and the race track. It was a time of free-and-easy entertainment. In fact, as the *Marion Star* might have put it in one of its felicitous phrases, a good time was had by all at the party.

As an inconsiderable member of a minority Harding saw no reason for killing himself with overwork. Out of 245 roll-calls in his first session, he responded to 112. When present he refrained from voting on thirty-five per cent of the mo-

[1] Statement of Walker S. Buell of the *Cleveland Plain Dealer* to the writer.

tions. The figures seem to indicate a want of interest or industry, a lax sense of duty. In fairness, however, they should
be read in the light of senatorial averages. From this angle
Harding makes a respectable early showing. As he settled
into harness, he became more negligent, content that someone else should do the hard pulling. Only eighteen Senators
of his time showed a higher percentage of absences on roll-
call, and of the new members who came in with him, he was
the ranking slacker.

'The conclusion that Harding was extremely dilatory in
this duty is inevitable,' says Doctor Alderfer.[1]

Analysis of the Ohio man's votes proves indubitably that
in all party measures he was still Old Reliable. He conscientiously opposed the nomination of two liberals, Brandeis to
the United States Supreme Court and George Rublee to the
Federal Trade Commission. He supported a bill which, if
passed, would have undermined the government's conservation policy. He was for a tax exemption which would
grossly have favored the private water-power companies. He
was against a measure which would have given the government, in case of war, the power to acquire water-power plants
for the manufacture of nitrates, and another to provide for
government manufacture of armor plate. But he upheld
naval preparedness and army increase, while voting No on
the proposition to warn Americans against travelling on the
ships of belligerent nations.[2]

Several important measures found him either uncertain
of his mind or loath to reveal it. He refrained from voting on
child labor, the eight-hour railroad bill, on the bill to forbid
our warships being used as collectors, by threat of force, of
private claims against foreign nations, on publicizing in-
come-tax returns, and on two tariff bills.

Broadly speaking — and one must generalize again since

[1] H. F. Alderfer: *The Personality and Politics of Warren G. Harding.*
[2] H. F. Alderfer: *The Personality and Politics of Warren G. Harding.*

in the darkening atmosphere of coming war a number of measures lost their partisan significance — he followed his leaders faithfully. Doctor Alderfer says:

> There were twenty undoubted party [Democratic] issues and on each of these Harding either voted No or did not vote at all.... Harding recognized that the function of the minority party was to criticize and obstruct. His votes show his record that of a static conservative, supporting new measures only when fostered by his party or when demanded by public opinion.

Harding's contribution to legislation in six years of senatorial incumbency is practically nil. History would not be altered in any way perceptible to the eye of future generations if he had never tried his hand at lawmaking. In all he introduced 134 bills. Of these 122 were vote-bait, pension or local measures. Twelve were of national scope but of minor significance, such as provisions for public instruction in Spanish, loaning of tents to relieve housing shortage, investigation of influenza, making available discarded rifles to the Sons of Veterans Naval Reserve.

True to form he was vacillating in his course when weighty matters were up for decision. His preference would always be against standing up to be counted. For example, out of thirty-two calls on various angles of the Prohibition question, he voted Wet thirty times. But in the final showdown he was counted on the affirmative for the Prohibition Amendment; he even went further and helped override Wilson's veto of the Volstead Act. It was not for conviction. He was himself a drinking man, though he claimed to be temperate, as every drinking man does. He publicly stated his belief that enforcement would prove ineffective, and later, as President, gave point to its ineffectiveness by consistent violations of the law for which he had voted. Why did he so vote? Because he recognized a public demand 'growing and insistent and persistent.' On minor phases where senatorial records would not make the front pages, he could afford to vote his convictions. When the voting public, of which he had a salutary fear, was aroused to watchfulness, he took the safe course and reversed himself. He was not so foolish as to risk the bandwagon transforming itself into a juggernaut and crushing his hopes beneath avenging wheels.

The Nineteenth Amendment also caused him discomfort and uncertainty. No student of his character can doubt that he disliked extension of the suffrage to women. It was a change, and he distrusted all change. The founders of the nation knew best. Why try to improve upon their tenets? He dodged as long as he dared. 'Utterly indifferent... neither hostile toward it nor for the suffrage cause.' Such was his definition of his attitude, expressed to a delegation of suffragists. Hoping that the party would take a stand and thus relieve him of responsibility, he patiently stalled. The best the women could get out of him was a promise, unremarkable for originality, that he would give the question 'earnest and careful consideration.' Indefinite evasion was not possible. Face the question he must. He voted aye on the amendment and, afterward, making a virtue and an asset of necessity, pointed with pride to his official support and sunnily suggested that a little reciprocity would be appreciated. This was some years after, when he was a candidate for the Presidency.

Personal popularity and political subservience brought him desirable if not too onerous committee assignments. These included Foreign Relations, Commerce, Territories, Naval Affairs, Claims, Expenditures in the Treasury Department, Pacific Islands, Porto Rico and Virgin Islands, Public Health and National Quarantine, Standard Weights and Measures, and Philippines of which he became chairman. Since he had never evinced any special interest in countries beyond our immediate borders, the number of 'travel' assignments suggests that he received them, not because of fitness, but to afford him participation in pleasant congressional junkets. Join the Senate and see the world.

As to his effective part in committee decisions, there is little evidence, since these proceedings are not public. It is logical to believe that his main value was as an adjuster, a smoother-out of difficulties and obstructions, the practitioner of those special arts which had so commended themselves to the grateful Governor Nash of Ohio.

In one respect, and by no means a contemptible one, he may stand as a senatorial model. Never was there a sweeter-tempered, a better-mannered member of that often contentious and not infrequently acrimonious body. The man from Ohio never took part in any of the unseemly squabbles. Nor was this urbane equanimity a superficial quality. Like all genuine and consistent courtesy, his was the expression of a deep-seated kindliness, a natural charity, tolerance, and trust in the essential decency of the human species. Early in his incumbency some of his sharper-tongued confrères occasionally took a fall out of him. As a pastime this soon lost its zest. It was so easy to turn the laugh on him that it was unsportsmanlike. Furthermore, he was so obviously, so innocently surprised and hurt when made the butt of wit or the victim of satire, that his assailant soon found himself up against stout defenders and not always of Harding's own party, for he could claim many friends among the Democrats.

In appearance he fitted his job to perfection. Mark Sullivan observes that no man could possibly be as much a Senator as Harding looked,[1] and a saying gained smiling currency to the effect that he was the only man in the world who could wear a toga and get away with it.

No personal aspersion or deliberately hurtful word was ever attributed to Senator Harding. Always he was ready to credit an opponent with a sincerity and honesty of belief

[1] *Our Times*, vol. VI.

equal to his own. And this was neither policy nor hypocrisy. He believed it. He was consistently deferential to the views of others; never opinionated as to his own. At times his intellectual humility seems a little overdone, perilously near to abasement, as when he says, 'I would not for a moment desire to take up and discuss any individual appropriation; I feel myself utterly unfit to do so'; or again, 'I rather suspect that I will not influence any vote on this measure.' His fellows might well have been tempted to ask, 'What is he doing in *this* gallery, then?' He answered that, too, in his way.

> Mr. President, I do not want any fellow Senator to misconstrue my remarks. I like the fraternity of this body. I like to know that when the waters are muddy, I will be considered. I like to participate in the 'Booster' proposition.

No one of his time more greatly contributed to the fraternity feeling of 'the most exclusive club in the world' than Warren G. Harding.

His official conduct does not measure up. Doctor Alderfer thus sums up his senatorial attitude on public issues:

> Complete indifference, a desire to follow the dictates of his party, a friendly interest in those who appear in behalf of a proposal, a period of cautious vacillation to await developments, a vote with the prevailing faction and the use of that vote to appeal for support from the winning group — all these are part of the method which he used to attack important problems concerning which he had no real interest.[1]

It is not unfair to Harding to say that his legislative course was shaped primarily by the desire to consolidate and assure his position. His formula was to conciliate, first, the party leaders; second, popular opinion as far as he could interpret it — not always an easy matter — keeping an attentive eye on the folks back home; to march in the ranks rather than push forward among the leaders; to play a modest alto horn accompaniment to *vox populi*.

[1] H. F. Alderfer: *The Personality and Politics of Warren G. Harding.*

His all-informing concern was to keep Warren G. Harding in the United States Senate.

Outside of immediate party control, his guide to conduct was the interests of Big Business. Government should be conducted, he believed, with an eye to the maintenance of the *status quo*, since Big Business supported the country, was the beneficent distributor of jobs of labor, and had given the United States the greatest prosperity in the history of mankind. Says Doctor Alderfer:[1]

> He held a vague and naïve faith that government and business were dissociated, or, at least, that relations between the leaders of these institutions were ethical.

Harding himself testified to the faith that was in him in these words:

> And I make the statement, Mr. President, that American business success, commercial and industrial, is not founded in any way on favoritism or privilege.

Again:

> But I make the statement, and I challenge its contradiction, that there runs through the ranks of the great captains of industry as high a type of conscience as can be found even on the floor of the United States Senate.

Senator Harding had not yet met E. L. Doheny, Harry F. Sinclair, and other lesser oil barons.

Any person who did not subscribe to the creed of business-worship was under suspicion of radicalism. Taxes upon wealth encouraged the undermining heresy, 'that those who have ought to be plundered.' Regulation of industry, even as a war measure, met with his instant hostility. The proposition to extend the Food Control Act spurred him to a defence of 'the inherited institutions of the fathers.' Government control of paper supply he deemed (as a publisher) a step toward Bolshevism. The soap-box was anathema to him. That

[1] H. F. Alderfer: *The Personality and Politics of Warren G. Harding.*

world-old '*cupiditas novarum rerum*' of which Cicero complained filled him with an equal distrust. 'This everlasting seeking after something different' was a dangerous symptom of unrest. Harding was not unrestful. He had seized his opportunities and made the most of them. Why couldn't everyone else be contented, too? If they weren't quite so well off, then frugality and adjustment to their condition in life was his prescription. 'No people in eighteen-dollar shoes is equipped for the march of civilization,' he told them. At the time he was marching in clothes made by a Fifth Avenue tailor and was considered one of the best-dressed men in the Senate.

As a corollary to his fealty to Big Business, he distrusted Labor. His employees never made any trouble for him. Why should other workmen be antagonistic to their bosses? It was part of his attractive if somewhat imperceptive modesty to see himself, not as the exceptionally just, generous, and humanitarian employer that he really was, but as the average wage-payer. Most business men were good fellows. A good fellow would naturally be square with his men. Therefore, labor discontent rose, not out of unfair conditions, but through the fomenting of trouble-makers; i.e., labor officials. Such, loosely, would be his syllogism. Still, Labor was a factor to be reckoned with. He must make a showing of support for it.

Statisticians compute his senatorial record as eleven votes unfavorable to Labor, seven votes favorable, and ten abstentions from taking sides.[1]

An outline of Harding's political, social, and economic expressions would take this general form:

> One hundred per cent party man.
> Ninety-five per cent standpatter.
> Honest and loyal adherent of Big Business.
> Anti-labor, though with caution.

[1] H. F. Alderfer: *The Personality and Politics of Warren G. Harding.*

Wet in belief and practice; Dry as a self-preservative.
Imperialist and expansionist.
Strong supporter of military and naval measures of defence.
Uncertain and ill-informed on international questions; with
a tendency toward isolationism.
Follower of the Penrose-Smoot-Lodge leadership.

These are, of necessity, generalizations. They disappear
with the declaration of war. Partisanship, in Harding's soul,
gave way to patriotism. He had been pettily partisan before;
he was to revert to that frame of mind afterward. But for the
duration of the war his loyalty was predominant. His Americanism, narrow in some aspects, bombastic in expression at
times, was none the less fundamental, constant, and profoundly sincere. It was his true piety.

Others of his confrères were more vociferous, more conspicuous, more dynamic. None was more loyal. He voted
for the war, as he made clear in his speech of explanation, not
because he was influenced by 'the alleged hysteria of a sub-
sidized or English-owned press' (note the instinctive caution
of that journalistic 'alleged'), nor in support of any 'campaign of the munitions makers, for there was none,' but for
the 'maintenance of just American rights.' Having thus
voted, he supported President Wilson with unswerving stead-
fastness in all major measures. He even used the term 'dictator' without misgivings, and in a favoring sense. Successful prosecution of a war called for a dictator he told a *New
York Times* interviewer. 'That dictator must needs be the
President, whether I like him or not. Why quibble over
accomplished facts?' [1]

Throughout he maintained a cool head and a calm judgment. Public furor evoked no response in him. He was no
hater, no patrioteering exhibitionist. He could boldly de-
nounce those phases of the Liberty Loan campaigns, which
descended to threats and oppression, as 'hysterical and un-

[1] *New York Times*, August 12, 1917.

seemly' — as, in fact, they were. The persecutions to which Americans of German affiliation were unjustly subjected, moved him to sadness. He could be loyal without sentimentalism; militant without savagery.

He sensibly believed that it was none of our business what form of government Germany or any other nation preferred, as long as it respected international law and the rights of others. The pretence that the German people were not behind their leaders, the myth of an official tyranny forcing a reluctant nation into battle, failed to fool him. He shrewdly surmised that when war was on and the war-spirit released, Germany and the United States were much alike. 'The idea of dethroning the Hapsburgs and the Hohenzollerns makes me weary,' he remarked.[1]

One of the two or three busiest and most harassed men in the country during our participation in the war was Herbert Hoover, Food Director. So overworked and overstrained was he that on one occasion when the State Food Directors from every state and territory in the Union arrived in Washington for a conference (except one unfortunate who was stricken with appendicitis on the way and was haled from his train to an operating room), he could not find time even to put in an appearance at the formal dinner given in the Food Administration Building for them. Yet he was obliged, for reasons of policy, to waste precious hours on members of the two houses of Congress who came chiefly to ask favors or try to place friends or followers on the payroll. It was a serious hindrance to his arduous job.

One morning the name of a Senator whom he did not know was presented. No word had been sent in advance. Mr. Hoover gave directions and Warren G. Harding was ushered in. Another complaint or request — was the thought in the busy executive's mind. The visitor may have sensed it, for he smiled and said: 'I haven't come to get anything. I

[1] *New York Times*, June 19, 1917.

just want you to know that if you wish the help of a friend, telephone me what you want. I am here to serve and to help.'[1]

He left the Food Administrator rather surprised and heartily wishing that there were more officials in Washington with the same ideas.

With the close of hostilities, Harding reverted to type. World-problems presented themselves to him as domestic issues had before, from the angle of party advantage. Take some position he must. Congress was divided into four general groups: the thick-and-thin supporters of Wilson, of the Treaty unqualified and of the League of Nations; the mild reservationists as exemplified by the legal-minded Hughes and the internationally experienced and sagacious Root; the strict reservationists, led by the bitter and often venomous Lodge; and the irreconcilables whose Republican exemplars were William E. Borah and Hiram Johnson. Harding, after some hesitancy, cast his lot and his votes with Lodge. He thought the strait-jacket reservations of that statesman would best 'safeguard the interests of the United States.' Hatred of Wilson was a motivating force in Lodge's strategy. In this his follower did not share. He hated no one. His views are expressed in Hardingesque terms of robustious patriotism:

> These reservations must be strong and unmistakable. I could no more support mild reservations than I could support mild Americanism. These reservations come of a purpose to protect America first and still save a framework on which to build intelligent co-operation.... I do not believe, Senators, that it is going 'to break the heart of the world'[2] to make this covenant right, or at least free from perils which would endanger our own independence. But it were better to witness this rhetorical tragedy than destroy the soul of this great Republic.

[1] President Hoover's eulogy at Harding's tomb.
[2] Wilson had said that rejection would break the heart of the world.

The emotional idealism of President Wilson was incomprehensible to him. He could feel warmly about people, but he could never 'make friends with an abstraction,' nor become wrought up over underlying principles, which to him would always be vague, impersonal subtleties.

To expect Wilson and Harding to see eye to eye on any matter would be absurd. One may surmise that the Senator would regard the President as an impractical idealist and a bit of a prig, while to the scholarly historian the Ohio editor would be just another cheap politician. Wilson's lofty purposes would be as inexplicable to Harding as Harding's warm and endearing humanity would be insignificant to Wilson.

In the reaction, moral and political, to the stress and sacrifice of war, the nation turned against the Administration. Wilson's ill-advised appeal for a Democratic Congress received a tart retort; the Republicans were restored to legislative power in 1918. Harding gladly recognized this as a mandate for resistance to the presidential appeal for enhanced authority.

> The people have looked with apprehension on the executive assumption of power, and feel that safety for popular government lies in Congress asserting itself.

Jealousy for senatorial prestige and authority was lively within him. He was one of four conferees to warn the President that reservations must be attached before there could be any hope of the Senate accepting the Treaty project. His sentiments are expressed in the report of the Foreign Affairs Committee:

> We are not quitters. We want to resume our own development.... A Senator may be just as jealous of his constitutional authority as a President of an international concoction. ... The Treaty changes echo the conscience of the Republic.

In a speech at Carnegie Hall in New York, he proclaimed the dominance of the body of which he was so proudly a member:

> At the present time the preservation of American nationality rests with the Senate, and I can assure you that the Senate will not fail.[1]

He signed the senatorial round robin, instigated by Lodge, and voted for the Knox peace resolutions, which would have stripped the President of power in the settlement, on the ground that this course would restore the constitutional powers of Congress and check the danger of one-man rule in the United States.

Committee work offered him ample opportunity to expand. There were experienced legislators associated with him who could have taught him much. Had he known to what he was destined, he might have thought it well worth while to familiarize himself, for example, with international relations. Long before the end of his term, the League of Nations and the peace treaty were poignant questions. He was in a position to command the best sources of information. For a man who wished to improve his knowledge, to broaden his views, to gather material for use in more important work than being a rather inert Senator, this was a chance in a thousand. Harding did not seize upon it. Why should he? He had no thought of rising higher. There was nothing more to be desired, in his view, than the position he occupied. Thus it was that a President, with little more knowledge than the average man in the street of the issues on which the world's future was to hang, came into office and face to face with those issues. The Senate taught him how to increase his popularity; it altered little if at all his views, his wisdom, or his ambition.

Harding's interest in his duties, measured over his whole term, seems to have waned after a fair start. Out of the total of 2692 roll-calls, he failed to answer 1163. On the basis of attendance he stands below the middle of the class, seventy-eighth out of ninety-six members. Nor does he figure promi-

[1] *New York Times*, May 19, 1919.

nently under the heading 'Remarks' which is the *Congressional Record's* roster of speeches delivered, long or short. Most of Harding's two hundred and twenty-five appearances were brief. Fond as he was of oratory, and a little vain of his forensic skill, his speaking record drops below the numerical average. Probably he was disappointed in the reception accorded to his 'bloviation.' He found his official audiences less responsive than the fervid crowds of party conventions or local rostra.

His style was still that of the hustings, flamboyant, diffuse, appealing to stock emotions and reliable prejudices, 'glory-talk' often ill-informed and loosely constructed, interspersed with ejaculatory 'Oh, Senators!' and 'Senators!' to accord, perhaps, with the supposititious toga in which popular imagination had garbed his impressive form. What he designed to be his *magnum opus* of senatorial effort was a speech on the Versailles Treaty.[1] It was ignored in the Senate and neglected in the newspapers.

Saddened, Harding turned back to his amusements.

[1] September 11, 1919.

★

VII. Design for Happiness

THE Hardings enjoyed Washington life. They had a car and a house. They were coming up socially. The Senator joined some agreeable clubs and was admitted to a select official group which took its politics lightly and its amusements seriously. He developed a liking for golf. The type of poker which he had learned in the back rooms of Marion suffered nothing in competition with Washington's best. Harding's game won universal respect and gratifying sums of money. It was said that he seldom rose a loser.

As for Mrs. Harding, she was gaily excited by her new opportunities. Before leaving Marion she had suffered from serious kidney complications. Under the stimulus of the Washington atmosphere she revived miraculously. Too much of her energy may have been nervous excitation. She tried to keep pace with her restless husband. Duty, as she interpreted it, demanded that she be at his side; safety, also, for she had definitely cast herself for the rôle of guiding spirit.

To Mrs. Norman Thomas, wife of her old employee, she confided on the occasion of their first meeting, that Warren Harding always did well when he followed her advice: not otherwise. For her companion's benefit she cited the counsel which Warren Harding's mother had given her; always to have reserve food in the icebox and never to let her husband travel without her.[1]

Ohio clannishness is operative in other than purely political relationships. The Longworths and the McLeans were 'nice' to the senatorial newcomers, and entertained them. Edward B. McLean, heir of John R. McLean of the *Cincinnati Enquirer*, was rich in his own right and richer by marriage with Evalyn Walsh, daughter of the gold-mining king and owner of that ill-famed gem, the Hope diamond. Their vast Washington house, noted for lavishness rather than selectivity, was the Capital's chief place of private entertainment. Mrs. Harding got a new thrill out of life in meeting there important people of whom she had read in the newspapers with the absorbed interest of the country mouse gazing from afar at the glittering scene. Harding was welcome also at Friendship, the McLean country house, where the festivities were of a livelier order.

Although not of the same brand of Republicanism, and of a different social stratum, the Nicholas B. Longworths (Alice Roosevelt) invited the Hardings to their poker séances. Mrs. Harding did not gamble, and was a very sparing drinker. But she went to all the parties. She could not bear to miss anything. Mrs. Longworth gives this pen portrait of her guests in that pungent chronicle, *Crowded Hours:*[2]

> From the time he came to Washington as Senator in 1915, he and Mrs. Harding came to our house a great deal, chiefly to play poker, a game to which he was devoted. Though Mrs. Harding did not play, she always came, too, and the job of the 'Duchess,' as she was called, was to 'tend bar.' Harding and Nick and the others would say, when they wished another drink, 'Duchess, you are laying down on your job.' And Mrs. Harding, who was watching the play of the hands, would immediately get up and mix a whiskey-and-soda for them.

[1] Letter from Norman Thomas to the writer.
[2] Quoted by permission of Charles Scribner's Sons, publishers.

A pen-picture of a rather grim Ganymede. As if in casual afterthought the daughter of T. R. adds this commentary, which is not without its overtones:

> The fact was that, though they came continuously to our house, I had never happened to go to theirs.

Some people in Washington apparently failed to estimate properly the social importance of the senatorial Hardings. Such recalcitrants were listed in a memorandum book of which Mrs. Harding told the amused Mrs. Longworth, 'These people were to realize that she was aware of their behavior.' [1]

It may be that even this early she previsioned herself in a position where she could repay slurs with interest. For the stars shone with promise for her. With three other ladies of senatorial rank, she visited a seeress calling herself 'Madame Marcia' and modestly describing herself as 'A President-maker and a President-ruler.' Mrs. Harding wished to know what fate was written in the heavens for a man born on November 2, 1865, at 2 P.M. With this date, a copy of the *Congressional Directory*, which all Washington fortune-tellers keep in stock, and a little guesswork, it would not be difficult for the prophetess to identify her caller.

What she interpreted from her stars was sensational enough. The man born at that time was a statesman. He would become President of the United States. But he would not live to complete his term. For good measure, Madame Marcia threw in a character sketch which could hardly have been pleasing to the wife: [2]

> Sympathetic, kindly, intuitive, free of promises and trustful of friends, enthusiastic, impulsive, perplexed over financial affairs. Many clandestine love affairs; inclined to recurrent moods of melancholia.

[1] Alice Roosevelt Longworth: *Crowded Hours.*
[2] *Liberty*, April 9, 1938.

Design for Happiness

The forecast was in no way phenomenal. Washington's professional astrologers make a practice of prophesying the Presidency for budding statesmen. It flatters susceptibilities, fosters goodwill, builds business. If the history fails to confirm the reading, no harm is done; the subject *might* become President. It is a fair guess that he thinks he ought to be. On the other hand, there is always a chance of hitting it right. After all somebody must be elected.

The character reading is of quite another order. It was surprisingly, even suspiciously accurate. The attribution of intuitiveness was the only slip.

How many or how serious 'clandestine love affairs' Harding had been through there is no way of determining. In his bachelor days his reputation had been no worse than that of his free-and-easy young associates. But after a few years of married life, vagrant tendencies asserted themselves. Whatever his sentiments of respect toward his Duchess, she ceased to satisfy his emotional, or perhaps his physical demands. To paraphrase the sportive ditty:

> His right eye was a good little eye,
> But his left eye loved to roam.

Had it roamed farther afield, trouble would have been saved, or at least lessened. It fixed itself upon the pretty wife of a leading local merchant. William Allen White notes that upon the triumphal Harding homecoming, when all the rest of the town had blazed into multicolored bunting, one large store front remained staringly blank, and ascribes this to 'a primrose détour from Main Street which the Duchess had chosen to ignore.'[1] Though the affair never attained the publicity of open scandal, it was the occasion of anxiety and eventually of action on the part of Harding's political supporters. People in Marion still believe that this in part accounts for Mrs. Harding's eagerness to get him out of that environment.

[1] William Allen White: *Masks in a Pageant.*

The affair is mentioned as showing that the far more momentous liaison in which his senatorial period was involved was not his first errancy from the strait and narrow path.

Nan Britton, aforetime contributor of school notes to the *Marion Star*, was now twenty years old. According to Gaston B. Means's always dubious testimony, Mrs. Harding had been suspicious of her girlish adoration and of Harding's penchant for welcoming her in his office and petting her.[1] Nan's own account is quite different. She describes herself as worshipping from afar, hanging about until she saw her idol emerge upon the street, when she would put herself in his way, hoping for no more than a smile or a casual word.[2]

On her father's death, Nan found herself footloose. Still goaded by her unslaked infatuation of six years' standing, she came to New York, and wrote to the Senator, ostensibly with a view to enlisting his aid in getting a job. In reality she sought an assignation. Here and hereafter I am following, in general course, her own version of the liaison.

Her circumstantial story has been the target of hot denunciation and cold denial. The denunciation is comprehensible enough. The denials take root from bias or an unwillingness to weigh the evidence. Truth, as regards the salient allegations, is patent in every chapter of *The President's Daughter*, the book which Nan Britton published in 1927, with its dedication to unmarried mothers and unsponsored children. Had Harding's sexual morals been above suspicion before or after the start of the Nan Britton episode, there might be some grounds for doubt. Overwhelming evidence, backed by documentary proof, would have been required, for example, to convict Calvin Coolidge of similar wrongdoing; it simply did not inhere in the character or standards of the man. Unfortunately, Harding could not be cited as a convincing character witness for himself.

[1] Gaston B. Means: *The Strange Death of President Harding.*
[2] Nan Britton: *The President's Daughter.*

In the rueful estimate of his father, Warren couldn't say No.

Nan would not have been an easy temptation to say No to for a man of Harding's vulnerable susceptibilities. She is described by Means, who was set to shadow her, as 'a most attractive young woman, blonde, fresh, vital.'[1] She was romantic, impressionable, and intelligent. The *New York Times* published a blank verse poem by her, an apostrophe to the eyes of her child by Harding and so, reflexively to her lover, which is not devoid of emotional and poetic quality:

> These are the eyes of one whom grief assailed,
> Whom disappointment crushed with its great weight.
> Around his head a halo memory casts,
> Reflecting that refiner's fire which purged
> Him clean, and made him what he was.[2]

Naturally, Harding answered her letter. It would not have been Harding if he had not. He replied benignantly that he would be glad to do what he could about the job, and would see her on his next trip to New York.

They met in a hotel lobby. Though more than fifty years old, Harding was robust and virile; the sort of male who is swift to perceive an opportunity and no laggard in profiting by it. So Nan wanted a job in Washington? What was the matter with New York? He frequently had business that brought him over, and he'd be glad to see something of her again. Judge Gary of United States Steel was a good friend of his. He'd see what could be done. He suggested that they go to his room and talk it over. She acceded without demur.

Between the lines of the Harding-Britton idyll, upon which a not unskilled collaborator strove with doubtful success to diffuse the rose-color of romance, it is plainly to be seen that in this case the woman was the pursuer, the man the not impossible he. The fact protrudes in bald definition that while

[1] Gaston B. Means: *op. cit.*

[2] 'Her Eyes,' by Ninon Britton, *New York Times*, August 30, 1926.

he was the genuine, if rather gross infatuation of her life, she was to him merely a physical indulgence. His errancy lacks the sentimental condonation of a grand passion. He was no Launcelot to her Guinevere, no Tristan to her Isolde. Nowhere in her story is there indication of any depth of feeling, any redeeming glow of romance on his part. She betrays this with (I think) unintentional ingenuousness when she narrates that, on their first parting, 'he tucked thirty dollars in my brand-new silk stocking and was sorry he had no more that time to give me.' [1] As a practical man he was taking his fun where he found it and settling for it on a value-received basis.

As for the woman in the case, no sentimental tears need be shed over her. The wronged maiden of melodrama rôle is not hers, nor, to do her justice, does she insist upon the trappings of woe. She wanted Warren Harding. She went after him. She got him. He provided for her plenteously while he lived. By his standards, he treated her not shabbily, and I think she had no quarrel with those standards. There is no taint of animus in *The President's Daughter*.

So Nan landed a sixteen-dollar-a-week job in the New York offices of the United States Steel Corporation. She also landed her senatorial fish, presumably without great delay. Much is made in the book of her girlish hesitancies, her maidenly delays and refusals. All of which may be taken, I think, with a large grain of salt. Allowing that Harding was her first lover, she was too enamored to raise needless difficulties. Reluctant virgins do not welcome married men to their rooms nor share Pullman berths with them. Everything points to the easy accommodation of a freely proffered gift and a ready acceptance.

They lived together off and on from 1916 through 1922, if not longer. Most often they were together in various New York hotels. There is a Frenchily farcical situation in one

[1] Nan Britton: *The President's Daughter*.

chapter setting forth the circumstances of a rendezvous interrupted by two hopeful blackmailers from the New York detective force, who invaded their temporary love-nest and
invited the terrified Senator to tell it to the Judge. All ended
happily, however, when the chagrined officers found that
they had bagged an important official, and beat an alarmed
and apologetic retreat.

Caution was cast to the winds. Harding took his mistress
on a tour in the Middle West, registering her as his niece, a
device so hackneyed as to be brashly transparent. She sometimes ran down to Washington, on which occasions he would
borrow an apartment for the evening from some obliging
friend. Among his chosen associates that sort of thing was
evidently accepted as a matter of course.

On October 22, 1919, their child was born. According to
the mother's version there was never any question of Harding denying his paternity, or any indisposition to support
both of them generously. Checks were not sent to her; a
trusted secret service man delivered the funds by hand. She
saw her lover at the time of the Chicago Convention which
nominated him for President. Later he gave her three five-
hundred-dollar bills in one lot. She was taking a trip in
Europe at his expense when he died.

Her quite justifiable attempts to secure recognition and
support for the child from the Harding family contribute a
page to history which the then dead President would assur-
edly have regarded as not 'becoming.'[1] What obligation
there was upon the surviving Hardings was moral; it was not
enforceable. It did not stand up when submitted to court
test. Nan sued for a share in the Harding estate and a jury
(it was an Ohio jury, to be sure) found no cause for action.
The proper attitude for loyal Ohioans to assume was that the
whole Britton affair was a hold-up. Harry Daugherty de-

[1] 'His acid test for everything...was to ask himself if it would be becoming.'
Boyden Sparkes in *New York Tribune*, August 2, 1923.

nounced the book as a fake. But Harry Daugherty asserted with stern and unsmiling mien that no taint of any woman-scrape had ever touched Harding. 'If there had been one, Harding would have told me.'[1] Doctor George T. Harding, the President's younger brother, presented a stony front to Nan's pleas for herself and the child and demanded letters. On the other hand, the young mother's statement that there were family contributions to the child's support is borne out by an interview with Daisy Harding, the President's sister, in the *New York News*, shortly after the publication of the book. She admitted that she had sent money to Nan Britton because she believed her account. Later she had her doubts. But this may have been due to the influence of her evidence-demanding brother.

Ingenious efforts to discredit the narrative were not wanting. One, Joseph de Barthe, wrote a book, *The Answer*, to prove that it was physically impossible for Harding to be a father. Establishing a negative is proverbially difficult. There are special and obvious difficulties in this particular department of life. Mr. de Barthe may be credited with a gallant failure.

With a view to weakening Nan's ascription of her child's paternity, her morals have been brought in question. Affidavits were procured to the effect that her conduct in her schooldays was loose. A nude bathing party in which she was alleged to have taken part was cited. The character of the affiants is not impressive. A Marion man named Klunk burst into print with a rebuttal of *The President's Daughter*, in which 'the Complaining Witness,' not identified by name but patently Nan Britton, is displayed in a decidedly Police Gazettish light. Nan sued on that, but the case came to naught, and Mr. Klunk fell down some hotel stairs and broke his neck. I have talked with high-school classmates of Nan Britton who knew her well until after she left Marion, and

[1] Mark Sullivan: *Our Times*, vol. VI.

they are unanimous in giving her a good character and reputation. Furthermore, Means, who shadowed her (or so he says) in the hope of finding something which could be used against her, wholly failed, which I take to be a fairly convincing testimonial (if true) to her illicit monogamy. The height of his achievement was stealing the baby's trinkets.[1]

Did Mrs. Harding know of the liaison? If so, when did she find out? Nan says that she went to see Harding in the White House, which would seem a needless risk unless she put in an appearance simply as 'home folks.' Means, in his book, confirms this and says that she also met Harding after his Presidency in the house of a very accommodating lady, who was supposed to be Mrs. Harding's intimate friend, but appears to have played both sides. The lovers were upstairs, he says, when Mrs. Harding dropped in by chance, and he, Means, was put to the exercise of his best strategy to get her out of the place safely.

Means insists that the deceived wife knew practically everything about the affair. It is certain that domestic relations at the time were strained, though this may have been due to other factors; for example, the wife's continuous nagging and bossism. I quote from the Means book, *The Strange Death of President Harding*, not because it can be accepted as authentic or reliable (the author was straining every nerve to establish his thesis that the President was poisoned by his Duchess and that jealousy of Nan Britton was a contributory motive), but as indicating a considerable possibility of the domestic situation. The time is the fall of 1921; the scene, Mrs. Harding's private apartment in the White House; present, Means, then an operative in the Bureau of Investigation of the Department of Justice; Mrs. Harding speaking:

> Warren Harding has had a very ugly affair with a girl from Marion named Nan Britton.... I became suspicious of this girl when she was but a child in Marion.... She was always

[1] Gaston B. Means: *The Strange Death of President Harding*.

doing everything on earth that she could to attract Warren's attention.... This girl, Nan Britton, has a child and she claims Warren is the father of it.

Mrs. Harding vacillated between insisting that she did not believe the story, and indicating that she did. She was constant, however, in averring that Harding was impotent to beget a child.

To a number of people the liaison was factually known; the secret service messenger who acted as go-between for Harding, the complaisant friends who loaned their quarters for the assignations in Washington, the two New York plain-clothes men who had raided the hotel room; some, at least, of those — not all of them could have been blind and deaf — who were with Harding on his Mid-West travels with his 'niece.' To expect that out of this heterogeneous lot none would have been indiscreet of speech is to overestimate human taciturnity.

For some time before this, according to Means, there had been a good deal of talk around the Department of Justice, in which Nan's name figured, and the loose-lipped Jesse Smith was cynically amused when Means pretended ignorance of the affair. There was a proverb current in Washington at the time: 'A Senator is known by the women he keeps.'

Associates far more evil and dangerous than Nan Britton joined forces with the future President while he was still an unconsidered figure in the national scene. Senator Albert B. Fall became his mentor and his political ideal. Charles R. Forbes, met on a senatorial junket to Hawaii, cannily laid the foundations of a friendship that was to close in catastrophe.

★

VIII. Daugherty Grooms
His Entry

DAUGHERTY, the indomitable, had never forgotten the presidential vision evoked by that first meeting with Harding. There was a theatrical slant to the clever manager's conception of political strategy; he believed in keeping this star in the spotlight.

What he would have liked, was to join his protégé in the Senate where he could keep an eye on him. Balked in this ambition, he concentrated upon establishing his control of the party machinery in Ohio. Here he worked to 'point' his man for the Republican Convention of 1916. Not for the nomination: no such visionary scheme entered the shrewd directorial mind. Daugherty's aim was the temporary chairmanship for his protégé. As a 'keynoter' Harding was eminently available. He could be relied upon to take direction. None of the leaders had anything to fear from him. He had made no enemies. Now he must make friends.

'Gee, but he'd make a great-looking President!' Daugherty had declared to Jesse Smith in an early morning talk at the Deer Creek shack. 'We'll put it over sometime, Jess.' [1]

[1] Mark Sullivan: *Our Times*, vol. VI.

There was need of a soothing and harmonizing influence at that Chicago Convention. Trouble was looming in the person of Theodore Roosevelt. The guiding spirits wanted no more of him. The edges of that gaping wound caused by insurgency, though they had been drawn together in the union of desire to beat Wilson, were still raw. But Roosevelt was too formidable to be suppressed. Another split would just about end the party, and there was the lively fear that unless the Bull Mooser had a voice in the convention's choice, he would lead a second mutiny. Harding was no Roosevelt man; he had proved that. But neither was he anathema to the Progressives. He would be for Charles Evans Hughes, upon whom both factions could unite, though sulkily on the part of the Old Guard, or for whomever else the leaders dictated.

Accordingly, when Harry Daugherty, at a meeting of the predominantly standpat National Committee which was considering the temporary chairmanship, put it to his fellow members, 'Why not Warren G. Harding?' there was no logical negative. The Senator from Ohio was chosen, not for achievement, but for the Brahministic virtue of abstention from strife.

Harding worked industriously on his speech, and was pleased with it. Then the leaders got hold of it, took it to pieces and remoulded it closer to the heart's desire. Harding was sorrowful but acquiescent. On the eve of its delivery he said to Finley Peter Dunne:

'It's rotten. I wrote a good one, but my friends in the Senate made me put things in — the tariff, reciprocity, public lands, pensions, and God knows what — and now it's a rag carpet.' [1]

It was a 'dead' convention; almost a 'dud' convention. The Old Guard were sullen because Roosevelt was forcing their hand on Hughes, whereas there were several other can-

[1] Finley Peter Dunne: *Saturday Evening Post*, September 12, 1936.

didates whom they would have vastly preferred. Nor were the Progressives particularly happy. Apathy was in the air. Reporters dubbed the Coliseum the Mausoleum. It was not more than comfortably filled. The keynote speaker started under a handicap.

From that source a rousing exhibition of verbal fireworks was forecast. Harding's speech was not that kind. It had at first all of his ease and charm, and nothing more; as it progressed, it became noticeably subdued to the medium it worked in. Demosthenes could not have withstood that fishy chill. Harding's platitudes and amiable generalities made little impression. He glorified the party with conventional paeans, but the phrases were trite, stale. The audience sat, listless, with spaced responses of perfunctory applause where required, while the orator accompanied his fine vocality with a series of six gestures, repeated over and over with the regularity of a metronome.

Most of the political scorers gave it a zero, though the *New York Times* thought it merited a better response than it received. Dunne considered it 'dismally unsuccessful,' and pityingly recorded that the orator 'suffered the additional humiliation of having his audience walk out on him.' Some one must have liked it, however, for Harding was made permanent chairman. He presided with dignity and competence and even received a few scattering votes for the nomination.

Daugherty was pleased. He figured that of the delegates present a full half would be acting in the same capacity four years later, a considerable overestimate, as it turned out. That they should remember Warren G. Harding was desirable and might be important.

'Every man in the convention went home with a vivid picture of the man, Warren Harding.' Such was Daugherty's optimistic interpretation.[1]

[1] Harry M. Daugherty: *The Inside Story of the Harding Tragedy.*

A more unprejudiced participant, Will Hays, agreed. As quoted by Mark Sullivan, he said:

> ... it was an important item in developing a national acquaintance among those who go to conventions, the organization men, etc. There is no doubt about the impression that speech of Harding's made on everyone who was in that convention. I never forgot that speech.[1]

Having finished his assignment, Harding, docile to what was expected, went on the stump in his home state and, as Daugherty records, 'made more enthusiastic friends.' For himself, perhaps, but apparently not for the candidate. Mr. Hughes lost Ohio and the election. The victory of Wilson by the narrow margin of California's close vote could hardly have been a crushing disappointment to Harding. Hughes was not at that time the Ohio man's ideal type of candidate.

One result of the campaign was to bring about a rapprochement between the editor of the *Marion Star* and the man whom he had denounced as 'the greatest faker of all time.' Now that T. R. was back in the fold, Harding's orthodoxy was appeased.

> We jointly deplored the result, but he did insist that we must all get together and save the country through a Republican restoration; that the Republican Party was the one agency through which to give the highest service, and the compact of our counsel and co-operation was made then and there, and in many conferences afterward I came to know how deeply he felt the necessity of all Republicans uniting to effect the party supremacy so essential to the nation's good.[2]

In this same speech the prospective candidate perpetrated that form of chicanery to which politicians are so prone, credit-grabbing. Speaking of Roosevelt, he said:

[1] Mark Sullivan: *Our Times*, vol. VI.
[2] Speech in Topeka, Kansas; March 8, 1920.

It was his personal rather than his political wish that I should stand sponsor for the amendment to the Army Bill that made it possible for him to take a volunteer division to France.

It was neither. It was Harding's own idea, and an essentially political one. The implication that Roosevelt had approached him to stand sponsor for his ambition to go overseas is as obvious as it is baseless. T. R. knew nothing in advance of Harding's intention to offer such an amendment to the bill. Not being devoid of sardonic humor, the Colonel must have been grimly amused when Lodge wrote him:

> The amendment to allow you to raise a division will be offered. Harding said the other day that he would like to offer such an amendment and I told Johnson that I thought it was a great deal better that Harding should offer it than either he or I, because we are known to be very close to you.[1]

The movement was quashed by President Wilson on the quiet insistence of high army authorities. The Rooseveltians were inclined to accept Harding's good offices as a gesture of apology and reparation.

As he settled enjoyably into club life in the Senate, Harding realized that he needed political capital. In the unsettled state of the nation in general and Ohio in particular, he felt no assurance that he could retain his membership. Questions that were on everyone's lips perplexed and worried him, because he had no convictions and lacked a broad enough view to judge which way the political cat was going to jump. He said to Senator Borah, leader of the isolationists, in the spring of 1918: 'Bill, I'd like to get in the fight against the League of Nations, but the people in my state are all for it, I'm afraid.'

He then suggested that Borah should make some anti-League speeches in Ohio. 'I'll arrange the meetings for you,'

[1] Theodore Roosevelt letters in Library of Congress.

he offered, adding with true Hardingesque caution, 'but no one need know that I did it.' [1]

If the lightning of pro-League wrath was to strike anyone, it might better be Borah than himself, he figured. The straightforward, hard-hitting Idaho Senator was disgusted.

Another and a greater impresario than Daugherty now considered Harding for the star part. In search of a 'man who will listen,' Boies Penrose of Pennsylvania thought that the Ohio man would certainly fill that requirement and might be built up to others. Leighton C. Taylor, private secretary to Penrose, gives this account of a momentous interview. [2]

> In the summer of 1919, on a hot afternoon, the Senator did not go to the Capitol.... He asked me to call Harding. When Harding came in, Penrose said: 'Take off your coat, Senator, and sit down.' The next thing from Penrose was, 'Harding, how would you like to be President?' I don't think anyone could have registered more surprise than Harding. He said: 'Why, Penrose, I haven't any money and I have my own troubles in Ohio. In fact, I will be mighty glad if I can go back to the Senate.' Penrose said: 'You don't need any money. I'll look after that. You will make the McKinley type of candidate. You look the part. You can make a front porch campaign like McKinley's and we'll do the rest.' From then on Penrose began to talk Harding, until Harding made a speech before the Manufacturers' Association in Philadelphia.... One of his comments was: 'Harding isn't as big a man as I thought he was. He should have talked more about the tariff and not so much about playing the cymbals in the Marion brass band.'

(Senator Penrose was slightly in error as to the home touch. Sounding brass, not the tinkling cymbal, was Harding's musical medium.)

A second try-out before Eastern audiences failed to further his cause. In his speech before the Ohio Society in New York

[1] Claudius O. Johnson: *Borah of Idaho*.
[2] William Allen White: *A Puritan in Babylon*.

City,[1] he delivered a resounding peroration of six points, exhorting his hearers:

> To safeguard America first
> To stabilize America first
> To prosper America first
> To think of America first
> To exalt America first
> To live for and revere America first.

He ended 'In the spirit of the Republic, we proclaim Americanism and acclaim America.'

That is a sample of Harding in his perfervid flag-waving moments. At his best, he was an over-ornate speaker; at his worst he was a purveyor of flatulent claptrap.

Styles in oratory change, and Harding's was already a little outmoded. The war had made people impatient of verbosity and bombast. The platform in America owes an unrecorded debt to the late Donald M. Ryerson of Chicago, founder of the Four-Minute Men, whose blighting influence upon American oratory can hardly be overestimated or overpraised. Within their rigid limitations of time, they taught the public that much can be said in small compass; the unbridled licence of the human voice has never been the same since. Harding was of another school. Given four minutes wherein to say something, he might well have choked to death. On the other hand, he could use up two hours in saying practically nothing. H. L. Mencken asserted that Harding's was 'the worst English I have ever encountered . . . it reminds me of a string of wet sponges.' And Senator William G. McAdoo gave full rein to his mingled exasperation and boredom in a philippic so withering that it roused a lethargic Senate:[2]

> His speeches leave the impression of an army of pompous phrases moving over the landscape in search of an idea; sometimes these meandering words would actually capture a strag-

[1] January 10, 1920.
[2] Mark Sullivan: *Our Times*, vol. VI.

gling thought and bear it triumphantly, a prisoner in their midst, until it died of servitude and overwork.

What is it in Harding's style which could so rasp critics of such diverse minds as Messrs. Mencken and McAdoo? A few excerpts will, I think, explain that irritation. They are cited, not as the average, which was merely commonplace, but as the most Hardingesque. I confess to a suspicion, perhaps unworthy, that these are passages which their originator would, himself, have selected, as exhibiting him in top form. For example:

> Since freedom impelled and independence inspired and nationality exalted, a world supergovernment is contrary to everything we cherish and can have no sanction by our Republic. This is not selfishness, it is sanctity. (Query: did he mean sanctuary?) [1]

Or this:

> We have not only wrought the most of liberty and opportunity for ourselves at home, but the firmament of the earth, occident and orient, is aglow with shining suns of new republics, sped to the orbs of human progress by our example.

Which recalls W. S. Gilbert's Agib

> . . . who, amidst barbaric scenes,
> Wrote a lot of ballet music in his teens.
>   His gentle spirit rolls
>   In the melody of souls,
> Which is pretty, but I don't know what it means. [2]

Again Harding:

> We have mistaken unpreparedness to embrace it to be a challenge of the realities, and due concern for making all citizens fit for participation will give added strength of citizenship and magnify our achievement. [3]

[1] *Marion Mirror*, June 24, 1912.
[2] W. S. Gilbert: *The Bab Ballads.*
[3] Warren G. Harding: *Inaugural Address.*

And once more:

> I would rather make Mexico safe and set it aglow with the light of New World righteousness than menace the health of the Republic in Old World contagion.

Here he rises and, as it were, flaps his wings:

> In deliberate and appreciative retrospection and gratifying contemplation the American who fails to see a progressive Republican Party is blind to the irresistible onward movement and deaf to the triumphant shouts of the all-conquering American people.[1]

Finally, this acme of alliteration's artful aid at its most artful:

> ... not heroism but healing, not nostrums but normalcy, not revolution but restoration, not agitation but adjustment, not surgery but serenity, not the dramatic but the dispassionate, not experiment but equipoise, not submergence in internationality but sustainment in triumphant nationality.[2]

Mr. Frederick E. Schortemeier, collector and editor of the Harding addresses, expresses his conviction that 'He [Harding] possesses a remarkable aptitude for the choice of accurate and meaningful words.'[3]

What special aptitude Harding possesses — and 'remarkable' is not too strong a characterization of it — is for the choice of the safe, sane, and sanitary cliché in all its banality. 'Agriculture, the foundation of our existence'; 'I must utter my belief in the divine inspiration of the Founding Fathers'; 'Womanhood, the glory of America'; 'The world has no use for a loafer'; 'God Himself had a purpose to serve in the making of the New Republic.' (It should be unnecessary to point out that Mr. Harding did not have in mind the magazine of that name.)

When he tried to be original, he fumbled his words, grand-

[1] *Cleveland Plain Dealer*, September 18, 1910.
[2] Speech before Boston Home Market Club, May 14, 1920.
[3] Frederick E. Schortemeier: *Rededicating America*.

iloquent and inept. Such solecisms as 'normalcy,' 'anti-
doted,' 'welcome you with unselfish hands,' 'rollicking in a
laughter,' 'brief but wholesome expression,' serve to justify
Mr. Mencken's disgust and Senator McAdoo's scorn, but
leave one speculating upon how much of his subject Mr.
Schortemeier has read.

Love of expression was not the only basis of the Harding
forensics. They had a sound and worthy economic justification. A *New York Times* reporter, asking him for a copy of
his speech before the Boot and Shoe Men's Convention in the
winter of 1919–20, was surprised to learn that the orator had
conned it by heart.

'Do you do this often, Senator?' he asked.

'As often as I get it to do,' was the sunny answer. 'Two
hundred dollars is a good deal for a poor country editor like
me.' [1]

As the time drew near for the great decision as to his candidacy, Harding grew more and more dubious. He did not
think he could be happy, as President, so he told his friend,
Colonel McClure. [2]

Mrs. Harding begged Daugherty not to push him forward.
She was fearful. It may be that she realized his unfitness.
It may be that she feared attacks if he set himself up as a
shining mark. Or, supersensitive as she was to the artifices of
commercialized witchcraft, she may have been terrified by
the prophecies of the Washington star-gazer.

Daugherty was obstinate. He was playing a long shot, and
he was determined to play it through.

---

[1] Statement to the writer by Louis Stark of the *New York Times*.
[2] Letter of Samuel G. McClure to the writer.

★

IX. Presidents Are Made, Not Born

Had Theodore Roosevelt lived, he would have been the Republican nominee in 1920. So thought Harding, in retrospect; 'by acclamation,'[1] he said. Roosevelt died in 1919, leaving the field wide open. A long and strong list of candidates was put forward: General Leonard Wood, Governor Frank O. Lowden, and Senator Hiram Johnson in the front ranks, with a secondary line of Governor Sproul and Senator Knox of Pennsylvania, Nicholas Murray Butler of New York, Senator La Follette of Wisconsin, Senator Borah of Idaho, and in the background of possibilities, Hughes, Hoover, and Coolidge. Against competition so formidable, Harding's modesty would harbor no hope.

Daugherty was no Harding. Nor was he modest. He was inspired by the arrogant optimism of the long-shot player. But the most promising long-shot cannot be played unless he enters the race. Harding's vacillating spirit through 1919 must have irked Daugherty's soul. He backed and filled. He would and he wouldn't. As early as February of that year there was a Harding-for-President dinner in Toledo,

[1] Speech at Topeka, March 8, 1920.

which was a failure in so far as it was designed to elicit a response from him. In July an Ohio congressman undertook to round up his colleagues on behalf of the undeclared candidate, to 'act at once so as to prevent complications that will otherwise arise.' Presumably the chief 'complication' was the local activity of the Wood agents on the hunt for delegates.

On October 6, Harding declared himself in a private letter as wishing to stick to the Senate, 'a position far more to my liking than the Presidency possibly could be.' Within a fortnight the Republican State Advisory Committee was trying to jockey him into an open avowal. They got it on November 1. He was a candidate for the Senate only, and politely bespoke their support. This forced Daugherty's hand. He went to Washington for a showdown with his principal.[1]

If not a success, neither was his mission wholly a failure. Always the necessity for positive decisions tried Harding's easy-going soul. He could not be persuaded to make one now. His Senate seat was a bed of roses; never in his career had he found life so good. Why risk a possession dear to his heart in order to gamble at long odds for a prize he did not really want and probably could not win? Nevertheless, he did not definitely reject the plan.

The self-appointed manager went ahead without assurance that he had anything to manage. Unknown to his principal he saw Penrose, Lodge, Knox, and other personal friends of Harding's in both houses of Congress. Co-operation was the burden of his song; Senator Harding could be trusted to co-operate, in other words, to take orders. It was soft music to the ears of the oligarchs who had too long been under the galling discipline of obeying instead of commanding. He did some useful ground-breaking with the National Committee, practising his best persuasions to the end that,

[1] H. F. Alderfer: notes.

if such members as exhibited interest could not accept the Ohio man for first choice, they should bear him in mind for second, third, or even fourth. He cooked up an interview with the Washington correspondents and got some useful publicity.

By those arts of persuasion whereof he was master — it must have been persuasion, for Florence Kling Harding could not be driven — he swung her from opposition to support. They were good friends. He respected her force and decisiveness. He knew how to play upon her feminine ambitions. Whatever misgivings she may have entertained regarding her husband, she would have had no doubts as to *her* fitness for the honors and responsibilities of the White House position. 'Never was a woman so greedy for the emoluments of office,' said an old acquaintance of her. To be the First Lady of the Land; what a prize to dangle before the dazzled eyes of the woman who had dared parental wrath and social exclusion to marry Warren Harding and who might now push him to the heights! What a justification of her daring and her foresight! She became Harry Daugherty's staunch ally.

Precipitancy on the part of the Wood forces furnished Daugherty with a cogent argument for positive action. Harding's Senate term expired in 1920. He wanted to be re-elected, didn't he? Very well, Wood's sortie in Ohio was going to imperil his re-election. How? It was very simple. If the Wood cohorts captured the Ohio delegation for their man, it would follow that Wood's adherents in the state would take over the party machinery. Daugherty and the Harding faction would be superseded. And where would that leave Harding as regards the Senate? Nowhere. The Wood crowd would pick their own Senator and it certainly would not be Warren G. Harding. Whereas if Harding entered the presidential contest and secured Ohio's support, which, as a favorite son, he could do, the control of the state would remain in safe (i.e., Daugherty-Harding) hands.

And what harm could it do to come out in the open? He could file his application for the Senate, just the same. There was everything to gain and nothing to lose.

Harding took a month to think it over. His conviction of inadequacy still persisted. When first the presidential lure had been spread before him, he had objected to Daugherty that he was not of that calibre, and had been only half-reassured by the tempter's response that what the party and country needed was not a big man — the time for that was past — but a reasonable, careful, common-sense citizen whom the ordinary man in the street would understand as being one of his own kind. Certainly Harding was taking his cue to be careful. Not until mid-December did he announce himself and then with hesitancy. In his letter to the Republican County Committee which had first endorsed him, he said:

> I venture to announce now no platform, nor to emphasize any obvious policy. Men in Congress make records which speak for them. Moreover, I still believe in representative popular government through political parties, believe in party sponsorship, believe conventions representing all the Republicans of the nation should make platforms, that nominees ought to be chosen as exponents of such platforms, and hold such declarations as inviolable covenants to the people.

Again he referred to his reluctance to forward his claims, promised that he would support any other favorite son who might appear, specified that he could not consent to the use of his name simply to control the Ohio delegation (this must have caused writhings on the part of Harry Daugherty) and that he would not take personal or promotional part in the pre-convention campaign, because of his official duties as well as because it would not be becoming.

His sensitivity to unseemliness did not prevent his calling on Robert Wolfe, proprietor of the *Columbus Dispatch* and of the *Ohio State Journal*, and perhaps the most influential publisher in the state. Wolfe liked Harding. He hated (politically) Daugherty, with whom he had a feud of long standing. Harding solicited Wolfe's support.

'All right,' agreed the newspaper man. 'That is, provided Harry Daugherty is not to have a leading part.'

'He's going to manage my campaign,' replied Harding.

'Then I'll do my best to beat you,' declared the uncompromising Wolfe.

He came out for Wood and was influential in preventing the favorite son from securing a solid delegation.

Money was now an acute problem. Daugherty collected it where he could. His own investment in Harding was already heavier than he could afford, $50,000 he told Finley Peter Dunne, adding that it was 'every cent I had in the world.'[1] By some potent magic he had conjured up a war chest of no mean proportions from Ohio admirers of the favorite son. One hundred and thirteen thousand dollars is the sum officially admitted.[2] No contributor is set down for a large amount. Carmi Thompson heads the list with $13,500. Daugherty modestly lists himself at $12,500. Harding's own ante, as he might have termed it, was $1000. A few donors merit mention because of their subsequent official or semi-official functions. Colonel James G. Darden, later a conspicuous figure in the Teapot Dome investigation, yielded up $6000. F. E. Scobey and F. E. Starek chipped in $500 apiece and profited by appointments respectively as Director of the Mint and Director of the War Finance Corporation. Jesse Smith enjoyed the richest return on his small investment of $500. The diligent collector did not limit his solicitations to his own state. While East, he 'touched' Harry Payne Whitney for $7500 and Harry F. Sinclair for a like sum, grudgingly granted.[3] He brought on to Washington

[1] Finley Peter Dunne: *Saturday Evening Post*, September 12, 1936.
[2] Senate Committee on Elections and Privileges, May 21, 1920.
[3] Finley Peter Dunne: *Saturday Evening Post*, September 12, 1936.

fifty staunch Hardingites, housed them at a hotel, and sent them forth to do missionary work among the committeemen. He organized a publicity bureau. He set field agents to work at home. Always at the back of his hard-worked brain he cherished the hope that when, as, and if the other aspirants killed one another off, the powers that be, weary of unprofitable battle, would turn to a man of peace.

'It's only a shoestring,' he told Mark Sullivan. 'Maybe both sides will turn to Harding. I don't know — it's just a chance.' [1]

These patient efforts began to produce an effect. From the ranks of the negligible obscure, Harding emerged to join the also-mentioned category. While he was still a rank outsider, Henry L. Stimson (afterward Hoover's Secretary of State), a keen observer, wrote to General Wood in December, 1919:

'Keep your eye on Harding. The gossip I get here is that his candidacy is more dangerous than you evidently anticipated, and it is being aimed directly at you.'

Originally it was Daugherty's plan to confine his efforts to Ohio. Wood's pressure in Ohio was resented by the admirers of Harding — it was considered not quite 'clubby' to poach on a favorite son's preserve — and Wood's adherents were spreading the damaging story that Harding's pretensions were merely a blind to further his senatorial ambitions; in other words, that his candidacy was not based on good faith. To offset this, it was decided that he should have a try-out in other states. Indiana, which was making its first trial of the direct primary, looked hopeful. The Ohio man was entered there, and also in Montana.

The Ohio test came first. It was one of those victories which can be interpreted as a semi-defeat. Harding's margin over Wood was less than 15,000 votes; his delegates 39 to Wood's 9. Daugherty, running for delegate-at-large, was beaten by a Wood man. A split delegation at home was an

[1] Mark Sullivan: *Our Times*, vol. VI.

inauspicious start, indeed. It might have discouraged a spirit less hardy than that of the old war-horse, Harry Daugherty. Toughened against defeat by his own experiences, he mistrusted that his principal would not take it so philosophically. Off he posted to Louisville where the candidate was exhibiting himself for the approval of the Kentucky Republicans. He found him low in hope: 'his face was a yard long.'

'Well,' said he to his promoter, 'it looks like we're done for.'[1]

Results in the neighboring state of Indiana dealt another blow. Harding was entered there in the hope of splitting the vote so that neither General Wood nor any other rival would win a majority. Under Indiana procedure this would mean an unpledged delegation. Then Harding's senatorial friend Harry S. New, afterward his Postmaster General, would use his wide influence to good purpose.

On primary night Mr. and Mrs. Harding were staying with the News in Indianapolis. As the returns came in, it became painfully evident that the guest of honor was making a very poor run, and finally that he would not get a single instructed vote from Indiana.[2] The luckless candidate was a picture of depression. Why had he ever let himself be jockeyed into so hopeless a venture? What he ought to do was to drop out in time, and concentrate his energies in making sure of his renomination for the Senate. A muttered remark from a local man confirmed him. Heaving himself to his feet, he slouched over to the telephone and called up his headquarters at Columbus. Mrs. Harding, who was at the far side of the room talking with Mrs. New, interrupted herself and called over:

'Warren Harding! What are you doing?'

'Getting Harry Daugherty.'

[1] Harry M. Daugherty: *The Inside Story of the Harding Tragedy.*
[2] *New York Times*, November 22, 1924.

'What for?'

At that moment a response came from the Ohio end.

'Hello! Hello!' said the disheartened candidate. 'This is Senator Harding. Is Harry there?'

The answer evidently was that Mr. Daugherty was near at hand and would be called. Harding let the receiver slump in his hand, when it was snatched away from him. Mrs. Harding was speaking, not on the telephone, but to him. According to the accepted version she said indignantly:

'Warren Harding, what are you doing? Give up? Not till the convention is over. Think of your friends in Ohio.'

This is, I believe, a Bowdlerized report. The account which I have had from friends of the News is less conventional and more realistic. With fire in her eye, the Duchess addressed herself, not to her faint-hearted husband, but to the politician at the far end of the wire.

'Hello! Hello! This is Mrs. Harding. Yes, *Mrs.* Harding. You tell Harry Daugherty from me that we're in this fight till hell freezes over.'

She slammed the receiver back on the hook. Somebody whistled. Somebody else laughed. Harding with a look of resignation resumed his seat. There was a silence. Mrs. New, a tactful hostess and a woman of the world, salvaged the situation with an inconsequential remark. Outside, later, one of the guests observed to her husband:

'It looks as if the Senator were in the race to stay.'

'You mean Mrs. Harding is,' replied the husband.

Ohio had been a dash of cold water, Indiana a slap in the face. Montana, the third state which he was contesting, gave him a derisory 723 votes out of a total of more than 40,000. Harding's 'press' slumped. He was practically counted out

For the disappointing Ohio result Harry Daugherty had an explanation ready. Sheer weight of cash, Wood money in this instance, was the answer. Two million dollars was his estimate of what the Wood forces were spending on posters, publicity, advertising, brass bands, hall rentals, orators, organizers, and general expenses. It is true that there were Wood organizations generously financed throughout the state. But, as the sworn outlay of Wood finances was $128,300, the Daugherty figures may be taken with a discount for the fervor of outraged virtue. It appears that his moral sensibilities were deeply wounded by the corrupting element of cash. He felt keenly that 'the foundations of the Republic were being destroyed by this method.' [1]

With his unerring political instinct, Harding's manager had hit upon the enemy's most vulnerable spot, exorbitant expenditures.

Covering the years in the uncertain processes of memory, Harry M. Daugherty claims in his book to have inspired the counter-offensive to the Wood war chest by a 'carefully guarded movement' to send an undercover man to Senator Borah and stir him to action, never a difficult design where there was taint of corruption in the wind. But here, I think, the Ohio strategist assumes a credit to which he is not entitled. It may be that he approached Borah indirectly on the issue of campaign boodle. There had been a previous and more direct approach. The facts are as follows:

Speaking in a North Dakota town three or four months previous to the convention, Hiram Johnson had hit out with his customary vigor at the flood of money gushing from Wood headquarters. Louis Seibold, seasoned political reporter for the *New York World*, saw an inconspicuous report of the speech and took it to the managing editor, Charles M. Lincoln. The two alert newspaper men agreed that there was a story in it if properly worked up. Official support was needed to make it available for print.

Lincoln called up Senator Borah at Washington with a

[1] Harry M. Daugherty: *The Inside Story of the Harding Tragedy.*

suggestion that a congressional inquiry would elicit interesting facts. Borah and Johnson were allies.

'The idea is all right,' agreed Borah. 'But I'd have to have something more specific to go on before I could move for an investigation.'

'Tell him I'll get it for him,' said Seibold.[1]

The political expert took train for Bridgeport to see John T. King, who, having been deposed from management of the Wood forces, was thoroughly disgruntled. He had already arranged to be at Chicago, representing Boies Penrose. The Pennsylvania boss was hostile to Wood whom he considered disqualified by lack of political experience. King turned over to the *World* man a list of the Wood contributors. It fairly bristled with 'fat-cats,' a species of political animal not in specially good odor. The *World* spread it on the front page.[2] The list comprised:

> Millionaire oil-man E. L. Doheny
> Millionaire metal-man Ambrose Monel
> Millionaire utilities-man H. M. Byllesby
> Millionaire copper-man William Boyce Thompson
> Millionaire steel-man and banker Dan R. Hanna
> Millionaire sports promoter E. E. Smathers
> Millionaire grocer A. A. Sprague

They were to raise a million dollars. Each paid in $20,000. In the background was Colonel William Cooper Procter of Ivory Soap fame and money, who, as developed later in a civil suit which brought a good deal of dirty linen to public view, had loaned $710,000 to the cause — which was $710,000 more than he ever got back.

Using this material Senator Borah roused the Senate with a blistering speech. There was no heading off an investigation, though the Wood cohorts had looked to Senator Calder of New York to perform that kindly office for them. The

[1] Statements of Messrs. Lincoln and Seibold, to the writer.
[2] *New York World*, March 27, 1920.

Kenyon Committee was appointed, went promptly to work, since there was no time to lose, and developed the following figures, duly sworn to by witnesses for the most part reluctant: [1]

Leonard Wood	$1,773,303
Frank O. Lowden	414,000
Hiram W. Johnson	194,000
Herbert Hoover	173,000
Warren G. Harding	113,000

For the Wood forces the revelation was a catastrophe. Governor Lowden's cause was also impaired, though not to the same extent; it was a later malignant joke of the same Money Devil that eliminated him.

Without the Kenyon Committee exposures, it is almost certain that the ex-army man, with his unimpeachable record of public service, the personal respect and liking which he commanded, and the efficient organization behind him would have swept the convention.

Only in after-effect was the full damage shown. Notwithstanding the money-blight, Wood remained the popular favorite. The *Literary Digest* polls, then regarded as a reliable index, published these pre-convention figures.

	First Choice	Second Choice
Wood	277,486	186,946
Johnson	263,087	161,670
Hoover	240,468	120,430
Lowden	120,391	129,992
Hughes	54,719	88,787
Harding	36,795	42,212
Coolidge	33,621	67,041
Taft	32,740	62,871

Wood led Harding in his own state of Ohio.

In the face of all discouragements, Harry M. Daugherty,

[1] Senate Committee on Elections and Privileges, May 21, 1920.

doubtless inspired by a wish to further useful propaganda, uttered a prophecy which was weird in its detailed accuracy.[1]

> I don't expect Senator Harding to be nominated on the first, second, or third ballots, but I think we can afford to take chances that, about eleven minutes after two, Friday morning of the convention, when ten or twenty weary men are sitting around a table, someone will say, 'Who will we nominate?' At that decisive time the friends of Harding will suggest him and can well afford to abide by the result.

Subsequently that was amended to 'fifteen men, bleary-eyed with lack of sleep and perspiring profusely'; and finally, in echo of Long John Silver's piratical chantey, 'Fifteen men on the dead man's chest,' to the widely circulated version, 'fifteen men in a smoke-filled room,' which became a synonym for backstage, underhand machinations. It may be, as National Committeeman Charles D. Hilles told Mark Sullivan, that the report was a paraphrase of a hasty interview between Daugherty and a *New York Times* man. Nevertheless, it must stand as Daugherty's startling success in the untried field of augury.

[1] *New York Times*, February 21, 1920.

★

X. The Man from Ohio

I

HARDING took train for Chicago on that June day reluctantly and without hope. Over the bridge table, en route, he told friends that he did not expect to win, had no ambition to be President, and wanted only to go back to the Senate. Mrs. Harding went along to insure against his backsliding. Harry Daugherty was already on the ground, energetically organizing.

One of Harding's first acts on arrival was to arrange for filing an entry at Columbus for the senatorial nomination. By law he had until Friday midnight. Before then, he was sure, all would be settled and he would be out of the presidential race. When Daugherty remonstrated, he lost his temper — a rare indulgence for him —and swore raspingly. It was as near as that Damon and Pythias ever came to a quarrel. In a panic of distress Harding cried:

'You don't want me to give up the senatorship, do you? I haven't got a ghost of a chance at the Presidency.' [1]

The field against which he was pitted was strong enough to daunt a firmer soul than Harding's. Leonard Wood and Frank O. Lowden seemed hopelessly to outclass the Ohio man.

[1] Charles Willis Thompson: *Presidents I've Known.*

Wood was admitted to be the most popular of the aspirants. He 'had everything.' He was a man of sturdy intellect, unimpeachable principles, ardent patriotism, and spotless record. Though not a West-Pointer — he had entered the army through the medical service and switched to the line later — he had the army regular's viewpoint and virtues. In the Spanish-American War he had been Roosevelt's superior officer, though public opinion always attributed the command of the picturesque Rough Riders to the more spectacular Teddy. As Governor General of Cuba, he furthered the brilliant campaign which cleansed Havana from yellow fever. As Chief of Staff of the Army he had preached and prayed for preparedness with a pertinacity which was appreciated only when the United States was drawn into the war. The Plattsburgh idea of officers' training camps originated with him. Denied active participation in the conflict, as his fellow Rough Rider had been by President Wilson, he grew in popular sympathy because of the feeling that he had been shabbily treated for political reasons. Another advantage accruing to him was that he was regarded by many as the rightful heir to the Roosevelt principles and policies.

Character, prestige, and ability combined to make him an outstanding figure. But the very qualities of his training operated to his disadvantage. He was primarily a soldier, with a military man's conception of government as a system of patriotic discipline. The nation was fed up with discipline. It was sick and weary of war and everything pertinent thereto. 'There's not enough money in the world to buy the nomination for a man with epaulettes on his shoulders,' said Harry Daugherty, wishfully speaking.

The word 'buy' was the poisoned edge. Too much money was Wood's bane. That fund of a million dollars, underwritten by the group of millionaires in the summer of 1919, inevitably became a convention issue. Nicholas Murray Butler stigmatized the goodly fellowship of soap, oil, tobacco, utilities, and other moguls as 'stock gamblers, oil, mine, and munitions promoters who wanted to buy the Presidency.' The attribution of the will-to-purchase was a little harsh. Presumably any other consortium with an equal fund would have operated along the same lines.

Apparently Colonel Procter conceived that the same methods which had so brilliantly exploited Ivory Soap could be employed to put over a presidential candidate. Colonel Procter was not a man who welcomed advice or suffered opposition patiently. There were men in his organization who could have warned him of the dangers of his course. John T. King was so offended by his autocratic methods that he resigned early from the campaign and managership to go over to Penrose and play a part as Nemesis in the *World's* exposure of the Wood 'fat-cats.' Congressman Norman Gould, Wood's Eastern manager, foresaw the danger that their own money might beat them, and bluntly warned his fellow executives, 'You can't wave a thousand-dollar bill like a flag.'[1]

The Procter theory was better fitted to commerce than politics. He continued to ignore advice and spend indiscriminately. A contemporary jester remarked of his methods that 'all the ivory didn't go into the soap.'

With less popular appeal than Wood, his competitor, Frank O. Lowden of Illinois, was his equal in character and his superior in practical experience. Both as Governor of Illinois and in the House of Representatives he had given an excellent account of himself. While a conservative by legal training and moneyed associations, he was never a slavish yes-man to the party bosses. There was plenty of money back of him too; he had married into the Pullman Car Company family.

Something of the taint of machine politics was upon him, however, because in promoting his candidacy he elected to

[1] Statement to the writer.

work through the already established Republican committees rather than submit his qualifications direct to the people on a broad scale. Labor did not like him, because he inveighed against labor domination. As a regular he commended himself to the Old Guard, in spite of having manifested independent tendencies of thought and vote on occasions. That he would be reliably compliant if elected was doubtful. But he was much closer to proper machine form than General Wood and was the best available weapon with which to eliminate the soldier, a project essential to the oligarchs, since they well knew that he would take no orders from them.

Two Californians, Herbert Hoover and Hiram Johnson, were lively entries. Hoover's humanitarian work in Belgium, followed by his masterly conduct of what might have proved a galling tyranny in more selfish and less skilled hands, the National Food Administration, had endeared him to thousands of his fellow countrymen. Those who had been associated with him officially felt for him an almost religious loyalty and affection. Scattering to their homes on all parts of the map after the war, these men and women formed a purely amateur but nevertheless inspirational organization for the rallying of Hoover support. Had the issue been left to the mass of voters, he might well have been the nominee in 1920. But nominations are not managed in that way. Conventions are controlled, not by the hot enthusiasms of popular favor as voiced by the gallery, but by the chilly mathematics of partisan dicker behind the scenes. Hoover had no organization back of him. His party allegiance was in doubt. The leaders would have none of him.

That schism led by Roosevelt which had rent the seamless robe of Republicanism in 1912 had been pretty well repaired. But there were still rifts. Because of these Hiram Johnson entered the contest at a disadvantage. He had been T. R.'s fellow candidate on the Bull Moose ticket, and would always be anathema to the die-hard element of the regulars.

He was a man of strong personality, rugged courage, and a savage fighter. There is much to support the belief, bitterly remembered for years after, that his failure to support Hughes against Wilson, after the Republican had short-sightedly snubbed the Californian in his own state, swung state and election against the party. Herein was further cause for implacable hostility. Johnson could count plenty of enemies. But he also had widely if rather thinly spread support from those who admired his fearlessness and fighting spirit, those who saw in him the standard-bearer of true progressivism, and, on the other side, many who followed him to the extremes of that bitter-end isolationism which was now the main tenet of his creed.

Horse-racing differs from politics in that nobody is allowed to shoot the leading horse, whereas all competitors go gunning for the leading candidate. Leonard Wood suffered the penalty of his initial advantage. That exceedingly hot snowball started by Messrs. Seibold and Lincoln of the *World* had gathered momentum in the Senate where Borah thundered of corruption, and rolled up an investigating committee report which startled the public with its revelation of a potential $1,770,000 in the Wood chest.[1] In every rival camp capital was made of the 'millionaire coterie.' The wise observers at Wood headquarters gave up hope, though they did not stop fighting, after the opening day.[2]

As the battalions lined up for the struggle, it became plain to the waiting nation that it was a Senate-controlled set-up. The oligarchy gathered at Chicago, ready to set in motion the steam roller, included such seasoned warriors as Lodge and Crane of Massachusetts, Smoot of Utah, Brandegee of Connecticut, Watson and New of Indiana, Curtis of Kansas, and Wadsworth and Calder of New York. The two Pennsyl-

[1] Report of Senate Committee on Elections and Privileges, May 21, 1920.
[2] 'By the second day, both Wood and Lowden were out of it.' — Statement to the writer by Norman Gould.

vanians, Knox and Penrose, were absentees. Knox was a possible candidate. Penrose was desperately ill, supposed to be about to die. But he retained enough energy in that gross and massive frame of his to maintain touch with the events eight hundred miles away when he emerged from the coma which threatened to be the end. He favored (for publication) Governor Sproul, Pennsylvania's favorite son.

The Senate ring did not want Wood, whom they could not control; they did not want Lowden, who, while regular, was too firm a character to take orders meekly; they certainly did not want the insurgent Johnson, with his suspect semi-radical following. As yet they had not made their choice. But it must be, as Penrose put it, 'a man who will listen.' Their first concern was to organize the convention for smooth control and eliminate the leading contenders.

As is typically the case where diverse forces are in operation, unexpected complications developed. For purposes of jockeying, the inner ring had smiled upon Hiram Johnson's round-up of delegates, willing to allow him a measure of support which they would withdraw in their own good time. But the California man had been making a lively campaign with unforeseen accesses of public support. He had become a quite possibly formidable entry. Out of twelve states on whose ballot his name appeared, he led in seven. In the primary states, though without machine support except in two, he polled the highest total vote of all the candidates, nearly a million.

The plan of the elder statesmen had been to help Johnson hold down Wood's prospects in some states, while Lowden captured enough votes to keep the General from sweeping the convention in the first charge. But here was a situation full of dynamite. With Johnson's growing power, if he and Wood made common cause they would easily be able to dominate the proceedings. The 'Senate Soviet,' as Charles Willis Thompson of the *New York Times* dubbed them, would have no chance against such a coalition. Happily for them the possibility of such a combination was eliminated by the Johnson-Borah onslaught upon the alleged misuse of 'big money,' with General Wood as the target. Johnson would bear watching, but Wood was the man to beat.

National Chairman Will H. Hays, shrewd, energetic, of high personal character, and popular with all factions, was relied upon to handle the many contests tactfully and to the best advantage. Out of 129 contests before the Credentials Committee, 88 seats were apportioned to Lowden (who now needed building up), 34 to Wood (to make a show of fair dealing), and 7 to Johnson. The play was, of course, to check Wood and maintain the balance. Already the lines were being formed for the deadlock which eventuated. Senator Moses of New Hampshire, a Wood man, made charges of unfair and autocratic methods in such heated terms that his principal felt it necessary to apologize for him. (There seems, however, to have been a good deal of basis for his accusations of railroading.) This did not endear the Wood group to the dominant Old Guard. In defence of the committee it may be said that the use of money among the Southern delegates, under the skilled management of Frank Hitchcock, who had learned something about such operations as Roosevelt's postmaster general, presented a fair target for criticism. Delegates from the hopelessly Democratic states — whose votes in the convention, of course, counted for as much as any other — were priced as high as five thousand dollars each. One of the ablest of the Wood lieutenants so stated to the writer.

'I have seen the checks going over the desk myself,' said he.

As Wood waned, Lowden waxed. Accordingly he was the next victim of senatorial machinations. Two obscure individuals from Missouri were the unconscious agents of destruction. Nat Goldstein and Robert E. Moore were delegates pledged to the Illinois governor. They received twenty-five hundred dollars each from headquarters 'to stimulate Lowden sentiment' in their localities. Presumably feeling that their own sentiment needed stimulus as much as anyone's, they pocketed the cash. At the subsequent investigation they insisted that they had no intention of keeping the money, but were only harboring it temporarily. Conceding this to be true, the effect was no less disastrous. Lowden was buying delegates! Such was the report that spread like oil. Of course, the candidate himself was in no way a party to the transaction; corruption was as little in his line as stupidity. It is ironic that a man so scrupulous about the use of money that he would accept no large contributions for his campaign, preferring to defray the expenses out of his own private purse, should have been the victim of this particular stigma.

It killed his chances as surely as the 'fat-cat' funds killed General Wood's. Whether they realized it or not, the chief contenders were out of the running. All was working to the satisfaction of the Elder Statesmen. While the process of elimination was going on, the process of selection was still in abeyance.

Some odd characters were working beneath the surface of the convention. The most picturesque was Jake Hamon of Oklahoma. Jake was an authentic if not a representative American type. At one time he was reputed to be worth twenty million dollars. To his home town, Newkirk, Oklahoma, he was Public Benefactor Number 1. All charities and good causes, the Boy Scouts, the Y.M.C.A., the Chamber of Commerce, the churches, found him a lavish donor. He was also a drunkard, a lecher, a bribe-giver, a thief of oil properties from the gullible Indian owners, a gambler for high stakes, and an ambitious political strategist. Nine years earlier he had taken as his mistress one, Clara Smith, then an eighteen-year-old shopgirl, and, combining business with pleasure, trained her to be an efficient confidential secretary. For official occasions, however, he stuck to his patient and condoning wife. This proved his undoing, since his announced plan for the inauguration, of taking the wife and leaving the mistress behind, annoyed Miss Smith to the point of shooting him — in self-defence, of course. A tearful and possibly appreciative jury so found, and acquitted her. The word in Oklahoma was: 'Somebody had to kill Jake. It's just as well it was Clara.'

This was the first of those tragedies of violence which so strangely mark the course of the pacific and violence-hating Harding.

Early on hand at the convention, Hamon represented oil, that same brand of oil which, flushing from Teapot Dome and Elk Hills into the bank accounts of Albert B. Fall, Harry F. Sinclair, and E. L. Doheny, so befouled the Harding Administration. Hamon was in Chicago to buy himself a cabinet position. He wished to be Secretary of the Interior, a job which he reckoned, with commendable approximation to accuracy, should be worth four hundred thousand dollars to an incumbent who knew how to make use of it. Notwithstanding that he was an avowed Lowden supporter, he got in touch with Harry Daugherty. He had been a guest of Daugherty's at the Deer Creek shack and was a friend of Harding's. Just when he switched allegiance from the Illinois to the Ohio candidate does not appear. Shortly before his death, late in 1920, he told his friends that he had 'signed the check which enabled Warren Harding to run for President.' This, however, was exaggeration. Gentlemen of Mr. Hamon's type are likely to brag a bit when exhilarated, as Hamon was by the election, in which he helped to carry Oklahoma at a cost — so he claimed — of four hundred thousand dollars. For he believed the election meant for him the profitable cabinet job he craved. Later he became plaintive, indicated that he had been double-crossed, and declared that, although he had helped Daugherty out with an immediate twenty-five thousand dollars to cover expenses at

Chicago, and had also put up ten times that sum with Senator Penrose of Pennsylvania, Harry Sinclair had beaten him in the race for Teapot Dome.[1] Sadly he characterized the whole thing as a raw deal, lamented that Harding had been framed, and that the post had been sold out from under before the election.

Unlike Hamon in every respect except preference for subterranean operations was Colonel George B. M. Harvey. He was an odd and incongruous figure to be found in that environment. He was not a delegate. It is doubtful whether he was even a Republican. If so, he was a raw recruit. He was, or claimed to be, an 'original Wilson man' and had ardently supported him until one of those tragically frequent quarrels which marred the course of the high-minded but often petty-tempered war President, shattered the friendship. President Wilson dubbed him 'an errand boy for Wall Street,' a charge to which the editorial policy of his short-lived but virulent *Harvey's Weekly* gave color.

Harvey was another Jesse Smith, on the intellectual plane. He loved the limelight. He delighted in the sense of being in the midst of vital activities; as Jesse might have put it, of 'sittin' in where there's somethin' doin'.' He affected formally statesmanlike attire, great, horn-rimmed spectacles, a pontifical carriage, and a weighty quietude of confidential speech. Where Jesse held you by the buttonhole whilst spluttering in your ear, George Harvey took you aside and privately addressed you in the manner of a public meeting. In scholarship and mental equipment he was the peer of any man at the convention, with the possible exception of Doctor Butler, but he was vain and, despite his carefully cultivated air of ponderous secrecy, often indiscreet. A malicious commentator said of him that he was so impressive, he impressed himself. Certainly he impressed the elders of that

[1] *Senate Investigation of Naval Oil Reserve Leases.* Government Printing Office, 1924.

senatorial convocation to a degree difficult to explain except on the ground that he typified, almost as completely as Lodge, the hatred of Wilson which informed the proceedings.

Another quiet but busy influence was John T. King. With Joseph Grundy of Pennsylvania, he was in charge of Penrose's headquarters. Justifiably vengeful because of his brusque dismissal by Colonel Procter, he had a personal interest in beating Procter's candidate, General Wood.

It is a reasonable assumption that specie played a part in the obscure tactics of Penrose and his henchmen. Penrose was a great believer in cash. On his death a packet of large denomination bills, aggregating $226,000, was found in his safety deposit box.[1] It is quite within the bounds of reason that he may have been quietly dealing in delegates. Money, however, did not figure directly in the proposal which, according to a story widely circulated at the time, he submitted to the leading candidate. This version is that he telephoned to Wood headquarters from his sick-bed in Philadelphia and offered his support in return for the privilege of naming three cabinet members. Wood declined to talk with him, and the offer was relayed by the man at the receiver.

Another man present said, 'Now, General, one word will make you President of the United States.'

Wood turned to the man at the telephone. 'Tell Senator Penrose that I am making no promises and will make none.'[2]

There is an improbability in this story. The conversation is supposed to have taken place on the critical Friday night. At that time, Penrose had barely rallied from a coma, was supposed to be moribund, and was certainly incapable of telephoning. However, his secretary may have been speaking for him. As will appear, this secretary did transmit directions to King about this time. The version is interesting as possibly supporting Jake Hamon's statement of coalition

[1] *New York World*, January 27, 1922.
[2] *Senate Investigation of Naval Oil Reserve Leases.*

with the Pennsylvania Senator on behalf of the oil interests. How important Penrose's long-distance influence proved is still a matter of controversy. Mark Sullivan and other competent historians minimize it, regarding his accession to the Harding cause as a 'bandwagon climb.' They point out the undeniable fact of his disabling illness, that the Pennsylvania delegation was accredited to Sproul whereas Penrose would have preferred Knox or Watson, and from this they deduce that his power as a boss was already waning. This latter seems more than doubtful. He was not maintaining an expensive Chicago connection for his amusement. The exact course of his factotum, King, is not known, but there is little doubt that he controlled a number of delegates to whom he transmitted his principal's orders. Six months thereafter Harry Daugherty considered him one of the two most powerful men in the Senate. And when the convention was over, Senator Kenyon of Iowa could sting the Republican leaders with the taunt that they were unable to act until they received word from a sick boss in Philadelphia.[1]

2

We sing with hearts on fire,
Oh, Harding! Salute!

chanted the Harding Glee Club of Columbus, seventy-five strong in full evening dress, serenading the other candidates with shirts and collars soft in the wilting heat.

Harding's heart was not on fire. It was chilled with hopelessness. 'He hadn't smiled the whole week,' said a Columbus newspaperman, covering the Ohio headquarters in the Congress Hotel.[2] Dishevelled, unshaven, and lonely, the candidate wandered unhappily about the streets. He gave directions to his friend, George B. Harris, about going to

[1] *New York Times*, June 16, 1920.
[2] Jacob A. Meckstroth.

Columbus to file his entry for the Senate race. These were his instructions:

'Keep in touch with headquarters. If I get the nomination, don't file. If I fail, use your own judgment. I don't care. I'm tired out and sick of politics.'

Even 'the most exclusive club in the world' had, for the time, lost its charm.

Mrs. Harding, too, was disheartened. 'He hasn't got a chance,' she confessed to a friend, and she frugally repined over the high cost of the headquarters at the Congress Hotel. Presumably she had not then heard of Jake Hamon's $25,000 check. Her husband, too, felt qualms over the $750-a-day rental, and was ready to give up the rooms.

'This convention will never nominate me,' he gloomily told Nicholas Murray Butler. 'I am going to quit politics.'

No thought of quitting entered the valiant soul of Harry Daugherty. All trains were met by his smiling welcomers. Every delegate was greeted, buttonholed, sounded out.

For Wood? That's all right. A fine man. But how about second choice? Give a thought to Warren Harding.

Johnson? Well, a lot of folks like Johnson. But suppose he don't come through; who's in your mind next? Lowden, huh? Yes, Lowden's got a good chance. How about third choice, then?

And so on down the line. Instructions were to keep smiling, knock nobody, leave a pleasant thought of Harding. Grandiose predictions were abandoned. A modest suggestion that the Ohio man was worth consideration in case the favorites dropped out was all. The publicity experts pulled their punches. No interviews were given out by Daugherty; he had done his public prophesying earlier. But he sent his singers around to serenade the rival headquarters. And he kept a spot-map of every delegate's room,[1] and had his men drop in for a friendly word or a cordial invitation to have a

[1] Harry M. Daugherty: *The Inside Story of the Harding Tragedy.*

drink. The effect produced was a pervasive impression that the Harding lot were pretty good guys. Popularity was quietly making, like ice on a zero night.

But for all the visiting and buttonholing, for all the sebaceous harmonies of the glee club, there was an atmosphere of chill in the costly Florentine Room of the Congress Hotel. No such bustle of enthusiasm, no such in-and-out of busy workers and happy swappers of victory predictions enlivened the Harding headquarters as kept those of General Wood, Governor Lowden, and Senator Johnson in a cheerful turmoil.

The convention was organized under strictly orthodox control. Will Hays, chairman of the Republican National Committee, while regarded as reasonably progressive and certainly not a standpatter, was entirely satisfactory to the Old Guard, who had no fear of his kicking over the traces. Jim Watson of Indiana was chosen to head the Resolutions Committee upon which devolved the most ticklish of the convention's problems. It was fixed that Lodge should be temporary chairman of the convention. He was advanced to the permanent chairmanship to beat the Progressive Senator Beveridge who was backed by Wood, and paid for his preferment by one flagrant parliamentary ruling in favor of the Senate cabal. All sub-committees were safe in Old Guard hands. They held the wires.

In preparing the platform the League of Nations was the delicate problem. Some of the wisest minds in the party were known to be for some kind of league, notably Elihu Root and Charles Evans Hughes. Leonard Wood also favored an 'American league.' Murray Crane, the foxy ex-Senator from Massachusetts, was the spearhead of the movement at Chicago. A triangular fight developed among the League supporters, the reservationists of the Lodge type, and the irreconcilables represented by Johnson and Borah. After a struggle behind locked doors, a strong anti-Wilson plank was rough-hewn to the pattern of the bitter-enders, mainly because of the fear of a bolt by Johnson, which would ruin the party's chances. Perforce, everyone professed to be satisfied. Watson was wildly cheered when he read the plank to the convention.

The one tenet upon which all factions could unite was anti-Wilson emotion. Henry Cabot Lodge gave expression to it in his keynote speech:

> Mr. Wilson and his dynasty, his heirs and assigns, or anybody that is his, anybody who with bent knee has served his purpose, must be driven from all control of the government and all influence in it. (Prolonged cheers.)

The voting strength of the delegates was 984; 493 were necessary to a choice. Six hundred and forty-three were uninstructed beyond the obligation of casting a courtesy vote for a favorite son until released. Three hundred and forty-one were committed by pledge to one or another of the four leading candidates. On this basis General Wood entered the field as favorite, with 124 pledges. Johnson was second, with 112; Lowden third, with 66, and Harding lowest, with his 39 of Ohio's split delegation. But these merely official figures did not represent the actual strength of the contestants. The experts based their calculations upon underlying prospects.

They allotted to General Wood upward of 250 votes at the start, which was too low a number. (Even the keen Harry Daugherty miscalculated and was alarmed when he discovered his error.) Lowden was credited with better than 200, and Johnson placed third with something less than 150. The sharps considered themselves generous toward Harding in allowing him between 60 and 70. In the background were the favorite sons, Butler of New York, Poindexter of Washington, Sproul and Knox of Pennsylvania, Coolidge of Massachusetts; also the names with scattered supporters such as Borah, Hughes, Lodge, La Follette, Taft, and Pershing. The votes controlled by this heterogeneous company were valuable mainly for trading purposes, though in the case of Sproul, Knox, and Coolidge, there were forlorn hopes attached.

Obviously General Wood was the man to beat, and Lowden the man to beat him with.

Trading began. Louis Emmerson, Lowden manager, accosted Daugherty with the offer of a Cabinet position in return for throwing the Harding vote to his candidate, a suggestion which the Ohio man politely declined. He had a better idea. Of course, he explained, he could not, as Harding's manager, permit his man's vote to approach the vanishing point. But he was willing to farm out a few Ohio votes to help check Governor Lowden's chief competitor.[1]

The nomination speeches were delivered on Friday, June 11. That setting forth Harding's qualifications was received with the most spontaneous applause, partly because the sponsor, ex-Governor Frank B. Willis of Ohio, combined the gifts of 'oratory, grand opera, and hog-calling,' to quote Mark Sullivan's witty characterization, partly because it lasted but eight minutes of close-packed high-class hokum, and largely because of Harding's personal popularity. All three rival leaders enjoyed more protracted 'demonstrations,' but those were staged and artificial. Meantime *vox populi* was whooping it up in the galleries for Herbert Hoover and making no impression upon the massed delegates below, who were there for business.

The first ballot was a jolt to the senatorial statisticians. Instead of the 250 votes attributed to Wood, he started with 287, and steadily accumulated support, until, on the fourth and final vote of the day, his count was 314½. Lowden followed with 289½, Johnson had 140½, and Harding trailed with 61½. Sproul of Pennsylvania was 18 votes ahead of Harding, but that was a negligible tribute of state loyalty.

Meantime there was lively trading on the curb. The New

[1] Mark Sullivan: *Our Times*, vol. VI.

York contingent, supporting its favorite son, President Butler of Columbia, though not unanimously, switched a number of its votes to Lowden to aid his build-up. This was counteracted by John T. King, operating under Penrose's long-distance manipulations, who swung some of the scattered votes controlled by him to Wood. William Hale Thompson, Chicago boss and Johnson supporter, not that he loved Johnson so much, but because he hated Lowden so hotly, was making overtures to Daugherty and others in the hope of beating his fellow Illinoisan. A. T. Hert, convention manager for Lowden, accompanied by Dan Mulvane, was scurrying from headquarters to headquarters, making tentative offers, arranging possible deals and swaps against Wood. There were lively rumors of bribe-money passing; sums specified, one thousand dollars to this man, five thousand dollars to another to swing a delegation; a moneyed Wood rooter proposing to open his purse and being harshly forbidden by the General. Hiram Johnson disgustedly opined that '1912 was a Sunday school convention compared to this.' Alice Roosevelt Longworth, an interested and always interesting commentator, described the situation as 'wormy with politicians — riddled with intrigue.'[1]

The oligarchs now called a halt. All was going as per programme. Wood and Johnson were satisfactorily neutralizing one another. Johnson was practically static. Enough had been done to make clear this point to the delegates; that further balloting would not materially change the result nor give any of the competitors a commanding lead. It was time to look coolly about for new material. Further competition at this time might bring on one of those angry deadlocks which engender inextinguishable enmities and imperil party harmony. Smoot of Utah conferred with Lodge. A motion to adjourn was offered. The ayes were comparatively few, scattered, and uncertain. Lodge called again. There was a

[1] Alice Roosevelt Longworth: *Crowded Hours.*

full-voiced chorus, 'No,' from both Wood and Lowden co-horts. Their fighting blood was up and they wanted to go on to a finish. No unprejudiced listener had any doubt of the convention's wishes. But that did not move the chairman. Blandly Senator Lodge declared the motion carried and an-nounced that the delegates would reconvene in the morning. No emphatic protest was raised; there was not so much as a demand for a roll-call. The assemblage knew its master's voice.

From now on the convention dwindles as a factor. It be-comes merely a confirmatory body. The motivating power shifts to a smaller stage.

★

XI. A Smoke-Filled Room:
2.11 a.m.

Frantic activities marked that night and the next morning along Convention Row. The candidates who divided the sentiment of the majority were already beaten, though they had not learned the unpleasant fact. Shrewd watchers scented danger, however. Politicians — good politicians — possess a sixth sense in such matters. Word-of-mouth warnings were being dispensed wherever groups gathered together. Time for action was at hand if anything effective was to be done.

At Pennsylvania headquarters, plans for a rousing Sproul night parade were formulated. The theory was that the situation was opening up; that a dark horse, urged forward now, might dash into the lead. All that was wanted to start the demonstration was word from the leaders — meaning, Boies Penrose. It did not come. His lieutenants on the ground, John T. King and Joseph Grundy, lent no support to the waiting celebrants; they were busy elsewhere on other missions. So recruiting for the parade of Sproul rooters lapsed and Melancholy marked them for her own.

Perceiving that Johnson's cause was waning, Borah tried

out sentiment for a Knox and Johnson ticket. Combining East and West, senatorial conservatism with the vigorous liberalism of the Californian, should appeal to many voters of all kinds, he thought. He found little sympathy for this view. Nor was Johnson receptive. The Senate cabal might beat him — indeed, he was already beaten — but they could not tie him to the tail of anybody's kite. Had he been minded to accept that function, other and better opportunities were at his command. Harding, Wood, and Lowden each dangled the vice-presidential bauble before his undazzled eyes. It had no allure for the immovable ex-Bull Mooser. *Aut Caesar, aut nullus:* first place or nothing for him.

Jake Hamon went to Wood with a proposition which did more credit to his nerve than to his judgment of character. Oil support, political and financial, sufficient to insure the nomination would be forthcoming if the candidate would promise to appoint him Secretary of the Interior and assure him a free hand on oil leases. The irate soldier told him to get the hell out of there lest a worse thing befall him.[1]

The late Percy Hammond, then dramatic critic of the *Chicago Tribune*, was told by one of Lowden's right-hand men that a similar offer was made to the Governor by two prominent delegates, with this curious difference, that one of the offices demanded was that of Director of the Mint. It was curtly rejected, and the proposition was then passed on to Harding, who was open to any bargain.[2]

Ignorant of the undercurrents that favored him, Harding was sunk in apathy at the close of the session. He had lost a few of his meagre array of votes, having sunk from an initial 65½ to a final 61½. Had he but known it, this was of little significance. Daugherty, who did not always confide in him, had 'loaned' a few votes. In Harding's position of low man among the leaders, he could afford this. When the leader in a

[1] *Editor and Publisher*, August 13, 1927; Edgar Mels.
[2] Account given to the writer by Percy Hammond.

convention race suffers a loss of votes, that is the beginning of the end for him. He is like a faltering horse. His bolt is shot; seldom if ever does he recapture the advantage. With a trailer this curious rule does not apply. Fluctuations within small limits in his case indicate only that there is trading in progress.

Seeking an interview with Harding after the adjournment, Jacob A. Meckstroth of the *Ohio State Journal* found him a picture of gloom:

> He showed great mental distress. Harding had a trick of holding his right hand to the side of his head as if to rest a tired brain. That was his posture when I saw him. Discouragement hung about him like a cloud. He was not interested in anything.[1]

Eight hundred miles to the east a sick man roused himself from a coma which, his physician then believed, was an immediate forerunner of the end. Dr. H. W. Carpenter thus reports the circumstances:[2]

> He [Penrose] was a very sick man. He collapsed ... he had been unconscious for hours. But even in that condition his mind was subconsciously turning over the problem at Chicago. He came to at last ... turned to Leighton C. Taylor, his secretary, and asked what they were doing at Chicago. It was the first question he asked after regaining consciousness. Taylor answered that they had been doing nothing, that a deadlock had been reached. The Senator lay a moment, thinking. 'Call up King,' he said at last to Taylor, 'and tell him to throw it to Harding.'

When that message was communicated to the quarters where it would have the most effect, the choice of the senatorial bosses was still in the air. That Penrose's word should not have carried weight is incredible. But there are no scales in which to weigh such imponderables.

Four of the unofficial steering committee dined together

[1] Statement to the writer.
[2] *New York Times*, January 9, 1922.

that Friday evening, Senators Lodge, Curtis of Kansas, afterward Vice President, Brandegee of Connecticut, and Colonel George Harvey. The dinner was held in Harvey's suite at the Blackstone Hotel. Opinion of the quartette was unanimous that Lowden and Wood had shot their bolts, and that their forces were set for a deadlock. Should they, then, adjourn the convention until Monday to afford more time for adjustments and decisions? Could they if they wished? Another such autocratic assumption might provoke mutiny. The delegates were growing restive. The heat had been punitive; expenses no less so. At what moment they might get out of hand and demand action that would release them to go home, no man could tell. No; it would not do. The deadlock must be broken.

With whom? Doctor Alderfer, who attended the convention, thus analyzes the requirements:

> The situation called for a candidate who had opposed the League of Nations, but one who would favor a league with some 'American reservations,' in order to keep that great body of Republican voters who wanted 'some kind of a league.' This candidate must also be a Republican who had remained loyal in 1912, but who was not too much of a reactionary who by his record might fail to win the confidence of the liberal element of the party. The nominee must, by temperament, record, and personality, be the complete antithesis of Wilson. He must be democratic and genial, not aristocratic and intellectual; he must be of that persuasion that the Senate would be able to assert its constitutional position; and he must be safe in that the Senators could trust him to listen to the reasonings of the leaders.[1]

Evening verged toward morning and found the party moguls still canvassing the poor pick of availables, in gloom, weariness, and incertitude. Other advisers came and went, proffering each his own suggestions, citing objections to those of the others. In and out there drifted, with the leases

[1] H. F. Alderfer: *Personality and Politics of Warren G. Harding.*

of distributable votes in their pockets, the Indiana Senators, New and Watson, the New Yorkers, Wadsworth and Calder, Weeks of Massachusetts, Reed Smoot of Utah, McCormick of Illinois; also Nicholas Murray Butler, Murray Crane, and Joe Grundy. Conspicuous absentees were Harry Daugherty and Will Hays. Naturally the backers of Wood, Lowden, and Johnson were not present. To welcome to an evening conference men whom you are planning to crack over the head with a club in the morning is one of the 'things that aren't done' at conventions.

Harvey was for Will Hays. But Hays, while he had proved an efficient cog in the machinery and was well liked by all the leaders, lacked public appeal. Someone, probably Grundy, mentioned Knox of Pennsylvania. Knox had a bad heart; he was too ill to be safely available, even had his Senate record not been too conservative for his own political good. Governor Sproul was too local. Senator Jim Watson was too hidebound a standpatter. Senator Lodge's venom against the League of Nations and all the Wilson policies had been so extreme as to alienate even the 'solid men of Boston,' and many of his old friends cut him on the street. Nicholas Murray Butler was a college president; hadn't the country had enough of college presidents in the White House? Hughes had already been defeated. Geographical considerations worked against Coolidge; he was too far East. Hoover? What was Hoover? Didn't he permit himself to be voted upon in the Democratic primaries, where, incidentally, he made quite a showing? Away with him to the limbo of such damned spirits as insurgents, bolters, and La Follette! No sooner was a figure set up for consideration than somebody doused it with a bucket of cold water — or mud.

A decision, tentative and provisional, but still a working agreement, was reached and a messenger left the room.

Passing Ohio headquarters at 11 P.M., the *Ohio State Jour-*

nal man saw Harding coming out on the arm of Myron T. Herrick. Mr. Meckstroth could hardly believe his eyes. Was this the pattern of despair who, only a few short hours earlier, had hardly emerged from his glum apathy enough to answer questions? Gone was all evidence of depression. The candidate's chin was up. He was jaunty, beaming, chipper. Herrick waved an exultant hand.[1]

'You can say,' he told the reporters, 'that Senator Harding will be nominated on the first ballot tomorrow.'

The pair jumped into a car and were whirled away.

Mr. Meckstroth is sure of the time. He consulted his watch. It leaves two hours unaccounted for. It was after one o'clock when Harding was delivered at the door of George Harvey's Blackstone Hotel suite a few blocks away, to hear the glad news. Where he and Herrick had been in the interim nobody appears to know.

The offer was not yet unrestricted. There was an important point to be clarified. Only Colonel Harvey and Senator Brandegee were in the room. Harvey, owlish behind his looming horn-rims, greeted the visitor, shook hands solemnly, said there were some questions to be answered, and he, Colonel Harvey, had been delegated to present the questions. In the opinion of friends who knew him well, he nominated himself for this delicate inquisition: 'It's just the sort of thing George would do.' With his portentous manner, his ambassadorial make-up, and his air of grave and reliable secrecy, he was peculiarly suited to the confessional rôle.

There are a dozen versions of the form which the query took. The one current in Ohio immediately after the event runs:

> Senator, we want to put a question to you. Is there in your life or background any element which might embarrass the Republican Party if we nominate you for President?

[1] Statement of Jacob A. Meckstroth to writer.

More Harveyesque — as it should be since it is Harvey's own repetition, recited to Mark Sullivan thirty-six hours after the event — is this form:[1]

> We think you may be nominated tomorrow; before acting finally we think you should tell us, on your conscience and before God, whether there is anything that might be brought against you that would embarrass the party, any impediment that might disqualify you or make you inexpedient either as candidate or as President.

'Rather stunned,' as Mr. Sullivan puts it, the subject of this searching inquisition asked for time to think it over. Harvey shut him in and rejoined Brandegee, who was waiting in the living-room.

On the same page Mr. Sullivan refers to a 'woman scandal.' The imputation is that the Nan Britton entanglement was in question. It may well have been this in part. But there was more. The dilemma in which Harding found himself had more than one horn.

Two people were then in Chicago, either of whom might have the power to ruin him politically. One was Nan Britton, the unmarried mother of his child. The other was, or held himself out to be, William Estabrook Chancellor, Professor at the College of Wooster in Ohio and author of leaflets which were then being peddled about at rival headquarters purporting to prove negro blood in the Harding line.

In Harding's political past there was nothing to inspire an inquisition by George Harvey or anyone else; nothing of which he was ashamed or afraid. Therefore it must be either the girl scandal or the negro story that was being put up to him.

Consider his position. He had not countermanded his entry for the Senate race. Presumably that had gone in in due form. (As a matter of fact it had at 11.58 P.M., since the candidate had neglected or, what is more likely, for-

[1] Mark Sullivan: *Our Times*, vol. VI.

gotten in the excitement of his sudden change of prospects, to give George Harris, his emissary, instructions. It was cancelled on the following morning.) He could still run for that office with reasonable assurance. Self-appointed conclaves do not peer with such particularity into the past of a mere Senator; self-nominated examiners do not segregate him and trouble his conscience with discomforting queries. It must have been borne in upon him with painful force that the implications of running for the Presidency were sternly retroactive. . . . Anything that might be brought up against him . . . any impediment . . . any disqualification . . . any embarrassment.

To persuade himself that the episode with Nan was not dangerous would not be difficult. For five years the liaison had existed without open scandal. If he gave these men his solemn word that it was all over between him and the girl, wouldn't that satisfy them? Need he go that far? Nobody had asked him about it in so many words. He could trust Nan. She wasn't the kind to make trouble for a man. He had always been square with her, and he could trust her to be square with him and keep her mouth shut. Only a few people actually *knew* about them, and they were friends he could trust. Others might suspect, but what could they prove?

There was the baby, to be sure. But it was to the interest of the two or three people who were in on that secret to keep it quiet. He'd look after the child; he'd look after both of them, for that matter. Lots of men had done the same thing and got away with it.

With the negro story, as he knew by bitter experience, it was different. No one could predict where that would crop up next. It never could be wholly suppressed. There were those unforgotten newspaper stories, that indestructible testimony from people who believed his family blood to be mixed.

Suppose he made a clean breast of it? Suppose he opened up his whole past, told them about Nan, laid bare the negro rumor; said to the waiting men: 'Here is the story. It has been printed several times. It has made me a lot of trouble and caused an estrangement between my wife and her father, who believes it. A lot of people believe it. It isn't true' (or perhaps, more conservatively, 'I don't believe it is true'). 'But it may be printed again by my enemies. I am willing to face the issue. It is for you gentlemen to decide.'

What would have been the result? One can only conjecture. But repellent though it be to one's sense of fairness, it is probable that such courage and straight dealing on Harding's part would have been penalized. Politicians are not noted for valor when confronted with issues of unreckonable potentialities. It took a Cleveland to say, 'Tell the truth,' when an ancient woman-scandal rose in his path. (The rumor of negro blood, by the way, circulated about him, too, absurd though it was.) Harding would probably have been dropped as a potato too hot to handle.

What arguments Harding brought to the defeat of his conscience only he could have said. He came out after ten minutes' cogitation and told Harvey and Brandegee that there was nothing; no obstacle.

From that moment he was as good as nominated. Cognizant or incognizant of its purely contributory function, the convention was now to be no more than a rubber stamp for endorsement. The 'fifteen men' had decided. Harry M. Daugherty had made good on his extravagant prophecy. He had won a victory unique in American politics.

He was able to do it because he was equipped with a candidate, possible and available. No one else was. The old adage was proven once more: 'You can't beat somebody with nobody.'

To scouting correspondents Harvey sketched out the position. The party leaders, whom he represented in the present negotiations, had expected Governor Lowden to capture the nomination. The unfortunate Missouri scandal had eliminated him. Publicity given to his disproportionate expenditures, together with anti-militaristic feeling, had spoiled General Wood's prospects.

Drawn battle between those two contestants, holding the convention at a deadlock, might have irreparably compromised party harmony, so essential to success. In this crisis, the leaders deemed it their duty to intervene and find the solution. Senator Harding of Ohio was the solution. That was all.

Messengers visited the other headquarters. To the Wood men they set forth that it was 'in the bag' for Harding. Would the General's supporters see reason? Why not get aboard while the getting aboard was good? There was a gathering of advisers to consider the situation. The decision was that Wood would fight until beaten on the convention floor.

Lowden was next tried out. Two of his own supporters, National Committeemen Hert and Warren, were the bearers of the bad news that the ruling spirits had handpicked Harding. The Governor's reply was that they knew the chances better than he, but that he would not drop out while there was a fighting hope. It was left at that for the time.

So confident was the Lodge-Brandegee-Smoot-Harvey combination now that Smoot gave out definite, though not quite accurate, details of how the wires were to be pulled at the coming session. Wood and Lowden would be permitted to make a showing. Wood's figures would grow a little, but not dangerously, on the opening ballot of the morning. In the afternoon, when the other contenders had been appeased by the graciously permitted exhibition of their apparent strength, Harding would be brought forward and pushed through to victory. That was the programme and nobody could stop it.

★

XII. Victory

Elimination of the other contenders as painlessly as possible to the end that no incurably inflamed wounds be left was now the object of the Smoot-Lodge-Brandegee-Harvey faction. How smugly certain of control they were may be judged from Smoot's Friday night announcement of their perfected Saturday plan.

In one respect the Smoot prediction went wrong. Wood's strength on the initial ballot of the morning (the fifth) decreased, nor did it ever again reach its high point of the fourth (Friday's final). Able now to shift a reliable bulk of delegates at will, the dominant clique may have chosen to exalt Lowden over his competitor, in recognition of his sportsmanlike acceptance of the death sentence to his hopes. He passed Wood, 303 to 299. Whatever delusions of victory his followers may have cherished, however, were dissipated on the next two roll-calls when the General, after catching up to him, 311½ to 311½, drawing mainly from the depleted Johnson, passed him by half a hair, 312 to 311½ on the seventh.

On the eighth the beginning of the end for the leaders was manifest. Both sagged; Wood to 299; Lowden to 307. Never had they dangerously approached the required plurality.

The reason for this was only too plain. Harding loomed.

Only one circumstance had threatened the slow and steady progress of the Ohio man. Four of the delegates from his own state, led by 'Rudy' Hynicka, an old-time lieutenant of Boss Cox of Cincinnati, and a gang politician, broke away on the sixth ballot and went to Wood. This was flat treachery. Presumably it was intended to start a report that Harding could not hold his own Ohioans, and thus inspire a final rush to his rival. Daugherty had advance notice of it. The loyal Ohio men were on watch. They had forestalled any evil effects by spreading the word that Hynicka controlled no more than this little handful.[1] The sortie proved quite futile.

Word passed electrically through the assemblage, 'Watch Harding.' It was like the excitement at a horse-race when one of the contestants who has been held back comes through with a rush on the rail. Harding was certainly coming. With 78 votes on the fifth ballot, he had risen to 89 on the sixth, 105 on the seventh (passing Johnson, who had sunk to 99½), and had jumped to 133½ on the eighth.

A recess was requested by the Harding forces at this juncture. Why, it is difficult to perceive. Their advance was well under way, and gaining momentum. One would naturally suppose that any check to its progress now would operate to afford the opposition time for getting together in a final effort toward checking the new threat.

Exactly that attempt was made. Wood and Lowden got in touch by telephone, met, hurriedly discussed developments. Wood could hold his ranks intact; could Lowden guarantee as much? The Illinois man was uncertain. Naming no names, he intimated doubt of some of his lieutenants. If he tried to divert his followers from his own candidacy, it would be interpreted as a release from their pledges and heavy defections to Harding or Johnson might follow. Upon one point the collaborating rivals agreed: if

[1] Harry M. Daugherty: *The Inside Story of the Harding Tragedy.*

Harding was to be stopped, it must be by a prompt merger of interests, the details to be worked out later. The first thing to do was to halt the balloting before the Harding wave gathered irresistible force. They agreed to force an adjournment to Monday. The combined Wood-Johnson-Lowden vote was more than adequate to the design.

Word reached Lowden and was relayed by him to Wood that Kentucky was preparing to swing to Harding. This pointed the absolute necessity of adjournment. It was the last chance.

The Kentucky National Committeeman was Alvin T. Hert, one of the Lowden managers. His subsequent course seems to justify Lowden's suspicion of sharp practice among his staff.

Interested watchers had observed Hert in quiet consultation with John T. King and Joseph Grundy, Penrose's handymen.[1] Both of these experts were, in their way, men of capacity and resource. But, as representative of Governor Lowden's interests, Hert laid himself open to suspicion by this unobtrusive — too carefully unobtrusive — association. Delegates of an analytical trend of mind wondered what was going on and thought that they knew when strange developments followed.

Working in desperate haste, the Wood-Lowden coalition sent a trusted messenger to Will Hays. He brought back word (right or wrong) that the National Committee Chairman was with them on the issue. It may be noted here that Hays had not been one of the 'fifteen men.' He was to use his influence for prolongation of the recess until the forces for adjournment were lined up. Then Hert was to present the motion to adjourn.

Hert was an inexplicable and calamitous choice. Search failed to locate him. There is reason to believe that he was

[1] 'All of us knew that Hert and King were hand-in-glove during those days.' — Statement to the writer by Norman Gould of Wood's headquarters.

at that moment in touch with Senator Penrose through King and Grundy, while the Lowden men were combing the locality for him. In any case, he was not in the Coliseum when Chairman Lodge mounted the rostrum.

Recess had now lasted overtime. Lodge warned the proponents of delay that he could not hold off indefinitely. Someone brought word that Hert was on his way to the hall. Reluctantly, Lodge agreed to allow ten minutes more. The period elapsed. No Hert. The gavel came down. The meeting was in order.

With the ninth roll-call came the break. Connecticut started it, switching from Lowden to Harding. Florida quit Wood for Harding. Other Southern delegates, nervous and uncertain, were caught in the sweep. It was known that a great deal of Wood money had been spent on them. But how long could they be trusted to remain true to that persuasion? Other rewards were now in prospect: postmasterships, marshalships, minor federal jobs, to be attained only by climbing on the bandwagon. There were rumors of wavering everywhere.

In the midst of the voting Hert arrived. Lowden and Wood men excitedly crowded around him. Where had he been? What was going on? How about the adjournment? The Kentucky committeeman shrugged them off and threw a bomb. He voted the delegation for Warren G. Harding in the midst of pandemonium. Afterward he explained that if Lowden had remained in the contest, the nomination must have gone to Wood. To defeat Wood rather than to support the man to whom he was pledged was his purpose.

The roar which greeted Kentucky's defection was partly acclaim, partly wrath. There was further turmoil when New York contributed part of its quota. The final count was Harding 374½; Wood 249; Lowden 121½; Johnson 82. The new leader had taken 50 votes from Wood, 185½ from Lowden, only 5 from the loyal Johnson hosts. It was by no means a choice. But it was the harbinger of victory. The bandwagon was rolling. Governor Lowden, always a sportsman, meeting Harding in the aisle, congratulated him.

All chance of adjournment was now gone. There was nothing to do but stand in the path of the wave and take it. The end came with the tenth ballot. Harding polled 692½ votes. Amidst the frenzied roaring of a mob now become a menagerie, a motion to make the nomination unanimous was put. The Official Report of the Proceedings records that 'applause, long and loud, greeted the declaration of the Chairman that Warren G. Harding of Ohio had been unanimously nominated for the President.' Chairman Lodge may have so declared. It was not the fact. La Follette's twenty-four stubborn Wisconsin stalwarts voted No.

The Senate oligarchs were soberly gratified.

'This year we had a lot of second-raters,' said Senator Brandegee. 'Harding is no world-beater. But he's the best of the second-raters.' [1]

The ranking is too high. As a Senator, Harding was a second-rater. As a potential President, he was a tenth-rater. Not a man who was mentioned in the convention but was better qualified for the job than he. Tragically, Harding knew it. But being Harding, he couldn't say No.

Naturally he was elated. 'I feel like a man who goes in on a pair of eights and comes out with aces full,' said he. [2]

'I can see but one word written over his head if they make him President,' cried Mrs. Harding; 'and that word is Tragedy.' [3]

The vice-presidential sequel was expected to be anticlimactic. It was sensational.

Irvine Lenroot, junior Senator from Wisconsin, was the

---

[1] Clinton W. Gilbert: *Mirrors of Washington.*

[2] *Literary Digest*, November 27, 1920.

[3] Charles Willis Thompson: *Presidents I've Known.*

choice of the inner ring. He was the logical complement to
Harding. Starting in politics as a La Follette lieutenant, he
had parted company with that leader, deeming him too
radical, but had preserved a sturdy liberalism of his own.
As offsetting Harding's proved conservatism, he would be a
reassurance to the more progressive wing of the party —
who also had votes. So he went on the programme, though
he had not been apprised of the fact.

Wine of victory had gone to the senatorial heads, unduly
swelling them. No thought penetrated to those overconfi-
dent minds that all might not proceed as per schedule. They
had only to pass the word among the delegates and their
selection would be duly ratified; such was their comfortable
assumption. Meantime water was flowing under the bridge,
bearing on its surface a name not in the calculations.

Whispers of instruction passed through the hall, 'It's
Lenroot.' The message was answered not in the expected
spirit of humble acquiescence, but with growls of dissatisfaction. Heat, or exhaustion, or boredom may have been the
leaven which turned the convention suddenly sour. The
Senate ring had already put across one member of their club
on the delegates. One Senator was enough; another was too
many. They did not want any part of Lenroot and Lenroot,
not having been consulted by the lordly bosses, made it
unanimous by not wanting any part of the Vice-Presidency.

The party elders had not foreseen anything of this sort.
How could they have been expected to? Commanders who
have just won a smashing victory do not look for mutiny in
the ranks.

There is nothing to indicate that the Coolidge boom had
been mapped out beforehand. But it went over with a crash
that left the experienced bosses gasping.

Calvin Coolidge had achieved national fame through the
Boston police strike of 1919, which, for turmoil and excitement, was second only to the Boston Tea Party of a century

and a half earlier. He had cleverly capitalized a crisis.[1]

Grossly underpaid and miserably housed, the police force had organized and joined the American Federation of Labor against the orders of a rather stuffy police commissioner who thereupon put the leaders on trial. When they were found guilty and discharged, the whole force walked out in protest. Looting and rioting followed. Coolidge as governor played a master hand at politics. He sympathized, for publication, with the hardships of the police. He denied officially their right to strike. While the crisis was looming, he disappeared so as not to incur the unpopularity of calling out the militia. An opening was made to order for him by a letter from Samuel Gompers, head of the Federation, asking for a fair settlement.

Pat came the answer, 'There is no right to strike against the public safety by anybody, any time, any place.'

It was sound, laconic Yankee rhetoric. Followed to a logical conclusion it would reduce the police and all other public servants to the estate of slaves. But the public mind will always respond to an apt phrase. Seventy thousand messages of acclaim flooded the Boston State House. Coolidge became the idol of anti-labor employers all over the country. But more than this, he had spoken for a great mass of ordinary citizens who, alienated by the excesses of reckless strikers, felt that Labor, fed fat on wartime wages, was becoming too arrogant and contemptuous of the public interest.

Undoubtedly this sentiment was prevalent in the Chicago Convention. The Republican Party traditionally represented property rights as the foundation of society. Governor Coolidge had demonstrated his support of property against the incursion of destructive forces. He had had the courage to tell Organized Labor where it got off. The convention bosses might whisper, 'It's Lenroot.' A more potent word

---

[1] William Allen White: *A Puritan in Babylon.* This book gives the most acute and comprehensive analysis of the Boston police strike.

countered theirs: 'There is no right to strike against the public safety; Coolidge is our man.'

Medill McCormick in nominating Lenroot had paid a tribute to the presidential candidate as 'a man of ripe experience, of deep learning, and of great power,' a recital which, probably delivered with tongue in cheek, evoked languid amusement. It was not a happy introduction to his brief speech which was received without enthusiasm. One, Remmel, from Arkansas seconded the nomination. So did Hert of Kentucky, Senator Calder of New York, and Governor Herrick of Ohio. It was demonstrably another Senatorial 'party.'

Up jumped a man unknown to that gathering, whose claim to recognition — and a sufficient one — was the possession of a trombone voice. The chairman obligingly recognized Mr. Wallace McCamant of Oregon. Mr. McCamant, as far as he could be heard above the clamor of departing delegates and the turmoil of the emptying galleries (and he could be heard farther than anyone else present), was naming Governor Calvin Coolidge of Massachusetts 'for the exalted office of Vice President.' The official records note 'an outburst of applause of short duration but great power.' Michigan seconded the nomination, and before they could gather for defence, the bosses found themselves facing a revolt. Maryland, Arkansas, Connecticut, and North Dakota raised an approving clamor. Illinois, Nebraska, Nevada, and Vermont joined in. It was an ovation. Before the vote was taken, the result was obvious.

The vote was 674½ for Coolidge to 146 for Lenroot. As soon as the Big Show was over, a large number of the members, including half a delegate, had grown weary and left the hall. This time the choice of the convention was made unanimous. Wisconsin went along.

In a small, rather dingy Boston hotel suite Governor and Mrs. Coolidge were receiving news of the proceedings. Harding's nomination had evoked no enthusiasm from them; Coolidge had been hopeful that the presidential lightning would descend upon Massachusetts, and was depressed when it struck in Ohio. He displayed a revival of interest when the sensational response to McCamant's trumpetings was reported. The telephone receiver was in and out of his hand at brief intervals. Presently he set it back, turned to his wife and said:

'Nominated.'

'You're not going to take it, are you?' she asked.

'I suppose I'll have to,' he replied.[1]

So it was Harding and Coolidge, a curiously assorted pair. The hard-bitten New England Yankee and the soft, easy-going Ohioan; the hedonist and the Puritan.

[1] William Allen White: *A Puritan in Babylon.*

★

XIII. Statesmanship à la Front Porch

I

NO EXTRAVAGANCE of enthusiasm marked the reception of Warren G. Harding's candidacy. The public expressions of sentiment were for the most part restrained, not to say perfunctory. Harding's own dubiety toward the position into which he had been pushed was matched by that of his party. Open dissatisfaction was not widely voiced, though some Republican organs did not hesitate to define the result of the convention as a standpat conquest. This was the view of the *New York Tribune*. Such newspapers as hailed the nominee with acclaim based their satisfaction on the assumption that he represented the antithesis of President Wilson in all respects. The country, they figured, wanted an anti. In so far as he typified anything, Harding stood for comprehensive opposition to a wavering Democracy.

Nobody was deeply impressed by the personality and record of the convention's choice. The *New York Evening World* opined that the Republicans had nominated not a man but an oligarchy. The *Evening Post* saw in the outcome the usurpation of control by the Senate ring, and the *Cleveland Plain Dealer* and the Hearst papers agreed. Penrose, Crane,

Watson, Lodge, Knox, and Smoot were credited with a sweeping victory and indicated as preparing to take over navigation of the ship of state. The *New York Times* stigmatized the nomination as 'the fine and perfect flower of the cowardice and imbecility of the senatorial cabal.' [1]

Broadly gauged, the feeling about Harding was that he was the Senate's egg. Now let them hatch him.

To this congenial task of incubation they set themselves. They had at their call what Harry Daugherty, looking back across wide vistas of battle, considered 'the most powerful national political machine ever set up.'

From Chicago Fred Upham, the party treasurer, sounded the call: 'Boys, get the money.' He hoped for fifteen millions. [2] While falling short of this mark, he nevertheless did well. To refute the Democratic charge that an oligarchy of wealth was 'buying a stranglehold on the government,' William Boyce Thompson, prettily known to his intimates as 'Guts' in tribute to his abdominal impressiveness, announced that contributions would be limited to one thousand dollars per donor. This was for publication only. Large sums were privately contributed or pledged. Some of these, in the form of bonds from oil companies seeking future benefits, were subsequently traced to the National Committee.

From the viewpoint of the managers, Harding was the ideal candidate. He was a pattern of conformity. What the Elders prescribed for him he would do and say without cavil. It would not be fair to call him a puppet; puppets do not sit in on the conferences of those who pull the wires. Rather he was an actor, cheerfully responsive to the direction of the playwrights. With his inbred deference to party authority he was always ready to take orders. In fact, he welcomed them. Never was Harding less happy than when he had to make decisions for himself on any question of principle or policy.

What type of campaign best fitted the circumstances was

[1] June 13, 1920.   [2] *Literary Digest*, September 11, 1920.

the immediate problem for the management. Penrose's advice was to the point as was customary with that brutally frank statesman.

'Keep Warren at home,' he said. 'Don't let him make any speeches. If he goes out on a tour, somebody's sure to ask him questions, and Warren's just the sort of damn fool that'll try to answer them.'[1]

Harding loved to make speeches; to go out and 'bloviate' as he called it. But his type of verbose and overornamented oratory was becoming outmoded. To turn him loose upon a public grown critical of ponderous clichés would be too risky. The Front Porch campaign was determined upon. The rôle assigned to the candidate was that of the modest, simple, sagacious, home-loving, home-staying statesman. He was to be 'just folks.' To the Mecca of Marion would come the devout and the Prophet would edify them with the sound doctrine of orthodox Republicanism. Thus everybody would be happy.

As for the itinerant platform work, let his team-mate attend to that. But the choice of Coolidge for this job was not a happy one. He possessed none of the requisites for moving the mass mind. They sent him on a try-out to the Northwest. The dry, twangy Yankee, with his flavorless platitudes was an unholy flop.[2] He was hastily transferred to Southern fields, where he could do no harm and might haply be of some help. Thereafter the professional spellbinders, always on call for such duties at a suitable recompense, took over the forensic fireworks.

The Front Porch device proved popular. There was an immense influx into Marion. Any and all were welcome and were made to feel so. Happily for Harding he had been working himself into physical trim to stand the strain.[3] He

[1] Walter Davenport: *Power and Glory.*
[2] William Allen White: *A Puritan in Babylon.*
[3] He had been playing 6 A.M. ping-pong and 5 P.M. tennis with Secretary Christian.

liked to meet people, to shake hands with his firm grip — he had fine, strong, well-muscled hands, a great asset to a public man who must withstand the manual pressure of thousands of greeters — to smile at his guests and receive an answering and often surprised warmth, for his smile was a genuine expression of humanism. There was nothing of the perfunctory about these informal ceremonies; he was not being 'folksy' from policy, but because he liked people and wanted them to like him. He was a natural handshaker in the good sense of that abused word.

'It is the most pleasant thing I do,' [1] he once told his devoted secretary, George B. Christian, Jr., after what would, to most people, have been a paralyzing two hours.

Bands came to serenade him, and were told of his own exploits in brass. Glee clubs sang to him while he smiled and beat time. He listened with fortitude to Al Jolson's campaign song, words and music by the famous mammy-singer:

> We think the country's ready
> For another man like Teddy.
> We need another Lincoln
> To do the country's thinkin'.
>
> (*Chorus*) Mist-ter Hard-ding,
> You're the man for us! etc., etc.

Those who had made themselves responsible for the public attitude and behavior of the candidate were now confronted with a decision both intimate and personal. The lady with whom he was believed to have made that incautious 'primrose détour,' referred to by William Allen White,[2] was still a resident of Marion. Her continued presence while the town was filling up with distinguished visitors and watchful newspapermen worried the managers. There had been far too much talk of her long-enduring friendship with the handsome

---

[1] *Saturday Evening Post*, October 13, 1923. George B. Christian, Jr.
[2] *Masks in a Pageant.*

and virile editor. Her social grade was such that she could neither be tactfully paid off nor summarily packed off like a no-longer-desirable member of the demi-monde. Friends of the candidate raised a fund, estimated by wide-eyed but probably misinformed local people at seventy-five thousand dollars, and the lady, together with her family, was dispatched to the safe distance of the Far East on a six months' tour to investigate conditions in the raw silk market. Thus was quashed an idyll.

Harding had other and more technical worries. Questions far beyond the grasp of his untrained intelligence beset him. What was expected from him was tact, caution, and the sedulous balance of a man walking a plank; such several planks, in this instance, as had been laid for him in the convention platform. He must keep in the middle of them, lest, in stepping off, he tread upon sensitive party toes.

Subtlety was foreign and dialectics distasteful to his character. The National Committee supplied two men well equipped to steer him on his difficult course, Richard Washburn Child, a successful fiction writer with political ambitions, and Editor George Harvey. So deftly did they employ language to conceal thought that Harding himself was befogged at times. Midway in one of his (or their) addresses, he slowed down, stumbled, retraced his course, and then, looking up from the manuscript with a frankly baffled smile, announced to his astonished audience:

'Well, I never saw this before. I didn't write this speech and I don't believe what I just read.' [1]

Politics might force him to shiftiness, but in matters of his own personality there was an impatient honesty about him. With an eye to the church vote, his managers invited a writer of some note to accompany the candidate to the Baptist Church, of which he was a trustee, and write an article exploiting him as a pious worshipper. It chanced to be Com-

[1] Statement by Professor William Estabrook Chancellor.

munion Sunday and he was not a communicant. He flatly
refused to go. Not for the committee nor anyone else would
he parade a religiosity which would have been a pose.[1]

Part of the stage-set of our political system is the official
notification to the candidate that he has been nominated. It
is an awesomely formal ceremony. A duly appointed committee journeys to the candidate's home, where they are
joined by the moguls of the party. The chairman delivers
his speech of notification, and the nominee, concealing his
surprise as best he may, responds with an address of acceptance.

July 22 was the date of the function. Members of the Republican National Committee from the forty-eight states
occupied the platform set up in the Marion public park.
Official bearer of the glad tidings was Senator Lodge. He was
'full of ironic allusions to Wilson, waspy malice against the
man then occupying the White House,' as Mark Sullivan
records.[2] No echo of this was heard in the nominee's reply.
Outside of the necessary declaration of principles, it was
gentle in tone, religious in feeling, and informed with sincerity, gravity, and emotion, 'an exalted and moving ceremony'
in Mr. Sullivan's opinion. The personality of the speaker and
the environment of local pride and affection doubtless contributed much to the effect produced upon those who were
unfamiliar with Warren Harding in his worthiest aspect, that
of the loyal and simple first citizen of his town. The shadow
thus projected into a greater field, of the first citizen of the
nation, was propitious.

A reading of the speech today, stripped of its emotional
trappings, leaves one with a sense of full adequacy as a human
appeal, but no more. It is Harding at his best, perhaps; but
Harding's best is thin and invertebrate as compared with the
literate power of Woodrow Wilson or the dramatic force of
Theodore Roosevelt. The speech concluded:

[1] Mark Sullivan: *Our Times*, vol. VI.   [2] *Ibid.*

Mr. Chairman, members of the committee, my countrymen all: I would not be my natural self if I did not utter my consciousness of my limited ability to meet your full expectations or to realize the aspirations within my own breast, but I will gladly give all that is in me, all of heart, soul and mind and abiding love of country, to service in our common cause. I can only pray to the Omnipotent God that I may be as worthy in service as I know myself to be faithful in thought and purpose. One cannot give more. Mindful of the vast responsibilities I must be frankly humble, but I have that confidence in the consideration and support of all true Americans which makes me unafraid. With an unalterable faith and in a hopeful spirit, with a hymn of service in my heart, I pledge fidelity to our country and to God, and accept the nomination of the Republican Party for the Presidency of the United States.

On the ingenuous principle that the man to oppose an Ohio editor is another Ohio editor, the Democrats nominated James M. Cox of Dayton. There was an undercurrent of pessimistic belief that it did not matter; that a change of party was inevitable. Mr. Cox was upright and competent. He had served two terms in Congress ably and conscientiously if not brilliantly. As Governor of Ohio he gave an administration marked by economy, efficiency, and progressive social legislation which had commended itself to both labor and industry. For Vice President, Franklin D. Roosevelt, young, energetic, and popular, was selected. As a curiosity of politics it is worth a passing note that historically both second-place nominees of 1920 proved more important than their principals.

Shortly after the convention Governor Cox went to Washington to visit the President. It was the loyal and courageous course to pursue. It patently aligned the candidate with the Wilson policies and undoubtedly contributed to his defeat. Following the Washington pilgrimage, he made an unequivocal declaration in favor of the League of Nations. This he repeated in a quick swing around the nation, covering eighteen states in just under a month. No enthusiasm greeted him. There was no enthusiasm anywhere in the country except the pleasant and personal warmth of the Front Porch; merely a mental and moral torpor, the dull smoulder of resentment over the aftermath of a war which had left behind it ashes of glory. 'The zero hour of our courage and faith,' William Allen White termed it. 'Cox will be defeated not by those who dislike him,' prophesied Franklin K. Lane, 'but by those who dislike Wilson.' [1]

Cox's unequivocal stand on the League forced Harding to assume a position. He assumed several. First he seemed to be for, then he appeared to be against. In his speech of acceptance he did go so far as to say that, if elected, he would end the technical state of war, no peace treaties having yet been signed because of the Senate's obdurate refusal to accept the Versailles Treaty. From there he went on:

> Then we may proceed deliberately and reflectively to that hoped-for world relationship which shall justify both conscience and aspirations and still hold us free from menacing involvement. With a Senate advising as the Constitution contemplates, I would hopefully approach the nations of Europe and of the earth, proposing that understanding which makes us a willing participant in the consecration of nations to a new relationship, to commit the moral forces of the world, America included, to peace and international justice, still leaving America free, independent, and self-reliant, but offering friendship to all the world.

The immediate reaction was disappointment on the part of the pro-League element. 'Harding Scuttles the League' was the *New York Times's* interpretation.[2] And another Harding, the cartoonist of the *Brooklyn Eagle*, depicted the G.O.P. elephant turning tail upon a sign marked 'Progress' and scampering off in a cloud of dust, while the candidate, on

[1] Franklin K. Lane: *Letters.*
[2] July 23, 1920.

its back, brandished a banner with the device, 'Lafayette, we have quit!'

Those who hoped to see America assume the direction of restoring stability to faltering Europe got together under the leadership of Elihu Root. The Committee of Thirty-One included such names as Charles Evans Hughes, Herbert Hoover, Jacob Gould Schurmann, William Allen White, George W. Wickersham, Ray Lyman Wilbur, Presidents Lowell and Butler, and H. W. Taft.[1] Their plan contemplated preserving the treaty with modifications to conform to Senate requirements and the Chicago platform.

Harding's record would have furnished them little ground for hope. It grew more astonishing and anomalous as the question pressed. In the Senate he had twice voted for treaty ratification with reservations.[2] But after his nomination, he promised 'complete reversal' of our foreign policy.[3] Four days later, he hinted at an association of nations on a basis not dissimilar to the Root plan. There followed the speech, published on August 29, which heartened the pro-Leaguers and exasperated the isolationists with its design for an international association for conference. George W. Wickersham thought that Harding had not wholly rejected the League.[4] Root noted that Harding had assured Hoover and Schurmann of his resolution to stand by his position of August 29.[5] They were pinning their hopes to thistledown. Minatory growls from the irreconcilables scared Harding. For a time he avoided the touchy subject. Borah, Johnson, and their ilk proved more influential with him than the Thirty-One. He dismissed the League as a fraud,[6] following up by the assertion that he was seeking 'not interpretation but rejection.'

[1] When one considers this array of presidential material the choice of Harding becomes so incredible as to be fantastic.

[2] *Literary Digest*, March 19, 1921.   [3] *New York Times*, August 16, 1920.

[4] *Ibid.*, September 5, 1920.

[5] Philip C. Jessup: *Elihu Root*, vol. II.

[6] *New York Times*, September 20, 1920.

Notwithstanding, a week later (October 15) the Root statement was released for publication. The Thirty-One still hoped to keep Harding straight on the issue.[1]

The formation of the Committee of Thirty-One, and the outline of its purpose before the formal issuance of the statement, put the Elders in something of a quandary. To ignore a group which represented the brains and conscience of the Republican Party was impossible. On the other hand, the isolationists were formidable. The leaders were faced with the nice problem of disguising a straddle as a policy. The solution, in which may be detected the literary finesse of Messrs. Child and Harvey, took the form of a counterplan.

A committee of 'the most experienced minds of this country, from whatever walks of life they may be derived and without regard to party affiliation,' would be summoned to draw up a formula for a world court. This was the germ plasm of the Best Minds theory which haunted the Harding Administration like a sardonic banshee. Such plan would be offered for the consideration of Europe. The League of Nations would be rebuilt in conformance with its specifications, on the twin foundations of a world Court of Justice and a World Association for Conference, using the mechanism of the League where convenient.

It meant little and came to naught. But it was useful for party purposes in that the pro-League element could now plausibly support the candidate, whereas the bitter-enders could still persuade themselves that Harding was with them in heart. Indeed, they were privately given to understand that this was the case.

For the rest, the candidate had adopted with precaution the general trend of the convention platform. He called for intelligent, courageous deflation and reduction of taxes based on a working budget system, but he favored an excess profits tax and high percentages on large incomes, which must have

[1] Philip C. Jessup: *Elihu Root*, vol. II.

caused a chill to some of Treasurer Upham's fat-cats. As to Labor, he expressed himself warily; the impression given was that he would not be partisan. A protective tariff, of course, with its 'saving Americanism,' but not so rigid as to hamper business by compromising our world trade. Since Prohibition could not be avoided, he testified that it was 'impossible to ignore the Constitution . . . unthinkable to evade the law.' [1]

The voice of the weasel was heard in the land.

Between the principals, the campaign was decorous, even courteous. The two men rather liked and respected one another. There has probably never been another campaign so free from mud-slinging or bitterness, never two contestants more faithful to the letter and spirit of fair play. For one example of the kind of criticism employed, Cox's good-humored and not unjust characterization of his rival will serve:

> Senator Harding is the kind of man who, on his way to the legislature, would empty his pockets to some poor creature, and then vote with the conservative Republicans for a bill that would maintain the conditions making possible the sufferings of the recipient.

Yet Harding, toward the close of the campaign, bitterly complained of 'the awful abuse I have been subjected to in Ohio.' [2]

The abuse was in his fears of what might have been made an issue, but was suppressed.

2

Performing a clerical job at Republican headquarters in Chicago, Nan Britton noticed 'a great pile of genealogical sheets,' [3] tracing in diagram form the Harding stock back to

[1] Entertainment headquarters at Marion flowed with alcoholic refreshments.
[2] To one of the Front Porch reporters.
[3] Nan Britton: *The President's Daughter*.

Stephen Harding, a seventeenth-century New Englander. Since her two-year-old daughter was of that blood, she was naturally interested and pleased. She was also puzzled.

So was the public, to which the genealogies were distributed. That the folksy Harding should be going ancestral on them did not make sense. It did not matter to them whether the Hardings came across the Atlantic Ocean on the *Mayflower* or down the Ohio River on a flatboat. They cared little or nothing whether the candidate was a direct descendant of Stephen Harding of Massachusetts, Peter the Hermit, or Pocahontas. So far as they had been informed, he was running for election to the Presidency, not to the Sons of the Revolution or the Social Register. The natural reaction was, 'What of it?'

Harding knew. So, by this time, did the Elder Statesmen. The whispering campaign about negro blood had attained a new high in activity. Stories such as the following were going the rounds: Two darkies meet on a corner.

> *Sambo* — Did yo' heah de big news, Ephum? Dey done nomernate Mistah Hahding at Chicago.
> *Ephraim* — Sho! Who'd de white folks nomernate?

Instead of ignoring, the party sages decided to counter the reports without defining them. Hence the sheets which Miss Britton aided in mailing out. It would have been wiser to follow the counsel of Boies Penrose. Perturbed lieutenants consulted him about the rumor.

'Sure it's only a rumor?' asked the Pennsylvania boss.

'Of course. A damnable lie.'

'Don't say anything about it,' advised the Pennsylvania boss comfortably. 'We've been having a lot of trouble with the negro vote lately.' [1]

When the exaltation of his victory at Chicago died down, Harding who, like so many buoyant natures, had a talent for

[1] Walter Davenport: *Power and Glory.*

worrying, began to brood. Learning that Robert Scripps, head of the powerful Scripps-McRea chain of newspapers, was in Cleveland, he called him up to ask whether his papers intended to handle reports about the alleged negro strain.

'The story was whispered all over Ohio at that time, as it had been loudly whispered every time before that when he ran for office,' writes Negley D. Cochran, then political adviser to Scripps for Ohio.

Scripps queried Cochran, who suggested that he tell Harding 'that we were not interested in the story, and, whether true or false, we had no intention of touching it — that we did not fight that way.'

This was Scripps's own feeling. He relieved the candidate's apprehensions with the assurance that he had nothing to fear.[1]

The story owed its revival in a genealogical framework to Professor William Estabrook Chancellor of the College of Wooster at Wooster, Ohio. Professor Chancellor was an author of some note. His educational and historical books were published by such houses as Houghton Mifflin Company, Putnam's, and Macmillan. He called himself, on what pretensions is a little obscure, an anthropologist, ethnologist, and genealogist. Professor Chancellor had no personal animus against Harding whom he knew only by sight. But he had an obsession on the negro question. Believing implicitly the local gossip about the Harding family, he made an investigation on the ground and published his conclusions in a series of single-sheet leaflets, true type of the genus broadside, so common as a disseminating agency of political and personal scurrilities a century earlier. They were poorly printed on the cheapest paper, 'flimsy' or low-grade pulp, and carried the names of Professor Chancellor and Wooster University. The format varied. One, headed 'Harding's Family Tree,' was diagrammatic. Another, 'To the Men and Women of

[1] Statement to the writer by Mr. Cochran.

America,' asserted that 'Warren Gamaliel Harding is not a white man,' and embodied the pious invocation, 'May God save America from international shame and from domestic ruin.' Affidavits from early neighbors of the Hardings supported the statements.[1]

Fifteen to twenty thousand dollars may have been spent in the distribution of what proved to be a totally ineffectual publication. Who paid the bills? Not Professor Chancellor, from his modest salary. A few justifiably infuriated Republicans ascribed responsibility to the rival candidate. Those who knew Governor Cox did not believe it; he was not that kind of man. Official Democrats of all ranks hotly denied any connection with the enterprise. Some unknown 'angel' may have financed the operations. If so, his secret has been incomparably well preserved.

Attempts to peddle the issue at the Chicago Convention had found no market. They were now transferred to Washington. A stranger with an introduction from a Democratic committeeman called on Joseph P. Tumulty, President Wilson's private secretary, and presented what purported to be documentary evidence of a racial mixture in the Harding stock.

'What's this for?' asked Mr. Tumulty.

'Campaign material. I thought the National Committee might be interested.'

'The National Committee wouldn't touch it,' said Mr. Tumulty.

'Why not?'

'Suppose Senator Harding is elected. What a terrible thing it would be for the country if it came out that we had a President alleged to be part negro! I'll have nothing to do with it.'[2]

---

[1] These affidavits, according to one of the signers, were not procured by Professor Chancellor, but were put out independently.

[2] Statement to the writer by Mr. Tumulty.

Mr. Tumulty thinks that President Wilson never knew anything about this. Someone in the Wilson Administration did and took action. The official machinery of repression, which had been brought to such proficiency in war persecutions, was later to be invoked against Chancellor. But his first troubles originated nearer home.

The peaceful and classic shades of Wooster College were convulsed by a tornado of protest, stirred up by the Chancellor leaflets. Letters and telegrams, signed by alumni, angry or alarmed or both, poured in from California, Iowa, Wisconsin, Illinois, Virginia, Kentucky, Pennsylvania, Maine, New York, New Jersey, and, of course, Ohio, demanding explanation of the broadsides. Who was Professor Chancellor? What proof had he? Why did the college allow itself to be mixed up in scandalous and dangerous partisan politics? [1]

Newspapers telephoned and telegraphed from New York, Chicago, San Francisco, Bridgeport, Richmond, and St. Louis. Reporters began to crowd into the quiet little city and were re-enforced by politicians, including representatives of the national and state committees of both parties, and excited alumni and alumnae. It was, for the time, the storm centre of national politics.

The president of Wooster College, the Reverend Charles F. Wishart, had been in office only a year. Here was a hot kettle of water poured into his inexperienced lap. Doctor Wishart kept cool and got busy. Attaching himself to a telephone, within twenty-four hours he had a quorum of the trustees on the campus for a special meeting. They summoned Professor Chancellor.

He appeared, obviously laboring under excitement, and stated his readiness to answer questions. His first defence was a disclaimer of the authorship. Under examination he

[1] The data on the college involvement are derived partly from the minutes of the board of trustees, partly from President Wishart.

admitted having made a study of the Harding ancestry and having supplied the substance of the genealogical 'proof' while still maintaining his denial of having put the material in any of the forms of print with which he was confronted. Harding's nomination, he asserted, was a plot to achieve negro domination of the United States. He volunteered that he himself had been the victim of negro persecution while Superintendent of Schools in Washington, D.C. Upon his hearers he produced an effect of emotional instability.

By a unanimous vote the board requested his resignation. He accepted their decision without protest. Four months' salary was voted him. He immediately gave up his classes, but remained in the house near the campus which he had bought. There was no question of academic freedom; his unauthorized use of the college's name on matter so perilously controversial rendered impossible his continuance on the faculty. The trustees decided against any pronouncement upon the truth or falsity of the publications, despite pressure on the part of some of the alumni who wished a flat repudiation and an official denial. This, the board felt, was beyond its proper province.

In his address to the students, explaining the resignation of one of the most popular of the faculty, President Wishart charitably attributed Professor Chancellor's offence to 'misguided zeal rather than evil intent.'

The sensation was over. Wooster emptied itself of its visitors. The politicians mulled over what they should do and decided to do nothing. But the newspapers were in a quandary. It was unquestionably a 'big story.' It was also a very dangerous one. Most papers suppressed it. Some important ones published long articles about the circulars without revealing their purport. Such curious, adroit, and interesting examples of journalistic pussyfooting stimulated a public curiosity which they left unsatisfied. E. L. Doheny, the oil magnate and a Democrat, contributed twenty-five thousand dollars to the Republican war chest to be used in the publication, at advertising rates, of full-page portraits of Harding's father and mother, thus further increasing the mystification. The whole thing loomed in the public eye like an iceberg in a fog, only a small fraction of which is perceptible, and that dimly.

In the annals of American journalism there has never been another case where so much was left unpublished on a topic of major and sensational interest. Special correspondents at Marion were daily sending out on the wires from five hundred to a thousand words for publication, and from fifteen hundred to six thousand words for the private information of their editors.[1] If the confidential data of the great dailies were preserved, history would be altered, supplemented, and illuminated at many points.

The local managers of the Harding campaign were hard put to it. Their best wisdom was that the question should be referred for determination to the person most concerned. Up to this time, so far as can be ascertained, Harding had made no assertion, yes or no, on the subject, nor any direct comment, unless the ineffectual visit of protest which he paid in the middle nineties to the rival editorial sanctum with a shotgun for argument may be so regarded.

The Front Porch method having been temporarily abandoned, late in the campaign, for a quick round of speeches, the candidate called a conference on his special train. The question was whether he should or should not issue a formal denial that there was a negro strain in his blood. Those present with him were Harry Daugherty, two trusted newspapermen, and two or three friends of the inner circle. The impression was that Harding was prepared to commit himself to a wholesale denial.

While the form of it was under consideration, Mrs. Harding unexpectedly entered. Glancing about with sharp sus-

[1] Statement of Walker S. Buell of the *Cleveland Plain Dealer* to the writer.

picion, she demanded to know what was being discussed. Someone told her. Instantly and imperatively she vetoed the plan. Nothing was to be put out; not a word.[1]

That ended it. Discussion was closed. No formal or official denial of the negro allegation was ever to be made by Warren Harding.

All the experts agree that politically the negro issue produced no adverse effects. If anything, it was a boomerang.

3

> Harding or Cox? Harding or Cox?
> You tell us, populi; you've got the vox,

warbled F.P.A. in his Conning Tower.

Populi did not seem to care greatly which. Lethargy possessed the electorate; the memory of the oldest voter ran not back to so spiritless a campaign. It worried the leaders. Everything worries politicians on the eve of election. They sought omens where there were no omens. People had already made up their minds and were busy thinking about something else.

The result made Republican doubts seem incredibly foolish. As the returns came in, all one way, it became patent that the traditional yellow dog could have been elected on that ticket. The first formal radio announcement ever broadcast in this country spluttered forth from Westinghouse station, KDKA, in Pittsburgh, announcing a record plurality of more than seven million.[2]

The overwhelming verdict was a mandate rather than a tribute to Harding. The country had made its choice, not that it loved Harding more, but Wilson less. Cox had manfully accepted the Wilson tradition; he was made the scape-

[1] Statement to the writer by one of the consultants who prefers to remain anonymous.

[2] *News Week*, February 13, 1939.

goat. Insensate hatred for the broken man in the White House piled up those ballots. Charles Willis Thompson wrote: [1]

> The people of the United States ... did not vote for Harding ... they did not vote for anybody; they voted against somebody; and the somebody they voted against was not a candidate; it was Woodrow Wilson.

Mark Sullivan said much the same thing in other terms: [2]

> Of this American mood [disillusionment] about the recent war, Wilson was the unhappy victim, symbol of the exaltation that had turned sour, personification of the rapture that had now become gall, sacrificial whipping-boy for the present bitterness.

It was a period of moral slump, the backswing from the idealism and sacrifices of war. Men's thoughts could not indefinitely maintain themselves on that lofty plane. Cumulative discontents blended in a savage resentment. The nation was neurotically suspicious; in a mood to blame everything upon the party that was in power. People felt the grind of hard times. Coal went to as much as twenty dollars a ton. All necessities were high. Pocketbooks were feeling the pinch, and when the American pocketbook is pinched, it kicks. Labor was growling at war profiteering. But Labor had been doing some fancy profiteering on its own account, in war wages. Now there was spreading unemployment. Industrialists incited the Government to repressive measures against labor organizations, under the convenient excuse of 'curbing the Reds.' People were unhappy, restless. They craved a change.

Here was ripe opportunity for the second-raters, the practical politicians, the realists of the 'Let's go!' school. In their own minds, if not in his, Harding was their exemplar, their potential tool. Fortunate, indeed, was the nation be-

---

[1] *Presidents I've Known.*   [2] *Our Times*, vol. VI.

yond its deserts that the satrapy of Republican masters, misrepresentative of the real character and virtues of the party's best, had not set up as its figurehead some demagogue of baser type than a Harding who would have been comparatively innocuous if left to his own devices, or if more wisely guided; some Foraker, or even Penrose. As the event turned out, Harding proved to be less of a puppet than the Senate had planned.

What manner of man is this whom the American electorate has so impatiently chosen for its leader? The country began to ask itself. No President had ever been elected of whom so little was known. His career in state politics had been insignificant. His record in the Senate was less than mediocre; it was negative. Not one measure of any importance, not a speech of any influence derived from him.

He was the first member to pass from the Senate to the White House, thus fulfilling an ambition thwarted in such giants of the Upper House as Webster, Clay, and Calhoun. Having stage-managed his nomination and pushed him to election, the oligarchs now built up a pattern of the new President for presentation to the country. One of his admiring though unofficial press agents attributed to him

> ... the firmness and steadfastness of a Cleveland, the princely grace and sympathetic kindness of a McKinley, the crusadic [*sic*] spirit of a Roosevelt, ever fighting for the rights of the people, the good humor and judicial temperament of a Taft, the keen intellect of a Wilson, the poise of a Washington, and the wisdom of a Lincoln.[1]

It was a large order for any man; definitely too large for the subject.

For Harding as incoming President is the same minor and well-meaning politician who made himself useful in hack-

---

[1] Unnamed eulogist quoted with approval by Joe Mitchell Chapple: *Life and Times of Warren G. Harding, Our After-War President.*

work at Columbus; who served a carefree, easy-going, inconspicuous term in the Senate; whose modest ambition it was to return to Marion and run his successful newspaper. He is uneducated, without precision or discipline of mind or power of analysis. In any broad sense he is unread.

What little schooling he had is unsupplemented by his contacts with life which are essentially superficial. His experience of men and cities is wide but shallow. Travel has not enriched him. For political ends he has covered a large part of his own country, continental and insular, and he has three times been abroad, but intellectually he has never traversed the boundaries of his own state, hardly those of his own home town. His is a parochial mind. He is unprepared for the duties of statesmanship. There is no subject, national or international, among the many which enlist the anxious thought of leaders, which he can confront with the authority of the specialist or the interest of the student. In one of the rare bookish allusions which can be found in his speech or writing, he personifies himself as 'Main Street come to Washington.' Pride, not deprecation, inspired the utterance. Marion's Main Street was, for him, the epitome of success, soundness, enterprise, orthodoxy, every worthy quality which he had in mind when he rolled out his unctuous encomiums of Americanism.

Harding's patriotism and partisanship were equally fervent. To his hazy and naïve conceptions, Americanism and Republicanism were one and inseparable. Republicanism was in his blood. His creed is set forth with convincing sincerity in scores of phrases of splendid and empty sonorousness. It was his misfortune to grow up in the faith at a time when the party leadership was at its flood in power and its ebb in principle.

Doctor H. F. Alderfer, in his penetrating study of Harding's political rise, regards him as an attractive and pliant lay-figure for his party, raised to unexpected authority, as if 'a clothing store model, after years of faithful service in displaying choice garments in the front window, should suddenly find itself manager of the store.'

For Harding the problems of the day were two-dimensional. His vision could not penetrate the plane to which his intellectual excursions were limited. To estimate the effect of evil politics in terms of injustice, crime, suffering, degradation of public and private standards and morals, calls for imagination. Harding lacked that quality. He could not project his mind beyond the immediate and concrete. He was unfailingly sympathetic to the individual. He loved humanity in detail, but had no conception of it as a whole, the reverse of Wilson who could be a martyr for the mass, but disliked most people.

Harding's conception of public service was to give a friend a job. It made the seeker happy. It enlisted a supporter in the party ranks. That the effect of the bestowal might, if the recipient were unworthy, involve wrong, oppression, injustice to ten thousand other men would be quite beyond his vision. Implications other than the most obvious did not occur to him. He never tried to see around a corner.

He loved life and wanted to enjoy it, a simple and natural desire, but one difficult to adjust to the rigors of the Presidency. Senator Jim Watson charitably explained that 'his lovable nature carried with it a certain weakness that led him easily into temptation and sapped his powers of resistance when beguiled.'[1] He was intensely loyal to his friends and confident of their good faith toward him. When they betrayed him, he raged or mourned. A friend said of him that he differed from George Washington in this: that Washington could not tell a lie, but Harding could not tell a liar. Clinton W. Gilbert pictured him:

> ... the square head, typical of that American whose artistic taste is the movies, who reads and finds mental satisfaction in

[1] James E. Watson: *As I Knew Them.*

the vague inanities of the small-town newspaper, who has faith in America, who is for liberty, virtue, happiness, prosperity, law and order and all the standard generalities ... who has his car and his bank account and can sell a bill of goods as well as the best of them.[1]

We, the sovereign people, had chosen for leader by an unprecedented majority, at a time of decisions vital to ourselves and hardly less so to the outer world, an amiable, well-meaning, third-rate Mr. Babbitt, with the equipment of a small-town, semi-educated journalist, the standards of a hand-shaking joiner and all-around good guy, the instincts and habits of a corner sport, and the traditions of a party hack; an expert on partisan mechanics, a sophomore in legislation, a tyro in economics and government, an ignoramus in world movements and trends.

It could not work. It did not work.

4

The College of Wooster was the scene of a dramatic postscript to the campaign. After getting the returns downtown, a jubilant mob set out for the campus with the intention of capturing Professor William Estabrook Chancellor and riding him out of town on a rail with tar and feather embellishments. But Professor Chancellor was popular with the student body. His dismissal had endowed him with the aura of martyrdom. News of the march reached the campus in advance. The students organized, in their turn.

When the vigilantes, several hundred strong, reached the Chancellor house, they were confronted by a student spokesman. He issued a warning. The house was defended at every point. Anyone attempting to break into it would be hurt. Lovers of peace had better go home.

The townsmen came on, but halted when the muzzles of

[1] *Mirrors of Washington.*

revolvers and shotguns appeared in the threatened windows. They withdrew, formed again, and listened to speeches of incitement. But there was a lack of leadership. Nobody appeared who was willing to be shot in that dubious cause. It was growing late. Slowly the marchers dispersed. So ended what might have been the bloodiest town-and-gown encounter in American academic history.

But quiet was not for the author of all these disturbances. Sometime after election a stranger called upon President Wishart, displayed a badge, and stated that he was connected with the Department of Justice. Information had been received, he asserted, that one William E. Chancellor of Wooster, formerly connected with the college, was planning to attend the inauguration of President-elect Harding and assassinate him. Could Doctor Wishart tell the visitor anything about it?

Doctor Wishart could and did tell him that the rumor was absurd. Professor Chancellor was a peaceable and law-abiding citizen, totally incapable of violence or crime. Unconvinced, the operative wished to see Professor Chancellor. Where was he? The college president gave him an address in Columbus. Later the man returned; told Doctor Wishart that Professor Chancellor had agreed not to go to Washington (whither, of course, he had not harbored any intention of going), and had promised to write no more on the subject of negro blood in any political connection.[1]

As a campaign issue the broadsides were now dead. They came to life in a more permanent form, to plague the new administration and incite it to an extraordinary exercise of extra-legal powers.[2]

When the result of the election was beyond doubt, Mrs. Harding exulted. Forgotten were her spiritistic obsessions.

[1] Statement of Doctor Wishart to the writer.

[2] The genealogical data, adduced in the Chancellor researches, will be analyzed in a later chapter.

She was to be the First Lady of the Land. Her medium had told her that, when she was only the ambitious wife of an undistinguished Senator.

The President-elect did not share her exhilaration. The burden of responsibility was heavy on his spirit. Amidst the general jubilation, in which such diverse characters as Harry Daugherty, Doctor Sawyer, afterward Surgeon General, and a delegation of printers from his newspaper, the *Star*, joined on the premises, Harding was thoughtful, almost morose.

For years he had been insisting, with occasional weakenings when Harry Daugherty or Senator Penrose dangled the bright hope before his eyes, that he had no ambition to be President. To his old friend, Samuel G. McClure, he said early in 1920: 'I am very happy in the Senate and much prefer to remain there. I do not believe I could be happy as President. I don't want it.'

Now, when Colonel McClure returned to congratulate him and wish him good luck and Godspeed, his smile of greeting faded.

'Yes, Sam; and God help me, for I need it,' said he.[1]

To another friend he said sadly, 'I have lost my freedom.'[2]

Observers who saw him daily were struck with his variable moods which, however, tended more and more toward gravity. In optimistic moments he felt that everything would be lovely. The Best Minds would set the course. He need only sift the advice of the leaders, select the best, and go ahead. A darker mood would supervene. He would droop, physically and psychologically. A worried supporter, William Boyce Thompson, was shocked by his depression, speculated whether he would live out his term, surmised that Calvin Coolidge might yet be President.[3]

The same thought seems to have been in Harding's mind.

[1] Letter from Colonel McClure to the writer.
[2] Sherman A. Cuneo: *From Printer to President.*
[3] Pound and Moore: *They Told Barron.*

Statesmanship à la Front Porch

The local Elks tendered him a congratulatory banquet. It was the sort of occasion which, in other days, would have found the popular 'W. G.' at his genial best, brimming over with good-fellowship and high spirits. Instead, to the concern of the gathering, he presented an aspect so solemn as to be little short of ominous. Speaking under stress of obvious emotion, he bade farewell to those good friends and to the old, easy, pleasant life to which he might never return. He realized, he told them, that the new path stretching before him involved profound changes. The demands upon mind and body might prove too much for him. He was going to do his best to live up to the requirements of the office. No man present had ever before heard 'W. G.' speak to such grave purport.[1]

And, on the day before he left for his inauguration, the Marion Lodge, Loyal Order of Moose, presented him with a life-membership card. To the committee of presentation the recipient spoke with tears in his eyes of the possibility of his being unequal to the ordeal before him. A member of the committee writes: [2]

> It appeared to me that he was reluctant to take up the responsibilities of the Presidency. . . . I left, somewhat depressed and with some foreboding, because I knew that he was not physically a rugged man.

Earlier than this, Bishop William F. Anderson of Cincinnati, a close friend of the Hardings, calling on the President-elect, had been impressed by a spiritual change like that which 'comes over a man in the experience of conversion at the altars of God.' The Bishop reported a conversation in

[1] Confirmed by Theodore H. Tangeman of Columbus, Ohio, who was present.
[2] Letter from Frederick E. Guthery of Marion to the writer. The importance of these two episodes lies in the light thrown upon Harding's physical condition, and the indication that, long in advance, he may have felt a premonition of the weakness that was to cause his death.

which Harding had poured out his troubled heart to a banker neighbor:[1]

> John, we've been friends for a long time. I want to say something to you. I am going off to my new office to bear responsibilities which no human being can carry in his own strength. I have always believed in the sincerity of your religious life. If you will talk to God about me every day by name and ask Him somehow to give me strength for my great task, I will be thankful beyond words.

Laying his hand on the visitor's shoulder, he added:

> I have been thinking a lot about these things, as I have come to the realization of the tremendous responsibilities which rest upon me. It is my conviction that the fundamental trouble with the people of the United States is that they have gotten too far away from Almighty God.

These are the words of a frightened and humble man. Harding was not innately nor profoundly religious. He supported and attended the church of his faith; that was the seemly thing for a man in his position. That he was a believer is as plain as that his life and conduct were not patterned upon the code imposed by his creed. Facing duties too onerous for fearless contemplation, he turned naturally to a compassionate Deity for support. There is something of childlike faith and confidence in his asking the intercession of a man whom he deemed better than himself, begging him to 'talk to God about me every day by name,' something moving in his expressed belief, which was perhaps more a wistful hope, that Presidents of the United States were, *ex officio*, so to speak, taken under divine guidance.[2] He needed it.

On midnight walks with newspaper intimates — he was always prone to be confidential with the newspapermen, feeling himself to be of their ilk — he would discuss what

[1] *New York Times*, April 3, 1922.
[2] Willis Fletcher Johnson: *The Life of Warren G. Harding.*

kind of President he hoped to be. He could not, he frankly stated, expect to be the best President that the country ever had, but he did want to be the best-loved. That would satisfy his highest ambition.[1]

[1] Statement of Boyden Sparkes to the writer.

★

XIV. Cabinet-Making

HAVING contrived the election of Harding, the Senate ring naturally regarded him as their creature, a conception in which he partly concurred, as indicated by his explicit intention of accepting guidance from the Best Minds. Nevertheless, they had the judgment to keep away from the Front Porch in the days following the election. To haunt those precincts now would be to give point to the Democratic allegations that the President-elect was no more than a senatorial marionette. This would not at all fit in with the picture they were building up of Harding as a sturdy, self-reliant, calm, and careful statesman, independent in thought and act.

Interest now centred on the Cabinet. Every prominent visitor was canvassed by the reporters as a possibility. Will Hays, who had so ably conducted the campaign as chairman of the National Committee, was a foregone conclusion as Postmaster General. It was a matter of common knowledge that Harding wanted Harry M. Daugherty as Attorney General, but was hanging back because of strong objection within the party. Few were as outspoken in opposition as Myron T. Herrick whom Harding wanted in his Cabinet.

'Is Harry Daugherty going to be in the Cabinet?' Herrick asked.

'Yes.'

'Then I can't accept.'

Harding vainly tried to persuade him to reconsider.

'Harry Daugherty will wreck your Administration,' said the blunt Ohioan.[1]

The subsequent offer of the ambassadorship to France surprised him. He accepted.

General Leonard Wood was the natural selection for Secretary of War. He declined. The portfolio of Navy was offered to Governor Lowden. He did not want it and would not take it. For the rest, the field was open and the contest on. Advocates of the various hopeful candidates girded themselves for battle. State and Treasury were the storm centres.

Elihu Root, whose insight into Europe's tangled and tragic pattern was more profound than that of any other American, was summoned and came to Marion. He had little comment to make on his interview. It is unlikely that the lucid and incisive intellect of the great lawyer and diplomat would find much in common with Harding's muddled thinking and half-digested impressions on world events. Mr. Root was not invited to join the Cabinet. He did not expect to be, with Knox, Lodge, Brandegee, and the others of the ring in control.[2]

Another visitor was Andrew W. Mellon of Pittsburgh, head of the great financial clan which has been compared to the Rothschilds. He arrived unannounced, walked to the Front Porch, since nobody had met him at the train and there was no taxi available, and sat around, modestly waiting in an anteroom until a reporter identified him and escorted him into the Presence. It is a fair measure of Harding's limitations that he had only a vague notion of who this giant of finance might be, until Harry Daugherty enlightened him. As Mellon had never held office, he had not come within

[1] Letter to writer from Maurice Léon to whom Herrick repeated the dialogue.
[2] Philip C. Jessup: *Elihu Root*, vol. II.

Harding's orbit. He deserved well of the party; a Mellon bank underwrote a part of the National Committee's deficit.[1]

The Pittsburgher talked with the President-elect, walked back to the station, and departed. He had modestly said that he didn't think he'd make a very good Secretary of the Treasury; too many interests. Harding's first choice had been Charles G. Dawes. No actual proffer of the portfolio was made to Mellon at this time.

With Harding remaining in a state of indecision as to these headline appointments, the competition and doubt intensified. Everyone who was called in consultation fervently wanted someone and more fervently disapproved someone else. The don't-wants were more vehement and troublesome than the wants. The pro-League of Nations element wanted Root or Hughes for Secretary of State. The oligarchs were against both. The *New York Tribune* guessed that a poll of Senate Republicans would not have given Hughes one single vote, an underestimate, since Fall was for him. So was Frelinghuysen. Penrose was against him, though with typical cynicism he did not think it much mattered who headed the State Department. The bitter-end isolationists were for Lodge but he was anathema to the moderates.

Harding's personal and original preference for the place was Albert B. Fall. Fall claims and Daugherty disputes that the portfolio of State was offered to him the day after the Chicago nomination. However this may be, Harding's high opinion of the man who was to envelop his Administration in the stench of oil graft is sufficiently attested by his statement to an old friend, Samuel G. McClure, a month after election.

'I suppose I shall have to appoint Hughes, though he is not a diplomat by temperament. Do you know, Sam, there is one man in this country who would make a great Secretary of State. He is one of the ablest international lawyers, but

[1] *New York Times*, February 7, 1921.

he is from the West, and I do not think it would be wise for me to go to the West for Secretary of State.'

Groping, Colonel McClure asked, 'Who is it?'

'Albert Fall,' was the answer which amazed the visitor.

'No,' he replied. 'It seems to me the man for the place is Mr. Hughes.'[1]

Harding's second choice for the State Department was no less grotesque. Colonel George Harvey was his candidate. Never lacking in good opinion of himself, the editor nevertheless had the becoming modesty to tell Harding that it simply would not do. Anyway, he did not crave that kind of preferment. What he had in mind was the pomp and circumstance of the Court of Saint James. He got it and proved to be the most indiscreet major ambassador in our diplomatic annals.

Knox was the cabal's choice for a Cabinet seat, but he was failing in health and preferred to take his ease in the Senate. He wanted Mellon in the Treasury. So, by this time, did Mellon himself, who had recovered from the fit of super-modesty which afflicted him at Marion.

The more liberal and progressive element of the party did not like Mellon or Hays, and were violent against Daugherty. In fact, nobody was for Harding's friend, manager, and mentor except the clannish Ohioans and Harding himself. As soon as Wallace was suggested for Agriculture, the live-stock men rose in revolt. Some bright mind conceived the notion that a great industrialist would be useful — presumably to other great industrialists — as Secretary of Labor, and for a time the name of Charles M. Schwab of Bethlehem Steel was seriously considered, though with no participation by him. As steel was then running on a twelve-hour-day schedule, organized labor was less than enthusiastic and nothing came of the project.

The *bête noire* of the party regulars was Hoover. The inner

[1] Letter from Colonel McClure.

circle had as little sympathy with his humanitarianism as they had faith in his party principles. Daugherty disliked him personally and doubted whether he was a real Republican. Persistent reports that he would be nominated to the Department of the Interior, for which by training and taste he was eminently fitted, irked the Elder Statesmen, except the few who understood that the place was already made safe for oil. Certain promises as to clearing up the National Committee's debt had taken care of that.

Wearied with conflict and indecision, Harding determined on a vacation in the South. Before leaving he had made up his mind as to the standard, enunciated later, if not as to the personnel of his official family. 'This is going to be a Republican Cabinet; you may count on that. And you may be sure it will be a Cabinet of which the whole country can be proud.[1]

He left in vacation mood. For companionship he took along Ned McLean, Jesse Smith, Harry Daugherty, and Senators Frelinghuysen, Hale, and Elkins. Senator Knox, when he heard of Harding's choice of senatorial companions, observed that he must be seeking 'complete mental relaxation.' Senator Fall joined the tourists before they reached Texas.

At Oklahoma City, Jake Hamon gave a banquet for the party, said to have set a new high in festivity, even for that profuse town. When the guest of honor, shortly after, learned of his host's death at the hands of his mistress, he could not restrain his tears.

Rainy weather in Texas depressed the spirits of the tourists. Panama was briefly visited. Conditions more to their liking were found in Florida. Harding was mischievously amused by the woes of a statesman (let charity cover his name) who, on his way to join the party, lost the valise of liquor, wherewith he had hoped to fortify his spirit against the rigors of Prohibition, to a Pullman hijacker. There were

[1] *New York Times*, February 22, 1921.

poker and bridge and hearts and drinks galore; parties every evening.

'Had a great party last night,' he wrote home. 'Everybody drunk but me.'

With the unknown problems of the Presidency before him, he was not going to let the prospect take all the joy out of life.

Responsibilities now pressed upon him. The time for Cabinet-making was growing short. Most discussed of the offices was now the attorney-generalship, which had not yet been formally assigned, though Harry M. Daugherty was the favorite in the betting. The Columbus lawyer and lobbyist was not regarded as measuring up to standards, either in professional attainments or in character. His legal status was mediocre; his abilities, while unquestioned in his own special field, were not such as would be specially serviceable to a government executive. He had been involved in a shady deal with a shadier lawyer, afterward disbarred,[1] to secure the release of Charles W. Morse, a crooked Wall Street multimillionaire, who, with the endorsement of two gullible (or collusive) government physicians, and the aid of a bar of soap which he privately ate, successfully counterfeited kidney symptoms and set forth a pitiful plea that he be allowed to die outside of prison. He did die outside of prison, fifteen years later, thanks to the pardon by President Taft procured through Daugherty's good offices, and employed the time advantageously in further depredations. Daugherty was obliged to dun him for the twenty-five-thousand-dollar fee. When these operations were made the subject of adverse comment, Mr. Harding denounced the critics as 'political blackguards.' All opposition merely confirmed his conviction that he wanted his political mentor and sponsor in his official family.

If one may believe Daugherty, writing on the subject of

[1] Thomas B. Felder.

Daugherty — not always a safe assumption — he was extremely reluctant to assume the post repeatedly urged upon him, and modestly advanced the superior qualifications of other possibilities. The circumstances of Harding's final and long-delayed decision in his case hardly bear out this claim.

At St. Augustine, Harding was in the habit of holding daily press conferences. At one of these he saw the newly arrived Louis Seibold, who had been running a series of biting anti-Daugherty articles in the *New York World*. Although he liked Seibold and continued to like him, Harding's face flushed at sight of him. There was challenge in his manner as he announced his choice for the Department of Justice, 'Harry M. Daugherty, a splendid man, an able man, and he will make a great Attorney General.' Pointedly addressing the *World* man in the phraseology of their common craft, he rasped:

'And you can set that up in block on the front page of your paper.'

That evening the new appointee was leaning against a pillar in the hotel lobby, looking the crowd over when Seibold came along.

'Louis,' said he pleasantly (Daugherty rarely bore a grudge), 'that was a great favor you did me today.'

'Yes?' said the newspaperman. 'How is that?'

'I've been trying to get Harding to make up his mind about me. He's kept sidestepping. Now he's named me and it was seeing you there that did the trick. I owe you one for that.'

'Well, I'm glad you feel that way.'

'Who have you got in your Cabinet forecast?'

The reporter ran over his list.

'Ever hear of a fellow named Denby?'

'Michigan man? Yes.'

'Put him in.' [1]

[1] Mr. Seibold's own account, given to the writer.

Daugherty was repaying what he strangely regarded as an obligation by giving his harshest newspaper critic a beat. Long afterward he was to set down his sorrowful conviction that his acceptance of the office was 'the tragic blunder of my life.' [1]

Edwin N. Denby was another tragic blunder. On his record he should have been an excellent Secretary of the Navy. A veteran of the Spanish-American War, he camouflaged his age when the United States entered the World War, enlisted in the Marine Corps, was sent to Parris Island, South Carolina, for training, thence to France, and ended as a major. He served three terms in Congress. By profession a lawyer, he made a quick million-plus in the automobile business in Detroit. His hobby was public service. He acted as probation officer in the Detroit Municipal Court for sheer love of the work. He was a conservative in politics and economics. But some inexplicable change came over him upon his elevation to high office. He grossly neglected his duties, and, by permitting himself to become a 'stooge' for Albert B. Fall, contributed to the worst *débâcle* of the Harding régime.

A senatorial investigating committee has entered a Scotch verdict of not-proven, upon the charge that the Chicago convention's procedure was influenced by oil. [2] The suspicion, however, was ineradicable, and was pointed by the choice of

---

[1] Harry M. Daugherty: *The Inside Story of the Harding Tragedy.*

[2] Report of Senate Committee on Public Lands and Surveys; Investigation of Naval Oil Reserve Leases. The contrary opinion of an observer at the spot, who was a delegate to the convention, is pertinent. William Allen White, in his *Masks in a Pageant*, writes: 'Oil had a room in an office building and presumed to summon potential presidential and vice-presidential candidates to that room where men good-naturedly discussed our foreign relations with Mexico in the oral examination which was given to those whom oil was about to bless with its support.... There can be no doubt in the mind of anyone who reads the testimony in the numerous oil suits brought later by the Government, that oil controlled the convention of 1920. It worked through the Senate cabal, led by the irreconcilables who were so busy hating Wilson that they became easy victims of the greed for oil.'

Albert B. Fall for Secretary of the Interior. Doctor Alderfer writes:

> Circumstantial evidence points to the conclusion that the choice of Albert B. Fall as Secretary of the Interior was the result of a collusion between oil interests and politicians which made possible the first swing to Harding in the convention of 1920. This has never been proven.[1]

Something caused Harding to hesitate, probably the fear of just such criticism. Fall became urgent. Harry Daugherty categorically accuses him of forging a telegram to Harding, urging prompt action in the appointment, and signing it 'Harry M. Daugherty.'[2] It is a measure of the senatorial standards of the day that the announcement of Fall's appointment was made the occasion for an unprecedented compliment, a *viva voce* and unanimous ratification. Fall was their ideal. Nothing could give a better indication of the senatorial morals, ethics, and politics of the period.

For Fall, if not actually disreputable, was at best a dubious figure. A century earlier he would have been catalogued as a 'warhawk.' In the Senate he had advocated 'policing' Mexico with our armed forces. His selection was stigmatized by the *Richmond News-Leader* as 'a gross affront to Mexico and a peril to peace.'[3]

Two appointees to the Cabinet had never before held political office, Andrew W. Mellon and Herbert Hoover. Their candidacies were curiously interwoven. Alike in being men of wealth — Mellon's twenty-fold that of the mining engineer — they were at opposite poles as to its use. The Pennsylvania magnate represented the impersonal power of money.[4] He cherished and augmented his wealth with jeal-

---

[1] H. F. Alderfer: *The Personality and Politics of Warren G. Harding.*

[2] Harry M. Daugherty: *The Inside Story of the Harding Tragedy.*

[3] *Literary Digest,* March 12, 1921.

[4] For a sharp appraisal of Mellon's complex personality, see *Mellon's Millions,* by Harvey O'Connor.

ous intensity. Sharing it for the public good was beyond the scope of his thinking. So far as is known, he was the only possessor of a great art collection who kept it unsullied by the general view, only grudgingly and suspiciously permitting a few selected outsiders the privilege of enjoying it during his lifetime.[1]

On the other hand, the Quaker engineer, without fuss or exploitation, had financed out of his own private purse the care and return of hundreds of United States nationals, marooned in Europe by the chances of the war. His record as the head of Belgian Relief and later of the Food Administration gave him unique status in the country.

Eager to obtain suitable representation for Pennsylvania, Senators Penrose and Knox were urging Mellon upon Harding. Nobody in particular was forwarding Hoover's claims, and Harry Daugherty was doing his best to block his path. But for once Harding was sensitive to public opinion as opposed to party pressure, though Hoover would hardly have been his personal choice. Harding did not feel easy with him. Many people did not in those days. His generosity of character was not expressed in a corresponding warmth of personality. An expansive joviality like Harding's would recoil from the quiet impassivity of the Californian. Nevertheless, Harding sincerely admired him.

Too faithful a subordinate and too loyal a friend to rebel against his chief, Harry Daugherty, when he found Harding's wishes definitely set upon Hoover for the Department of Commerce, volunteered to help. Old Guard hostility, mustered by Lodge, Knox, and Penrose, and supported by Hoover's fellow Californian, Johnson, was a formidable barrier. Cautioning the President-elect to keep silent on his intention, Daugherty hurried to Pennsylvania to interview the two Senators. They were resentful when he set forth his position as representing Harding; if they wanted Mellon in

[1] He did, however, leave it to the nation in his will.

the Cabinet they must withdraw their opposition to Hoover.
'Penrose got my ultimatum — no Hoover, no Mellon. And
rose to heights of profanity I have never heard equalled.' [1]

It was wasted eloquence. The emissary stood pat. Finally
Penrose grinned. 'All right. You win,' he admitted.

Crediting Daugherty with accuracy as a reporter of his
passage at arms with 'the two most powerful men in the
Senate,' he continued to treat 'em rough. He would not even
announce nor permit them to announce Mellon's impending
appointment. Two days later, Harding obliged. Thus was
Hoover's path smoothed.

'It was not a popular appointment among the men who
took an active part in the nomination and election of President Harding,' Daugherty morosely records.[2]

John W. Weeks of Massachusetts was selected as Secretary
of War. His official record comprised four terms in the House
of Representatives, and one in the Senate, where he was
known as a conscientious student of legislation. He was an
engineer and banker and was identified with the Old Guard.
His appointment was in the nature of reward for services
rendered. Through his good offices a Boston bank in which
he was interested was reputed to have underwritten part of
the campaign deficit.[3]

For another species of benefit Harding would have liked to
give a Cabinet berth to Alvin T. Hert. It was the Ken-
tuckian's betrayal of Lowden at Chicago that started the
Harding landslide. Apostasy of this sort does not commend
the perpetrator to his fellow politicians. Bitter opposition
arose. Harding defended his friend. 'There are few abler
men than he. A man who makes a practice of politics per-
forms a patriotic duty and we ought to have more like him in
this country.' [4] However, Hert dropped out.

[1] Harry M. Daugherty: *The Inside Story of the Harding Tragedy.*   [2] *Ibid.*
[3] *New York Times*, February 7, 1921.
[4] *Ibid.*, March 1, 1921.

The business interests of the farmers were represented by Henry C. Wallace, publisher of a prosperous farm journal in Iowa, as Secretary of Agriculture.

Designated to the Department of Labor, James J. ('Puddler Jim') Davis represented nothing but political expediency. Although he held a union card, he was actually an affluent banker and was distrusted by the radicals of organized labor as too conservative. In their view Charles M. Schwab might as well have got the job.

As a whole the Cabinet represented the business ideal. It was a rich man's Cabinet. The *New York World* estimated more than six hundred million dollars owned or controlled by its collective membership, but this was a considerable exaggeration. It was wholly satisfactory to Industry, big and little. Where the Wilson Administration had placed emphasis upon human rights and international co-operation, the Harding régime, as forecast in the personnel of the official family, would emphasize property privilege and 'introverted nationalism.' Only Hughes and Hoover saved it from wholesouled commitment to the irreconcilables. The *New York Tribune* viewed it as 'a disappointment, tempered by Messrs. Hughes and Hoover.' Newspaper comment as a whole was temperate to kindly.

What criticism was uttered was not taken well by Harding. One Washington correspondent irreverently observed that he was 'getting pouty.' He was certainly getting annoyed.

'It isn't fair,' he protested. 'This premature criticism is a serious menace to popular government.... I see in all this a wrong effort to undermine public confidence in the incoming administration before it has a chance to perform.... It strikes at the root of government and strikes dangerously.' [1]

As its creator had forecast, it was a Republican Cabinet. His confident prediction that it would be 'a Cabinet of which

[1] *New York Times*, March 6, 1921.

the whole country can be proud' was destined to correction for error.

The spectacle of a President subjected to the humiliating dread of blackmail is not flattering to national pride. Harding underwent this ordeal, though happily without publicity. A few letters written by him, while in the Senate, to a Washington woman, were offered for private sale — very private. The original asking price was one thousand dollars. The letters were frivolous, no worse. They exhibited the writer in the rôle of senatorial playboy, humorously fretful over the compulsion of devoting so much time to official routine.

Nothing essentially compromising was contained in them. The damaging element was the character of the woman. She was seeking to cash in on her own shady repute.[1]

Harding, in Florida, was reluctant to leave until the threat was eliminated. Trusted friends undertook negotiations. The immediate result, as is frequent in such cases, was to raise the price to five thousand. At this point it was discovered that the bargainer was politically vulnerable through a member of her family. Counter-pressure was brought into play and the documents were surrendered without price.

The effect upon Harding's morale was deleterious. Throughout his Presidency he knew that other and more damnatory data were in existence, and he could not tell when exposure might threaten.

[1] A lawyer and a Washington correspondent who have seen the letters agree that there was not, *per se*, anything damaging in them. The recipient was later made the subject of an undercover 'investigation' by Jesse Smith and the Department of Justice.

★

XV. Pattern for Normalcy

WHATEVER misgivings Harding may have felt in pre-contemplation of the Presidency were temporarily resolved when he reached Washington for the inauguration. He was in high spirits as he rode through the ranks of cheering thousands, beside the wasted figure and ravaged face of Woodrow Wilson. Once he even managed to conjure up a difficult laugh from his sombre companion.

A story both stupid and cruel went the rounds of the Capital, amidst the sniggers of the Wilson-haters, to the effect that Harding had deliberately snubbed the man he was displacing, by failing to make provision for him in the ceremonial. It was stupid because it belies Harding's fundamental kindliness. Toward a man sick and broken he would have been considerate to the point of tenderness. President Wilson's confidential secretary commented upon Harding's 'keenest consideration and courtesy' during that trying passage.[1]

What gave rise to the unpleasant legend was lack, not of kindness, but of tact on the part of the incoming executive. Owing to his decrepitude, Mr. Wilson was unable to mount the steps of the White House at the end of the shared ride

[1] Joseph P. Tumulty: *Wilson as I Knew Him.*

and asked that he might enter by a ground-floor door and take the elevator. Harding, of course, assented, but it never occurred to him that the courteous gesture would have been to accompany the man who was now, in a sense, his guest. He ascended the steps, buoyant in his vitality, leaving the other to make the elevator trip alone.

In the exuberance of the occasion he had quite simply forgotten. But he did not forget to think of his sick predecessor in a matter of greater importance. Rear Admiral Cary T. Grayson had been President Wilson's physician. One of President Harding's first official acts was to assign Doctor Grayson to Washington so that he might continue to care for his distinguished patient.

It is customary for the wife of an outgoing President to invite the new mistress of the White House to tea, and to give her useful pointers on the complicated housekeeping of the Mansion. The interview between Mrs. Harding and Mrs. Wilson was not a pleasant one. Mrs. Harding's first *gaucherie* was asking if she might bring her hostess, Mrs. Edward B. McLean, along. Meeting a polite rebuff, she came alone, and, perhaps realizing that she had made a *faux pas*, was uneasy and voluble. The termination of the encounter is thus recounted by Mrs. Jaffray, the housekeeper, who was called in and found both women on their feet, Mrs. Wilson flushed of face.

'Mrs. Harding, this is Mrs. Jaffray,' said she, and without a word of farewell, turned and left the room.

The caller addressed the housekeeper bluntly, 'Well, I won't want you any more, for I have already made other arrangements.[1]

Later Mrs. Jaffray received a letter from the Hardings, asking her to remain. She did, and made some pungent notes on the new and restless tenants.

Possibly Mrs. Wilson's name was among those in that little

[1] Mrs. Elizabeth Jaffray: *Secrets of the White House.*

red book which the 'Duchess' had shown to Alice Longworth, marked for reprisals because they had not paid to the
wife of the Senator from Ohio that deference which she had
deemed her due.

Economy was the order of the day in Washington. President Wilson had dispensed with the Inaugural Ball in his
second term. Since his successor was committed to retrench-
ment, it would have been unbecoming to revive it. This
could hardly have been pleasing to the First Lady, who was
feminine enough to love display and pageantry. It was a sad
blow to Jesse Smith, already installed as a White House
familiar. He was to be vice-chairman of the Inaugural Ball
Committee and wear a badge on a ribbon. As substitute,
the Ned McLeans, who were social sponsors for the Administration, gave a huge unofficial fête; but although Jesse
was a guest, his insignia lacked glow in a private establishment, however grand in scale.

An episode of the inaugural reception shows the new
mistress of the Executive Mansion at her best. Coming down
before the event, to see that all was in order, she found the
servants drawing the window-shades. Asking why, she was
told respectfully that, unless this were done, the people outside would crowd around and peer in.

'Let 'em look if they want to,' said Mrs. Harding. 'It's
their White House.' [1]

Her husband was equally democratic by instinct. When
his staff wished to protect him from the hordes of visitors
whom curiosity brings to the White House, he was impatient.

'If these people want to see me, why shouldn't I see them?'
he demanded. [2]

The private life of the Hardings, if a presidential pair may
be said to have a private life, marked a departure from the

---

[1] Mary Randolph: *Presidents and First Ladies.*
[2] Irwin H. Hoover: *Forty-Two Years in the White House.*

more rigid formality of the preceding incumbents. When the incoming couple paid their call on Mrs. Wilson, the visiting wife sat up very straight and stiff in her chair. Mr. Harding slouched in his, as Mrs. Wilson noted with displeasure, his leg slung over the arm of the chair.[1] Throughout their occupancy of the White House it was the same: Mrs. Harding sat up just a little too stiffly, and the President characteristically slouched when not on exhibition.

The familiars of their play-hours were a motley crew. There were Charles R. Forbes, on his way to jail; Senator Frank Brandegee, on the decline to a reckless bankruptcy and the saving grace of suicide; Jesse Smith with his vapid grin, his jocund 'Whaddayah know?' and his palms itching for the easy graft which did not save him from a bullet through his brain; Secretary Fall, staking out his path to the penitentiary; Elias Mortimer, who precipitated a scandal second only to Fall's before he killed himself; Edward B. McLean on his way to mental collapse; and others of various repute, but all with a like taste for revelry.

Twice a week regularly there was early dinner followed by a stiff poker game. At least once a week the President indulged in his favorite sport outside the home walls. Of the Poker Cabinet regulars, the faithful attendants were McLean, Forbes, Jesse Smith, Harry Daugherty, Fall, Albert Lasker of the Shipping Board, Senators Frelinghuysen and Hale, and Surgeon General Sawyer, who attended more often than he played. Occasionally Controller of the Currency Crissinger sat in, as did Charles G. Dawes, Postmaster General Hays, and even Secretaries Wallace and Mellon,[2] while out-of-town participants were George Harvey, Harry F. Sinclair (who also did his bit in jail), and chewing-gum magnate William Wrigley, Jr.

[1] *Saturday Evening Post*, February 25, 1939.

[2] Mr. Mellon was wont to protest his ignorance of the fine points, but he usually, according to Walter F. Brown, an occasional participant, came out a winner.

Sometimes Mrs. Harding lent the stimulus of her presence to the occasion, but did not take a hand.

Easy fellowship prevailed. To the President of the United States in these moments of recuperation Forbes was 'Charlie,' McLean was 'Ned,' Mortimer was 'Mort,' Sinclair was 'Harry,' Lasker was 'Bert,' Smith was 'Jess,' Sawyer was 'Doc.' All called their host 'Mr. President.' That much sense of the proprieties survived the reek of whiskey and tobacco. Mrs. Harding was also on given-name terms with several of the gamesters. Harry Daugherty called her 'Ma.' Ned McLean habitually addressed her as 'Boss.' Charlie Forbes adopted her husband's sobriquet of 'Duchess.' [1]

White House family life had been easy and relaxed during the occupancy of the Theodore Roosevelts; but it had maintained the standards of gentlefolk, too sure of themselves to alter their ways materially, while still conforming to the exigencies of executive position. Now Theodore Roosevelt's daughter, certainly no prude, was shocked 'to see the way President Harding disregarded the Constitution he was sworn to uphold.' Prohibition being the law of the land, no liquor was served downstairs, but there was much gossip of high jinks around the poker table. Writes Alice Roosevelt Longworth: [2]

> No rumor could have exceeded the reality; the study was filled with cronies, Daugherty, Jess Smith, Alec Moore, and others; the air heavy with tobacco smoke, trays with bottles containing every imaginable brand of whiskey stood about, cards and poker chips ready at hand — a general atmosphere of waistcoat unbuttoned, feet on the desk, and the spittoon alongside.

High the game might run; it was not stiff enough for the host. He sought an extra fillip of excitement in side-bets. Calling to see the President one evening, Louis Seibold, then

[1] Irwin H. Hoover: *Forty-Two Years in the White House.*

[2] From *Crowded Hours*, by Alice Roosevelt Longworth. By permission of Charles Scribner's Sons, publishers.

a Washington correspondent and forgiven for his earlier strictures upon Harry Daugherty, was complimented upon a tie-pin he was wearing.

'That's a nice pearl, Louis. What do you think of this one?'

Seibold examined with interest the pearl in the Harding tie, which he guessed to be worth four or five thousand dollars. 'That's something else again, Mr. President,' he answered. 'I haven't often seen as fine a one.'

'Won it at the poker game Wednesday night.'

'You must have been holding 'em.'

'Not so good. I got this, spading with the man on my left.[1] He took it out of his pocket and said, "I'll put this up against a hundred dollars." It looked good to me,' continued Mr. Harding, 'so I took him up. I won with a four of spades.'[2]

Back in Harding's Ohio days, poker was one method of repaying political obligations. Writing of his legislative experiences at that time in Columbus, Frederick C. Howe says:[3]

> There was little venality in the Assembly. It was not necessary. Some men were kept in line by being permitted to win substantial sums at poker.

In the Wednesday night poker where the pearl pin changed hands, there had participated a Cabinet official and the chairman of a national board. Whether either of them was the man on the President's left is a matter of speculation. Equally so is the question of whether Mr. Harding was wittingly or unwittingly following an old Ohio custom. What is fact beyond speculation is that he was receiving odds of forty or fifty to one on his side-bet.

[1] Spading consists in betting that one's hand will contain a spade higher than his opponent's.

[2] Told to the writer by Mr. Seibold.

[3] *Confessions of a Reformer.*

Pattern for Normalcy

Ill health prevented Mrs. Harding from extracting the full enjoyment from her status. Only a hard will and nervous energy kept her going. No more fitted to her position than her husband to his, she overdid it; she tried too hard to be a great lady. Uncertain of herself, she took refuge in volubility and effusiveness. She did not understand, as did her successor, the simple and gracious Mrs. Coolidge, that standards of breeding and taste are the same everywhere. Her housekeeper thinks that she

> ... could never quite accustom herself to the greatness and importance of her position ... it was all a difficult rôle for her. ... At times she had about as little self-control as any grown person I have ever met.[1]

She was prone to be overrouged and overcoiffeured, often overdressed. Jesse Smith was her arbiter of the elegances. He chose her gowns, bringing to the congenial task all the stylistic artistry acquired in long years behind the counter in Washington Court House, Ohio. Alice Longworth, who frankly admits not caring much for either of the Hardings, thus describes her:[2]

> She was a nervous, rather excitable woman whose voice easily became a little high-pitched, strident. ... She usually spoke of Mr. Harding as Warren Harding. It is impossible to convey her pronunciation of the letter *r* in print. Something like Wur-r-ren Ha-rr-ding.

Social contacts for a presidential couple are pretty well restricted by official exigencies. Outside of these, the Hardings' preferred associates were the Edward B. McLeans and their large and not stringently selective coterie. It was a set of high livers and free spenders, restless, garish, greedy of excitement. Laws and observances meant little to them; they formulated their code of conduct on their own predi-

[1] Mrs. Elizabeth Jaffray: *Secrets of the White House.*
[2] From *Crowded Hours*, by Alice Roosevelt Longworth. By permission of Charles Scribner's Sons, publishers.

lections. Like most of the rest of us in those days, they patronized bootleggers. They played bridge or poker for high stakes. At the McLean mansion was shown an early film — said to be the first showing — of the Dempsey-Carpentier fight in violation of the law forbidding the interstate transportation of prizefight pictures.

'I do not believe I could be happy as President,' the Senator from Ohio had told his friend, Colonel Samuel G. McClure. He tried hard to belie his own prophecy. He did his desperate best to have a good time, which is perhaps not quite the same thing as being happy. It was a failure. He was a misfit in his environment. Even his simplest, most deeply implanted habits were out of place. He could not keep dressed up for that party. His wife's uneasy insistence upon adjustment to grandeur irked him. Sometimes he craved those delicacies of Marion days, wienerwurst and sauerkraut. They were banned as unsuitable. He wanted toothpicks on the table. Contrary to etiquette. He sorely missed his assuaging chew of tobacco and devised secret caches in the upstairs rooms where he could stow away his plugs, safe from the questing eyes of the suspicious Duchess.

'She says cigars are all right, but it's undignified to chew,' he wistfully told a caller,[1] tucking a cut away in his cheekpouch.

Time is not supposed to hang heavy on the hands of a President of the United States. But there were evenings when Warren G. Harding felt himself at loose ends; he missed the old, relaxed fellowship of an environment more familiar and less restricted than the White House. In the June following the inauguration, Surgeon General Sawyer planned a jovial little poker party in his suite at the Willard. Charles R. Forbes and George B. Christian, Jr., were present, a high ranking army officer and a pair of heavy calibre officials. Proceedings were pleasantly under way when the door was

[1] Louis Seibold.

thrown open. President Harding stood there, an aggrieved expression on his face.

'You fellows can't sneak off and have a party without me,' he protested. 'I'm here for the evening.'

The climax of the game came when the President ran four nines up against a rival four jacks. Notwithstanding, he insisted that he had enjoyed the whole evening and suggested that he be notified in advance next time.[1]

Later in the year a group of newspaper correspondents who had covered the Front Porch campaign held a reunion dinner at the National Press Club. Halfway through the feast a bug-eyed negro attendant appeared at the door of their private dining-room.

'Mr. President of the United States is outside an' wanta know can he come in,' he breathlessly announced.

The caller was welcomed and the dinner continued without further interruption or any change of atmosphere.[2]

A favorite companion of the sometimes lonely man — one suspects that all Presidents suffer from loneliness — was Laddie Boy, a shaggy, homely, highbred Airedale terrier. No other dog was ever to take quite the place in Harding's affections held by the martyred Edgewood Hub. But the Airedale was an affable sort of person. As there were no White House children, Laddie Boy became the focus of that peculiar and rather engaging sentimentalism which plays, like a softer white light, about a throne. The newspapers gave columns of space to him. Poetasters sung his canine virtues. His 'letters' to his blue-ribbon father and to certain distinguished stage dogs (some press agent having become inspired) were read by millions. A smiling public learned that Laddie Boy brought the newspaper to his master in the morning, breakfasted and lunched with him, sat guard in his

---

[1] If this episode has a slightly A. A. Milne flavor of royalty oversimplified, the writer can only say that it was retailed to him by the lucky holder of the four jacks.

[2] Told to the writer by Walker S. Buell who was presiding at the dinner.

office, and accompanied him to the golf course, barking his reproaches if the President stubbed an approach or missed an easy putt. Newsboys contributed pennies for a statuette of him after Harding's death.

Privacy, Harding soon found, was a luxury denied to Presidents. He had, indeed, as he forecast on learning of his victory, lost his freedom. The supervision of the ubiquitous secret service men irked his nerves. He complained to Nan Britton, who was smuggled in to see him, that he was 'a prisoner.' The famous major-domo of the White House, 'Ike' Hoover, says that he 'despised being watched.'

Sports offered him needed relief from domestic frets. As often as he could get away he played golf at the Chevy Chase Club; often two or three times a week. He was a hardy enthusiast; nothing short of a downpour could drive him from the course, once he had set out. His game was reliable rather than brilliant, running from 95 to 100. With a handicap of 22 he just missed a victory which would have been enormously popular — for he was a good sportsman — in the Washington Newspaper Golf Association tournament, and which would have been his had not clicking cameras on the home green caused him to commit the solecism of looking up on a short putt. The President Warren Harding Cup, presented by him for the National Public Links championship, perpetuates his memory in the sport.

Boxing, motoring, fishing, and baseball were his other hobbies, particularly the latter. It used to be said that he spent more time over the Washington team record than the *Congressional Record*. He was a frequent attendant on the games and had Babe Ruth as White House guest several times. Chick Evans, the golf champion, was also an invited guest. Samuel Hardy brought a team of crack tennis players to the White House court, but the President had lost interest in tennis, since he was no longer active enough for its strenuous demands.

His enthusiasm for the prize ring was maintained. At one of the poker sessions Albert Lasker and Ned McLean waxed sentimental over the sad plight of ex-heavyweight champion, Jack Johnson, facing a fine on his release from Atlanta Penitentiary.

'Don't worry,' said the President. 'I'll remit it.' [1]

In an eloquent speech designed to 'sell' Mr. Harding to the nation, Will Hays summed up his first six months in office, drawing an appealing portrait, manly, human, simple. Said the speaker:

> Day by day the country senses the qualities of the man in the White House, and if they are qualities that appeal to the good in the common mass of men, the country tends to reflect them on as a pattern. [2]

The implications in that address are a credit to Mr. Hays's verbal felicitousness and official loyalty. They represent the strategy of the leaders who had put Mr. Harding where he was, and must now, for their own credit, present their choice as a model of respectability and worth. Already those leaders were beginning to feel qualms. The Washington whisperings were not all propitious.

The American people are a sport-loving folk. But a sport in the White House was something new.

[1] *New York World*, January 4, 1927.

[2] *World's Work*, November, 1921, reporting Hays's speech at Cleveland in September.

★

XVI. Big Job: Little Man

EVERYONE wished well to the incoming President. The stalwart figure, the handsome, genial face, with its kindliness of glance, its smiling mouth, its frank expression, the patent humanity, simplicity, and sincerity of the man, made up a picture of typical Americanism which filled the eye. No President ever enjoyed a greater initial popularity. Much was in his favor at the outset; a hope in all sections of public opinion and in many a faith that he would be able to restore equilibrium and prosperity through establishing that 'era of good feeling' which he had forecast; the personal friendship of the congressional leaders; and not least, the strong favorable prejudice of the Washington correspondents, who understood and liked him as he understood and liked them, in the caste-fellowship of working newspapermen. No other President up to his time met with such consideration or was treated with equal tolerance for his blunders. I do not mean to imply that news was distorted in his favor. But wherever his course was dubious, he received the benefit of the doubt in fullest measure, and charity covered, as long as it was possible, a multitude of errors which, had he been regarded with a less affectionate lenity, would have stood against his official account.

Big Job: Little Man

In a moment of optimism, the President-elect had expressed the opinion that government, after all, was a pretty simple business.[1] He was now to put that hopeful theory to the test. Friendly counsellors thought the prospect more dubious.

'Never has any President come to the tremendous office with so much unfinished business and so many fresh problems of moment,' warned the *Philadelphia Public Ledger*.

Due to Wilson's collapse, post-war economic complications, and the 'quarrelsome inertia' of Congress, the mechanism of government was practically stalled. Vital readjustments were necessary. Business men were demanding, 'What is to be done to restore good times?' The unemployed were crying, 'When do we get our jobs back?' The more decent-minded of a public, now widely given over to the lawlessness of evasion, impatiently wanted to know, 'When does Prohibition begin to prohibit?' All voices joined in the wail, 'Reduce the cost of living.' More specifically, constructive action was required on waning national finances, taxation, disarmament, tariff, the peace treaties, and the League of Nations.

Looking beyond our borders, the view was no more reassuring. Our relations with Mexico were touchy. Senator (now Secretary) Fall and the oil barons had been pressing for intervention. There was unrest in Cuba. War clouds were forming in the Orient where Japan and Russia were making faces at each other. Europe's diplomacy of tooth and claw was fostering those inequities and engendering those vengeances which now, a generation after, are liquidating themselves in a new and more dreadful blood-bath. Germany was prone. Soviet Russia, an unknown quantity, was knocking at our door for recognition. England was peevish at us for our Yankee smartness — a little more sharp than honest — in the matter of Panama Canal tolls. Foreign cartoonists

[1] Willis Fletcher Johnson: *Life of Warren G. Harding*.

delighted in picturing Uncle Sam as a Shylock because we exhibited the shocking bad taste of wanting our cheerfully loaned money back.

People looked to the Administration to set everything right.

'The whole world hangs upon Mr. Harding's every word,' declared the *Advocate of Peace*.

Mr. Harding had no helpful word to contribute. His inaugural address was vague where it should have been definitive.[1] He was feeling his way, leaning upon others. 'Ike' Hoover, a shrewdly analytical judge of men, commented upon the ease with which Harding's congressional cronies were able to convince him that whatever they wanted was right. He followed others because he lacked a program. Domestic dilemmas and foreign complications alike were obscure to a mind which had never found occasion to be studious or analytical. Harding simply didn't know what it was all about.

His pathetic admission to one of his secretaries illustrates the confusion of a mind appalled by the mass of material presented for its digestion. The immediate subject of his consideration was tax reform over which Wall Street was at odds and the party financial sharps wrangling among themselves.

'I can't make a damn thing out of this tax problem,' he complained. 'I listen to one side and they seem right, and then — God! — I talk to the other side and they seem just as right, and here I am where I started. I know somewhere there is a book that will give me the truth, but hell! I couldn't read the book.'[2]

---

[1] Doctor Alderfer, who has made a stylistic analysis of Harding's speeches, thinks that this is the last state paper actually composed by him. In the writer's opinion also the subsequent official output exhibits few if any Hardingesque 'bloviations.' I. H. Hoover (*Forty-Two Years in the White House*) says that Harding wrote few of his speeches.

[2] William Allen White: *Masks in a Pageant*. By permission of The Macmillan Company, publishers.

On tariff his brain was little if any clearer. He announced that he was for 'a two-cent tariff'[1] and his puzzled supporters looked at one another and asked in pained voices what the devil he meant by that. Poor President! Before he had been in office a week, twenty thousand pages of expert opinion on subjects of prospective legislation were dumped on the desk before his stricken eyes.

He astounded an interviewer, Bruce Bliven, with this obiter dictum:

'The United States should adopt a protective tariff of such a character as will help the struggling industries of Europe to get on their feet.'

Fearful that something had gone wrong with his hearing, Mr. Bliven asked for a repetition and took down the words as the President repeated himself verbatim. He published it in the *New Republic*, as spoken.[2]

Arthur S. Draper, correspondent of the *New York Tribune*, had come back from Europe to conduct a round-table on 'Foreign News' at the Williamstown Institute of Politics. While in London he talked confidentially with such men as Lord Robert Cecil, Sir John Simon, Austen Chamberlain, Ramsay MacDonald, and leading editors and publishers. After a press conference at the White House, he was detained to see the President. He had expected to have a talk of fifteen or twenty minutes with Harding and Secretary Judson C. Welliver, but the President swept it aside by saying:

'I don't know anything about this European stuff. You and Jud get together and he can tell me later; he handles these matters for me.'

On learning, however, that Mr. Draper had encountered a former *Marion Star* man in London, the President was much interested and held him in talk to hear all about his old employee.

'Jud and I had a long lunch together,' writes Mr. Draper,

[1] *New York Times*, June 16, 1921.
[2] *New Republic*, vols. 38 and 39: 'The Ohio Gang.'

'and he told me how difficult it was to get the President interested in foreign affairs. . . .' [1]

Harding's own self-estimate is pertinent. To David Lawrence he expressed the humble conviction that he was 'a man of limited talents from a small town. . . . Oftentimes, as I sit here, I don't seem to grasp that I am President.' [2]

In his official capacity the new President bore himself with dignity and gravity. Members of his Cabinet were struck with his seriousness; he seemed to them to be approaching his heavy task with a full appreciation of its import. He was eager to win and hold the respect of men whom he recognized as his mental superiors. Without question this was his instinctive attitude toward at least three of his official family. The dignified Secretary of State, the unobtrusively forceful Secretary of Commerce, the shy but impressive Secretary of the Treasury were, to him, Mister Hughes, Mister Hoover, Mister Mellon; or, more simply, Mister Secretary.

From them, rather than from his intimates, Daugherty and Fall, he took his official tone. The stage was set for statesmanship, and the President readily took on the form and color of his environment. He was sorely and righteously offended when the late Will Rogers, in a radio burlesque of a Cabinet meeting, represented him as boasting of his golf and interrupting discussions of weighty affairs to telephone an inquiry about the baseball score. Jokes about his drinking and poker parties flicked him on the raw.[3] He thought them unseemly.

His Cabinet had the appearance of a great asset, in the beginning. It could be roughly divided into two groups; the officially loyal — Hughes, Hoover, Mellon, Wallace, Denby, Weeks, and Davis; and the personally devoted — Daugherty, Hays, and, so far as anyone then knew, Fall. Fortu-

---

[1] Letter from Mr. Draper to the writer.
[2] Willis Fletcher Johnson: *The Life of Warren G. Harding.*
[3] Finley Peter Dunne, in *Saturday Evening Post*, September 12, 1936.

nately or unfortunately, according to the viewpoint, Harding had a weak Congress to deal with. Leadership was lacking in the Senate. Lodge, the titular leader, was slipping. Penrose, the most powerful intellect and the most skilful manipulator in the body, pottered about in clothes grotesquely too large for a form shrunken by the dissipation and disease that was soon to carry him off. Knox, Smoot, Warren, and McLean of Connecticut all wielded influence rather than authority. Factional dissensions split the majority party.

In the lower house Speaker Gillett had passed the peak of his power, as had Fordney, chairman of the Ways and Means Committee. Nicholas Longworth and James R. Mann, neither of whom was identified with the Harding crowd, were forces to be reckoned with. While the House was more conservative than the Senate, there was enough insurgency in both to cause legislative uncertainty and, for a time, legislative impotence.

All signs were set for positive action by the Executive. A Wilson, a Roosevelt, a Cleveland would have taken full advantage of such conditions, perhaps over-advantage. Harding had modelled himself upon the inert and negative McKinley. By his own interpretation of his function, he was there to serve the nation through the party; the leaders of the party with an indubitable mandate as leaders of the nation, would show him how best to proceed. One of his secretaries viewed him at this time as 'voluntarily allowing the power of the Executive to fall lower than it has for the last twenty-five years,' while at the same time giving him credit for being 'of great virility ... conscious of his present power ... of undoubted courage.' [1] From this estimate another of his secretaries, Mr. Welliver, differs in part. He thinks that President Harding 'never appreciated the extent or effectiveness of the moral force he might have wielded.' [2]

[1] W. H. Crawford: *World's Work*, May, 1921.
[2] William Allen White: *Masks in a Pageant.*

Mr. Crawford's words, 'voluntarily allowing,' express President Harding's conscious attitude of mind. He saw himself as one of an aggregation, all committed to the same end. There is a legend that, after the election he said to a little group of political friends:

'We're in the Big League now, boys. We're going to play ball.'

From every member of his Cabinet, his secretariat, his Administration, he confidently expected the same team-work which he meant to and did contribute within the limitations of his conception and his capacity.

Not all of his team-mates were as altruistically disposed. They were out for the spoils. Ever amenable to party demands, the President responded. One of his first acts was to cheer the faithful by an executive order shifting thirteen thousand postmasterships from the protection of the Civil Service regulations, under which Wilson had placed them. 'The spoils system is back in high speed,' snapped the *New York Times*.[1] If one may believe Harding's assurances to the Academy of Political Science in New York,[2] nothing was further from his intentions; he promised that economy and efficiency would prevail in the Administration. Perhaps he did not mean to be taken too literally. Postmaster General Hays, however, seems to have accepted the pronouncement in good faith. He organized his department for service, thereby mitigating the effect of the executive order and disappointing many hungry office-seekers.

As Senator, Harding had adopted a *laissez-faire* policy. Now he was in a position where slackness was impracticable. Neither lazy nor negligent toward his new duties, he nevertheless did not bring an efficient method to their performance. The task was too big for him. Instinctively he leaned upon others. 'Ike' Hoover wrote of him:[3]

[1] March 12, 1921. [2] *Literary Digest*, June 4, 1921.
[3] *Forty-Two Years in the White House.*

He never seemed to be very concerned with the fate of a measure under consideration, depending more on these so-called friends to take care of his interests.

Penrose had expressed the will of the party leaders in saying, 'We are going to put in a man who will listen.' Harding was willing to listen; he had always a well-grounded ear; now he was more than ever anxious to hear counsel. But the powers that had elevated him had nothing valuable to say to him. When they did speak, it was in voices so diverse and discordant that the result was confusion. On tariff, on taxation, on the sorry heritage of war their program was threatening to bog down because of intra-party squabbles. Sensing that he was more popular than they, the leaders hoped that he might assert the authority and prestige of his office to restore order. Would he come to the aid of the party?

This was outside the bargain. He had not expected the Best Minds to delegate their functions. Worse, the Senate, forum of said Best Minds, was dividing into mutually re-criminative factions, acting like a lot of unruly children. Even in the House, when he turned to it as the more conservative body, sour notes impaired the party harmony.

Harding could go to the front for his friends. He was ready to stand up and fight on such issues as the defence of a Daugherty or a Forbes. But to battle for a principle was beyond his political tradition.

Republican newspapers were clamoring for tax revision. Responsive to their arguments, the schedule-makers put taxation first on the legislative programme and tariff last. Before election Harding had declared for heavier rates on large incomes. Secretary Mellon converted him.

As one of the world's richest men, Mr. Mellon logically and conscientiously conceived his official duty to be the conservation and protection of wealth. Under his influence the President reversed himself and advocated a maximum impost of thirty-two per cent. This was bad politics. The memory of the 'quickie' millionaires of the war still rankled. Pointing out that the House would insist upon a severer ratio, Congressmen Fordney and Longworth persuaded Harding to accept an increase to forty per cent, which they thought they could carry through. They were mistaken. Led by the malcontents of the Middle West, where large fortunes are comparatively rare, the 'wild asses of the desert,' as Senator George Moses was to call them in a spirit of irritability rather than of tact, took the bit in their insurgent teeth and ran out on their President. The fifty per cent maximum in the new income imposts was his first major defeat.[1]

After the tax bill was enacted, no one liked it. It was nobody's child, everybody's stepchild. In both houses the Democrats sneered and the Republicans snarled. The pro-Administration *Herald* thought it 'a thoroughly bad job.'

Although permanent action on the tariff was postponed, something had to be done to carry on. The Emergency Tariff Bill became a law on May 27, 1921. It was a sorry makeshift, a compromise arrived at by the familiar pull-devil, pull-baker method. It was no more popular than the tax effort.

Harding put forth two pet projects of his own, the Department of Public Welfare and the Ship Subsidy Bill. Congress was not kindly disposed. It declined to recognize the President's leadership in the field of legislation. The Senate was becoming critical of his 'personal' appointments, which it regarded as encroaching upon its own prerogatives; it asked questions about his tampering with the Civil Service. Presumably as indication of independence, it turned down both Public Welfare and Ship Subsidy. Harding accepted the rebuffs. He was not a fighting man.

Compensation and comfort were found in the success of

[1] *New York Times*, November 13, 1921.

the Budget and Accounting Bill. When, with the President's support, it became law, he appointed Charles G. ('Hell-and-Maria') Dawes, Budget Director. For the first time business system was introduced into, and a business check set upon, government expenditures. The effect was swift and definite. Within six months taxes were reduced at the rate of a round billion a year, notwithstanding which the public debt was cut down in about the same ratio.

Another mark to the credit of the President (though entered on the debit side of his political ledger) was his stand on the Soldiers' Bonus. For a time he showed a disposition to play safe. Acridly reminded by the *New York Times* [1] that if he expected to stem the raid on the Treasury and enlist help from legislators it must be 'by the application of some pressure other than that of an arm around their shoulders,' he announced his opposition and fought so valiantly that he delayed the passage of the bill for a year.

At the end of six months' incumbency, President Harding was able to felicitate himself upon economies initiated, tariff and tax problems on the way to solution (here he was overoptimistic), and prosperity returning. Well-disposed, as a whole, Washington correspondents concurred in his self-approval. Mark Sullivan, casting up half-yearly accounts, decided that the President had 'undersold himself to the public.' He admitted that Mr. Harding had not taken over leadership, but saw no evidence of subservience to the senatorial cabal, and credited him with 'good housekeeping and business management.' [2]

'No one doubts that the present Administration will make a record never equalled before,' he wrote, a forecast sadly borne out by subsequent developments, though not within the meaning of Mr. Sullivan's encomium. He also estimated as 'the best Cabinet we have had in a generation' a body of

[1] July 9, 1921.
[2] *World's Work*, November, 1921.

men which was to see one of its members a convicted criminal, and two others dismissed in disgrace.

All this is cited, not in disparagement of Mr. Sullivan, whose reputation for perspicuous observation and honest evaluation is established, but to show how eager was the desire and hope for a successful administration. Ninety-five per cent of the nation, probably, would have endorsed his estimate.

Confusion and obstruction were threatening, but not yet obvious. The 'era of good feeling' which Harding had invoked was still in progress. Praise and support were plentiful; criticism mild to the point of charity.

Had the President chosen to assert himself positively at this time, he might possibly have established real leadership, though it is doubtful whether he would have had the force to maintain it. The party guides were still unable to get together on any of the 'three T's that all spell Trouble,' tariff, taxation, and treaties. The House was battling the Senate on duties. West was hostile to East. Bloc was at sword's point with bloc on almost any issue. Under the incitement of Fighting Bob La Follette, twenty-seven senatorial recalcitrants had formed a working coalition. They held the balance of power. They could neither be bought nor bluffed. Penrose, the trusted adviser and 'trouble-shooter' of the Old Guard, discouraged, disgruntled, and misanthropic, angrily admitted his impotence and cursed that of his colleagues. The spirit of rebellion spread to the lower House where a band of insurgents, less powerful and close-knit than their Senate congeners, were nevertheless capable of making trouble in plenty. All of this the President, as titular leader of the party, was called upon to face.

It might have been worse. However perturbed and divided the Best Minds might be, however troubled and muddled the presidential thinking, the nation was still favorably inclined. In the early fall elections, Massachusetts and New Mexico remained sturdily Republican. Harding was encouraged.

★

XVII. Ohio, Here We Come!

THE capture of the City of Washington by the State
of Ohio is unrecorded history. Harding's election was the
signal for the descent of the locust swarm, hungry for pick-
ings. The small fry came in the wake of the large. 'W. G.'
could be trusted to look after his friends.

Standard criticism centres upon the evils of political and
partisan appointments. Washington and, eventually the
country at large, was to learn that personal selections may
be worse.

For no other reason than that he was a friend and neighbor,
President Harding appointed Daniel R. Crissinger to be Controller of the Currency, and later made him Governor of the
Federal Reserve. He was not even a Republican. Twice he
had run for Congress on the Democratic ticket. An inconspicuous country lawyer, with a brief and fortuitous experience in banking, he exhibited no qualifications for or capacity
in either of the high posts to which his friend advanced him.
He had contributed modestly to the campaign chest, and had
been active in the movement to 'make Marion unanimous
for Harding.' Another boyhood friend and campaign contributor was Edward F. Scobey, who became Director of the

Mint. Mr. Scobey had gained his experience in fiscal technique as Sheriff of Pickaway County, Ohio.

To place a temporarily jobless brother-in-law, the President transposed the fat office of Superintendent of Federal Prisons from the Civil Service list by executive order, and conferred it upon the Reverend Heber Herbert Votaw. The reverend gentleman's peculiar fitness for the duties consisted in ten years' service as a Seventh Day Adventist missionary to Burma. He was later to contribute his mite to the general disrepute of the Administration by attempting to block the investigation of the drug ring supplying Atlanta Penitentiary with dope.[1] His wife, Carolyn Harding Votaw, drew a departmental berth and helped to stir the witch-brew of scandal that scalded so many reputations in the Veterans' Bureau exposé.

Through Mrs. Harding's favor, Doctor Charles E. Sawyer was brought on from Marion to be the White House physician, with the rank of Brigadier General. His professional reputation was hardly commensurate with the office to which he was elevated. He was a homoeopath of no more than local note, a graduate of the same medical college as the President's father.[2] By his care and skill he had saved Mrs. Harding's life — or so she believed — at the sanitarium on the outskirts of Marion which, well-managed, had made him prosperous. A little popinjay of a man, vain and dressy, he was nevertheless honest and not without a saving sense of public service.

Without official appointment, but confidently under the Ohio aegis, came Howard Mannington. A former Assistant Secretary of State of Ohio, a Daugherty-Harding henchman and handler of the lesser campaign funds, he had served effi-

---

[1] *Senate Hearings: Select Committee on Investigation of the Attorney General.* Government Printing Office, 1924. Hereinafter the hearings will be designated merely as 'Investigation of the Attorney General.'

[2] Cleveland Homeopathic College of Medicine and Surgery.

ciently as personnel manager of the Front Porch experiment. He was in Washington to realize on his services to the mighty.

Seeing him off at the train, a friend remarked enviously, 'You ought to be in a position to get pretty much anything through down there, if it's right.'

Mannington winked. 'Hell! If it's *right*, they won't need me.'

Mannington rented the famous Little Green House on K Street in partnership with another Ohioan named Caskey.[1]

In Harry Daugherty's train came two personal friends, Jesse Smith to share his living quarters and look after his private interests, and William J. Burns of the detective agency which took his name, to turn the Federal Bureau of Investigation into a medium of political blackmail and oppression. Both were frequenters of the Little Green House.

So was Elmer Dover. Political gossip whispered that he came to Washington to be 'President Harding's Colonel House,' but there is no evidence that he acted in this capacity. His official job was Assistant Secretary of the Treasury, where he was *persona non grata* to Secretary Mellon. He was purged out after an official scandal.

An anomalous Cincinnatian by the anomalous name of Jap (if he was otherwise christened the fact appears nowhere on the record) Muma, who acted on Ned McLean's behalf as a sort of general newspaper factotum, and on his own as an operator of quietly unlawful enterprises, was, like Mannington, an unofficial adjunct to the Ohio activities.

To become a member of the Ohio clique it was not essential to hail from that state. The native Buckeyes were hospitable; they were always ready to welcome, without too much insistence upon geographical origin, the outsider who could show that he had in him something profitable.

Colonel Charles R. Forbes, that fine flower of Capital night-life, was accepted in the charmed circle from the day

[1] 1625 K Street.

of his arrival. He was perhaps the most personal of all Harding's appointments. Imported from Spokane, he was the fair-haired boy of the White House. Harding loved him like a younger brother, and he stood almost as high in Mrs. Harding's graces. He had captivated both on their senatorial junket to Hawaii years earlier, where he was assigned to show them the sights of the place. He and Harding were pals from the first. To the sexual blandishments of which he was so profuse, Mrs. Harding would have been immune; she was Caesar's wife in that respect. But she fell for his camaraderie, his boisterous, high-pitched familiarity, his flattering hand on her arm and his jovial 'Hello, Duchess. What about a little drink for a thirsty hombre?' She was credited with influencing Harding in his appointment to the Veterans' Bureau. Both were stricken when his monumental corruption was exposed. Strange to say, Forbes, too, was a Democrat and owed his position to Wilson when he first met the travellers, but 'verted and worked for the Harding cause in the State of Washington to which he had returned.

E. Mont Reilly, on account of services rendered to the Harding campaign and without other warranty for a difficult executive position, was made Governor of Porto Rico. His administration developed a series of scandals which terminated only with his resignation under fire.

While Albert J. Lasker had aided in the campaign, his choice for chairman of the United States Shipping Board was chiefly personal. His nautical experience was gained in the advertising agency business. But he had other recommendations; he played a stiff game of poker and was one of the regulars of the White House soirées. His administration of the Shipping Board was said by its critics to be characterized by the freehandedness which marks the liberal poker player.

The hopeful Ohio émigrés who flocked to Washington in the Harding-Daugherty train and their friends made the

Little Green House on K Street their headquarters. Generically they were known as the Ohio Gang. Harry Daugherty, while disclaiming any association with the K Street rendezvous, declared that he esteemed the term, Ohio Gang, as a badge of honor.[1] It was not so regarded in other quarters.

The place became quite a social centre. Senators, Congressmen, and Cabinet members dropped in to have a drink from the supplies obligingly furnished by Government officials who diverted confiscated wet goods thither, and to play in the sky-limit poker game. Thomas W. Miller, who came to grief by trying to make too much money as Alien Property Custodian, was a frequent caller, as was John T. King. To Jesse Smith it was a second home. Gaston B. Means, Department of Justice operative and the most plausible and persuasive confidence man of his day, used it for business purposes. Charlie Forbes drank and gambled there, as did his Nemesis, Elias H. Mortimer, the unofficial White House bootlegger. It was a port of call for big liquor operators, office-buyers, jobbers in bribery, and all the sorry, furtive drift of the political underworld. There is contradictory evidence as to whether the President was ever in the house. In any case, he was not one of the regulars. He played his poker elsewhere.

The Ohio Gang traded in liquor withdrawal permits, protection to bootleggers, appointments to office, illegal concessions, immunity from prosecution, pardons, paroles, privileges, and general graft. Howard Mannington ran the headquarters. He put out a shingle. He purported to be a lawyer, which he was not. His partner, Caskey, was. Caskey did the work and Mannington handled the loot, while Jesse Smith skimmed the profits. They soon became the best if not the most favorably known triumvirate in the city.

The Little Green House slumbered not nor slept. It was open for business by day, and for pleasure mingled with

[1] Harry M. Daugherty: *The Inside Story of the Harding Tragedy.*

business by night. Greeks came, bearing gifts. Also Italians, Armenians, Jews, Irishmen, Germans, Swedes, and native-born Americans; all the internationale of bootleggery. 'Good God! how the money rolls in!' Jesse Smith used to hum in his leathery voice, as he stood on the corner greeting his hundreds of acquaintances, for he was a man of note. If they wanted something, sooner or later they must come to Jesse or Mannington or Caskey.

M. P. Kraftmuller was a typical patron. Operating as a go-between for bootlegging drug houses, he dealt in liquor withdrawal permits through Mannington and Company. The General Drug Company of Chicago paid him twenty thousand dollars for a batch of these useful documents. As his commission he retained one-third and turned over the balance to Mannington, who gave Caskey fifteen hundred dollars. On another deal Mannington got twenty-five thousand dollars for himself and partner.[1] There were a dozen lesser transactions of the sort daily with other commission men. The parties of the third part were accommodating Treasury Department agents who issued the permits for a consideration. Modest though Lawyer Caskey's cut was, he soon laid by enough to buy himself a fine mansion.

Appointments and pardons were Jesse Smith's early specialties, though all was goldfish that came to his net. Charlie Forbes saw in this House of Graft a Department of Justice file, containing applications for federal judgeships, over which Mannington was poring. The student of the entries explained that a part of the prospective appointments were turned over to him for decision — that is, for sale. It was Forbes's understanding that when an appointment, not otherwise disposed of by political necessity, was put up to the Attorney General, he would refer it to Jesse or Mannington. The question would then arise as to the applicant, 'How is he fixed?'[2]

[1] *Investigation of the Attorney General.*   [2] *New York World*, December 4, 1927.

Also at disposal of the K Street triumvirs was a file from the Department, listing federal convicts who might be candidates for purchasable pardons. Most of the names were those of bootleggers. Presumably the response to the stock query, 'How is he fixed?' would be encouraging in these cases; they would be counted upon to react liberally to suggestions of release. A difficulty here was that President Harding approved of pardons only in exceptional cases. However, there were ways of getting around that. In the case of one, Philip Grossman, upon whom Mr. Harding had turned thumbs down, the release was accomplished behind his back by the pardon sharps.

Exemptions, too, were a source of profit. George L. Remus of Cincinnati, 'King of the Bootleggers,' testified that he paid Jesse Smith in all more than a quarter of a million dollars for immunity from prosecution, and then did not get it.[1] Even when he was sentenced to Atlanta, the persevering Jesse pried further tribute out of him on the ground that he could get him out.

The investigating attorney inquired: 'And who did he say assured him of that?'

'The General,' was the bootlegger's reply. (This was Jesse's formal locution for Attorney General Daugherty.)

Remus's subsequent career is one item in the long roster of violent crimes connected with the Harding régime. He murdered his wife on the public street in circumstances of peculiar atrocity, and in a few months, by the operations of typical Ohio immunity, was a free man.

The K Street place was a House of Mirth as well as a House of Graft. It was the liquor supply centre for the good scouts who played around with Jesse and his circle. Charlie Forbes got his supply there and on the grand scale, for he was entertaining royally in those days. Surgeon General Sawyer could always be assured of a hearty welcome. Ac-

[1] *Investigation of the Attorney General.*

cording to Forbes the Attorney General used to drop in. But the Attorney General himself denies it, saying that the place was run by a couple of Ohio men of his acquaintance, but that he never went there. In any case, the aegis of the Department of Justice was over the premises.

Express wagons rolled up in broad daylight, with agents from the Department escorting the driver (sometimes revenue officers from the Treasury Department acted as guards), discharged their precious cargoes of liquor in plainly labelled boxes, and departed.[1] Open house was the order of the day and night. Late-session poker parties often ran over into the next day. There were plentiful drinks of the best, and ladies, if not of the best, at least of the most accommodating. Any important or well-vouched-for visitor could be sure of hospitality, and could make reasonable arrangements for supplies which could be had cheap since they cost the purveyors little or nothing, being confiscated contraband.

Connected with the K Street house by links of influence was the smaller and more discreet residence, loaned to the cronies, Daugherty and Smith, by their rich and obliging friend, Ned McLean.[2] Hither came the highly placed of the Capital, including the Hardings. The tone of these parties was decorous and elegant. The occupants were living at the rate of fifty thousand dollars per annum, so Jesse, who handled the accounts told his Roxy.[3] They shared the expenses. That Jesse could well afford his portion is obvious. As to his housemate, the matter is less clear. He had been down almost to his last dollar when he took office.[4]

Soberly respectable though it was to outward view, the little house on H Street served as 'front' for the less reputable little house on K Street. Surface appearances count for more in Washington than elsewhere. To be known as a

---

[1] *Investigation of the Attorney General.*   [2] 1509 H Street.
[3] *Investigation of the Attorney General.*
[4] Finley Peter Dunne: *Saturday Evening Post*, September 12, 1936.

friend of the powerful is, in itself, an indication of power. Thus the McLean house respectability was used as a cloak for the Ohio Gang's profitable iniquities. Did a prospective contributor-under-pressure to the graft fund express doubt of the gang's ability to deliver? Mannington or Caskey or Means was in a position to say:

'So you think we're giving you the runaround, huh? Well, you meet me tomorrow evening at seven back of the Shoreham.'

Watching at the rendezvous, they would see Jesse Smith drive up in the Attorney General's car and enter with his latchkey.

'Do you know whose house that is?' the cicerone would continue. 'Well, that's Daugherty's. And Jess Smith lives there with him. He and Harry Daugherty are just like that,' with fingers intertwined in illustration. 'But that ain't the half of it.'

Presently the White House car would appear, guarded by the ever-present secret service men. Out would step the President and Mrs. Harding. Perhaps as the door opened, there would be a glimpse of the Attorney General in evening dress. Or the Postmaster General might follow, or a pair of Cabinet officers or a group of Senators.

He was, indeed, a hard-boiled sceptic who would not accept such evidence as warranty of the gang's ability to deliver.

More simply the doubter might be invited to examine a newspaper photograph, picturing that ardent fan, the President, about to throw out the first ball of the season at Griffith Park, with Jesse Smith seated in the place of honor on his right, while Cabinet members bowed their diminished heads in the background.

There is something grimly ironic in the fact that Harding, himself free of the taint of corruption, should have served as guaranty for the most flagrant group of bandits known to

Washington since the days of Ulysses S. Grant. There is no doubt that he was for a long time ignorant of those Ohio operations already becoming notorious among the *cognoscenti*. So many things go in Washington that the White House never hears, or, if it does hear, only long after the fact. The late Richard Oulahan, one of the wisest of Washington correspondents, once observed that any President is bound to be the worst informed man in Washington, because there are so many people interested in keeping information from him.

Directly Harding was blameless for what was going on. Indirectly he cannot be wholly exculpated. A President is measured, weighed, and catalogued by the character of his chosen intimates. Washington is peculiarly susceptible to this kind of reflex. Will Hays's philosophical observation upon the tendency of the public to mirror the good qualities of the White House occupant is equally true on the obverse side. Harding's levity of bearing, his laxity of conduct, his moral lapses, were known to the 'wise boys.' One of the Hearst managers was retailing prevalent gossip when he told C. W. Barron: 'Harding was made a fool of. He liked a game of cards and he liked the girls.' [1]

And Ike Hoover summed up, with curt contempt: 'Harding was a sporting ladies' man.' [2]

All this encouraged men wholly lacking in moral or financial principles to believe President Harding such another as themselves. He was 'regular'; one of the boys. He knew what it was all about. A good guy like that wasn't going to make any trouble if a fellow wanted to pick up a piece of money on the side. He was a pal of Jess Smith, wasn't he? He played poker with Charlie Forbes and helled around with Ned McLean and that crowd, didn't he? He'd been known to go out with the gals. Mort Mortimer and Howard Man-

[1] Pound and Moore: *They Told Barron.*
[2] *Forty-Two Years in the White House.*

nington and that bunch had a pull with him. There was nothing to fear from a Big Boss who played the game. They could go as far as they liked.

So reasoned the frequenters of the Little Green House on K Street. The political underworld implicitly believed that the President of the United States was a member in good and regular standing of the Ohio Gang.

★

XVIII. Borrowed Glory

Two men whose literary adroitness had helped Harding to juggle and shift his pronouncements on foreign policy during the Front Porch campaign received their reward in ambassadorships. Accredited to Italy, Richard Washburn Child made a good record. But Colonel George B. M. Harvey, as our representative at the Court of St. James, went wrong.

He was his own selection for the post. Quitting the Democratic Party because President Wilson had denied him this particular plum, he had kept his eye steadfastly fixed upon it, preferring it to the portfolio of State which the grateful Harding had offered to him. Bumptious, unstable, sensational, and loose of tongue, the ex-editor, as the most authoritative mouthpiece of our European policies, was the wrong man in the wrong place at the wrong time. Commenting in the Senate upon his appointment, Pat Harrison said:[1]

> His whole life has been one of inconsistency and vacillation. He never remained true to any purpose, loyal to any friend, or steadfast to any conviction. He is wedded to no principle and bound to no conscience.

There was need of a high standard of judgment and discretion on the part of our spokesman in London. Europe was

[1] April 10, 1921.

anxiously awaiting our co-operation in the effort to find some formula for permanent peace. We had done nothing about the League of Nations except to make it a furious campaign issue. Nor had anything further been heard from Mr. Harding about his tentatively projected World Association. We had not even disposed of the peace treaties. Technically we were still at war with the prostrate Central Powers. England and France wanted to know where we stood.

Colonel Harvey conceived himself to be the man to tell them. The Pilgrims' Dinner in London had become a celebration of goodwill between the two great English-speaking nations, with hands-across-the-sea as its slogan. Ambassador Harvey chose this occasion to explain, with all the impact of his official status, the position and sentiments of the United States for the benefit of the startled Britishers, in what one of his hearers described as 'a spirit of combined supernationalism and subalcoholism.' His country had entered the war, he informed the assemblage, to save not democracy but its own hide.

'We were not too proud to fight, whatever that may mean. We were afraid not to fight. That is the real truth of the matter.'

Even if true, the time, the place, and the emphasis were unfortunate. He warned England against the absurdity of believing that America could be 'beguiled into the League of Nations. . . . A majority of seven million is against it.' [1]

The peculiarly undiplomatic diplomat had weighty precedent for his outbreak. No other than Warren G. Harding had said, two years earlier:

'It is a lie from the beginning that we are in the war for democracy's sake.' [2]

Now his *Marion Star* exulted, 'Colonel Harvey is voicing true Americanism.'

Few Americans agreed. Without respect to party lines,

[1] *Literary Digest*, June 18, 1921.　　[2] *New York Times*, January 22, 1919.

there was a storm of protest across the country. It proved that world problems had been penetrating into the national consciousness. All factions, including the extreme isolationists, could unite on one point, the hope of lifting the burden and threat of increasing armaments. There were formidable obstacles. The virus of international distrust was keeping the nations at fever heat. Harvey's outbreak, coming as it did at a time when the Administration was desirous of building up confidence in this country's goodwill, was a gratuitous contribution to misunderstanding. It served notice on our allies that our aims were one hundred per cent selfish, our interests and acts purely centripetal. The falsity of this view was now to be manifested.

Ill feeling between Japan and the United States had been growing steadily worse. The Yankees of the East, expanding, were threatening encroachment upon the Yankees of the West in their Oriental expansion. Anti-Japanese outbreaks in California were met by bitter attacks from Japanese officials and newspapers. The threats took concrete form in the launching of the mighty *Mutsu*, the most formidable battleship ever built up to that time. To apprehensive minds the prow of the Japanese monster seemed pointed at the Philippines. The islands were vulnerable; indeed, they were indefensible. Source of intermittent trouble and financial drain though they had proved, it was not in the national temperament to stand by and see them gobbled up by alien force.

Hence we had entered upon a naval program to meet the supposed Yellow Peril. This brought England into the race. Traditionally she must keep pace with any competitive advance. Britannia could hardly rule the waves with a navy become obsolescent. She, too, must build. Of such rivalries war is bred. And we had had enough of war.

No rôle was more grateful to Harding than that of peacemaker. On the League of Nations issue he had been vacillant and self-contradictory, consistent only in inconsistency. Notwithstanding his earlier 'rejection' of the League of Nations and his stigmatizing of it as a fraud, he had embodied in the original version of his Inaugural Address a paragraph inferentially committing the United States to eventual entry into it. At least, so Mrs. Harding, brandishing a blue-pencil above the draft submitted to or pre-empted by her, considered. She cut it out.[1]

Falter as he might when confronted by opposition, to the hope of disarmament and international pacification he was still hospitable. Opportunity was presented to him — one might say, forced upon him — to forward the cause. Chroniclers of the day apportion the credit for the Disarmament Conference between the President and his Secretary of State. The prime mover was neither of them; it was Senator William Edgar Borah of Idaho.

Through his long service on the Foreign Relations Committee Borah was thoroughly informed on world conditions. He believed that the time to call a halt was before it should be too late. He had introduced a naval limitation resolution in December, 1920, and brought it up again in January, 1921, in the form of a six months' suspension on naval construction. Elihu Root, sympathizing with the purpose of the movement, advised delay until after Harding's inauguration. To this Borah objected and pressed forward to his end by offering an amendment to the Naval Appropriations Bill. For some reason, difficult to interpret on any ground other than that he wished the credit for himself, Harding used his influence with the Senate Committee on Naval Affairs, and the amendment was quietly squelched.[2] But not for long. In a sudden change of spirit the Senate unanimously accepted the proviso three days before inauguration and called upon the President to convoke an international conference.

[1] Harry M. Daugherty: *The Inside Story of the Harding Tragedy.*
[2] *New York Times*, May 4, 1921.

Had Harding, upon assuming the duties of office, been willing to come out in open opposition after the Senate reversal, he might still have succeeded in his tactic of obstruction. That far he would not go. And the Naval Affairs committeemen, who had acted to kill the Borah plan at first, would not now move without him. Senator Poindexter, a member of the committee, on returning to the Capitol after having been summoned to the White House, said to his friends that he would not take the responsibility of opposing the resolution unless the President would publicly avow that he did not desire its passage.[1]

Borah's biographer, Claudius O. Johnson,[2] believes that the Senate's shift is to be explained by a belief that the House would reject the plan. If so, it was singularly misplaced confidence; the House passed it with only four dissenting votes.

Impotent to check or divert the movement, Harding shrewdly capitalized on it. In essence the measure was bound to appeal to his concern for the future, his hatred of war, his rooted creed of conciliation and adjustment. As in ward politics so in world affairs he believed in getting together — in talking it over — in exchange of views, concessions, allowances — in compromises upon non-essentials to the end of achieving the essential — in the friendly, flexible, productive merging of minds for the common good. Here we see him revert to that early recipe for getting things done which had made him so valuable a legislative influence in the Ohio days. He would now put it at the service, not of the party, but of the world.

He was ready to go even farther. Why not expand the scheme of pacification, while they were about it, to include armies as well as navies? Borah agreed. Secretary of State Hughes was called in. He gave his unqualified endorsement of the project, and applied to it those solid intellectual qualities of synthesis for which he was becoming famous. Thus

[1] Letter from Senator Borah to the writer.   [2] *Borah of Idaho*.

was born the Washington Conference for the Limitation of Armament.

England, France, Japan, and Italy were invited to participate; also several of the lesser powers. The date was November 12, 1921. The nations sent their greatest; Balfour for England, Briand for France, Tokugawa for Japan, Schanzer for Italy. They were matched in character and intellectual power by the Americans, Hughes and Elihu Root; not quite matched by the remainder of the quartette, Lodge and Oscar Underwood. Borah was not asked to serve. To the meeting came such a congeries of military, naval, and political experts and foreign and domestic stars of journalism as had never before gathered. The ceremonies were opened by the President of the United States in a brief speech of welcome which both moved and exalted that experience-hardened congress. On the previous day he had spoken at the ceremonies for the 'Unknown Soldier' at Arlington. Now he said:

> Here in the United States we are but freshly turned from the burial of an unknown American soldier, when a nation sorrowed while paying him tribute. Whether it was spoken or not, a hundred millions of our people were summarizing the inexcusable causes, the incalculable cost, the unspeakable sacrifices, and the unutterable sorrows; and there was the ever-impelling question, How can humanity justify or God forgive? Human hate demands no such toll; ambition and greed must be denied it. If misunderstanding must take the blame, then let us banish it.[1]

The modesty, the serenity, the profound sincerity of the speaker, struck out a spontaneous response. Unemotional as was Charles Evans Hughes, his eyes glowed as he grasped his chief's hand. Briand, Balfour, Viviani, and others pressed

[1] Comparison between the simplicity and beauty of this speech and the turgid rhetoric of the Inaugural Address bears out Doctor Alderfer's theory that the President no longer composed his own official matter. Oswald Garrison Villard (*Fighting Years*) says of Harding's Unknown Soldier eulogy: 'He read admirably the able speech prepared for him.'

forward with eager felicitations. Onlookers gained the impression, as Harding made his way through the fervent crowd, that he was more than surprised; that he was abashed. Artifice of the hustings spellbinder to stir casual audiences had always been at his command. In Washington it had been sadly different; as orator he had signally flunked the applause of listening senates, which, if they listened at all, did so out of negligent good nature. Unexpectedly, startlingly, he now won for himself recognition of diplomacy's ablest and most critical minds by the exercise of an emotional simplicity on a level far above any diplomatic tactic. At that moment Harding reached the shining apogee of his career. He became a world figure. In foreign eyes he diminished from that stature little, if at all, to the day of his death.

The Conference was thus started in a glow. After so propitious an opening it seemed that acerbities might be quelled, rivalries mitigated, and the spirit of goodwill and conciliation mark the sequel. It was a brief dream. Thunder was brewing on the left where sat Secretary Hughes.

Diplomatic intentions almost invariably seep out to the knowledge of those attentive observers and analysts whose business it is to know what is in process before it happens. This instance was an exception. Nobody knew what was coming except a very few taciturn insiders, bound to secrecy. Mr. Hughes could be, at need, the most secretive of officials. Mark Sullivan likens the proposal with which he astounded his listeners to a 'lightning stroke flashing cleanly through an atmosphere of murk.'[1] With Jacksonian curtness, the American Secretary of State informed his listeners that the way to reduce is to reduce. A simple and (to most of those present) disruptive plan was presented for the consideration of the assemblage; that the great navies of the world be 'frozen' into immobility at the ratio then extant; that construction of all warcraft be abandoned; and, pushing to an unheard-of

[1] *Our Times*, vol. VI.

extreme of radicalism, that some ships already afloat be junked. Colonel Repington, the British military expert, who was present officially, felicitously worded the dawning impression when he remarked:

'Secretary Hughes sunk in thirty-five minutes more ships than all the admirals of the world have sunk in a cycle of centuries.'[1]

Indeed, so destructive a proposal in the interest of constructive peace had never before been heard across a council table.

Immediately upon conclusion of the speech, a motion to adjourn over the week-end was proposed and carried. It was, of course, a trick, shrewdly matured in advance by the Americans who had set the stage, to forestall immediate trouble. Instinctive reaction from, let us say, Admiral Lord Beatty, head of the British Navy who, hunched forward in his chair, bristling and flushed under the horrid shock of such heresy ('it is proposed that Great Britain shall stop further construction of the four new *Hoods*' were the calm-voiced words which fell upon his scandalized ears) might have precipitated such a wrangle as to empoison all further proceedings. The over-Sunday recess would afford time for mental digestion and nerve recuperation.

Boiled down, the plan called for a maintenance of the 5–5–3 ratio of warships for the leading naval powers, England and this country being about on a parity, with Japan having three-fifths their rating. The allowance to France and Italy alike was about half that of Japan. There were also restrictions upon the maximum tonnage of ships and the weight of ordnance. Fifteen years was the life of the treaty. As a corollary there was offered the Four Power Treaty whereby the United States, England, Japan, and France were to respect all extant national rights of the signatories in the Pacific, this to run for ten years. The enormous advantage

[1] *Our Times*, vol. vi.

of this to the United States (and also to England, though this was not emphasized) was that it automatically terminated the Anglo-Japanese Alliance which would have aligned England, at least theoretically, on the side of the Asiatics in case of war with this country.

Almost without exception the newspapers of civilization, through the pens of the distinguished and often authoritative correspondents assigned to the Conference, rallied to the Hughes-Harding-Borah cause. Thus an immense and promising public opinion, even a public demand, was linked into a prospective chain of peace around the world.

Whittling and boring began at once and continued throughout the twelve weeks of Conference deliberation. The French were the offenders. France, still fevered and abnormal from the dreadful wounds of the war, translated her sufferings of the past into fears for the future. She wished, in fact she all but demanded, an undertaking on the part of this nation and Great Britain that they would come to her aid with military force in case of future German aggression. When this proposal, obviously impracticable as regards the United States, was rejected, France went into a fit of international sulks from which she had not emerged at the close of the congress. She blocked President Harding's hopeful scheme for reduction of land armaments. She refused to accept a genuine and useful limitation upon submarine warfare, out of a spirit, as it seemed to some critics, of sheer perversity, since she had always been inferior in this branch of navigation. Peering now, with taut nerves, beneath the troubled surface of 'Mare Nostrum,' she has cause for bitter repentance of her obstinacy and intransigeance.

Notwithstanding all efforts at emasculation, the adjournment of the Conference left a world, avid of peace, with the comfort of newborn hope, unhappily set too high. Mark Sullivan could write with happy conviction: 'Naval competition was ended, a naval holiday was ordained, and offensive naval warfare was made impossible.'[1]

Many other wise and informed commentators, the world over, held that roseate view. They could not see into a future wherein every ocean was to bristle with threat and the nations of the globe move forward toward bankruptcy to the anvil chorus of the shipyards, beating out the rhythm of menace.

At the worst, the Borah-Harding-Hughes plan gave to humanity a breathing spell of hope, and new, if not lasting, security.

'Less of armament and none of war,' said the President of the United States.

Not until two weeks after his death were the final treaties ratified by the Senate.

Borah, the originator of the Conference, is the forgotten man. The father of the plan was not invited to take part in the christening ceremonies.

[1] *World's Work*, March, 1922.

★

XIX. Creaking Mechanism

WHEN depressed, President Harding was accustomed to seek diversion in the companionship of Charles R. Forbes. The robustious humor and fluent spirits of the 'court jester to the Best Minds' was a reliable restorative. Forbes was shocked, on a winter evening, at his friend's melancholy. It was after one of the poker dinners.

'I went with the President to the rear lawn of the White House,' he reports, 'and he cried.' [1]

Becoming confidential, the President dissolved in self-commiseration. He expatiated on how unhappy he was, how empty his life had been. Nan Britton would have her readers believe that, at this period, her lover was pining because he could not get free and marry her. But this lacks substantiation either in corroborative testimony or in any evidence of a matrimonial attitude of mind on his part.

On his first Christmas Day in the Presidency, Harding sent a message through his favorite sister, Mrs. Votaw, to Forbes.

'Come over,' she telephoned, 'Wernie wants to see you.' She always called her brother 'Wernie.'

Forbes found his crony in the dumps. 'This is a hell of a Christmas' was his greeting.

---

[1] *New York World*, December 4, 1927.

'What's the matter?'

'Everything's the matter.'

Outside, the caller met Surgeon General Sawyer. 'My God! They had a hell of a row this morning,' whispered the little doctor.[1] Forbes did not need to ask who was meant by 'they.'

If one could believe Gaston B. Means, an excess of credulousness against which precaution is always advisable, it was about this time that he was employed by Mrs. Harding to investigate Nan Britton.[2] This would seem to dovetail in with the climax of domestic relations mentioned by Doctor Sawyer. Lesser crises were frequent.

'She [Mrs. Harding] was at all times jealous and at most times suspicious of Harding,' a family friend told Mark Sullivan.[3]

Some part of the growing acrimony which Mrs. Harding exhibited toward her husband, and sometimes toward others, may be attributed to her semi-invalidism. Against this she struggled valiantly. Not only was she scrupulous in all social obligations, but her sense of duty transcended official requirements. One of her self-allotted tasks was to visit the disabled veterans at the Walter Reed Hospital, taking them flowers from the White House gardens. It was an event in hospital life when she came; the men were devoted to her. Here she was her kindly and matriarchal self as she had been to her newsboys in the struggling days of the *Star*. When, on the special occasion of the Veterans' Garden Party, she found a new costume laid out for her, she rejected it.

'I'll just wear this old hat instead of my new one,' she decided, 'because the boys are accustomed to it and, as soon as they see it, they know where I am.'

---

[1] *New York World*, December 4, 1927.
[2] Gaston B. Means: *The Strange Death of President Harding*.
[3] *Our Times*, vol. VI.
[4] Mary Randolph: *Presidents and First Ladies*.

Forbes gathered that all the presidential troubles were not home-made. There was grief in the business of being Chief Executive. Things were going on that he did not like, Mr. Harding signified, but he was impotent to stop them. Echoes of revelry from the Little Green House on K Street may have begun to reach his ears. Certainly criticism of many of his official acts must have come to him. More than once, as he measured his inadequacy against the increasing complications of his position, he may well have sighed for the ease and freedom of the golden Senate days. There were few unavoidable responsibilities in that halcyon phase of his existence.

Dark though his own Christmas was, he had lightened the day for another public man who was his antithesis in every political and social concept, and his like only in that both possessed a gentle spirit. Eugene V. Debs, leader of the Socialist Party, was serving a ten-year term in Atlanta Penitentiary for obstructing the conduct of the war. Technically, his conviction was in order. If now it smacks of medieval brutality, we must remember that to suppress the right of the individual to speak as conscience dictates seemed, at the time, to be an essential concomitant to maintenance of the winning spirit. The United States Supreme Court had upheld the sentence.

Debs's record in jail was more than exemplary. By sheer force, depth, and sweetness of character he became a prison angel. 'Everyone wanted him to get out and everyone hated the thought of his leaving' is the testimonial of a prison official. By common agreement his influence was the most salutary and mollifying ever known within those walls.

Legally correct the Socialist's sentence might be; to Harding's sensitive humanity it was a rankling injustice, an undeserved martyrdom. This without his ever having come within the radius of the man's extraordinary personality. He talked it over with Harry Daugherty.

After studying the data, the Attorney General sent for the convict to come, without guard, to Washington. They met in his office. Debs recanted nothing, expressed no contrition. He spoke with frankness and courage and Daugherty listened and questioned. Between the practical politician and the evangelistic radical there was little in common except sincerity and courage. Yet Daugherty held him there while other matters of more political importance waited; sent out for luncheon for him — a little fruit was all the guest wanted — and resumed the conversation afterward. Debs returned to prison without any promise. But the hardboiled Daugherty was convinced. He knew a man when he saw one.

His recommendation was that Debs had sufficiently expiated his offence and that his sentence be commuted to expire with the year. President Harding improved on the suggestion, and released the prisoner in time for him to spend Christmas with his wife.

Sensitiveness was never a weakness of Harry M. Daugherty. To criticism and abuse alike he turned a pachydermatous hide. But when his relentless foe, the *New York World*, jeered at his action as a grandstand play, he was for once sore and hurt. The slur was unjust. No one can read the passage in Daugherty's book about his interview with Debs and deny its spontaneous honesty. The saintliness, the lambent spirituality of the convict both impressed and moved a man who made no claim to being either saintly or spiritual.

Harding had, of course, acted in accordance with his natural kindliness. Where human suffering was in question, he could always be trusted to run true to his best form. In concrete presentment, where no imagination was called for, he would instantly discern and revolt from injustice. A deputation, led by Norman Thomas, Oswald Garrison Villard, Paul Kellogg, and Robert Morss Lovett, calling on him to urge leniency for conscientious objectors, was received sympathetically and as regards Thomas, former employee of the *Marion Star*, with unaffected warmth.[1] When Villard congratulated the President on his clemency to a group of unhappy pro-Germans who had received sentences of thirty-five and forty years for nothing more criminal or subversive than 'shooting off their mouths' in dispraise of this country's participation in the war:

'Why, you know, I couldn't do anything else,' said the President. 'Those fellows didn't mean any harm. It was a cruel punishment.'[2]

Government, in Harding's view, was essentially a personal function. He saw it, not as a formula, but as a mechanism. His mind, unequipped to cope with the abstract, turned instinctively to the factual. Men were concrete entities. He believed that he understood men. His theory was that you gathered about you, in order to carry on the processes of administration, your friends or those whom your friends recommended, and depended upon their good faith to carry out your policies.

Himself loyal to excess, Harding leaned upon the loyalty of others with dangerous credulity. In this faith he had completed the first year of his Administration without damaging disillusionment. Difficulties had risen in his path, but they were such as are inherent in any complicated political situation. He still commanded that easy popularity which was to him the *summum bonum* of existence. But certain symptoms began to cause him a degree of worry.

Congress and President were not working smoothly together as 1922 dawned. Party leadership was wavering. The two Pennsylvanians whom Harry Daugherty deemed the Titans of the Senate, Penrose and Knox, were dead, the former leaving as monument and memorial to his political methods that strong box with its mysterious fund in thou-

[1] Oswald Garrison Villard: *Fighting Years*.
[2] Statement of Paul Kellogg to the writer.

sand- and ten-thousand-dollar bills. Aggressiveness and purpose in the Senate were now taken over by the insurgent bloc under command of La Follette of Wisconsin. Between it and the titular head of the party there was little community of interest or understanding. Its power was chiefly obstructive; it could not achieve much in the way of positive legislation, but it could and did hamper Old Guard programs.

The House was divided and without strong command. A powerful Executive could have turned these conditions to his own profit and purpose. Harding had neither the will nor the vision. His confidence in the competence of the Best Minds to find ultimate solutions was unimpaired. But, to the awakening nation 'the Best Minds, Inc.' was beginning to be a sorry jape. Perceiving the danger, the leaders hoped to spur the President to unite the party by asserting authority. Doctor Alderfer writes:[1]

> They appealed to him to take a firm hold and assert his control. He was reluctant to do this on account of his promise to refrain from administrative usurpation of legislative functions. The manner most commonly suggested was a public appeal to Congress to enact legislation which the Administration endorsed. It was believed by the leaders that the President was more popular than the party in Congress and that it was possible for him to assert leadership in a fashion that would arouse the enthusiasm of the country and force the recalcitrant legislature to action. He made several attempts to accomplish this result. . . . He wrote letters to congressional committees to influence their activities. But letter-writing did not grip the public or scare the Congressmen. Something more spectacular was needed. It was necessary to emulate Roosevelt or Wilson. He conferred with leaders in Congress in the hope that sweet reasonableness and a benediction of understanding would make the initiative, direction, energy, and driving power of White House control unnecessary.

[1] *The Personality and Politics of Warren G. Harding.*

In what appears at this distance to have been an inspiration of petty spite over Executive inaction, the legislators passed two bills which, of minor importance in themselves, were indicative of intent to whittle down presidential authority or possibly to test presidential mettle. One of these was an instruction, in fact a command, that Harding should appoint a dirt farmer to the Federal Reserve Board. The second, even more impertinent, directed him to refund the foreign debts. This is a treaty process and, as such, is delegated by the Constitution to the authority of the President. Following his bent for avoiding trouble, Harding yielded without a fight in both instances. In the minds of his disappointed friends it was an exhibition of misplaced meekness.

Nevertheless, he continued to try. That plan for an association of nations which he had tentatively put forth a month after his inauguration and which had been assailed as 'a toothless whatnot, a miserable makeshift,' by the *New York World*, was now brought forward in another guise. As part of its mechanism, the League of Nations had organized a Permanent Court of International Justice (known to Americans as the World Court) in which it was hoped that the United States would join. Entrance into the League was not a requisite; there was no apparent reason for our remaining outside. The President transmitted to the Senate a recommendation that we accept membership. Up rose the isolationists, the irreconcilables, the bitter-enders. All the old shibboleths were resurrected. Let America mind America's business and the rest of the world go to hell and destruction in its own way. Why should we be betrayed into fighting Europe's battles? Besides, what about those war debts?

Never decisive, always underinformed on international relations, Harding had approached the question of participation with diffidence; he now retreated from it in panic. The big voices of the 'Battalion of Death' had intimidated him. James Truslow Adams said bitterly:

> Faced by the responsibilities of a moral leadership in the world such as had never before come to any nation, America backed out of the room, frightened and stammering.[1]

Upon one sorely contentious and politically perilous measure Congress found him rock-firm. His stand against the Soldiers' Bonus was consistent and courageous. After a brief and futile trial of the 'arm-around-their-shoulder' persuasiveness, he announced his opposition to any bonus bill which did not definitely provide for revenue to meet it through new taxation. Pleas and threats failed to move him. If the bill passed, he would veto it. Congress hinted at refusal of army and navy appropriations. Too sound a poker player not to recognize a bluff on sight, the President stood pat. Both houses passed the bill by large majorities. Harding vetoed it and treated them to a notably direct and vigorous message.[2]

> Congress fails, first of all, to provide the revenue from which the bestowal is to be paid. . . . To add one-sixth of the total sum of our public debt for a distribution among less than 5,000,000 out of 110,000,000, whether inspired by grateful sentiment or political expediency, would undermine the confidence on which our credit is builded and establish the precedent of distributing public funds whenever the proposals and the numbers affected make it seem politically appealing to do so.

Thereupon the House Democrats, seizing upon the opportunity for pettifogging politics, ganged up with the recalcitrants of Harding's own party to override the veto. But the Senate, where the original bill had carried, 47 to 22, narrowly sustained him, thereby accomplishing a saving — unhappily only temporary — of between four and five billion dollars.

[1] *Epic of America.*   [2] September 19, 1922.

All was not peace in the Cabinet. Rumors of impending resignations, involving five portfolios, kept cropping out in print. The most persistent one related to the Secretary of the Interior. It met with prompt and authoritative denial.

'Like every other politician, I am going to hang on to my job,' Mr. Fall blithely informed the newspapermen.[1]

He had good reason to. The job was already promising handsome returns, though his grafting enterprises had not yet come to a head. Nevertheless, there was a Senate request for information regarding certain leases of Government oil lands.[2]

He met it with consummate *sang-froid*. Yes; he had leased the Teapot Dome reserves to private interests. What was more, he was about to make a like disposition of the Elk Hills oil. No; there had been no competitive bidding. As explanation of this unusual and probably illegal procedure, he hinted at issues of great and dangerous moment, meaning a quite possible war with Japan, and intimated that he knew better than his interrogators what he was doing: their proper course was to keep their hands off. He got away with it.

Within the Cabinet, also, he was making trouble. The State Department found it necessary to snub him for attempted interference in Mexican affairs. Tentative encroachments upon the national holdings in Alaska, suspected to be in the interests of timbergrabbers, brought on such a fierce attack from the conservationists in the Department of Agriculture that he appealed to Harding to protect him from them.[3]

He could better have been spared from the Cabinet than the member who did resign. The appointment of Postmaster General Will Hays had been received with general disapproval. It was regarded as a purely political move. So it was. But it turned out well.

[1] *New York Times*, February 11, 1922.
[2] April 21, 1922.   [3] *New York Times*, March 12, 1922.

In the face of the presidential 'spoils' order removing Civil Service restrictions from thirteen thousand postmasterships, Hays announced that efficiency and not party service would be the yardstick of his department. His avowed purpose was to 'humanize' the postal service. Labor was no longer to be regarded as a commodity, nor the employee as a piece of mechanism. Any postal worker, no matter how unimportant, could get a hearing from him. The result, unpleasing to the politicos, restored a morale that had been slipping and standards of efficiency that had been deteriorating. He astonished his critics among the liberals by restoring to mailing privileges a Socialist publication which had been banned by the Democratic Administration. The American Federation of Labor endorsed his administration for its enlightened attitude. The National Civic Reform League praised him for his stand against the spoils system.[1]

With unlimited opportunities to profit by his long service in the Republican high officialdom, Hays had remained a comparatively poor man. Much money, some of it dubious, had passed through his hands. None of it stuck. Now the motion-picture industry offered him $150,000 per year to become its 'czar,' a position he still holds. He could not afford to refuse. So the Administration and the country lost one of its most useful officials. With his departure the spoils system returned.

As it swung into action, Senator Pat Harrison offered a resolution calling upon the President to furnish a list of the executive orders through which he had set aside Civil Service regulations for the purpose of manipulating appointments. It came to nothing officially, but it helped direct attention to a scandalous abuse of power on the part of one of Harding's peculiarly unfit appointees, Assistant Secretary of the Treasury Elmer Dover of Ohio.

Dover possessed no qualifications for his important place.

[1] *New York Times*, November 17, 1921.

The Republican National Committee disapproved his selection; it had basis for judgment, since he had served it as secretary. He was *persona non grata* to his chief, Secretary Mellon, who got rid of him as soon as it was decently possible but not until after the damage was done.

Following the statement of Postmaster General Hays that he intended to humanize his department, Dover derisively boasted that he was going to Hardingize his. His idea of Hardingization was peremptorily to discharge Director James L. Wilmeth, after twenty-four years of devoted and distinguished service to the Bureau, and with him twenty-seven other executives, 'for the good of the service'; i.e., for the sake of the spoils. To make it worse, the action was coupled with unfounded insinuations of falsification in an issue of government bonds. Because of the character and record of the men thus impugned, there was immediate and widespread resentment. Partial amends were made later by the restoration of the ousted executives to Civil Service standing, but the effect upon the morale of the Administration, already weakened, was shattering. Once more the corrupting effect of the Ohio type of appointment was exemplified.

Brother-in-law Votaw was another sad example of misplaced confidence in a personal appointee. Atlanta Penitentiary, for which, as Superintendent of Federal Prisons, the ex-missionary was responsible, had long been infested by a dope-peddling ring. When J. E. Dyche was appointed warden, he found in operation among the convicts an extensive traffic in narcotics, which was making addicts of the new prisoners as they came in. Proceeding to root this out, he forced the resignation of two guards, had two others indicted, and obtained a confession of complicity from the assistant prison physician, himself a prisoner on parole when appointed to the office.

Effectually to control the trade, however, it was necessary

to track down and shut off the sources of supply from without. He appealed to the Department of Justice, and for a time secured their co-operation; but after the indictments, they slackened up. The warden found his efforts blocked. For a year he had been hammering at the Reverend Votaw, who was anxious that there should be no undesirable publicity. Finally, when it became a matter of running down the outside drug ring, the superintendent proved actually obstructive. Director Burns of the F.B.I. testified that his men were ready to go ahead, but were hampered by Votaw. Orders went out that there should be no further action until the indicted men were brought to trial, which, as matters were then proceeding in some phases of Department of Justice action, might mean long delay. Warden Dyche protested to the superintendent. The result was that he lost his job.

'I was perfectly amazed,' said the warden. 'Mr. Votaw was a minister of the gospel; he was a brother-in-law of the President . . . if there was anybody that ought to want to see that institution cleared up it was Mr. Votaw, and when he took the position he did about stopping the investigation, I was dumbfounded.'[1]

Hints of the evil conditions somehow reached President Harding. Possibly the warden had found a way. Casting about for a man whom he could trust, Harding hit upon Charles R. Forbes. He asked Forbes to go quietly to Atlanta and report privately to him. The report remained private. That it reflected upon the Department of Justice as well as the Superintendent of Prisons is apparent from Attorney General Daugherty's wrath. He informed Forbes that conditions in Atlanta were none of his, Forbes's, damned business.[2]

As Director of the Veterans' Bureau, Forbes himself came

[1] *Investigation of the Attorney General.*
[2] *New York World*, December 4, 1927.

in for criticisms by the powerful veterans' organizations, which were growing suspicious. Congressmen, with reports of neglect and maladministration and hints of worse things, visited the White House. They wanted both Forbes and Surgeon General Sawyer, his second-in-command, supplanted, though the latter was not included in the suspicions of graft. The two officials had quarrelled and were indulging in mutual recriminations. To all reflections upon either Mr. Harding turned a deaf ear. Nothing could persuade him that the head of the Bureau was not filling a difficult and complicated post with brilliant success. As for Doctor Sawyer, the President had known him all his life. No Congressman could tell *him* anything about the old Doc! Visitors who took this line found President Harding surprisingly captious and impatient.

Labor was becoming suspicious of the President. Despite his unimpeachable record as a fair employer — more than fair, indeed; kindly, generous, and progressive — the unions believed him unfriendly in principle. This was not without justification. His sympathies were naturally with capital. When he tentatively proposed regulation of trades unions, he was hotly denounced as inspiring 'propaganda for industrial feudalism.' [1] The Brotherhood of Locomotive Engineers declared him 'an enemy to organized labor.' [2]

Industrial unrest increased. A coal strike was called which lingered on through the hot weather with outbreaks of violence, and ended in a practical victory for the strikers, due largely to the stupidity and arrogance of the mine operators. (Harding was no partisan of theirs in this instance.) The railroad strike, called on July 1, was more serious.

The issue was a wage cut of $60,000,000, ordered by the Railroad Labor Board as a step toward liquidating the exorbitant and ruinous scale of war standards. Four hundred thousand railroad shopmen walked out. Disorders, acci-

[1] *New York Times*, June 20, 1922.　　[2] *Ibid.*, June 5, 1922.

dents, general dislocation of schedules, due in part to sabotage, followed. After several weeks of danger and discomfort to the public and after a warning proclamation had been issued by the President, Attorney General Harry M. Daugherty appeared before United States District Judge James H. Wilkerson in Chicago, and applied for an injunction. He accused the labor unions of seventeen thousand crimes and, from the tone of his self-appreciation in a later recital of the event, was doubtless, like Warren Hastings, astonished at his own moderation.

Judge Wilkerson was one of the judges appointed on recommendation of Daugherty.[1] The injunction issued from his court is a model of its kind. Hitler or Mussolini might be proud to claim its authorship. It forbade, among other activities on the part of the strikers, any 'display of numbers or force, jeers, entreaties, arguments, persuasions, rewards,' for the purpose of influencing workmen. Union officials might not issue any strike directions, employ any funds or speak any words designed to prevent a strike-breaker from substituting for a striker. Picketing was tabooed. The strikers, however, were, as a contemporary commentator observed, still permitted to eat, sleep, and breathe.[2]

After a petition to restrain local officials from enforcing the injunction was denied in the District of Columbia court, the strike petered out. Had other courts generally followed the Wilkerson pattern in labor disputes, strikes would now be permanently outlawed and organized labor rendered impotent.

The seventeen thousand criminals discovered by the Attorney General are still at large, if alive, since, by some oversight, they were never prosecuted.

That victory haunted Mr. Daugherty; not his conscience, certainly, for he acted in the full conviction of righteousness,

---

[1] Harry M. Daugherty: *The Inside Story of the Harding Tragedy.*

[2] The injunction was issued September 21, 1922.

but his memory. Invited to address a meeting made up largely of labor men at Canton, Ohio, he turned sick and giddy while speaking. Before him stood a large bouquet of flowers. Recovering himself, he concluded his address, which was well received — American audiences, however prejudiced, respect and admire courage — but in afterthought was convinced that the floral offering concealed 'a deadly gas trap.'[1] The Reds were after him!

They continued their persecutions. Incited by labor groups, Representative Oscar E. Keller of Minnesota, an absurd creature who might have been imagined by Gilbert and set to music by Sullivan, brought impeachment proceedings against the Attorney General. The Judiciary Committee, to whom his resolution was referred, asked for specifications. After faltering, evading, and actually and physically attempting to run away, Congressman Keller brought in fourteen points so tenuous and vague that the committee by a vote of 12 to 2 refused to take any action. Nevertheless, the attack disturbed Mr. Daugherty. He attributed it to those vengeful Reds. As to any and all charges, he countered with the assurance that 'at the proper time' all would be explained. It never was. More definite subsequent accusations he repelled with the characterization:

'Red Senatorial gas bags poured poison fumes into the air until an honest man could scarcely breathe.'[2]

His conviction that he was being hounded expanded to cover all schools of political thought. Those who opposed him were creatures of the Soviets and dynamiters. Then he turned around and accused Big Business of persecuting him because he was on the trail of frauds, a feat of imagination notable even in so lissome a contortionist as Mr. Daugherty. Arthur Brisbane and the Hearst newspapers supported him in his belief.

One count in the abortive Keller charges, that of 'deliber-

[1] Harry M. Daugherty: *The Inside Story of the Harding Tragedy.*   [2] *Ibid.*

ately conniving at the looting' of the naval oil reserves, fore-shadowed the Teapot Dome scandal which was indelibly to smirch the Harding régime.

Organized labor never forgave Harding for the Daugherty-Wilkerson injunctions. The most conspicuous of the Ohio appointees, Daugherty, never an asset to the Administration, became a detriment.

To offset the hostility engendered by his Attorney General's radical anti-labor stand, which he had tacitly supported, Harding now undertook a step in behalf of the workers in the most reactionary of industries. The United States Steel Corporation, as leader of and pattern for the industry, had long been a target of labor leaders, reformers, progressive economists, and soapbox agitators alike, because of its seven-day week and twelve-hour day rising to a twenty-four-hour day once a fortnight. Its president, Judge Elbert H. Gary, a lawyer turned steelman, was an industrial feud-alist of the extreme type. He had rejected a request of the American Federation of Labor, backed by President Wilson, for a conference to consider the working schedule. Pressure brought to bear by the Survey Associates [1] from without and by Stockholder Charles M. Cabot and Vice-President William B. Dickson (who, as a former mill worker, knew about labor conditions) from within, had eliminated the seven-day week. Nothing was done about the long day. Glibly Judge Gary declared, 'The twelve-hour day must go. The public demands it.' [2] It was lip-service only; the twelve-hour day would go when the industry was forced to abandon it, not before.

Thinking to employ his well-tried methods of conciliation and adjustment, Harding wrote to Gary to 'tender any prudent assistance.' It was not within his conception of the properties to inspire or even suggest legislation correcting

[1] *Survey Graphic*, January, 1938.

[2] Ida M. Tarbell: *Life of Elbert H. Gary*.

the abuses. That would be an unwarranted invasion of business rights. But perhaps if he could persuade the magnates to talk it over across a friendly table, something might be accomplished. Invitations were sent out to some fifty members of the American Iron and Steel Institute for a White House dinner of consultation and discussion.

There was astonishment and distrust from Pittsburgh to Gary, Indiana, wherever furnaces flamed. What was this man, Harding, doing? the invitees asked themselves. Did he think he was another T. R.? Was he trying to brandish the Big Stick above the head of Steel as Roosevelt had over that of Coal? What had they helped to elect him for? Not this sort of thing certainly.

Judge Gary could have assuaged their alarms. He knew Harding. It was to the ex-corporation lawyer and present steelman that the Ohio Senator had applied when he wanted a job for Nan Britton which would keep her at a safe distance from Washington. The Judge had obliged.[1] He understood the President too well to apprehend any serious trouble from him.

Rounded up by him, forty-one captains of the industry attended the love-feast. A statement was given out, cautiously admitting the desirability of abolishing the twelve-hour day, 'if and when practicable.' A special committee was duly appointed to consider the question. The committee thus duly appointed duly reported that no change was practicable. It had been all a gesture. Judge Gary continued to make gestures of his own; he was determined, for publication, to do something about it 'at the earliest time practical,' but he felt bound to point out that this would 'involve many adjustments.' In the language of the day, the steelmen were giving Harding the runaround.

Nevertheless, something had been accomplished. Public attention was again focused upon the sorest spot in American

[1] Nan Britton: *The President's Daughter.*

industrialism. Paul Kellogg, of the *Survey*, gives President Harding credit for putting his foot in the door at a time when it seemed likely to be definitely closed against reform.[1] Even the most autocratic of industries is in some degree susceptible to public opinion. Theodore Roosevelt and Woodrow Wilson had proved that. For the time, Harding accepted his defeat. But he was not through with Steel.

An intimately personal angle to a vexed political problem now added its complications. Prohibition was much on the President's mind. It was much on everyone's mind. The nation had sulked itself into a state of tacit rebellion against the obnoxious Volstead Law and the still more obnoxious oppressions of the enforcement agents. The scofflaws were justifying that not too felicitous appellation by reducing the law to a mockery. The example set by the White House was emulated in all ranks of society.

Home brewing took rank as a major industry. Bathtub gin bade fair to become the national beverage. Night-clubs flourished in every city; blind tigers throughout the country-side. Bootleggers piled up millions. Gangsters rose to power in municipal politics. Hijackers infested the motor roads. Police and public officials developed new and richer sources of graft. Corruption and law-breaking were stimulated to their highest development; the nation's morals reached their lowest. A joke became standardized for any locality.

> *Stranger* — Officer, where can I get a drink?
>
> *Cop* — Any door in this block but the place next the corner. That's a church.

Prohibition advocates urged the President to set an example through a personal announcement. It was an awkward dilemma for a man like Harding. Slack of habit, loose of standards though he was, he maintained an uneasy if not always effective sense of the dignity of his high office. How

[1] *Survey Graphic*, January, 1938. This issue gives an excellent summary of the whole protracted negotiations.

to conform to the responsibilities and properties expected of a President without uncomfortably altering his established way of life was the problem. He was not as patient of personal as he was of political limitations and restrictions. Now, it appeared, he was expected to adjust his habits to the distasteful negations of a law in which he had never believed, although giving it lip-service. The Drys were saying ugly things about White House laxity. They even wanted him to take the pledge!

They were not without reason on their side. In order to secure support for his candidate, Harry Daugherty had made campaign promises to the anti-saloon forces, which had in part been fulfilled by appointments in the law-enforcement departments. Without repudiating these obligations, the President did not take kindly to the extension of them to his private and daily life. The ratification of the understanding as to appointments should have been enough.

It was not enough. The active agent of the Anti-Saloon League was Wayne B. Wheeler, its counsel and evangel. Wheeler was a blend of Savonarola and gadfly. Entrée to the White House was his by virtue of his office and the vote-control of his organization, and he used it to pester the President with urgencies which perhaps no other man in Washington would have ventured. In language blunter than the protected executive ears were habituated to, he kept harping upon the theme that Capital circles were ringing with the gross violations of the Prohibition Act in what should be the citadel of the law. When was the White House going to give up its wild parties?

Vainly did Harding deny that there was any official drinking there. The small store of personal liquor which he admitted to keeping at hand was his own stock which he had a right to own, a dubious interpretation of the law. The ace Prohibitionist argued vehemently that the Chief Magistrate should set a shining example to the citizenry not only by abjuring all alcohol, but also by public affirmation of his abstinence, a thesis which his hearer half-heartedly endorsed without adopting it. Suspicion forces itself upon the mind that he was a little afraid of the crusader. Or perhaps it was his own conscience that intimidated him.

In legalistic distinctions as to drink he still found a subterfuge. On a hot summer night of 1922, Mark Sullivan was summoned to the White House to give his opinion on the coal strike, which was deadlocked. He was received in one of the first-floor rooms. Mr. Harding was in an exasperated mood.

'Those goddam operators are so stiff-necked you can't do anything with them,' he complained, and sought the correspondent's views as to which side public opinion favored.

After some discussion he sighed and said, 'Oh, well! Let's go upstairs and have a drink.'

He led the way to his bedroom. Mrs. Harding came in and highballs were brought. Half apologetically the President explained himself to the visitor.

'We both think that we ought not to drink in the White House. But we feel that our own bedrooms are our house and we can do as we like here.'[1]

A depressing realization was beginning to intrude upon his reluctant consciousness. He discovered that no man, however tactful at fulfilling both functions, can be at one and the same time a good fellow and a good President. This contravened an old and cherished theory. As Ohio legislator and lieutenant governor he had been popular with all factions. In his senatorial personification it had been the same; by virtue of a smiling exterior, the outward and visible sign of an unquenchable inner warmth, he had proved the feasibility of being all things to all men, within the framework of party docility. How different was this job, into which he had been hoisted by the hands of others on his bootstraps! In the White House it did not suffice to be kind, generous, loyal to

[1] The episode was narrated to the writer by Mr. Sullivan.

friends, genial to opponents, a good sport, pliant to the Best Minds, eloquent before a public grown too discriminating to respond to 'bloviation' by their Chief Magistrate. More was expected of him. Inaction, amiable inertia, amenability to suggestion, readiness to do as he was told: these no longer served; they brought about incomprehensible criticism and hostility.

The November elections barbed the point. A sound working majority in both Senate and House was sharply reduced; by seven members in the upper house and sixty-nine in the lower. In both the insurgents made gains. The newspapers interpreted the upset as 'a peremptory warning to the party in power to do better.'

To Harding it was a rude jar. He took the lesson to heart. From now on no major errors are to be counted against him. It was the misdeeds of his trusted friends and subordinates whereby he was to be judged, perhaps overharshly, by an aroused public.

Distrust of himself had always beset and hampered him. Indications develop that he began to suspect some of those upon whom he most depended. It may be that, all along, Harding was shrewder, less blind, more watchful of those who surrounded him with flattery and protestations than has been generally believed. The accepted theory is that he died in blessed ignorance of any betrayal other than that of Forbes, still confident of the loyalty of his friends. The first suggestion of misgivings is cited by Joe Mitchell Chapple, and the time placed as November, 1922. The date is noteworthy, because, so far as other evidence is available, he had as yet no specific reason to mistrust those about him.

'Some day' — so Chapple quotes Harding — 'the people will understand what some of my erstwhile friends have done to me in these critical times when I depended so much upon them.'[1]

[1] *The Life and Times of Warren G. Harding, Our After War President.*

XX. Bibliocide

EARLY in 1922 there appeared and vanished one of the most sensational books in our political history. The Government snuffed it out of existence. It purported to show that the President of the United States was part negro.

Several peculiarities distinguish the volume. It carried no copyright line. No author stood responsible for its form. It was undated. There was not even a price specified. Ostensibly it was published by the Sentinal (*sic*) Press. But the Sentinal Press lacked incorporation or address. The ordinary channels of trade knew nothing of it. Bookstores did not handle its output. Today the work is probably the rarest book issued in twentieth-century America. Yet it does not rank as a 'collector's item.' The rare book trade does not know of its existence.

The opus was an offshoot of Professor William Estabrook Chancellor's political and genealogical activities. After his forced retirement from the College of Wooster, Professor Chancellor lived very privately. With a view to supplementing his earlier volume, *Our Presidents and Their Office*, he had been working on his Harding data, even before election.[1] The addenda to *Our Presidents* never appeared, but the material was not wasted. The suppressed book used it.

[1] *New York Times*, October 30, 1920.

The style of the title-page is as follows:

Warren Gamaliel Harding

President of the United States.

A Review of Facts

Collected from

Anthropological, Historical, and

Political Researches

by

William Estabrook Chancellor

formerly

Professor of Economics, Politics, and Social Sciences

of

Wooster College, Wooster, Ohio.

This book is sold and distributed by agents of

The Sentinal Press.

To casual reading this would seem to identify Professor Chancellor as the author. It does not. He is named only as the source of the material. He disclaims all responsibility for the publication.

> I did not write this book. I did not authorize its publication. .... I do not know who issued the book. I have no copy of it. No one ever paid me a dollar for it, nor did I ever contribute a dollar to its issuance.[1]

If this be true, the Sentinal firm is guilty of forgery as well as piracy. A statement signed in facsimile handwriting which certainly resembles Professor Chancellor's, forms a foreword.

> The Sentinal [*sic*] Press has acquired unreserved legal title to my original papers relating to my investigations into the ancestry and life of President Warren Gamaliel Harding. Such references as may be made to me as the source of information concerning facts therein should be credited as authentic.
> William Estabrook Chancellor

It might be possible for Professor Chancellor to prove that he is not, in the full sense, the author. That is a pure technicality. Not only is he the source of the data, but the style is often strongly similar to his.

Late in 1921 — the date is not certain, but presumptive — Professor Chancellor came to Dayton to see his counsel, Hugh A. Snepp. Mr. Snepp is dead. His brother, the Reverend Samuel Snepp recalls that two strangers negotiated with the lawyer in the matter of the Chancellor data.[2] He thinks that the men were from Cincinnati. There was no Sentinal Press in Cincinnati at that time.[3] There was, however, an enterprise similar in name (Sentinel) operating obscurely in southern Ohio, where it disseminated Ku Klux literature

[1] Letter to the writer.

[2] Statement to the writer.

[3] For research in the matter of the vanished press I am indebted to the courtesy of Miss Mary R. Cochran, of the Public Library of Cincinnati.

and other violent propaganda. Mr. Joseph W. Sharts of Dayton, who knew the Snepps, writes:

> From my vague recollection of what Snepp [Hugh A.] remarked, I should say the Sentinal Press was some printing firm here in Dayton that was keeping under cover.

So successfully did it keep under cover that the identity of the promoter has never been revealed. Suspicion logically arises that publication may have come from the same press which so convulsed the alumni of the College of Wooster with its broadsides in the fall of 1920.

'Warren Gamaliel Harding, President of the United States,' was a 'subscription' book. It was hawked about through those arts of suggestiveness and innuendo known to the lower branches of the trade. The peddlers were of the door-to-door type who handle pornography, illicit drugs, 'rubber goods,' and other surreptitious items. They operated in Cincinnati, Cleveland, Columbus, and Dayton, but not in Marion where their enterprise would have been unpopular if not hazardous.[1] The price appears to have been whatever the traffic would bear.

At the outset political support was sought. Two of the promoters called upon Secretary Greer of the Democratic State Committee in his Dayton office.

> They were tough-looking fellows. Said they were working out of Cincinnati, and their book was a quick mover. I didn't like their looks, and I liked their proposition still less when they put it to me. I was to act as state agent, appoint sub-agents, and rake off a fat commission. I invited them to get out and stay out. From what I heard they found a pretty good market in Dayton.[2]

[1] 'There were fights in the streets of Marion and a Harding supporter beat up a judge on suspicion of his having said that Harding's grandfather was black.' *New York Tribune*, November 1, 1920, reporting the outbreaks against the Chancellor leaflets.

[2] Statement of Mr. Greer to the writer.

Copies appeared in Washington. A former Government official remembers seeing one on the Shoreham Hotel bookstall, priced at five dollars. Unidentified men called upon several of the newspaper correspondents, trying to interest them in giving publicity to the issue. The attempts failed. One of the agents boasted that the book ought to be worth a hundred thousand dollars.[1]

At once the Government swung into action. It will be remembered that, after the issue of the campaign broadsides, the Department of Justice sent an operative to Ohio to threaten Professor Chancellor.[2] It now set out on the trail of the book. The only direct evidence of the methods employed at the source comes from Gaston B. Means.[3] His version is that the Federal Bureau of Investigation force located the Sentinal Press — he does not say where — took over what books they found 'at a price,' transferred them to Washington in a guarded express car, and there burned them, 'copyright and all,' which is peculiar, since even had there been a copyright, its inflammability would be open to doubt.

Somewhere, presumably from the unrevealed publishers, the Government got hold of a list of subscribers. A force of operators, both from the Department of Justice and the Post Office Department, was sent out from Washington. Without regard to the merits of the book, there was no more warranty in law for official interference than there would have been for the confiscation of so many Gideon Bibles. The emissaries combed the State of Ohio. In some cases the volumes were bought from the owners; in others, they were 'borrowed' and never returned. Political and business pressure was brought to bear. I have heard of several instances where the books were actually seized. The result was a clean sweep. Not a library in Ohio, not a state collection, not a

---

[1] To Mark Sullivan.
[2] This was under the Democratic Attorney General, A. Mitchell Palmer.
[3] *The Strange Death of President Harding.*

historical museum or repository, owns a copy. As for the plates, one story has it that they were dumped into the Ohio River at dead of night. No second edition is likely to appear.

Lawyer Snepp's connection with the publication was discovered and the forces of suppression got after him. Mr. Sharts writes:

> The officials closed in on poor old Snepp.... There were bits of news in local papers designed to create the impression that he was a low, unscrupulous character, which he certainly was not.... Snepp, as I understand, was subjected to a severe questioning by certain men who came here for the purpose of finding out all details and stopping or preventing publication. ... You may appreciate the amount of sheer terrorism that can be packed into such an investigation, designedly used for intimidation.[1]

Historically the work is unimportant. It proves nothing as to Harding's lineage. It is violent in treatment and confused in method. As an example of its incongruities, compare these two passages:

There is no disposition ... to insist that Warren Harding is by race a negro. It is evident to all that the man is mainly white. What we insist on is that the race consciousness of the Hardings in Blooming Grove caused them to remain negro and that George Tryon Harding, II, never thought of calling themselves (*sic*) white until after the death of Amos Kling, father-in-law of Warren. Warren, his brother and sisters were reared and treated as colored people.

Our first negro President.... A people threatened by contamination of the blood ought to care for the truth about its head man.... Big, lazy, slouching, confused, ignorant, affable, yellow, and cringing like a negro butler to the great, such is the man who has been used by Lodge, Smoot, Penrose, Knox, Harvey, Daugherty to ruin Woodrow Wilson for the time being and to crash the hopes of mankind for world peace.

Whatever Professor Chancellor's qualifications in the highly specialized field of genealogical research, it is undeniable that he made a first-hand study of the Hardings. Be-

[1] Letter to the writer.

fore the appearance of the Wooster leaflets, he spent a fortnight in Blooming Grove and the vicinity, interviewing the
oldest inhabitants of the region and tracing down family
lines.[1] Though he advances loose and sometimes contradictory claims that there was a negro strain in several
branches of the clan, his main contention is that the second
wife of George Tryon (or Tyrone) Harding, born in 1799,
was a negress. All the Harding genealogies list Elizabeth
Madison Harding, whose son, Charles Alexander Harding,
was President Harding's grandfather. Chancellor alone refers to her also as Mary Ann Dickson or Dixon, and as Hul-
dah Tryon; and he alone mentions the African strain, which
he supports by the word-of-mouth testimony of survivors
old enough to have known Elizabeth Madison Harding. He
describes the grandfather of the President as having 'curly,
kinky hair, swart complexion, a wide, big body, and great
nostrils.'[2]

Because of the strong bias on the negro question which
impairs Professor Chancellor's judgment and impugns his
testimony, I should heavily discount any of his statements
in this department.[3] But Doctor Alderfer, who is beyond
suspicion of bias (and who considers the negro-blood theory
quite unproven), covered the same territory in the early
1920's, and substantiated the tradition and the belief, still
generally held, in the racial intermixture. The writer, in
1938, confirmed the survival of the opinion among the older
residents of Marion, though they were naturally reluctant
to be quoted. One of the *Star* reporters of the early 1900's
said to him:

'It was generally believed that there was negro blood in
the Harding line, but that W. G. had outgrown it.'

[1] It may or may not be significant that local pride has not been sufficient to mark
Harding's birthplace by any indication.

[2] *Warren Gamaliel Harding: President of the United States.*

[3] He advocates racial disfranchisement and segregation.

All this matter of general belief, of tradition, of persistent rumor, of opinion and prejudice is adduced, not as *evidence of the existence of negro blood in the Hardings*, but as evidence of widespread opinion about them, which materially influenced the President's character. In the early Marion days he must have suffered sorely under the insults of his father-in-law, the contemptuous references in print, and the social barriers which for so many years he could not surmount. Doctor Alderfer observes that 'it is, paradoxically enough, the effects of this rumor rather than its verity that are of importance.'

> Harding never attempted to fight the rumor itself. Either he might have been so impressed with its force as to believe it in part, or he must have realized the impossibility of combating it in words. Although he ignored it in a public way, there is no doubt that its effects on his personality were of great importance. When one reads some of his vituperative, insulting, coarse editorials of the early period of his editorship, it is impossible not to see that his anger, rage, and hatred for his tormentors was being transferred from the real issue to those which the general trend of events had substituted. Never able to face conditions squarely, his emotion was drained off through other outlets. . . . There is no doubt that this factor was of great importance in the development of his personality, that it tinged all his local activities.[1]

That Harding was uncertain in the matter is suggested by a story which I have heard from two independent, and I believe reliable, sources, to the effect that he once said to the late James Miller Faulkner, political reporter of the *Cincinnati Enquirer* and an old friend:

'How do I know, Jim? One of my ancestors may have jumped the fence.'

Harding never issued a denial of the rumor, though he considered doing so at least once. Other denials have been

[1] H. F. Alderfer: *The Personality and Politics of Warren G. Harding.*

plentiful. Unhappily for their cause the refuters did not get together. The theory of the Republican National Committee was that the Harding children in Blooming Grove brought to school an affection known as 'nigger itch,' and were playfully dubbed 'niggers' for that mischance.[1] Some of the campaign reporters dug up a story to the effect that Harding's sisters and brother got into a schoolyard squabble, wherein the epithet 'nigger' was contumeliously bandied between the factions, and that the stigma stuck to the Hardings. Why not to the opposition as well is left unexplained.

These well-meaning and ingenuous explanations have no force in the face of the facts. The assertion of negro blood long antedated Warren Harding's birth. Helen Harding Meredith traces it back to the 1820's and the vengefulness of a neighbor who, accused by Amos Harding of petty theft, started the aspersion to get even.[2]

It cropped up again in the middle of the nineteenth century. In 1849, central Ohio was stirred by a sensational murder. David Butler and Amos Smith, partners in a smithy, quarrelled over a small debt. Smith taunted Butler with having 'a nigger wife.' Butler snatched up a wrench, hurled it at his partner, and killed him. Mrs. Butler was a Harding.

The issue of slander was raised by the defence. Taking a broad-gauge view of its province, the jury found that it was not slanderous to call Mrs. Butler a negro, since the Hardings were always so considered, but that, even if it had been untrue, it would not have justified the killing. For seven years the case was fought in the courts. Butler was convicted, served two years, and was pardoned. There is extant an affidavit by Calvin G. Kiefer, a cousin of the victim, sub-

[1] The late James Keeley of the *Chicago Tribune* is credited with this bit of ingenuity.

[2] *The Hardings in America.*

stantiating the cause of the slaying and stating that Butler's wife was George T. Harding's sister.[1]

In the Harding genealogies there is an omission which may or may not be significant. None of them contains the name of President Harding's namesake, Warren Gamaliel Bancroft. One biographer mentions him, erroneously identifying him as President Harding's 'mother's sister Tillie's husband.'[2] A more reliable source is a statement by Harding's father:

'Grandmother Elizabeth Madison Harding was responsible for the Hardings' naming their son Warren Gamaliel after an uncle, a Methodist preacher.'[3]

Professor Chancellor states that Warren Gamaliel Bancroft was a negro preacher.

Faced with the issue of the Chancellor papers, the trustees of the College of Wooster wisely refused to take any stand, or make any pronouncement, though urgently pressed to do so, on the Harding family strain. It was not within their competency. That view, I believe, is applicable to the historical consideration of the matter, where basis for final judgment is inadequate. Harding's own manly doubt may stand as pattern. And, as Doctor Alderfer points out, the truth or untruth is of secondary importance to the fact of the general acceptance of the rumor in Harding's environment, and the effect of this upon his life and activities.

If negro blood there were in his line, he honorably and courageously lived down the handicap.

To return to the expunged edition, Harding himself may never have known of its existence. It is quite in key with Harry M. Daugherty's protective loyalty, with his swift, decisive, secretive tactics, to have put the offending volume

---

[1] This affidavit, together with others, unless they have been removed, are in the Marion County Court House.

[2] Clement Wood: *Warren Gamaliel Harding*.

[3] *Syracuse Post Standard*, November 1, 1926.

to death without ever troubling the subject's mind by mentioning it to him.

Of the two copies known to have survived the holocaust, one is now in the New York Public Library. It belongs in the category of curiosa.[1]

[1] The protective Harding ban was in modified force years after his death. The writer's novel, *Revelry* (1926), which parallelled the Harding Administration in its events but made no mention of the racial matter or the personal scandals, was barred from Washington news-stands, and the play, adapted from the book, was suppressed in Philadelphia.

★

XXI. Fall of a Favorite

THE glory of heroes is soon departed. The public which welcomed with oratory, banquets, and ticker-tape our fighters, returning victorious from Europe, quickly forgot those of them most sorely in need of care. Two years after the Armistice the plight of war's human débris was pitiable. Over 300,000 wounded and disabled were the partial price of our adventure. Of these the most desperate cases were 71,000 mental patients and 38,000 tuberculous victims. F. W. Galbraith, Jr., National Commander of the American Legion, estimated, on the basis of an investigation, that there were 10,000 of the disabled in cellars, poorhouses, and insane asylums. T. W. Salmon, a disinterested and competent investigator, thus reported: [1]

> Veterans with nervous or mental troubles were without provision for care and were quartered in institutions for the criminal insane, addicts, and vicious degenerates, without Federal supervision.

No agency in Washington was equipped to handle a problem of this magnitude. Nor was there any special public interest in it. The war was over. 'Let's forget it' expressed the attitude of a people sated and bored with emotion.

[1] *Literary Digest*, January 22, 1921.

The President did not feel that way about it. His humanitarianism revolted from such neglect. He acted wisely and constructively in welding the disparate, overlapping guardianships into one official entity, the United States Veterans' Bureau. He acted most unwisely in his selection of the Director.

Plausible, jovial Charles R. Forbes was slated for advancement on the strongest possible qualification; namely, that he was a pal of the President. His own preference was for membership on the Shipping Board, but Harding wrote him regretfully and with mysterious you-understand-why references,[1] that it was impossible. He could have the governorship of Alaska. He did not want it. The ministry to Peru was his friend's next suggestion; also declined with thanks. Patience and pertinacity won their reward in an appointment to the War Risk Insurance Bureau. When the merger of agencies was completed he was advanced to the command. The Veterans' Bureau was a semi-independent branch of government, responsible directly to the President. It swallowed up the Federal Hospitalization Board, whose chairman, Brigadier-General Charles E. Sawyer, thus became subordinate to Forbes. At that time 'Doc' and 'Charlie' were on chummy terms.

World War organizations had endorsed Forbes. Favorable opinion was not unanimous. Harry Daugherty was more than dubious. An influential party leader, upon hearing of his impending appointment, called the President on the telephone and in vigorous language predicted grief for the Administration if that doubly qualified so-and-so were put in office.[2] As always where his personal affections were engaged, Harding was immovable.

Forbes exhibits one of those combinations of qualities which seem contrary to any rational formula of human

[1] Harding to Forbes, April 7, 1921.
[2] Statement of Walter F. Brown to the writer.

nature. He was both hero and crook. His military record began with desertion from the Army and continued with a term in jail. He abandoned his wife as well as his service. Successfully concealing his delinquency, he got a commission in the World War, became Signal Officer of the 33d Division, rose to a lieutenant-colonelcy, and performed so notably the difficult and hazardous job of maintaining communications, often under fire, that he well deserved and won the award of a Congressional Medal. There is no taint upon his war record.

Upon his discharge he went into the contracting business and turned up in Hawaii with a Government appointment from President Wilson which brought him into touch with the Hardings while they were on a senatorial junket.[1] Returning to the United States, Forbes consolidated his position with Harding by switching party allegiance and working for the candidate in the State of Washington. After the victory he was in line for a fat appointment. No one stood higher in the graces of both the Hardings than he. The President considered him 'a fine, outstanding man' and believed that he had it in him to demonstrate 'constructive service and the making of a brilliant record.'[2]

So we find him in the Capital, a pursy, rufous, convivial, highly energized individual of forty-one, full of snappy stories and insinuating gossip, boisterous in mirth and fellowship, a magnetic talker, a ready public speaker, popular with men and alluring to women, with every needful quality of the universal good fellow and high-class confidence man, equally at home at an Executive Mansion poker party, a Little Green House wassail, or a semi-official dinner with the Daugherty-Jésse Smith ménage. Will Irwin dubbed him 'court jester to the Best Minds.' Beneath the genial glow of that exterior lay a serious purpose. Charles R. Forbes was there to cash in.

[1] In 1914.   [2] *New York Times*, January 10, 1925.

Opportunity could hardly have been more favorable. He was in mid-current of the greatest flood of expenditure that ran under any official bridge. More money was allotted to his agency than to any other governmental department; nearly half a billion dollars a year. Up to the time when he was forced out, a billion and a quarter dollars had been appropriated.

Why the Director of the Veterans' Bureau was not under suspicion from the start is a puzzle. He was spending money like the traditional drunken sailor, on a salary of ten thousand dollars a year. Perhaps in the orgy of splurge characteristic of an easy-money period such as the Harding régime, his lavish entertainments were not specially conspicuous. He gave luxurious parties in smart Washington restaurants. For week-ends he would take half a floor in a great Atlantic City hotel, wherein to play host to official Washington and his wife, visiting celebrities and Broadway stars, though he sometimes forgot to settle accounts afterward.[1] He played poker for high stakes, and could win or lose with equal imperturbability a couple of hundred dollars on the cast of a seven at crapshooting. In that Golden Age of a playboy officialdom he was a shining figure.[2]

Appointments to the Veterans' Bureau under Forbes were not exclusively on the basis of merit. Charles F. Cramer, a California lawyer, was brought East to become legal adviser, and, as it turned out, participant in certain of the Forbes operations which were decidedly extra-legal. Mr. Cramer bought Harding's Washington house, at a price which was not, as afterward charged, above the market. Ralph Tul-

---

[1] A Broadway star of the day told the writer of her surprise at receiving from the hotel where she, her mother, and her sister had spent a week-end as Forbes's guests, a bill for several hundred dollars.

[2] For much of the personal data on Forbes I am indebted to Mr. Will Irwin, whose series of articles on the Veterans' Bureau scandal, issued by the North American Newspaper Syndicate, February and March, 1924 (see *New York World*), is the best presentation of Forbes's Washington activities.

lidge secured a $3500-a-year job as a mechanical engineer. His previous engineering experience was obtained on the driver's seat of a milk wagon, but he qualified for the new position through the fortunate circumstance of having a sister to whom Forbes was, in the opinion of her husband, unduly devoted. Francis B. Smith, a 'special expert,' contributed a total of two hours' work per year, for which he was paid $4800 Government salary. R. A. Tripp, a field agent, earned his pay by keeping 'soused to the gills,' as he wrote a fellow agent; his guiding principle was 'to hell with central office work.' With a staff selected on such principles, a high degree of efficiency could hardly be expected.[1]

One of the Bureau attachés, assigned to personnel duty, was the President's favorite sister, Carolyn Votaw. Considering the relations between the Hardings and Forbes, it is natural that she and the Director should have been on friendly terms. She introduced him to Mr. and Mrs. Elias H. Mortimer. Mortimer we have already met in the Little Green House on K Street as a semi-amateur purveyor of liquor. Professionally he was a commission man for contractors who wished to do business on easy and quiet terms with the Government. A representative of Thompson & Black, contractors, of St. Louis, he had a special reason for ingratiating himself with Forbes.

His wife Kathryn, was young, pretty, gay, and the sister of the milk-wagon engineer mentioned above. At times her husband referred to her as a niece of the Hardings; at other times she was a cousin.

Friendship ripened quickly among the four. They were soon on given-name terms; 'Kathryn,' 'Carolyn,' 'Mort,' 'Charlie.' In restaurants and other public places the quartet became a familiar sight. There is some reason to believe that the Reverend Heber Votaw, who was not included in

[1] These details are from the *Proceedings* of the National Civil Service Reform League; 42d Annual Meeting.

the gaieties, disapproved. That irascible man of God, according to Mortimer, threatened to throw the Director out of his own tenth-story window for some reason which was discreetly hushed when the witness was about to explain.[1]

Having, in the intervals of social life, familiarized himself with the set-up of his department, Forbes perceived limitless vistas of profit if he could get the Bureau's building operations into his own hands. Seventeen million dollars, afterward more than doubled, had been appropriated for veterans' hospitals. Purchase of sites and letting out of contracts had been entrusted to the Army authorities. Forbes had a better plan to present to the President. Veterans' hospitals logically should be under the control of the Veterans' Bureau. It appealed to Harding's unsuspicious mind as reasonable. He assented. Presumably he did not know that the regular Government architectural staff had already built nineteen hospitals efficiently and economically. Forbes had built none. In any case, whatever he wanted was right with Harding. The plan was made an executive order. An architectural sub-department of incredible inefficiency was set up in the Bureau.[2] Forbes was authorized to make the contracts.

In the spring of 1922 he set out on a junket across the country. For good and sufficient reasons, business as well as social, he invited the Mortimers to go along. He and Mortimer, acting respectively for Charles R. Forbes and for Thompson & Black, were working out a private plan in connection with the hospital appropriation. Mrs. Votaw was not included in the jaunt.

'Forbes did not want Mrs. Votaw to know anything of his trip,' testified Mortimer. 'He objected because he had had trouble with Mrs. Votaw who was then engaged in welfare

[1] United States *vs.* Forbes and Thompson: United States District Court, Northern District of Illinois; January, 1925.

[2] As an example of the Forbes staff work, the plans for the Livermore, California hospital were scrapped as impracticable after two years and $100,000 had been wasted.

work for the veterans...her presence might interfere with his plans.' [1]

It was one of those social errors which, minor though they may seem, have catastrophic repercussions. Left out of the glorious whoopee which the journey developed, Mrs. Votaw kept track of the proceedings from a distance. Surgeon General Sawyer, now become hostile to Forbes, was also interested. [2]

On the financial side, Charles F. Cramer, counsel for the Bureau, remained at his post to look after his chief's interests.

'We will have to take Cramer into this situation,' the Director explained to Mortimer. 'We want Thompson to stay here in the East with Cramer. Cramer and I are very close. I can trust him.' [3]

At Chicago the three junketeers met Thompson. There was a cash transaction involving the transfer of five thousand dollars from Thompson to Forbes, on account of future divisions. It was further arranged that Thompson & Black money, handled by Mortimer, should finance the trip. (These dealings were afterward viewed in an unfavorable light by a jury.)

With such a start the trip could not be other than a brilliant success. Forbes came back to report glowingly to the President on the work accomplished. Harding was so pleased that he thought of rewarding his friend's efficiency by making him Assistant Secretary of War, which would hardly have suited his financial book.

The ointment of Forbes's self-satisfaction harbored a fly in uniform. This was Surgeon General Sawyer, who, as Chairman of the Federal Hospitalization Board, was his

---

[1] United States *vs.* Forbes and Thompson, *supra.*

[2] In Mr. Irwin's opinion there is little doubt that Mrs. Votaw and Doctor Sawyer made common cause against Forbes.

[3] United States *vs.* Forbes and Thompson, *supra.*

colleague. Doctor Sawyer had been nosing around during Forbes's absence. Forbes declares that he organized a spy system within the Veterans' Bureau. Both men were now under fire from veterans' organizations, grown impatient of the conditions of inertia and neglect. The American Legion demanded Sawyer's dismissal: Harding would not consider it. He was equally stiff-necked as to criticism of the Director. Harry Daugherty himself was snubbed when he impugned the favorite's fitness for his office. [1] A publicity agent was employed to put in a year's work on articles laudatory of the Veterans' Bureau.[2] Forbes was still the fair-haired boy of the White House.

How Harding could have continued to be so fatuously trustful is an enigma. Tales of the cross continent jaunt had followed the travellers back to Washington. There had been a swimming party in full evening dress. There were festivities all along the route on a scale of alcoholic hospitality which astonished enen Mortimer (who was paying the bills). There were shipments East of California wines. There was the incident of the bestowal by Forbes of a medal in the name of the President upon a gentleman named Alexander, for services unspecified. As Harding had never before heard of Mr. Alexander, he was mystified at receiving a letter of thanks from the grateful Californian. All this Forbes succeeded in explaining away. Everything was all right. The contracts were all right. Forbes himself had personally examined every site. Any time the President wanted the complete reports, they were there for him with every figure ready for check, all duly approved by the counsel for the Veterans' Bureau, Charles F. Cramer, whom the President knew to be reliable. Forbes hinted that the 'squawks' were inspired by jealousy.

Harding accepted it all. Short of hypnotism, it is hard to imagine how he could have done so.

[1] Mark Sullivan: *Our Times*, vol. VI.　　[2] Statement of the agent, Ben Grey.

Further money which Forbes expected as a result of the Thompson conference was not yet coming in. For ready cash there was recourse near at hand. Immense Government storehouses at Perryville, Maryland, were filled with supplies and equipment, which were to be shipped out as requisitioned, or otherwise disposed of if not needed. In the proviso for excess articles lay the Director's opportunity. Some of the goods were old, deteriorated, or damaged; these were proper subjects for sale at any price which they might fetch. But the bulk of them were usable, much of them in prime condition. Not only this, but they were sorely needed. All over the country the hospital staffs were crying for supplies to replace those which had been worn out or used up: bedding, gauze, bandages, drugs, soap, pajamas and other necessities.[1]

As part of the material had come from army and navy sources, those two services, together with the United States Public Health Service, could claim a twenty per cent ownership of the stored goods. A liaison officer was maintained at Perryville to conserve their interests. Contracts for the purchase and disposition of Veterans' Bureau supplies were handled by the Quartermaster General's Department of the Army. Forbes now represented to the President that it would be a saving of time and red tape if this function were transferred to him. Harding agreed. As there was some legal doubt, Attorney General Daugherty was applied to for a favorable opinion. He gave it, with what distaste for the sour dose may be imagined.

In November the liaison officer was approached by Forbes as to the sale of what was represented as surplus and practically worthless material. Upon this assumption the guardian of the Government's interests assented to the sale. All the formulae of such procedure were carried out with one exception; the goods were never advertised to the trade. Forbes had made other arrangements.

[1] Irwin articles, *supra*.

Fall of a Favorite

The Thompson-Kelley Company, of Boston (no connection with the Thompson of Thompson & Black) were the beneficiaries of a private arrangement. To what extent Director Forbes benefited will never be known. Without any publicity, the sale arrangement was made. Two other firms got wind of it and put in bids. Over this insignificant and futile competition, the Boston concern received the award within five days of the entering of their bid. Swift work.

Terms were unusually advantageous. Nearly one hundred thousand pairs of winter pajamas, for which there was already a crying need in the hospitals, were shipped to Boston at thirty cents per pair. These had been donated by the Red Cross. At any fair appraisal they were worth four or five times that amount. Twelve thousand old but still serviceable sheets brought six cents apiece. Those sheets would have been a boon to any of the many institutions which were short of bedding. Eighty-four thousand more sheets which had never been removed from the original packages, having cost the Government $1.27 a pair, brought, under the Forbes-Thompson-Kelley schedule, about 27 cents. Contemporaneously the Veterans' Bureau was buying sheets at $1.03 a pair. Obviously there was a profit for someone in these transactions, but for the Government it was sheer loss. In one instance a shipment of bedclothing just received was transferred to the Boston address without ever going through the formality of unpacking.

Oiled paper in prime condition, billed to Uncle Sam at 60 cents per pound, was disposed of by Uncle Sam's liberal representative in the Veterans' Bureau at 5 cents, 5387 pounds of it. Over 45,000 rolls of gauze, as good as when the factory turned it out at a price of $1.33 per roll to the taxpayer, passed through the transforming hands of Director Forbes and lost eighty per cent of their original valuation by the time they reached Boston. Surgical departments of many institutions needed that gauze. They had to wait.

Some $3,000,000 worth of such merchandise was disposed of by this informal method for about $600,000 to the Thompson-Kelley firm.[1] On the buying side, too, Forbes dealt in the same liberal spirit. One enterprising agent sold him enough floor wax to last a century.[2]

Rival concerns were naturally up in arms. They complained to Director Forbes and were unceremoniously ushered out. They appealed to Doctor Sawyer who said he would look into it. Presumably he had already been gathering data on the subject. What he found at Perryville he deemed definite enough to lay before the President.

At last Harding was obliged to listen. Here was no pressure-inspired Congressman to be brusquely cut short; no hearsay-repeating Harry Daugherty to be told, 'That can't be.' Doctor Sawyer knew the Bureau from inside. Troubled but still unconvinced, Harding, on November 24, 1922, ordered the sale of supplies at Perryville temporarily stopped.

Forbes, aggrieved, hurried to the White House. What was this, his friend and sponsor asked, about the non-competitive sale of hospital supplies? Forbes admitted that there might have been some looseness of administration. That was unavoidable in a high-speed, complicated organization such as his. Even a little graft of a minor order might have crept in. But he was, he assured his friend, on the job. They couldn't get away with anything for long. Everything would be all right. The shipments would be looked into and, if they weren't on the level, they would be stopped at once. The President might safely dismiss the matter from his mind.

Nothing would have pleased Harding better. But it was not a matter easily dismissed. The Bureau was buzzing with talk of the feverish activities. Loose-tongued underlings

[1] *New York Times*, March 5, 1923.

[2] The data on purchases and sales are from the Senate Investigation of the Veterans' Bureau, October and November, 1923.

were boasting. One of them blithely prophesied that when operations got into full swing he would be in the market for a Rolls-Royce car. To Cramer, then on the Pacific coast, his wife telegraphed on November 12: [1]

> Think Colonel is a traitor. Has ordered Perryville cleaned out this week.
>
> Lila

Finding that his assurances were insufficient, Forbes decided upon a bold stroke. (Or, perhaps it was not so bold as it appeared.) The War Department had an interest in the Perryville stock. He asked the Secretary of War to delegate an officer to check the operations. Major John D. Carmody of the Quartermaster's Department was designated. What his method of investigation was does not appear. It may be assumed that it was somewhat superficial. Forbes had little to fear from any such inquiry; the theory inevitably obtrudes itself that he had foreknowledge of this when he asked for the check-up. Major Carmody reported that all was in order and the shipments legal and proper. It is said that he never went near Perryville. [2]

Thereupon President Harding declared the charges against Director Forbes an 'abominable libel' [3] and on December 12 lifted the embargo. Merrily the cars rolled along again, laden with materials for lack of which sick veterans all over the country were suffering.

Many people were now on watch. Surgeon General Hugh S. Cumming of the Public Health Service visited Perryville in company with Surgeon General Sawyer. [4] As they reached the place they found freight cars being loaded with 75,000 towels for Thompson-Kelley, billed out at 3⅜ cents apiece. Not only had the towels cost 19 cents, but the Public Health Service, with a twenty per cent interest in them, was short

[1] *New York World*, February 16, 1924.
[2] *New York Times*, November 7, 1923.
[3] *Ibid.*, December 16, 1922.   [4] *New York World*, February 16, 1924.

of that very article at the time. Sheets, of which there was also a shortage, were going out. Able now to say, 'This I have seen with my own eyes,' Doctor Sawyer took his facts to the White House. Again the embargo was clapped on. Sadly Forbes accepted his friend's decision. Even then the outflow did not stop. It was probably too late for Forbes to check it. He was in the toils. The Boston profiteers had him. If they brought suit to enforce the contracts, he would be ruined. He must go on, covering his tracks as best he could by doctored bookkeeping and suppressed figures.

The inexplicable feature is that Harding clung to some remnants of his faith in Forbes. His one thought now was to save his friend and avert the scandal which an investigation must bring. The Perryville sell-out was permanently stopped. Reorganization of the Bureau was announced.[1] On the flimsy pretext that the disabled veterans still in Europe needed attention, Forbes was assigned to go abroad. Though his resignation was in the President's hands, Harding could not as yet nerve himself to announce it.

Forbes slipped away for Europe late in January, 1923. While still abroad he resigned. Brigadier-General Frank T. Hines was appointed to the place and did a good job of cleaning up a difficult and involved mess. Forbes testified later that even after he had cabled his resignation, the President asked him to continue in office.[2] He was definitely out on the last day of February.

During the brief trip abroad he was seriously ill. Officially his ailment was given out as heart trouble. Those who knew him well ascribed it to shattered nerves.

Shortly after his return, a visitor to the White House who had an appointment with the President was directed to the second floor apparently by error, and, as he approached the Red Room, heard a voice which sounded as if choking with

[1] *New York Tribune*, January 31, 1922.
[2] Senate Investigation of Veterans' Bureau.

anger. Entering, he was appalled to see Harding gripping the neck of a man who was huddled against the wall.

Harding was saying: 'You yellow rat! You double-crossing bastard! If you ever —— '

Whether or not the visitor exclaimed, he does not recall, but he thinks he must have done so, as the President whirled about. At once he loosed his grip on the man, who staggered away, his face discolored and distorted. To the new arrival, Harding said curtly: 'I am sorry. You have an appointment. Come into the other room.'

At the conclusion of the interview, as the caller left the place he asked the doorman: 'Who was the gentleman that went out just after I came in?'

The man replied: 'That was Colonel Forbes of the Veterans' Bureau, sir.' [1]

In his *New York World* article, published after Harding's death, Forbes attempted to implant the belief that the President retained his friendly feeling for him to the last. It is not true. Mrs. Harding told E. Mont Reilly that her husband 'never recovered from Forbes's betrayal of himself and the Administration.' [2] It was his first experience of treachery; probably his bitterest. The two cronies never saw one another again.

In graft and in the multiplied waste which is its invariable concomitant, Will Irwin estimates that Forbes's malpractices represent a loss of $200,000,000 to the nation. Harding's friendships were costly.

[1] Will Irwin and the writer separately heard almost identical accounts of this fracas from widely diverse sources.

[2] *New York Times*, October 24, 1923.

★

XXII. 'As the Sparks Fly Upward'

NINETEEN-TWENTY-ONE, passing into nineteen-twenty-two had seen President Harding full of vigor, zest, and purpose. Nineteen-twenty-two, giving way to nineteen-twenty-three, found him a changed man, a man beginning to break, to lose faith in himself and confidence in his régime. Those nearest him noticed a despondency and indecision in his bearing. He took no action without councils and conferences. The most optimistic of his supporters could not fail to perceive that there was no leadership in him.

The November elections had served as a sharp reminder of responsibility, a warning of dissatisfaction on the part of the electorate. With losses of sixty-nine seats in the House and seven in the Senate, though the Republicans retained a nominal majority, the Administration had lost control, since the insurgent wing, growing in assertiveness as well as authority, more than ever held the balance of power. Among the leaders the feeling of slipping control approached melancholia.

This applied chiefly to Washington. Out through the country opinion of Harding was still favorable. His veto of the bonus, sustained by the Senate, commended him to the far-sighted conservatives. So confirmed a liberal as William Allen White published a commendatory article [1] asserting his belief that 'our President is ruling the nation and doing a better than fair job.' Samuel G. Blythe noted captious criticism in certain quarters and called for a fair deal for the President.[2] The intellectual and moral leaders of Republicanism exhibited a growing respect for Harding as the Administration progressed. Elihu Root, who, late in 1920, 'did not believe that Harding was of big enough calibre for the Presidency,'[3] changed his mind and wrote: [4]

> I knew him very slightly at the time he was elected and I was afraid he was going to be too anxious to please everybody, but he has shown himself to have a decision of character and cheerful courage that are most gratifying. I have stopped having depressing thoughts about him and have turned my private, individual worry current on to Congress which is not quite holding up its end.

In party circles nobody had any conception of the extrapolitical activities beneath the not-yet-abnormally troubled surface of Washington.

Responsive to the worries of those about him, the President called a secret emergency meeting of trusted advisers, to bring about better teamwork. Among those invited were Lodge, Smoot, Brandegee, McCumber, Longworth, Fordney, Speaker Gillett, and Everett Sanders. Vice-President Coolidge was not there.

The project of holding caucus on important votes was brought up. It annoyed Lodge who sensed in it a slur on his titular leadership of the Senate. He was holding conferences

[1] *Collier's*, March 4, 1922. Mr. White further offers the somewhat startling opinion that Harding 'plays no favorites. Even his social friends have no political influence with him.'

[2] *Saturday Evening Post*, July 28, 1923.

[3] Philip C. Jessup: *Elihu Root*, vol. II.

[4] Letter to William Allen White, May 23, 1922.

whenever necessary, he pointed out. In rebuttal, some of the others charged that he was slack about taking his associates into his confidence. The undercurrent of sentiment and expectation was that here was the President's opportunity to take over command.[1] He did not do so. The caucus idea was dropped. The meeting had accomplished nothing except to demonstrate the slow party disintegration.

Among the Best Minds there was disaffection. Senator Brandegee split sharply from the President on his League and treaty policies, if they may be so termed.[2] Harding's personal appointments had always irked the Senate. Now one of them brought about a difference with his Secretary of the Treasury. Friendship and the fact that they used to steal melons together in boyhood apart, there had been no discernible reason for the appointment of Neighbor Daniel R. Crissinger to be Comptroller of the Currency. When it was proposed to advance him to the important and responsible post of Governor of the Federal Reserve System, Secretary Mellon protested. Harding stiffened. That was his invariable attitude where friendship was put to the test. The appointment went through and proved one of the worst in a bad list. To Crissinger's ignorance and ineptitude, as later evinced, Mark Sullivan attributes a considerable share of the responsibility for the mad bull market which culminated in the crash of 1929.[3]

The tariff was not working well. Farm prices had slumped, in spite of high duties on agricultural products. But the farmers could not reasonably object when the manufacturers, seeking their share, demanded higher duties. The result was 'an extreme of protection which few had thought possible,' as Professor Taussig put it.[4] The Fordney-McCumber bill

[1] Statement of Everett Sanders to the writer.
[2] *New York Evening World*, January 25, 1923.
[3] Mark Sullivan: *Our Times*, vol. VI.
[4] F. W. Taussig: *Tariff History of the United States*.

had introduced the so-called 'flexible provisions' empowering the President to increase or decrease rates. This was another burden. He lacked expert knowledge of the intricate subject.

In all these controversial fields he strove to bring about the easiest and most peaceable settlements. Whether or not he was yet aware of his condition, he lacked the physical stamina for a fighting program. In January he suffered a sharp attack of influenza, followed by digestive disorders and kidney symptoms. The condition was not so severe as to occasion alarm, but it left the patient still further depressed. He would have been grateful for a let-up in the pace, and set about adjusting his personal habits to a more restful basis.

A pistol shot shattered the hope of respite. Charles F. Cramer, whose wife had warned him by telegram of the corrupt dealings at Perryville, came back to Washington and found himself hopelessly involved through his partnership in the Forbes side-deals. When he learned that, in spite of the well-meant clean-up, there would be a senatorial investigation, he knew that he had reached the end of his rope.

The Cramers were living in the Wyoming Avenue house. The President was on genial terms with the quiet, industrious, middle-aged lawyer and his high-spirited young wife, known to her intimates as 'Bonnie.' He was an occasional visitor to the home which had once been his.

Forbes had left Washington, but would be called back to testify. Cramer realized that there was no hope of his escaping the witness stand. Thinner of skin than his chief, he could not face the test.[1]

On March 11 he finished his day's work at the office, came home to dinner, and devised an errand of pretended importance which required his wife's presence in New York. She left on the midnight train. After seeing her off, he went

---

[1] Deeply though Cramer was involved with Forbes there is no proof of criminality on his part.

home and shot himself through the head. The body was not found until morning. Shortly after the discovery an agent from the Department of Justice was on the spot. Burns's men had a habit, in those troublous days, of arriving early when anything untoward occurred and revelations might threaten.

Washington throbbed with rumors. The most persistent one dealt with the activities of the agent on the spot. The story took several forms, all alike in essentials. The version which presents the highest degree of probability, since it comes through the secret service (not, however, Gaston B. Means!), is this. The Federal Bureau of Investigation man examining the premises, found on a bedroom mantel several letters in the suicide's handwriting, one of which was addressed to President Harding. Taking it to the Department of Justice for instructions, he was ordered to deliver it personally into the addressee's hand.

It was early. The President, still out of condition from his illness, was not up. Roused, he put on a dressing-gown and came to the Blue Room to meet the messenger. He was pale and shaky. The agent said:

'Mr. President, I have a letter for you.'

'Who's it from?'

'Charles F. Cramer. You know that Mr. Cramer is dead.'

'Yes; I know.'

'Here is the letter, sir. It was found in his room.'

Harding stared at the messenger. His face worked. 'Take it away. I don't want it.'

The operative bore the letter back to the Department of Justice, where it was destroyed.

Capital gossip of the day was busy with two subjects of prime importance. One rumor was that several Cabinet resignations were pending; the other that the President was worn out and would not seek a renomination. It may have been this latter which impelled Harry M. Daugherty to a gratuitous action. He gave out this statement for publication:

> The President will be a candidate for renomination. He will
> be opposed by only one other candidate except for one man
> who always is and always will be a candidate.... The Presi-
> dent will be renominated and re-elected because the country
> will demand it.[1]

The strategy of Daugherty's timing would appear to be
sound. What more likely, when the President was dispirited
and discouraged, sensitive to criticism and wounded by reflections upon his Administration which he considered un-
justified, than that a summons to future battle would restore his flagging forces?

Political seers generally regarded the hat-in-the-ring challenge as premature and probably unauthorized. There is no
evidence that at this time Harding wished another term,
though afterward there was some conventional talk of his
having desired an 'endorsement' at the hands of the people.
Reports that there had been an actual quarrel between the
two friends over the issue were erroneous, though Harding
considered that there had been too much precipitancy. However, for better or worse, Harding was now a candidate. To
the duties of the Presidency, he had added the burden and
test of being a formal candidate.

As for the whispers about a Cabinet break-up, they were
justified not by the five resignations which the wiseacres
prophesied, by but one alone. Albert B. Fall resigned at the
end of his second year and went openly into the oil business.[2]

Much criticism has been directed against those who sat in
Cabinet meetings with Fall for having lifted no voice in
reprehension of his corrupt deals, the special targets being
Secretaries Hughes and Hoover, and Vice-President Cool-

---

[1] *New York Times*, March 18, 1923.
[2] Went to Europe on a commission for H. F. Sinclair.

idge.[1] What Hughes and Coolidge thought of Fall at this time is not known. But Hoover is on record. Within a few days after the resignation, he wrote a letter, beginning, 'My dear Fall,' and continuing:

> In my recollection that department has never had so constructive and legal a headship as you gave it.[2]

As an engineer Hoover was better equipped to judge of the operations of the Interior than any other of his colleagues. The inference would seem to be either that the writer of the letter had some ulterior motive — and this would be far to seek — or that the retiring Secretary of the Interior had so cleverly concealed his trail of malfeasance that no suspicions had been aroused. Doctor Hubert Work, who later succeeded Fall, an amiable and ineffective person, did little or nothing to correct the abuses.

Before Daugherty's hat-in-the-ring gesture, a presidential 'voyage of understanding' across the continent and up into Alaska had been projected. Now that he was a candidate, there was added reason for Harding's showing himself to the people. The journey would afford the ailing couple[3] a complete change and two months' absence from the thousand daily pressures of the Capital. It was a surprise to Washington circles to learn that Harry Daugherty and Jess[4] Smith, that inseparable pair of white House intimates, were omitted from the tentative list for the tour. Whispers revived that the President was still displeased with his too forehanded nominator. As for Jess, nobody understood his

---

[1] Coolidge, on Harding's invitation, sat in all Cabinet meetings. He was the first Vice-President to do this. He was characteristically taciturn and inert.

[2] Harry Daugherty gleefully cites the letter in his book, *The Inside Story of the Harding Tragedy*.

[3] Mrs. Harding was erroneously supposed to be in weaker health than her husband at this time.

[4] To a wide circle of intimates, Smith was familiarly known as 'Jess.' Hereafter that convenient diminutive will be used.

exclusion: he was supposed to be riding high, wide, and handsome in the official parade.

He was not. Somewhere the President had heard what, to every insider in town had been jocular gossip for many months, that Jess was swanking around town like a turkey-cock, acting as if he considered himself the National Government. It shocked the President.

'I am informed,' said he to Harry Daugherty, 'that he is running around with a gay crowd, attending all sorts of parties, using the Attorney General's car at all hours of the night.' [1]

The charge, with slight alterations as to the car, might justly have been alleged against the presidential critic himself, less than a year before. But Jess, however invulnerable in his own magnificent conception of himself, did not enjoy presidential privilege. His career of splendor was over.

How blackened the Smith name was, Jess discovered only when Harry Daugherty brought him the incredibly bad news that he was expunged from the White House roster. He was further advised that, for the good of all concerned, it would be well that he should leave Washington. It was a brutal blow to poor Jess. So far as he knew, everything was lovely. He was having a wonderful time. He was living the life of Riley. To be sure, nosy Senators with their fool questions about him had jockeyed him out of his special quarters in the Department of Justice Building, but he was still the Attorney General's 'bumper,' with all the dignity, prestige, and immunity of the great office back of him when people with cash to trade for favors were to be impressed. Money was pouring in upon him; such money as he had never dreamed of out in Ohio. People practically forced it upon him. No misgivings as to the ethical bearing of these transactions seem ever to have troubled his simple soul.

And now this! What had he ever done to his great and

[1] Harry M. Daugherty: *The Inside Story of the Harding Tragedy*.

good friend, the President, that all should be taken from him? He faced a life from which the glory was departed, a career turned to dust and ashes. Washington Court House, after this greater Washington, was a place of exile, of outer darkness to which he was being committed as if he were a criminal. What was it all about? What had he done that everybody else around him wasn't doing? Graft, to his mind, was a normal principle of politics. Everywhere in the record it stands out that Jess Smith was, in all such matters, morally imperceptive. He did not know right from wrong, nor distinguish between foul money and fair.

He sank into black depression. His health was not good. A diabetic tendency, aggravated by his far from hygienic personal habits, had so undermined his system that after an appendectomy the wound failed to heal. Refusal to accept the sentence of exile did not occur to him. Harry Daugherty had told him he must go. That was final. Whatever Harry said must be right. For his wounded spirit there was but one refuge, Ohio, where he could rejoin Roxy Stinson. Thither he went, and presently Daugherty followed. There was a party at the shack on Deer Creek.

Daugherty had not been well. In February, the solicitous Jess had reported him 'still very weak. I don't see how he is going to be able to go South next Monday.' [1] At the shack he hoped to get rested. After luncheon he was accustomed to take a nap.

Early one afternoon a caller arrived on business which Jess deemed important enough to warrant an interruption to the Attorney General's slumbers. Daugherty was furious. He berated his alarmed 'bumper' and even threatened to go back alone in the car leaving Jess to his own resources, though he relented later. Jess was like a whipped puppy.

'Harry has turned on me,' said he to Roxy, in tears.

Back in town he bought a revolver and cartridges at Car-

[1] *Investigation of the Attorney General.*

penter's hardware store, to the surprise of the merchant who knew his morbid dread of firearms.

'This is for the Attorney General,' he explained.

At the next meeting with Roxy, he seemed quiet and calm. He told her that everything was all right.

What follows lacks satisfactory explanation. Why should Jess, banished by presidential fiat, have ventured back to Washington? Possibly to pack his belongings, though he had had ample time for that before. In any case, he went back and established himself in the Daugherty-Smith apartment at the Wardman Park Hotel. He did not pack. It would have been superfluous.

Harry Daugherty did not stay at the apartment with him, but spent the night at the White House. Concerned as to his old friend's condition, he arranged for Warren F. Martin, his official secretary, to remain at the apartment.

This was the night of May 29. In the morning of Decoration Day, Mr. Martin was awakened by a sharp noise near-by. At first he sleepily thought that a door had slammed or that something heavy had fallen. Unable to drop off again, he rose and went into the living-room, beyond which was Jess's bedroom. As usual, the door was open; Jess had gone to bed with his fears of loneliness. He now lay, curled on the floor, his shattered head in a metal waste-basket.

The news was telephoned to the White House. It was a ghastly day, followed by a more ghastly evening when half a dozen pallid people sat around, trying to make conversation, and Harry Daugherty groaned from time to time. Justified though the President was in banishing Jess Smith as a measure of protection, the act must have now appeared to him as at least a contributory cause of the suicide.

Suicide? Was it suicide? All Washington was asking itself the question. The shot in the early morning silence of the Wardman Park Hotel was the starting gun for a rush of surmises, queries, alarms. The ugly word 'murder' was on the tongues of men wherever they gathered to discuss the tragedy.

For the safety and mental peace of many important people, Jess Smith dead was indubitably preferable to Jess Smith alive. He had splurged too much; that sort of thing attracts attention and eventually starts inquiries. He knew too much. He talked too much. He had been loose of tongue and braggart of claims in circumstances where silence is the only safety. Worse, his actions for some weeks had given indication of queerness. His mind seemed, at times, to be abandoned to vagaries. There was speculation as to whether drink and dissipation might not be undermining him. An irresponsible Jess Smith who might 'spill' could do incalculable damage, could spoil the most profitable and promising graft which had been developed for many years. Furthermore, he had been dealing on a large scale with desperate characters and had not always carried out his bargains with them. Suppose they decided that he had double-crossed them? Suppose, again, he was viewed in the light of a potential threat by people in established and profitable positions? Any well-informed person on Pennsylvania Avenue could tell you offhand a dozen people who would breathe easier with the Ohio grafter out of the way.

There were circumstances in connection with the death that were dubious. No autopsy was performed. The Department of Justice took efficient charge and all was hushed up as soon as possible. One curious fact that came out was the destruction of a mass of papers. Somebody had burned them. Testimony was adduced which seems to indicate that Jess himself was the incendiary. Harry Daugherty supported this theory. It was far from conclusive.

'To my surprise,' he wrote, 'I found that Jess had destroyed all my house accounts and my personal correspondence. In fact, there was hardly anything left pertaining to my personal affairs.' [1]

[1] Harry M. Daugherty: *The Inside Story of the Harding Tragedy.*

There were investigators in Washington who would have liked to go through those Smith-Daugherty records.

In so far as suspicion attached to the nature of Smith's death, Daugherty's alibi, had he needed one, was impregnable. He was asleep in the White House at the time.

Charles F. Cramer's suicide had been a sensation. Coming soon after it, Jess Smith's fate, so similar, was ominous. Putting one and one together, the gossip-mongers surmised an E. Phillips Oppenheim plot to put away such people as knew more than it was safe for them to know. Who would be the next? they asked. The Veterans' Bureau counsel was comparatively obscure, with connections that were narrowly bound within his own department. But the Ohioan was one of Washington's show figures. Through his association with the Attorney General he had become a power. He was known to be well within the charmed circle of White House habitués, a chum of Ned McLean's, hail-fellow with half the Cabinet, and a boon companion of President Harding's. It was not yet known that he had fallen from that high estate.

In a personal sense his passing was a shock to a wide circle of most curiously heterogeneous friends and acquaintances. This ignorant, unlettered, boorish, genial, garrulous, back-slapping drugstore sport from the sticks, arrayed in the smartest apparel purchasable, and pervading official and semi-official drawing-rooms like a shambling butterfly, touched a responsive chord in widely diverse natures. The list of those who wrote or wired condolences comprises such names as T. Coleman Dupont, Will Hays, Mark Sullivan, John Hays Hammond, John Oliver La Gorce, Albert D. Lasker and Wayne B. Wheeler, the Anti-Saloon leader. What did they see in him? Those whom I have asked find themselves at a loss to explain. His friendliness, his spontaneity, his overflowing juvenile zest in the splendid expansiveness of existence, without other qualities to back them would seem hardly enough. To this extent he casts illumination upon the Harding environment, that in no other administration of modern times could a Jess Smith imaginably have attained such position and recognition.

That Harry M. Daugherty was shocked and grieved by the fate of his associate is well attested. Yet according to Roxy Stinson, who was practically Jess's widow, he did not attend the funeral.

Was Smith murdered? The suspicion, so widespread at the time, is still firmly believed by many of the survivors of that unsavory era. Several times in the course of her testimony, Roxy Stinson patently tried to implant the idea that her ex-husband did not die by his own hand. But other statements by her constitute the strongest indication of suicide; indications amounting, I think, to practical proof. He was 'down,' physically and mentally. His brief career of glory had reached its end in bitter reproof if not open disgrace. The shining radiance of presidential favor was withdrawn. His protector and idol, Harry Daugherty, had exhibited an unprecedented harshness toward him. Their ways had parted. Life held little for the transplanted playboy.

His mind had shown signs of weakening. At times he succumbed to accesses of unreasoning terror, believing that he was followed by mysterious persons with obscure and terrifying intent. He dreaded to be out after dark. Returning from an evening engagement with Roxy, he would insist on walking in the middle of the street. People on railroad trains who did not know of his existence were objects of alarmed suspicion. 'They have put the spot on me,' he said to Roxy, but added darkly that he knew what to do. Everything was going to be all right. To all this she testifies.[1]

It was all planned in his quivering mind, she believes, when he bought the weapon at Carpenter's store, to take back to Washington with him. All points to suicide motivated by a

[1] *Investigation of the Attorney General.*

mixture of hallucination, dread of unknown threats, physical depression and nervous humiliation from the circumstances of his unhealed wound, and incapacity to face a future in which jail was one of the possibilities. It must have been a powerful, perhaps an insane, impulsion which drove the timorous, inconclusive Jesse, with his intuitive horror of guns, to send a bullet into his brain.

So died the Happy Grafter.

Two grisly tragedies within the close circle of his intimates accentuated Harding's desire to be quit of Washington. Meantime a brew of other troubles was coming to a boil.

★

XXIII. 'Department of Easy Virtue'

WHO is Jesse Smith and what are his functions in the Department of Justice?' inquired Senator Caraway one day in the Senate.

Had he voiced his query at headquarters, the answer, if it expressed the prevalent opinion of the rank and file, would have been that the object of his curiosity was the deputy Attorney General of the United States, without portfolio. Jesse Smith was regarded as the mouthpiece of Harry M. Daugherty. To the staff of the Department he was the very voice of authority. His suggestions, whether to bureau heads or stenographers, had the force of commands.[1]

[1] *Investigation of the Attorney General.* The witness is a confidential secretary in the Department of Justice; also the wife of Edward B. McLean's confidential secretary. There were other interlocking interests such as this in the department:

Sen. Wheeler — You say you took his dictation in Mr. Smith's private office on the sixth floor of the Department of Justice. Where was that office?

Mrs. Duckstein — Around the corridor from the Attorney General's office.

Sen. Wheeler — Did he have that office all by himself?

Mrs. Duckstein — Yes, sir; he had that office all by himself.... It was known as Mr. Smith's room. He had a messenger outside the door who attended to his callers.

Sen. Wheeler — What position did you understand that Smith had there in the department?

Mrs. Duckstein — Well, I thought, and I think everyone else did, that he was the confidential adviser and friend of the Attorney General.... He was a sort of second in authority under the Attorney General.

Jess, as he was universally known to his intimates, whom he numbered by the score, maintained an office in the Department Building. He enjoyed the use of the Attorney General's official car. He dictated his letters to a Government-salaried secretary and they went out under frank on the letterhead of the Attorney General. He travelled on a departmental pass. He instigated and directed investigations of both officials and private citizens, which special agents of the Bureau of Investigation carried out. Letters such as the following testify to his status:[1]

Department of Justice   Office of the Attorney General
WASHINGTON, D.C., *June 7*, 1921.

Maj. Alex M. Lochwitsky,
    New York City.
Dear Sir;
    I have your letter of June 4. At the present time we are not considering any applications for positions in the bureau of investigation, and I can hold out no temporary employment to you, nor even a job. I can only say again as I have said before, that when the department is reorganized and the force built up, your application will be considered along with the others. Please do not construe this letter as being an offer of a job. I do not want you to labor under any misapprehension of the facts.

Very truly yours,
JESS W. SMITH[2]

He even dictated a letter for the President of the United States to sign, authorizing the employment of two special agents to conduct investigations. The letter was duly signed. This is the more noteworthy in that the President must have known Jess's non-official footing.

There was ample warranty for Senator Caraway's inquisitiveness. Because of it, Jess had him 'investigated' by the Department sleuths, but they turned up nothing useful; i.e., discreditable.

[1] *Investigation of the Attorney General.*
[2] Even for official purposes, Smith had now adopted the form 'Jess.'

One notable exception to the general understanding as to Smith's status and importance was the Attorney General himself. He told Mark Sullivan, after Jess's death, that he never knew of his occupancy of the office or use of the Department personnel and equipment.[1] To a cynical mind, Mr. Daugherty's ignorance might seem to belong in Mr. Ripley's Believe-it-or-not column. The charitable assumption is that Mr. Daugherty's memory played him false. Mrs. Duckstein could have stimulated his recollection. Here is her evidence.

> *Sen. Wheeler* — Did you see the Attorney General and Mr. Smith together on a good many occasions?
>
> *Mrs. Duckstein* — Why, I saw them going in and out of the building and getting into the car. And I have seen Mr. Smith in the Attorney General's office frequently. . . .
>
> *Sen. Wheeler* — Did he go into the Attorney General's office without an announcement, just walk right in?
>
> *Mrs. Duckstein* — Yes; he would always walk right in.[2]

What may have simplified Jess's operations and given him a freer hand is the fact that the Attorney General was rattling around in a job far too big for him. Chief Justice Taft expressed an opinion generally held by the legal profession when he attributed to Daugherty 'ambition for too high a place . . . lack of real ability and capacity.'[3] And Elihu Root, commenting upon Harding's overstressed loyalty to friends and supporters, said:[4]

'He should have known that Daugherty wasn't fitted to be Attorney General of the United States, but he hadn't the nerve to take a course which would appear to be deserting his friends.'

Probably realizing this, for he was too shrewd for self-deception, Daugherty dodged and shirked, not because he was lazy or negligent, but because he knew himself to be out of his depth. One of the energetic young Congressmen of his

[1] *Our Times*, vol. VI.   [2] *Investigation of the Attorney General.*
[3] Taft Letters. Library of Congress.
[4] To his biographer, Philip C. Jessup.

time, John Taber of New York, found him the only Cabinet official difficult to see. 'Toward the end of his term it was almost impossible to get to him. No excuse; no explanation. He just wasn't available for business.'[1] And another Representative, an Ohioan and Republican, never came in contact with him during his term except in casual encounters.[2]

Not so with Jess Smith. He was on the job. He missed few opportunities. Anyone who wanted to do business with him could find him in that office of his, whereof the Attorney General knew nothing. In fact, he exhibited a surplus of energy. Lack of reasonable caution was the weakness which finally undid him. Sudden rise to influence and affluence is apt to blunt the instinct of self-protection: the well-fortified grafter comes to regard himself as immune.

Until he came East, Jess was just a simple, small-town shopkeeper. He did not mix in politics. He ran an honest business. His compelling and naïve ambition was to be seen in the company of the great. The transposition from Washington Court House, Ohio, to Washington, D.C., was too much for his balance. He went in for the loot with the simplicity and abandon of a cat at a cream pitcher.

In the early days of his glory Jess lived with Harry Daugherty in the snug little house on H Street, loaned by Edward B. McLean for their use. The sport of the country town and the playboy of the great world were kindred spirits. Jess was invited to visit the McLeans at Bar Harbor.

'Ned McLean and I think the same about a lot of things,' he told his ex-wife, Roxy Stinson.[3]

McLean, also, was a regularly constituted official of the Department of Justice, although, unlike Jess, he contributed nothing to its activities. His was a complimentary appointment, as Special Agent of the Bureau of Investigation. 'I

---

[1] Statement of Congressman Taber to the writer.
[2] Statement of ex-Congressman Roy Fitzgerald to the writer.
[3] *Investigation of the Attorney General.*

got a code, a little card, and a badge,' he bashfully informed a Senate Committee.[1]

Honorary emolument of this sort was a distinction allotted to special friends of the Attorney General. Involving no duties or responsibilities, it conferred departmental privileges, assured special consideration by the authorities in case of minor trouble, and initiated the fortunate possessor into the mysteries of the Government cipher. There is an engaging touch of childhood's happy days about the whole matter; one wonders whether the participants did not meet in midnight conclave and have a password and a grip. Fred Upham, of 'Boys, get the money' fame, was another initiate.

In his less romantic functions, McLean was owner by inheritance of the prosperous *Cincinnati Enquirer* and the influential *Washington Post*, known to the light-minded as the Court Journal.

The oddly named Jap Muma, also from Ohio, was general factotum for McLean, who knew the newspaper business mainly by hearsay. Jap was also in some measure a social entrepreneur for the McLean entertainments. In this capacity he imported to Washington, in violation of the statute, the films of the Dempsey-Carpentier fight, which had their first showing at one of the McLeans' vast parties, attended by Washington's high officialdom. Presumptively the governmental guests were unaware that they were lending countenance to an illegal performance.

Muma developed his film displays into a business enterprise, under the protection of the Department of Justice, having shrewdly let Jess Smith in on the profits. Jess figured that his share ought to be worth $180,000.[2]

Following the fight in which the giant negro Johnson beat Jeffries for the world championship (that same Johnson whose later incarceration enlisted the sporting sympathies of President Harding), all fight films were barred from inter-

[1] *Investigation of the Attorney General.*   [2] *Ibid.*

state traffic. The new law was designed to save the imperilled prestige of the white race!

Laws have loopholes. This one penalized merely the transportation and delivery of fight films from state to state. Once across the border and released, the picture could be exhibited with impunity. Muma and a sharp lawyer, said to have been recommended to him by the Attorney General,[1] worked out a device whereby the film would be shipped to a scapegoat who would submit to arrest and plead guilty. Thereupon a fine would be assessed and paid. Any exhibitor in that state could now safely put the picture on his list.

Complaisance if not actual corruption on the part of the federal courts was an essential to the working-out of the plan, since judges and district attorneys must be found who could be trusted merely to fine instead of jailing the scapegoats.[2] That the system of connivance operated successfully in more than twenty states casts a sinister light upon the federal judiciary of the day.

Though Ned McLean and his festivities were too important to be subject to the law, further transactions in this field brought the promoter within the ken of the authorities. Rudely aroused to the fact that a pair of Government men who could not be 'fixed' were on his trail, the Jap burst forth into a classic lament for his imperilled freedom.[3]

'Fine! Jap Muma, general manager of the McLean newspapers. Personal friend of the Attorney General. Old acquaintance of President Harding; called him "Warren"; calls me "Jap." Fine! On my way to Atlanta as a conspirator. The master mind!'

His apprehensions were premature. At the behest of his employer, Special Agent McLean (with badge, card, and

---

[1] *Investigation of the Attorney General.*

[2] Judges Landis in Illinois and Anderson in Indiana were to be shunned by the fixers, since they would enter into no deals. *Ibid.*

[3] *Ibid.*

code), the higher-ups of the Department of Justice took the tremulous Jap under its protection, and the evidence against him was buried in its files.

Gratifying increase in the law practice of several associates of Attorney General Daugherty was presently noted by the Washington bar. As Attorney General, Mr. Daugherty could not, with propriety, retain his membership in his home-town firm of Daugherty, Todd & Rarey. He resigned. Notwithstanding this loss, the firm prospered. Mr. Rarey, Daugherty's son-in-law, received an appointment in the New York City office of the Alien Property Bureau. There was an important underground connection between this agency and the Department of Justice, though it does not appear that Mr. Rarey had any part in this. Mr. John E. Todd, the other partner, found his law practice suddenly so enhanced by official business connected with the Department of Justice and the Alien Property Bureau that he was obliged to spend much of his time in Washington.

Whether correctly or incorrectly it was an accepted theory in certain circles that Mr. Todd was the lawyer to handle difficult cases. He was by no means invariably successful. Nevertheless, the business continued to come his way. Cecil H. Kerns, president of a bootlegging drug concern, sentenced to Atlanta, retained Mr. Todd at a fee of five hundred dollars a month, because, as he explained, of his influence at Washington.[1] Kern's prison term was cut short by parole. Colonel Thomas B. Felder (later convicted and disbarred), Daugherty's associate in the dubious pardon of Charles W. Morse, was frequently retained by interests which were liable to prosecution by the Department of Justice. Doctor Alderfer comments upon the suspiciously small proportion of such cases that ever came to trial.[2] Apparently Colonel Felder had at command certain powers of immunity.

[1] *Investigation of the Attorney General.*
[2] H. F. Alderfer: *The Personality and Politics of Warren G. Harding.*

Daugherty had selected William J. Burns to head the Federal Bureau of Investigation. It was a bad appointment. In official intention the Bureau was an agency for the detection of crime. Under Burns it became a weapon for use against the forces of law and order. Let an individual or a constituted body, such as an investigating committee, attempt to clean up or pry into evil conditions, and the Bureau set in movement its formidable machinery of espionage, menace, and oppression.

'Government by blackmail,' Senator Brookhart termed it, and Boyden Sparkes observed that for the first time 'private detective ethics had been introduced into a high place in the government.'

Shortly after the Senate adopted Senator Wheeler's resolution for investigation of the Department of Justice,[1] Burns's agents were in Montana working up a flimsy case against the Senator, and secured his indictment on a charge of unlawfully accepting a retainer to influence the issuance of oil and gas property permits by the Secretary of the Interior. The jury exonerated him almost without discussion. Nevertheless, one of Daugherty's men spread the report that he had 'smeared Wheeler in such shape that he had him sewed up.'

Any official who became offensive, dangerous, or obstructive to the Attorney General, the Director of the Bureau of Investigation, or their interests or friends, was liable to be made the object of petty persecutions. Senator La Follette, the elder, was known to be hostile to Daugherty. Operatives under the direction of Burns looted his office and rifled his papers. Elias H. Mortimer intruded upon the pardon graft which was a special perquisite of the Ohio Gang. The Bureau agents got after him. Congressmen Johnson and Woodruff criticized the Attorney General for inactivity in prosecuting war frauds, and were subjected to undercover espionage by

[1] March 1, 1924.

departmental operatives. The purpose was not honest investigation, but blackmail, as set forth by one of the experts in the procedure.

> If you found something damaging on a man you would quietly get word to him through some of his friends that he had better put the soft pedal on the situation. That is the way the information is generally used when you find it.[1]

Upon request the Department of Justice was ready to put its peculiar facilities at the service of other departments. Cabinet members Daugherty and Fall were never very good friends. Nonetheless, when Colonel Jim Darden, whom we have already met as a contributor to the Harding war-chest, threatened to interfere with Fall's oil graft, an F. B. I. man was detailed to snoop for compromising information about him. When Senator Walsh was pressing hard on Fall in the Teapot Dome investigations, a Department of Justice secret service agent (J. Edgar Hoover and the movies had not yet popularized the term, G–man), named Blair Coan, was sent to Montana to see what he could dig up or promote. Among other efforts he requested a Helena attorney to swear to an affidavit implicating Senator Walsh.

'He said he wanted something on Walsh,' testified Attorney Grorud,' so that he could smear him, because he wanted to stop him in the oil investigations.'[2]

This same Coan wrote a book proving, to his own satisfaction and presumably that of Mr. Daugherty, that the whole case against the Attorney General was a plot engendered in Red Russia.[3]

The first requirement of an employee of the Department was not that he should be efficient against law-breakers, but that he should be tactful in the prosecution of his inquiries. Of the agents who probed into Jap Muma's operations in the

---

[1] *Investigation of the Attorney General.* Testimony of Gaston B. Means.

[2] *Investigation of the Attorney General.*

[3] *The Red Web*, a work of superheated imagination.

prize-fight film industry, one, Holdridge, was so hampered that he resigned and another, Navarro, was transferred to Haiti.

Burns's favorite for the dirty work of the Bureau was Gaston B. Means. Daugherty admits that he appointed Means 'with misgivings,' upon the recommendation of Burns, who needed that sort of aide. As the Department was then in possession of a dossier from the District Attorney of New York County setting forth Means's peculiar record, there was more ground for the misgivings than for the appointment.

Means was a career man in crime. When he was about thirty years old, he fell from the upper berth of a Pullman car, one chain of which had been filed half through, and collected on the abnormally large insurance policies which he held. After a remarkably lingering recovery, he went to New York, where those extremely credulous and inept German diplomats and spies, Count von Papen and Captain Boy-Ed, were conducting their plots and committing their blunders. He so impressed the Germans that they paid him a large salary and installed him in a luxurious Park Avenue apartment with a life-size portrait of the Kaiser in the dining-room.[1] This was before the United States entered the war. Upon the discovery of various highly undiplomatic enterprises on the part of the diplomats, they departed by request, leaving their Park Avenue agent jobless.

Riding up and down in the elevator, he had scraped acquaintance with a rich widow named King. He filled her mind, which was too weak for the burden, with weird tales of international spies, persuaded her that she was a marked woman, and established himself as her bodyguard. In the course of time he induced her to follow him to his home in

[1] This bare outline of a varied career is derived partly from Means's testimony, partly from his writings, and partly from the statements of friends and classmates of his in the University of North Carolina.

North Carolina, on the pretext that to remain in New York, shorn of his protecting presence, would be simply to court destruction.

In his home town of Concord, North Carolina, he took her to the woods one evening for 'target practice.' The night was pitch-black, there was no target, but there was a pistol, although the widow had a horror of firearms. The weapon was discharged and she was killed. Arraigned on a charge of murder, Means was able to prove that he came from a prominent North Carolina family and had an uncle who was an officer in the Confederate army. Naturally he was acquitted. Subsequently, two wills turned up, purporting to be signed by Mrs. King, but showing evidence of the Means influence. Both were declared fraudulent by the courts.

On his modest official stipend of $88.33 per week Means rented a Washington home at $1000 per month, owned a $5000 car driven by a liveried chauffeur, and lived on a par with his friend, Jess Smith, though his social contacts were less impressive. It was Means who acted in a confidential capacity for both Burns and Smith. In the Senate investigation of Daugherty he 'told all' — probably much more than all, for he could never be depended upon to speak the truth when a lie of livelier interest occurred to him. Festive souls in local bar-rooms used to chant:

> Who spilled the beans?
> 'I,' said Gaston Means.
> 'I was behind the scenes.
> I spilled the beans.'

He testified that in the summer of 1921 a Japanese representative of Mitsui and Company paid over to Smith $100,000 in bills.[1] The Standard Aircraft Company, controlled by the Mitsuis, was at the time threatened with litigation by the Government. Charles R. Forbes, dropping in

[1] *Investigation of the Attorney General.*

to see Jess one day at his office, created such a draught that several thousand-dollar bills were blown from a pile on the desk. Forbes reckoned that in all there would be about seventy-five of them. The custodian of this wealth remarked that it was 'the General's.' [1] Some time later Jess wrote gleefully to his Roxy that he was banking $175,000 of 'Eastern money' in the Daugherty-controlled bank at Washington Court House.[2]

All this comes from witnesses of unreliable character. But Jess's guilt in the American Metal case is indubitable.

It has been mentioned that there was an unofficial liaison between the Department of Justice and the Alien Property Custodian's office. The active participants were the Attorney General, his partner, Jess Smith, John T. King, and Alien Property Custodian Thomas W. Miller.

Mr. Miller was regarded as one of President Harding's soundest appointments. A lawyer of good though not eminent standing, a Yale graduate, a communicant of the Episcopal Church, a member of leading Philadelphia clubs, a man of unblemished character and record, he might have stood as the type of the gentleman in politics. Gentlemen, when they get into politics, sometimes do ungentlemanly things.

Among the enemy-owned corporations, confiscated by the Government when we entered the World War, was the American Metal Company, a German concern. Under the regular process, the company was liquidated and the proceeds of about six and one-half million dollars, invested in Liberty Bonds, which were in the control of the Alien Property Custodian. A German named Richard Merton appeared in Washington, representing the American Metal Company, to claim the return of the six and one-half million dollars, on the flimsy pretext of a pre-war oral transfer to a Swiss,

[1] *New York World*, December 4, 1927.
[2] *Investigation of the Attorney General.*

and therefore neutral, corporation. He took his case to John Foster Dulles of New York who gave him scant encouragement. What Merton needed for his operations was not a reputable lawyer, but a not too reputable political go-between. He found him in the person of John T. King.

King has already been met with as vote-peddler at Chicago for Penrose. He was a shrewd, smooth political-financier, shady in both phases. Merton commissioned King, who was not a lawyer, to look after his interests. King made a deal with Jess Smith representing (unofficially, of course) the Department of Justice, and with Miller representing the Alien Property Bureau. There was money in it for all of them, he set forth.

Procedure at that time required that a claim, after being passed by the Alien Property Custodian, must then go to the Department of Justice for the approval of the Attorney General. This was usually a slow process, owing to pressure of business. In this case it was expedited, in fact 'greased.'

Merton filed his claims on September 20, 1921. Approval was immediate. The papers, accompanied by a favorable recommendation, went to the Department of Justice on September 21. They came back, officially passed, on the twenty-third. The mechanism was working swiftly and smoothly.

All was now clear — and perfectly legal. Within a few days, Miller drew two checks on the Treasury, aggregating $6,453,979.97; also two lots of Liberty Bonds to the total value of $514,350. With checks and bonds he travelled to New York for a celebratory dinner given by Merton for him, King, and Smith. So grateful was the host to one and all that he distributed $200 cigarette cases as mementoes. A more private memento was $391,300 in bonds, and $50,000 in cash to that adept ironer-out of difficulties, John T. King. Here the record is somewhat uncertain. King turned over to Jess Smith certainly $50,000 and perhaps $100,000. The price of the Alien Property Custodian's official virtue was $49,000. About $40,000 worth of the bonds turned up in the Daugherty bank in Washington Court House, as the property of Attorney General Harry M. Daugherty.[1] When criminal action was brought against both the Alien Property Custodian and the Attorney General, Mal Daugherty helpfully allowed his brother to burn the bank records. This saved him in what was perhaps the tightest spot of a life by no means devoid of hazards.

Out in Oklahoma the Miller Brothers, of the famous Ranch 101, were indicted for swindling the Indians, wards of the Government, out of valuable oil lands. They had powerful connections in both the Republican and the Democratic camps. Secretary Fall wrote to Attorney General Daugherty, asking delay. The plan was to release two of the indicted men who actually had not profited by these particular frauds and impose fines upon the others in consideration of pleas of guilty. The justice of this latter procedure is not apparent. The Millers were notorious in Oklahoma for this sort of chicanery. One of them was a convicted counterfeiter. At the lowest valuation, the land out of which they had jockeyed the Indians was worth $380,000; any fines assessed would have left them with a handsome profit. H. M. Peck, a local lawyer of repute, appointed as Special Attorney for the Department of Justice, stood out for prison sentences.

Serious trouble loomed for the Millers. They retained Lawyer John E. Todd. According to the testimony, he earned his fee by appearing only in an advisory capacity on a minor phase of law.[2] Nevertheless, the signs began to favor the Millers. In the face of Mr. Peck's thorough familiarity with the case which he had prepared, the Department of

---

[1] Decision of Judge O'Donohue declaring the Government refund to the American Metal Company fraudulent; District Court of Appeals for the District of Columbia, No. 6978.

[2] *Investigation of the Attorney General.*

Justice planned to substitute for him one of its regular staff. Information to this effect stirred up Senator Harreld. He warned Attorney General Daugherty that there would be open scandal if Todd appeared for the defence and Peck were dropped from the prosecution.

Daugherty professed surprise at learning that his former partner was connected with the case — just as he had expressed surprise on being informed of Jess Smith's activities in his Department. The Attorney General's capacity for amazement was unlimited. On his advice Mr. Todd withdrew from the case. He did not, however, return any part of his two-thousand-dollar fee. Special Attorney Peck was continued for a time. But the Attorney General adopted the extraordinary measure of wiring to him to accept the Miller plea of guilty, with the fine agreed upon. Peck protested and was superseded.[1] The original arrangement was carried through and the Millers walked out of court, free men. Incidentally, two investigators for the Indian Bureau, who were overactive in securing evidence against them, were discharged from the service.

In Texas, Special Agent B. C. Baldwin of the Bureau of Investigation, stationed at El Paso, undertook to check gunrunning into Mexico. He also attempted to enforce the Prohibition Law. In the first instance he ran counter to some of Secretary Fall's former associates, and the oil interests who were fostering an abortive revolution, in the latter, to one of Attorney General Daugherty's family. One, Harry Hamilton, a Prohibition agent, had worked up a nice little business raiding moonshine outfits, confiscating the plants and selling the stills back to the bootleggers. Agent Baldwin arrested him. Thereupon Dave Walker, a United States Marshal and brother-in-law of Harry Daugherty, was called into the case and it was quietly dropped. Director Burns sent out an official order instructing all Special Agents not to investigate

[1] *Investigation of the Attorney General.*

federal officials without specific orders. As usual, the Bureau of Investigation was engaged in shielding the crooks against prosecution. As for the arms-smuggling industry, the El Paso office was closed, and the traffic in arms-across-the-border continued, unhampered. Baldwin was forced out of the service soon after by being transferred to Butte, Montana. Being an asthmatic, he could not live in the rarefied air of that altitude. He resigned.[1]

Pardons supply some curious examples of the Daugherty methods. Lou Frank was a prominent lumberman of Nashville, Tennessee. He falsified his income tax return to the extent of $60,000 and falsely swore to the figures. He doctored the firm's books to cover the fraud. Thus he was guilty of evasion, perjury, and forgery. There was no room for doubt. He pleaded guilty.[2] In the circumstances his sentence of five thousand dollars fine and six months in jail does not seem excessive. He never served a day of his sentence. Attorney Daugherty recommended to the President a remission of the jail sentence and the President obliged. He couldn't say No. One of the sorriest exhibits of a sorry showing on the part of Department officials on the stand, was their attempt to adduce some valid reason for this extraordinary clemency.

But Mr. Harding eventually reached a point of conscience or perhaps wrath where he could and did firmly say No.

'President Harding, in the latter part of his Administration,' states James A. Finch, attorney in charge of pardons in the Department of Justice, 'would not pardon anyone unless he had served some part of his sentence, no matter what the situation was.'[3]

If the President would not, the Department of Justice found a way of getting around the difficulty in contemptuous disregard of his principles. One, Philip Grossman, a Chicago violator of the liquor law, was sentenced to a year in the

---

[1] *Investigation of the Attorney General.* [2] *Ibid.* [3] *Ibid.*

penitentiary and a fine of one thousand dollars. Before his term began, application was made for a pardon. Harding rejected it. A further attempt was made, backed by Fred Upham and Senator Medill McCormick. Roused, the President sent a specific message:

'No further consideration can be given this case until some part of the sentence is served.'

No part of the sentence was ever served; not a day. The fine was paid and the bootlegger walked out of court.[1] Later President Coolidge commuted the sentence.

Choice of a lawyer was important in liquor cases. Two large-scale bootleggers, Kerns and Tolhem, were tried and convicted together. After the trial they were quietly advised to put their case into the hands of S. R. Bolen, a Special Assistant to the Department of Justice. Tolhem did so. Kerns preferred his own counsel. Both counsel made motions for a new trial before the same judge. Kerns's application was rejected. He went to jail. Special Assistant Bolen served his client better. His motion was not accepted: the contrast in the two decisions would have been too patent; but it was 'taken under advisement.' It remained in that kindly legal shelter while Kerns served part of his sentence.[2] He might have served all had he not, as indicated above, seen the light and employed a member of the Daugherty firm to get him out.

The conduct of the Wright-Martin Aircraft Corporation case added nothing to the repute of the Department of Justice. Evidence had been gathered over a long period by Captain H. L. Scaife, a Department expert, to show overpayments to the company of three and a half million dollars. On two sets of contracts, this was to be made the basis of a suit brought by the Government through the Department, for the return of the overcharges. The suit lagged. Nothing was done. Captain Scaife found himself blocked in

[1] *Investigation of the Attorney General.*   [2] *Ibid.*

every endeavor to get action, not only within the Department, but also in the War Department, supposed to be working with the Attorney General's office, in the interests of the Government. Finally he resigned in despair and disgust.[1] His report on the case vanished from the departmental files. Other Government departments found it inadvisable to trust the Department of Justice with important documents. They were likely to disappear as had Captain Scaife's dossier. This, however, was nothing new. The same thing frequently happened under the previous Democratic régime. Daugherty and Burns did not invent all the tricks; they inherited and improved upon some.

When he took office, Harry M. Daugherty owned five hundred shares of Wright-Martin stock. In the next year he had increased his holdings by two thousand shares.[2] It is impossible to establish any connection between this ownership and the torpor of the Attorney General's office in handling the claim against the aircraft concern. But the propriety of the head of the Department of Justice holding stock in a corporation subject to suit by him as head of the Department hardly requires proof.

Thomas F. Lane, legal assistant to the Chief of the Army Air Service, assigned to special duty in the Department of Justice, exhumed some important evidence in the Standard Aircraft case, toward which the Department was displaying an extraordinary tenderness, possibly explicable on the ground of the alleged payment of $100,000 to Jess Smith. Mr. Lane's superior took over his papers and forbade his appearing before a Senate committee which was specially interested in Standard Aircraft. 'That is orders,' he was told. He gave testimony before the committee. Thereupon he was dropped from the service and his papers confiscated. Major W. O. Watts, who assisted two inquiring Congressmen in their investigations into war frauds, was let out for

[1] *Investigation of the Attorney General.*   [2] *Ibid.*

'disloyalty.' [1] Loyalty to the Government service was interpreted as disloyalty to the Department of Justice.

Giving testimony in response to the questions of investigators, even under subpoena, was regarded and punished as insubordination. Mrs. Duckstein, Burns's secretary, was summoned before the committee investigating the Attorney General, and testified under oath as she was compelled to do or be adjudged in contempt. The next day she received a letter from J. Edgar Hoover, Acting Director of the Bureau, peremptorily demanding her resignation. [2] Notwithstanding that Gaston B. Means had been Burns's favorite for a certain type of confidential work, the Bureau of Investigation prosecuted and sent him to jail, after his 'bean-spilling' revelations had startled Washington. There was, however, ample cause for jailing him aside from his evidence.

One of the ablest and most upright of Daugherty's lieutenants was Assistant Attorney General John W. H. Crim. [3] In the Old Hickory Powder Company case, in which war frauds were alleged, he found his work constantly hampered, and wrote to the United States District Attorney in Nashville, Tennessee:

> It now appears from what transpired that there cannot be any question that it was the intention of someone to frustrate any investigation. . . . I have prevented just such tricks being worked a great many times.

The obstruction was mainly the work of the War Department, which appeared bent on shielding the Dupont Company, owner of the Old Hickory Company, though there was some collusion in the Department of Justice. Finding himself unable to make progress, Mr. Crim resigned, though he

---

[1] *New York Times*, March 2, 1924. The efforts of the complaining Congressmen were smothered in the Rules Committee.

[2] *Investigation of the Attorney General.*

[3] He was recalled to the Government service to prosecute Charles R. Forbes, whom he convicted.

never alleged this as the cause. On the contrary, he retained his faith in and loyalty to his chief, to the end. His character sketch of the Attorney General makes an interesting addition to the record. He is testifying before the Senate committee:[1]

> Harry Daugherty was not the man who could take a pencil and say, 'Crim, you say the situation is so-and-so.' He was not that kind of an executive. He had not that training.... His policy usually ... was to get everybody around him who might know something about a matter, and then discuss it and talk it out, and then say, 'Now go ahead' ... but there was one thing I always felt ... that the last thing on earth that Harry Daugherty would ever be guilty of was disloyalty to an assistant.... He would say to me, 'Crim, you are too aggressive; hold on; wait. You are pushing me too hard; I have got to see others before I can do this. We must talk this over at the Cabinet meeting ... well, now, hold on now.' We would compromise by his going over to the White House or something of that sort.... And oftentimes I have seen him put on his hat and go to the White House ... not often, but a number of times when the matter of granting things occurred ... go to the White House and come back and say, 'Now I could not see the President. He is tied up today. I will take it up with him as soon as I can.' ... But on this question of loyalty to an assistant or selling the Government in any way for money, why, gentlemen, it is utterly impossible....

Upon assuming office, Attorney General Harry M. Daugherty was far from affluent. He had gone broke helping to finance the Harding campaign from his own pocket.[2] His taxable property was listed in his Ohio return for 1920 at $8030, with liabilities of $27,000,[3] yet, from the inception of his official career, he contrived to live like a man of wealth. Chairman Brookhart, of the Senate committee which endeavored to solve the mystery without any assistance from Mr. Daugherty, comments: 'The tax returns of Mr. Daugh-

---

[1] *Investigation of the Attorney General.*

[2] Finley Peter Dunne: *Saturday Evening Post*, September 12, 1936.

[3] *Investigation of the Attorney General.*

erty, himself, show that he had no property; he was in debt
more than he was worth when he became Attorney General.
The evidence shows that we found in his brother's bank live
certificates of deposit to him of nearly $75,000, which would
be accumulated within these two or three years, on a $12,000
salary.'

As Jess Smith ran the Daugherty-Smith ménage, kept the
books, and paid the bills, he was in a position to estimate
their scale of expenditure. Fifty thousand dollars a year is
the initial rate which he names. Rental was not at first included, since they lived, rent-free, in one of Ned McLean's
houses. Later they paid the Wardman Park Hotel $7800 a
year for a housekeeping suite.

How Smith was able to afford his half is glaringly apparent. The sources of the Attorney General's competency are
less patent. That there must have been either extraneous
income or realizable expectations of emoluments is an inevitable inference. Mr. Daugherty was by no means im-
poverished, upon his resignation, from the strain of living at
a $25,000 pace on a $12,000 income. Ample opportunity to
explain his system of finance was open to him; he avoided
the witness stand as a wary animal shuns a trap.

Under the régime of Harding's appointee, the Department
of Justice reached its lowest ebb in morale, morals, and
efficiency, and this in spite of many able sub-executives.
The blight of the Daugherty-Jess Smith-Burns system was
over it all.

Senator Ashurst applied the term, 'Department of Easy
Virtue,' to Harry Daugherty's administration. It was
justified.

★

XXIV. Menace

GOLF partners noticed a deterioration of the President's game early in 1923. At the outset of his term he had been a rain-or-shine enthusiast, undaunted by adverse conditions, and as keen on the last putt as for the first drive. Now he was listless. At the end of nine holes, or even earlier, lassitude overtook him. Not infrequently he would give up on the twelfth or thirteenth green. His fellow players inclined to attribute this to worry. They were mistaken. The cause was physical.

Harding's heart was giving out. For several months he had been unable to sleep without propping himself high on packed pillows. That uncanny diagnostician, Doctor Emmanuel Libman, meeting him at a dinner party in the fall of 1922, privately told friends that within six months the President would be dead of a coronary ailment, already far advanced.[1] He only slightly underrated the subject's powers of resistance.

How far Harding suspected his own condition is difficult to surmise. He was a person of marked fortitude in physical matters, little given to complaining. It is significant that he cut down on parties and the indulgences that go with them.

[1] *The New Yorker*, April 8, 1939.

He was seeing little of Nan Britton. In January she came surreptitiously to the White House, where he made arrangements for her to go to Europe at his expense.[1] It was their last tryst.

To physical debility was added mental distress, enhanced by a degree of concern for his own fortunes. Not alone from the jarring testimony of the November elections, but also from the politician's innate sense of what the public is feeling, he realized that he was gradually losing caste with the man in the street. It was an intolerable thought. He who had been well on the way to realize his naïve hope of becoming the best-loved of Presidents discovered how swiftly the public smile can turn to a scowl.[2] But he had confidence in his ability to mend all this, given a fair opportunity. Let him only come face to face with his fellows and explain himself to them, man-fashion, and all would be well. He could make them believe the truth that was in him. Harding preserved a solid faith in himself; not in his achievements in office, which were inadequate and had fallen far short of his hopes thus far (he could perhaps do better in a second term), but in his purpose, his pure intentions, his goodwill to do the best in his power for the nation that he served and loved.

The desire grew within him to travel, to elude the ruthless drive of work and worry. For nearly two years he had been on the treadmill, compelled to labor consistently and continuously. It was a new and harsh experience for him. Nothing in his temperament fitted him nor in his training disciplined him for the ordeal. Demands upon him had never been exigent before. He had selected a course of life which required only easy and congenial effort. Now he was tired, worn. He had earned if not a rest — rest is a respite beyond presidential attainment — at least a change.

[1] Nan Britton: *The President's Daughter.*
[2] Samuel G. Blythe, a warm admirer of the President, commented on the increasing criticism in his *Saturday Evening Post* article of July 28, 1923.

Two grisly tragedies within the circle of his immediate friends accentuated his longing to be quit of Washington for a time. Added to the shock of the Jess Smith and Cramer suicides was the disillusionment of the Forbes betrayal. Perhaps he could forget it if he could get out and 'bloviate' once more; meet the great American common folk, mix with friendly crowds. It would be a relief to his spirit. People did not weary, they stimulated him. Antaeus-like, he drew strength from those earthy contacts. The pressure of friendly hands, the repetition of good wishes from earnest and loyal faces, the fervent 'God bless yous' of the old folk, the cheers of welcome and the acclaim of farewell, combined to form an atmosphere in which he breathed more deeply and richly, inhaling a new faith in himself, a fresh sense of support and adherence. Official life constrained him. He had had too much of it. He wanted to meet people in the mass. The trip itself would be recreation. He could pick out guests for the train who would make up a pleasant poker table or a four at bridge, and maybe he could work in some golf betweentimes.

Though he had begun to consider the trip early in the year, he could not plan to leave his post before spring, and, as problems accumulated, the date must be postponed to early summer. Before leaving, he set his house in order. This he did with a completeness which suggests an apprehension on his part of failing strength, a revival of the post-election foreboding that he might not live to fill out his term. Yet, at the same time, he was looking forward to a re-election. No other hypothesis fits in with his sale of the *Marion Star*.

The *Star* was Warren G. Harding's pride of accomplishment. It was his life-work, the growth of his faith and effort. Always it had been his explicit ambition to come back to the editorial desk, hang up hat and coat, tuck away a plug of tobacco where it would do the most good, and get to work. Over and over again he declared this intention. It was no pose. Once again it may be stated that in thought, tastes, aspirations, standards, and instincts Warren G. Harding was a newspaperman. Politics was a side issue, an accident of his statesmanlike front and the ambitions of his wife and his closest friend. Only his intention to spend four more years in the White House would move him to give up the *Star*. But he could not be President and properly guard the interests of the paper. An offer of $550,000 was made. He accepted it, one may guess with sadness and a sense of sacrifice.

Long afterward, when every deal in which Harding had been involved was under hostile scrutiny, this price was made the subject of criticism and even accusation. It was suggested that a political debt was being paid off obliquely.[1] At first thought the price seems inordinate for a newspaper in a city of thirty thousand. But the *Star* was a phenomenally profitable enterprise. More than this, there was an understanding that Harding would conduct an editorial column, a feature of unique value to the publication and a potential source of highly profitable syndicate returns, since any matter from a presidential pen would have a ready sale throughout the country. At the agreed price, the purchaser's investment was sound. As there had been a considerable distribution of stock among the employees, by no means all of the sum went to the chief owner.

There was need of ready money. Harding had been playing the market heavily, too heavily, and with ill-fortune. There is no law which forbids a President of the United States to gamble on Wall Street. But it is not a procedure likely to meet with the approval of the circumspect. Ever sensitive to public opinion, ever hesitant toward any action which might be deemed unseemly, Harding covered his tracks through the familiar ruse of a 'blind' account carried by an Ohio firm

[1] Frank A. Vanderlip, a Republican and a political purist, who had been consistently suspicious of the Administration, made this charge, but was forced to withdraw it.

with a Washington office, Ungerleider and Company.[1] The local manager was the former secret service operative who had acted as cash-and-carry go-between for Harding in his communications with Nan Britton. Shortly before his departure, the President called up the Ungerleider office.

'How does my account stand?' he asked.

'You are down in our books for $180,000, Mr. President,' was the reply.

Harding was startled. He asked a few more questions. There was an understanding that the matter would be taken up on his return from the West.[2]

Prima facie, the unfortunate market ventures are proof that the President was not using the unlimited opportunites for 'sure-thing' gambling which his office would afford to an unprincipled incumbent.

Something other than financial worry was haunting him. His perturbation and incertitude of spirit at this time (June, 1923) are indicated by the circumstances of an interview with President Nicholas Murray Butler of Columbia University. In response to a rather insistent invitation, Doctor Butler, at no small inconvenience since he was about to leave for Europe, came down from New York to see the President. From the nature of Harding's request, Doctor Butler inferred a wish to consult him upon some matter of major importance. Several times during the conversation Harding seemed to be leading up to some communication of this sort, but each time shied away as if unable to bring himself to the point.

After an hour of this, given over mainly to trivia, the visitor left, thoroughly mystified. His impression was that the matter in the President's mind was personal rather than political.[3]

[1] The establishment of the Washington branch followed Harding's inauguration; it was abandoned shortly after his death.

[2] These details came from a gentleman afterward associated closely, though unprofessionally, with the adjustment of Harding's market operations.

[3] Report of the interview confirmed by Doctor Butler.

Walter F. Brown, Harding's associate and friend of Ohio days, afterward Postmaster General in the Hoover Cabinet, was in charge of the speaking arrangements for the trip. Calling at the White House for a final consultation, he found the President in an upstairs room. Some sort of party had been in progress; a table was loaded with bottles and glasses. The caller was invited to help himself.

'Aren't you having anything, Mr. President?' he asked.

'No,' answered Harding gravely, 'I'm not. I've decided to cut it out as long as I'm here.'[1]

The matter of his personal habits and their incompatibility with his office had finally come to a head. In January he had told several of the reporters whom he knew best, off the record, that he had given up liquor, but they were inclined to be skeptical. This time, however, he had determined upon his course. There is presumptive evidence that the presidential impediments did not include alcoholic supplies on the tour westward.[2]

At the pre-tour conference Mr. Brown was worried about the President's condition and concerned over the grilling schedule of addresses, banquets, and receptions which he had laid out for himself. En route, Harding added to these by impromptu talks from the car platform. This at a time when rest was an imperative need. But he had lost the capacity for rest.

Physicians are familiar with a type of chronic indigestion wherein the sufferer is plagued by an inordinate craving for food which his system is incapable of assimilating. Harding's mind was in a similar state. He must continually be feeding it with effort, with action. It was racing like a detached engine. Sleep, broken and unrefreshing, did little to restore him. It might have been thought that with the death of Jess Smith, his friend had fallen heir to his tremors and terrors, his fear of the lonely dark, his dread of solitude. Harding felt

[1] Statement of Mr. Brown to the writer.   [2] See Chapter XXVI.

a continuous and feverish need of people about him. When left alone, he brooded. He must always be doing something, seeking relief in a factitious gaiety and nervous garrulity. He was a man beset and distraught.

Mrs. Harding, still an invalid, was worried about him. Doctor Sawyer, professionally as well as personally alarmed, in vain urged him to relax, to give brain and nerves a chance to recuperate. He was unable to.

The day before leaving, Harding sent for Harry Daugherty and made his will. It was arranged that they should meet in San Francisco. Daugherty does not seem to have shared the concern of other friends. In his book [1] he writes: 'The President was as happy when he left Washington on his Alaska trip as he had been at any time during his term of office.' But on another page he comments that Harding 'seemed mortally tired.'

It is probably not true that he was happy. If he was, his happiness was short-lived.

The special train, drawing the presidential car, 'Superb,' left Washington on June 20. Aboard were Mrs. Harding, with her trained nurse; Doctor Work, Secretary of the Interior, and his wife; Surgeon General Sawyer; George B. Christian, Jr., the President's secretary, with his wife; Doctor Joel T. Boone of the Navy, Ned McLean, and a few others invited for personal reasons; secret service men, Washington correspondents, stenographers, and a Navy band for meetings.

The early part of the journey was inauspicious. The Harding oratory, depending as this type of elocution always must, largely upon personal magnetism, suffered from his depleted vitality. Audiences were polite but apathetic. 'Canned speeches' the *Times* termed his carefully prepared efforts. Broadcasting was coming into vogue. The microphone annoyed the speaker; he seemed suspicious of it, al-

[1] *The Inside Story of the Harding Tragedy.*

most timid in its presence. He was unhappily conscious of not being at his best. What was left to him if he lost his power to make friends and influence people with his fluent platitudes, his ready and appealing smile?

As the expedition bored farther into the West, there was improvement. People were more responsive, more sympathetic. St. Louis received him kindly. So did Kansas City. His heart condition was unimproved. William Allen White noticed that 'his lips were swollen and blue, his eyes puffed, and his hands seemed stiff when I shook hands with him.' [1] Here at the hotel an interview took place which may well have been for Harding the first premonition of catastrophe.

An elderly woman, veiled and furtive, eluded the reporters and was ushered up to the President's floor. She was Mrs. Albert B. Fall, wife of the ex-Secretary of the Interior. Senator and Mrs. Arthur Capper were with the Hardings when she appeared. Senator Capper recalls clearly the circumstances.

> She seemed to be greatly disturbed and talked quietly with the President for a few minutes; then they dropped into one of the private rooms in the suite occupied by the Hardings. They were there for nearly an hour. [2]

Harding was profoundly agitated. Afterward on the train he paraphrased (unknowingly, it may be assumed) the classic complaint of the Maréchal de Villars to Louis XIV: [3]

'In this job I am not worried about my enemies. It is my friends that are keeping me awake nights.'

What was said in the long and secret talk which left the President scared and shaken may never be known. But the subject can be assumed with certitude. It could have been nothing else but Oil.

[1] Letter to the writer.   [2] Letter to the writer.
[3] 'Defend me from my friends; I can defend myself from my enemies.'

★

XXV. Oil

I

ONE of the picturesque figures of Harding's Washington was Albert Bacon Fall. Ranching, office-holding, and an occasional venture in oil engrossed his energies in New Mexico before he came to the United States Senate. Born in Kentucky and raised in the open West, he looked both parts. He was a go-getter, a bit of a bluff in his quiet way, with a touch of the Bad Man from the Border, dressing the rôle in broad-brimmed hat and flowing tie, and playing it with a slow drawl from beside the cigar which he habitually held in his teeth, and a piercingly direct glance from his bright-blue, alert eyes.

With his fellow Senators Fall had been popular. He had shown considerable forcefulness and acumen, but no outstanding ability; nothing to explain Harding's extravagant estimate of his mentality. As a member of the queerly assorted Cabinet which the President had composed out of compulsory fitness, political pressure, partisan urgency, and personal predilections, Fall was not as well-placed as in his former office; he did not accommodate himself smoothly to the new mechanism. He ran counter to men whom he could neither cajole nor bully. This may in part account for his resignation, halfway through his term.

For a successful and ambitious politician Fall was in poor financial condition when he entered the Harding Cabinet. His ranch at Three Rivers,[1] New Mexico, was run down, the house dilapidated, the roads hazardous, the stock and equipment depleted. Taxes were due from 1912. There were debts. Mr. Fall was reputed locally to be 'broke.'[2]

A quick turn for the better puzzled the neighbors. Progressively the ranch took on an air of prosperity. The house was put in repair. Cement gutters and expensive wire fencing flanked the driveways. Blooded stock appeared on the grazing lands. All arrears of taxation were paid up and two new parcels were added to the property, one at a cost of $91,500, the other of $33,000. Prosperity had come around the corner to meet Secretary Fall. All this was done in two years. The salary of a Cabinet officer was $12,000 a year. He had no known outside source of income to explain the rise in his fortunes.

But he had two friends, or, to employ the expressive theatrical parlance for a rehabilitation which was certainly dramatic enough, two angels: E. L. Doheny and Harry F. Sinclair, oil magnates. They are the answer to the problem in arithmetic posed above.

Pro forma we may accept a Senate committee report that proof is lacking to connect Fall's appointment with the presence and influence of oil interests at the convention which nominated Harding. Some weight must be given, however, to inferences indicating that Doheny and Sinclair or their agents knew quite well what they might expect of the new administration. President Harding and his Cabinet had not been in office a month when the blueprints for extensive looting operations were drawn up and approved. One agency was

[1] Officially the name was Spanish: Tres Rios.
[2] *Senate Hearings before the Committee on Public Lands and Surveys: Leases upon Naval Oil Reserves*, Government Printing Office, 1924; hereafter to be abbreviated to *Oil Lease Hearings*, 1924 Report.

the Continental Trading Company, later incorporated in Canada.[1]

Canada's laws were not at that time less stringent than our own. But our federal authority for prying into phases of incorporation on foreign soil would necessarily be limited. Mr. Sinclair and his oil fellows, H. M. Blackmer of the Midwest Oil Company (still at this writing a lugubrious expatriate, yearning to return to this country but not daring to), Robert M. Stewart of the Standard Oil Company of Indiana (since deposed from the presidency and the directorate for his share in the shady business), and James E. O'Neil, president of the Prairie Oil Company (dead in enforced exile), operating as the Continental Trading Company, entered into an obscure and complicated arrangement to purchase a third of a billion barrels of oil in Texas at $1.50 per barrel and sell it, apparently to their own companies, at $1.75.[2] When the profits thus gained reached $3,000,000, the contract was to terminate. That point was never reached. But the Continental did accumulate a fund which was, in part, invested in Liberty bonds. The course of those bonds left a malodorous trail across contemporary political history.

Properly to understand the employment of the fund, it is necessary to examine the system of our government-owned oil-land control. As soon as oil began to supplant coal as fuel for ships, lands containing petroleum, withdrawn from public settlement as part of the national conservation policy, were assigned to the use of the Navy and control vested in the Secretary of the Navy. Thus, the Teapot Dome field in Wyoming was sequestered in 1915. The Elk Hills field in California had been set aside in 1912. Three Presidents, Roosevelt, Taft, and Wilson had scrupulously observed the

---

[1] The devious operations of this company are set forth in the Senate *Oil Lease Hearings,* 1924 Report.

[2] By his return to the stockholders of Prairie Oil, of $800,000 of these bonds, O'Neil inferentially admitted the illicit nature of the transactions.

policy of retaining the nation-owned, Navy-controlled oil intact for future use. Even in the World War these wells were not tapped. The only incursion was a General Leasing Act, passed in 1920, which authorized the Secretary of the Navy to permit leases within the limits of the reserves where he deemed it necessary.

The chief reason for this was casual drainage, oil having the tendency of all liquids to run downhill. Thus, privately operated wells adjacent to the public lands might in some cases reduce the level of the Navy's oil by contiguous pumping. A very few isolated leases were granted by Josephus Daniels, Wilson's Secretary of the Navy, all on a small scale, to protect the field. The latitude afforded the Navy Department under the 1920 act was necessarily broad. Nothing in the enactment prevented wholesale leases to private operators, though none had ever been made. Presumably because of the possibilities inherent in the law if liberally interpreted, the oil interests were present at the Chicago convention. Herein lay Albert B. Fall's opportunity.

Fall was a man swift and decisive in action. In furtherance of his plan, he must first acquire control of the under-earth petroleum. He went to the Secretary of the Treasury and suggested a transfer of the properties to the management of the Department of the Interior. Mr. Denby was agreeable. He appears to have been actuated by a desire to conduct his important office with a minimum of effort and responsibility. His associate, Mr. Fall, wished to administer the oil properties. Why not? Probably the Interior Department was better equipped to handle such problems than the Navy. Besides, it was just so much less trouble for him. Poor Denby did not know much about oil. He did not, for that matter, know much about anything. His was a small and feeble brain behind a noble façade of brow.

Others in the Navy Department, more suspicious on the subject of oil, were perturbed. What Denby himself charac-

terized as 'considerable resistance' to the transfer developed.
Neither the General Board nor the Council of Bureau Chiefs
had a good word for the project. Commander Stuart, one of
the Navy's oil experts, protested and was transferred far from
Washington at Fall's request to Denby.[1] Admiral R. L.
Griffin, Chief of the Naval Bureau of Engineering, with ten
years of experience in handling the oil reserves, having heard
the rumors (he was not consulted in the matter) spoke out
his mind to Secretary Denby early in April.

> I told him that I was very sorry to hear it; that the Navy
> had for ten years or more been fighting to retain the oil that
> we had in the naval reserves ... that in all the controversies
> that had taken place regarding these naval reserves we had
> always met with opposition from the Interior Department and
> that if he turned the administration over to the Interior De-
> partment we might just as well say good-bye to our oil.[2]

The Admiral had a just and shrewd appreciation of Secretary Fall's purposes if not of his precise designs.

Fall drafted an executive order of transfer for the President to sign and dispatched it to Denby for his endorsement.[3]
Admiral Griffin, suspicious of some such development, got
hold of the draft and inserted in it a proviso requiring approval of the proposed leases by the Secretary or Acting
Secretary of the Navy before they should become operative.
This would have ruined all Fall's careful plans. So he simply
struck out the protective clause and substituted the harmless
phrase, 'after consultation and co-operation with the Secretary or Acting Secretary of the Navy.' What he meant by
consultation and co-operation he explained in a letter to E. L.
Doheny, who was interested to the extent of one hundred
million dollars.

> There will be no possibility of any future conflict with Navy
> officials and this department, as I have notified Secretary
> Denby that I shall conduct the matter of naval leases under

[1] *Oil Lease Hearings*, 1924 Report.   [2] *Ibid.*   [3] May 11, 1921.

the direction of the President, without calling any of his force in consultation unless I conferred with him personally upon a matter of policy.

Which seems a pretty high-handed attitude for one Cabinet officer to assume toward another. One might almost credit the Secretary of the Interior with hypnotic powers. How otherwise account for Secretary Denby's supine acceptance of this contemptuous displacement, his readiness to be the goat for operations which were to ruin his career? He took full responsibility for the executive order. 'It was wholly my initiative.'

Though an appalling ignoramus as to his own department, Denby was an upright and honorable gentleman. He would always take the straightforward course. He wrote a letter to the President frankly setting forth the opposition of some of the Navy officers to his course, and appended to it Admiral Griffin's formal protest.[1] Neither letter nor protest reached Harding. Someone suppressed them.

President Harding saw only the emasculated form, after it had passed beneath Secretary Fall's blue pencil. It was falsely represented to him as having Denby's endorsement. The letter, presumably from the Navy Department, addressed 'My dear Mr. President,' and requesting that the transfer of powers be made, presents the double peculiarity of being without either date or signature. An investigator in the Department of the Interior reported to his superior under date of April 15, 1921:

> I have made a considerable effort to ascertain whether the attached was signed by the Secretary of the Navy or one of his assistants, and the date thereof, but without definite results. I was referred by one of the divisions of the Navy Department to a Mr. Ogle (?) who, without much effort, produced their file upon the subject. He advised me that while they have a copy it is without evidence of date or signature.[2]

[1] May 26, 1921.   [2] *Oil Lease Hearings*, 1924 Report.

Further, there was an omission of a line in the Navy Department's copy.

The go-between in these transactions was Assistant Secretary of the Navy Theodore Roosevelt. He seems even then to have been uneasy as to the procedure. He told Admiral Griffin that he had done the best he could with Secretary Fall, but found him difficult. It must be borne in mind that up to this time and for long after, Fall's reputation was without blemish.

If Denby was easy, Harding was easier. Yet he must have felt some manner of misgiving. To his crony, Charles R. Forbes, he said:

'Well, I guess there will be hell to pay, but those fellows seem to know what they are doing.' [1]

He was right on both counts. There was hell to pay, and those most concerned knew perfectly what they were doing. The man who had no conception of what they were doing was Harding himself.

Nevertheless, he signed. This is what he signed:

> ... the administration and conservation of all oil and gas bearing lands in Naval Petroleum Reserves Nos. 1 (Elk Hills) and 2, California, and Naval Petroleum Reserve No. 3 in Wyoming (Teapot Dome) ... are hereby committed to the Secretary of the Interior subject to the supervision of the President, but no government policy as to drilling or reserving lands located in a naval reserve shall be changed or adopted except upon consultation and in co-operation with the Secretary or Acting Secretary of the Navy. The Secretary of the Interior is authorized and directed to perform any and all acts necessary for the protection, conservation, and administration of the said reserves, subject to the conditions and limitations contained in this order and the existing laws or such laws as may hereafter be enacted by Congress pertaining thereto.

It is at least doubtful whether the President possessed the legal right to modify an act of Congress such as the General

[1] *New York World*, December 4, 1927.

Leasing Act. To make it perfectly clear, however, that he stood back of his Secretary of the Interior, he issued this endorsement:

> At the request of the present Secretary of the Navy to the Secretary of the Interior, and thereafter directly to the President of the United States, the President on May 31, 1921, directed the Secretary of the Interior to administer such naval reserves for the Secretary of the Navy.

When there was doubt in legislative minds concerning the delegation of control, Harding wrote to the Senate: [1]

> I think it is only fair to say in this connection that the policy which has been adopted by the Secretary of the Navy and the Secretary of the Interior in dealing with these matters was submitted to me prior to the adoption thereof, and the policy decided upon and the subsequent acts have at all times had my entire approval.

> WARREN G. HARDING

Had the President lived, he might, in the opinion of many of his apprehensive friends, have been impeached. The charges would have been supported by this ill-advised wholesale endorsement of a policy thus palpably introductory to operations subsequently proved fraudulent and corrupt.

All the groundwork had now been prepared for private transactions in public property. Both the Elk Hills and the Teapot Dome oil reserves were at Secretary Fall's disposal. Fall was a careful business man. He was making no commitments until he had the cash in hand or reliable assurances of it. His first customer was Edward L. Doheny of the Pan-American Petroleum Company. Mr. Doheny wanted Elk Hills. He figured that the oil in that field ought to be worth $100,000,000 to him.

Graft knows no party. Doheny was a Democrat. He and Fall were old friends. They had even formed a sort of loose partnership in the old, lean days. Doheny, a man of keen mentality — actually an uneducated intellectual who had

[1] June 7, 1922.

directed his great powers to accumulation and exploitation — had piled up millions in oil. He was a born money-chaser; could not wean himself from the hot pursuit after he was weary and worn-out and had acquired more than any human being could use. But his self-drawn picture presents quite a different personality, set forth in a spirit of deprecation for the benefit of an investigating committee:

'There is nothing extraordinary about me. I am just an ordinary, old-time, impulsive, irresponsible, improvident sort of a prospector.'

This impulsive and irresponsible old-timer, on November 30, 1921, sent a small black satchel to Secretary Fall. The bearer was his son, E. L. Doheny, Jr.[1] The satchel contained $100,000 in cash.

Transfer of funds in this manner was nothing out of the common in Mr. Doheny's life. As for the amount, it was 'a bagatelle to me ... no more than $25 or perhaps $50 to the ordinary individual,' he told the committee. Mr. Doheny, it will be readily perceived, was a man of means. A loan of $100,000 and a small black satchel to a friend was all in the day's work.

What he considered a loan presented unusual features. True, it was covered by a note, but the document, when it turned up, lacked a signature. The name had been torn off so that, in case of the death of Mr. and Mrs. Doheny, the executors 'would not be able to press Mr. Fall and make the loan an injury instead of a help to him' — the lender's explanation. Generally speaking, an unsigned note commands little attention from banks or courts. When eventually the missing fragment, inscribed 'Albert B. Fall,' appeared, it threw no new light upon the essential peculiarities of the transaction.

---

[1] The murder and suicide which coincidently ended the lives of Doheny, Jr., and his private secretary, obscure both as to circumstance and motivation, is another of the tragedies that haunted the Harding régime.

The lease, for which the bribe-money was paid, had been assigned in July, but no hint of it reached officialdom until the following April. Mr. Doheny proceeded to draw out the Navy's oil. The terms upon which he operated were much less favorable to the Government than those obtaining in other and smaller leases of the same sort. His company might still be drawing profits from the process had not Fall's too sudden affluence called for explanations which he was unable to provide. Finally, when cornered, he admitted the 'loan.' But the courts declined to take so lenient a view of the small black satchel and its contents.

The leases were voided and Mr. Doheny never cleared his anticipated $100,000,000.

Next in line for trading facilities was Harry F. Sinclair. Teapot Dome was his objective.

Social notes of New Mexico record that on the last day of December, 1921, a month or so after the Canadian incorporation of the Continental Trading Company, Mr. Sinclair, with his counsel, Colonel J. W. Zevely, came to New Mexico in the Sinclair private car, and called at Secretary Fall's Three Rivers Ranch, already in process of rehabilitation. They talked of a Teapot Dome lease. Sinclair saw big money in it; more than $100,000,000, he computed. Fall readily promised him the lease. In so doing he ignored the law which calls for competitive bids.

The Texas Company was interested in part or all of the Teapot Dome outflow. But the Texas Company had no Liberty bonds for distribution. Secretary Fall was not interested in the Texas Company.

Sinclair left, well content. The Continental Trading Company had made its trade. Part of the income from the quarter-per-barrel profits of the somewhat complicated deal of which it was agent was used in the purchase of Liberty bonds, three lots aggregating $280,000. How financial experts of the experience of the oil men could figure that bonds are safer as a medium for bribery than cash is puzzling to the lay mind. Bonds bear numbers. The coupons are traceable.

The Teapot Dome lease was signed on April 7, 1922. On May 10, Continental-owned Liberty bonds in the sum of $198,000 were transferred to Fall's son-in-law, M. T. Everhart, and followed up with $35,000 more in the same medium. Of the total disbursement, $90,000 worth were deposited for the Secretary's account, and $140,000 more were delivered to the M. D. Thatcher Estate in Pueblo, Colorado whence they found their way to Fall. All were traced and identified by the betraying numbers. Sinclair also presented his friend with some blooded stock. Later, the New Mexico rancher received $85,000 in cash from the oil magnate, but this may be regarded (by the charitable-minded) as merely a transaction between friends, since Fall had resigned his office.

To uninformed logic this might smack of bribery. Not at all! Not if one listens to Mr. Sinclair. It was merely an investment on his part. He was buying a one-third interest in the ranch with a view to transforming it into a pleasure resort. That was his story and he stuck to it through thick and thin, including a couple of jail sentences for contempt of the Senate and contempt of court, one of them due to his unwillingness to enlarge upon the theme. Before criminal action was brought he was asked:

'Is there any profit to be received in this transaction that Mr. Fall received, any benefits or profits, directly or indirectly, in any manner whatsoever in connection with you?'

Sinclair answered: 'No, sir; none, unless he had received some benefit from the cattle.'

Perjury? No; apparently merely a matter of Mr. Sinclair's peculiar interpretation of what constitutes a benefit.

The highest court in the land took a less lenient view of the operation than the Sinclair version, when the leases were voided on the grounds of 'collusion and conspiracy.'[1]

[1] United States Supreme Court decision, December 28, 1927.

For the time Fall had his bonds; Sinclair had his lease; everybody was happy.

On the day of the signature of the lease, Admiral Robison, who seems to have represented the interests of the oil men rather than of the Navy throughout, made a statement for publication that the Navy Department had signed no oil lease. It appears that he and Fall had an agreement to keep the Sinclair deal as quiet as possible for fear of 'meddlesome Congressmen.'

Their caution, though unsuccessful in the long run, was well founded. A 'meddlesome' Senator, Kendrick of Wyoming, put some pertinent questions to Secretary Fall, but could get no satisfaction from him. The newspapers began to take notice. Belatedly Fall admitted the lease to the Mammoth Oil Company (Sinclair). Senator La Follette joined in the meddling. He put through a resolution of inquiry. The Senate invited Fall to explain.[1]

A man as carefully groomed for action as was Fall would of course be prepared with a plausible reason for the wholesale diversion of Government property. He considered himself 'a business agent of the Secretary of the Navy, acting in what I regarded as a military matter under the President of the United States.' On this theory there devolved upon him the duty of conserving our oil for a future crisis (hinting at war with Japan, relations being strained at the time), and his policy of conservation was based upon his alleged belief that there was danger of drainage from private well-boring along the border of the reserves. This was a pretext without adequate scientific support. Not only the Navy specialists, but such recognized authorities as Doctor W. C. Mendenhall of the United States Geological Survey and K. C. Heald, chief of its oil and gas section concurred in a definite opinion that any such drainage would have been inconsiderable, that fear of it was groundless, and, in Doctor Mendenhall's un-

[1] October 25, 1923.

compromising words, 'any leasing in consequence was un-justified.'

Admiral Robison, mentioned above, was the one impor-tant Navy officer of prominence who approved the leases. He announced this on the ground of belief that the oil supply was being depleted by drainage into outside wells. Asked upon what he based his belief, he had his answer pat. Ed-ward L. Doheny had told him so! The Admiral resigned from the Navy later to accept a lucrative position with the Sinclair companies.[1]

As to the leasing without the usual formalities of competi-tive bidding, Secretary Fall was what might be termed cocky about that:

> *Question, by Senator Walsh* — Your reason for not calling for bids was what?
>
> *Answer* — Business purely. I knew I could get a better price without calling for bids.
>
> *Question* — Do you think if you had advertised, designating whatever terms and conditions you saw fit, and invited bids, that you would not have gotten any?
>
> *Answer* — Oh, I might have gotten bids. There was only one bid I could have gotten that I could have considered, how-ever, in my judgment, and that is the bid that was finally accepted.
>
> *Question* — Who was the authorized legal adviser of the In-terior Department?
>
> *Answer* — The Secretary of the Interior, largely, himself.
>
> *Question* — In this matter what other oil companies did you consult?

But Mr. Fall wouldn't tell this. Military secrets, he indi-cated. The fact was, of course, that he had consulted no other oil companies. The whole deal was safely 'in the bag' for Doheny and Sinclair.

When his right to assume such authority over the reserves was questioned, he wrote with superb self-assurance to the

[1] *New York Times*, October 1, 1929.

President that the Judge Advocate General of the Navy had vindicated his authority.[1] Like other contributory elements of Mr. Fall's defence, this exhibits the weakness of being untrue.

Profits other than those pumped from the nation's oil lands were available to the insiders. Following the completion of the lease which Admiral Robison and Secretary Fall had so light-heartedly denied, there was a sensational boom in Sinclair stock. From a low of 18¾ in January, 1922, Sinclair Oil soared to 38¾ in June of that year, an appreciation of nearly 120 per cent in less than six months. It was this operation which led Jess Smith to observe lugubriously to Roxy Stinson:

'Some fellows — five fellows made thirty-three million the other day in two or three days,' which was a considerable foreshortening in time.

'Were you and Harry in on it?' she asked.

'No. That is what we are sore about,' he replied. 'They were our friends, too.'[2]

Jess, at the time, was running a 'blind' account with Hibbs & Co., local brokers, under the name of W. W. Spaid Account, No. 3, which showed a picayunish profit of some $3000 in Sinclair Oil. W. W. Spaid Account, No. 2, was a joint account of Smith and the Attorney General. No. 4 was Harry M. Daugherty's own 'blind' account.[3]

Fall's legalistic self-sufficiency was to be a great help to the hard-pressed Attorney General when he was under investigation for failure to prosecute the oil frauds. With unassailable veracity he was able to state that he had not been consulted[4] and to point to the record of Fall's testimony. He could claim to be, in his official capacity, quite innocent of any knowledge.

In acting as counsel for himself, Fall provided a variant

---

[1] Letter of June 3, 1922. [2] *Investigation of the Attorney General.*
[3] *Ibid.* [4] Telegram to Senator Lenroot: February 1, 1924.

upon the old saw. As his own lawyer he had for client, not a fool, but a man who was just a little too smart for his own good.

Belatedly answering Senator Kendrick's query, the Department of the Interior admitted the Teapot Dome lease, and added that negotiations for the lease of Elk Hills to E. L. Doheny were in process. This was somewhat after the fact. That deal had been agreed upon nine months before.

2. *Here Come the Marines*

Among the genial visitors who discussed and fabricated politics in the Deer Creek shack outside Washington Court House and who afterward attended upon the Front Porch was Colonel James G. Darden. He was a former textile operator from the South who had dabbled in oil. He did not come on his visit to Ohio empty-handed. His five-thousand-dollar contribution to the Harding war-chest was turned over to an entertainment committee who converted it into liquid supplies for the thirsty faithful. Colonel Darden deserved well of the party.

One of his oil properties was located within the confines of the Teapot Dome reserve. This is no unusual circumstance. Claims to oil rights, some valid, some insufficiently established, some downright fraudulent, were often alleged against the Navy's holdings, with the result that where the private right was clear, operations were permitted under the General Leasing Act. In doubtful cases the claimant could have his day in court. This was the accepted method under the Navy's administration of the reserves. It was different under the Interior's.

Having long known Harry M. Daugherty, Colonel Darden called at the Department of Justice to talk over his case. He wanted protection for his men who were already drilling, or, failing this, at least a fair hearing.

'It is a shame,' he complained to the Attorney General, 'that Fall is going to drive us into a lawsuit on this land.'

Little encouragement was to be had from his old acquaintance. 'The court is the only recourse as I understand it,' said Daugherty. 'He is determined about this.' [1]

Nothing as slow and dubious as court proceedings was in Secretary Fall's quick-action brain. He knew a better way. Sure of his ground now, he wrote to the President that Darden and others were threatening to operate part of the Teapot Dome property and ought to be ejected. Harding, with his unfailing accessibility to chicane on the part of his friends, fell into the trap. He replied:

'I have my call out for an interview with Mr. Darden. If he does not comply with friendly recommendations, we will immediately take steps to eject his company from the Government property.'

Welcome, indeed, must have been that word 'eject.' It would not have suited Fall's book to have the matter thrown into the courts; he was at least dubious as to the legality of the presidential transfer which underlay the whole process. Action was what was needed. Possession was nine points of his scheme. Without delay he replied to Harding's letter, saying that prompt measures were imperative, since the Department was unable to get service on Darden,[2] and that he would use the Marines unless there was objection.

Meantime, Darden was making what defence he could of his little holding of one hundred and sixty acres in the disputed territory. He gives this account of his visit to the White House. Harding opened the talk by asking:

'Jim, how about this property which you think you own in Teapot Dome?'

'I don't know,' replied the oil man. 'I couldn't tell you.

---

[1] *Oil Lease Hearings*, 1924 Report.

[2] Another instance of Secretary Fall's disregard for facts. Colonel Darden was at the Lafayette Hotel and could have been served at any time.

We feel naturally that we own it, because we spent some money to get it.'

'Fall doesn't think you own it,' returned the President. 'He is T.N.T. What are you going to do?'

'I guess we have to go into court, Mr. President,' said Darden.[1]

He never got that far. A factor more potent than the law was on the march. The Marines were coming.

Assistant Secretary of the Navy Theodore Roosevelt sent them, but Secretary Fall of the Interior was the motivating spirit. He told the Navy official that there were squatters on the Teapot Dome property; he and the President wanted them driven out by the Marines. Further, he said that there was precedent for such action; Secretary of the Navy Daniels had taken the same step in a similar case. Here again Fall was taking liberties with the facts; Secretary Daniels had done nothing of the kind. Mr. Roosevelt was the one to supply the precedent, which, however, has not since been followed. At the time he had no reason to suspect Fall of taking liberties either with the truth or with the Navy properties.

Wishing to avoid trouble in the field, Roosevelt asked the advice of the local commandant of the Marine Corps, General Lejeune, on the selection of a trustworthy officer for the assignment. General Lejeune recommended Captain George K. Shuler. The selection was reported to the President with the assurance that the nominee would be both firm and tactful.

'Good!' said Mr. Harding.

Captain Shuler's first intimation of the martial junket was when his commanding officer sent for him and asked him how he would like to go to Wyoming. The place was Casper and the mission 'rather delicate.' The Captain thought he would like it. At the Department of the Interior Secretary Fall was waiting for him.

[1] Darden's testimony: *Oil Lease Hearings*, 1924 Report.

'I have got a job for some Marines,' the Secretary informed him. 'We have a naval reservation out in Wyoming, the Salt Creek country, and there is an oil company that is going in there and they are trespassing; that is, they are drilling a well. We know they have no rights there.'

The young officer did not know much about oil, but he was ready for instructions. Secretary Fall further volunteered that he had taken the problem to President Harding that very morning and that the President was reluctant to interfere because an officer of the company that was trespassing was a close personal friend and had contributed to the campaign.[1] Captain Shuler is the happy possessor of a narrative style that would have delighted the late Captain Marryat. He is now recounting his interview to a fascinated senatorial committee:[2]

> Mr. Fall told me that he had told the President that his friend [the trespasser] was a lowdown S.O.B. and Mr. Fall said that the President told him that he supposed he was all that when he sent him his check [the five thousand dollars, transformed into liquid refreshment], and Mr. Fall said that he had told the President, 'Mr. President, by God, he was.' But, he said, the President finally consented and that was why the Marines were to go out.
>
> He said, 'What would you do if they served an injunction on you, signed by a Federal judge?'
>
> I said, 'Mr. Secretary, I have never seen an injunction and wouldn't know one if I saw it, and if they served one on me, I would file it.'
>
> He said, 'I guess you will get along all right out there.'

It was a reasonable guess. Captain Shuler got along very well, indeed, with the aid of four enlisted men, all veterans of the war. Mr. Ambrose of the Bureau of Mines also went along, and when they reached Casper, there were some other

[1] Colonel Darden.
[2] *Oil Lease Hearings*, 1924 Report.

Interior Department people waiting for them with automobiles. Let the Captain take up the narrative again.

> We went out to the Salt Creek district, about forty miles ... There was a rig up there, a drilling rig, and they had built a barbedwire fence around it. ... I went up to the fence and yelled out and asked where the boss was, and a man came over and said he was Harry McDonnell or O'Donnell. I said, 'Do you represent the Mutual Oil people?' He said he did. I said, 'I am the commandant of this Navy district.' I assumed that title, being the only representative of the Navy Department around there, and somebody had to be commandant, so I took the title. I said, 'I have orders to stop the work in this part of the reservation.' He says, 'Well, I have orders to keep everybody outside of this fence.' I said, 'Well, I have orders here from the Secretary of the Navy that I think will supersede any orders you have.' I said, 'Do you realize that I am absolutely serious about this thing and I am going to back up what I say?' He looked at the Marines; they had pistols and rifles and everything that goes with it. He said he thought we meant business. I said, 'You have got to stop drilling.' He said, 'I can't give the order.' I said, 'Who is your boss driller?' So he called over a fellow named Harry Martin, and I said, 'Are you in charge of the operation?' He said he was. I said, 'How long will it take you to stop this work?' ... He said 'Five minutes.' I said, 'I will give you ten.'
>
> So he went right in and stopped the rig from working, and Mr. Tough gave me a Government seal, and Mr. Tough and I placed the seal on the line, and I was told by the Bureau of Mines representative that that seal was absolutely sacred; it was a Government seal and no one would disturb it. About that time the field superintendent of the Mutual Oil Company came along, and I told him what I had done. He was rather peeved, but wanted to know if he could take the small tools and things that might be stolen if they shut down. I told him he could take anything he wanted, just so he left the ground.

So having established the Government's absolutely sacred right to the Mutual Company's oil, Captain Shuler and the Department officials went to luncheon with the oil men, and the Captain tacked up 'No Trespassing' signs and reported to Washington that the job was done.

Going back into history, some fairly piratical enterprises appear upon this nation's record. But so far as research shows, Captain Shuler's expedition presents the first example of piracy on behalf of private enterprise within our own borders.

Harry F. Sinclair was the beneficiary of the march of the Marines. Colonel Jim Darden was the loser. Assistant Secretary Roosevelt wrote congratulations to the conqueror of that stricken field:

'You did excellently well and confirmed our pride in the Marine Corps to measure up to whatever it was put up against.'

Secretary Fall would doubtless have concurred, had he seen the note.

3. *A Footnote on One Type of Journalism of the 1920's*

After the lion, the jackals. An excrescence upon the Fall-Sinclair intrigue, itself somewhat tumorous, brings to light three exponents of American journalism in a phase common enough a century ago, but supposed to have become extinct in the nineteenth century.

The *Denver Post*, a yellow newspaper owned by Frederick G. Bonfils and Albert Tammen, lived largely by blackmail. Both owners had checkered careers. Tammen was an ex-circus performer, Bonfils a former professional gambler with a conviction against him under the alias of Wynn for operating a lottery. They brought the methods of the circus and the underworld into journalism. Their repute, personal and professional, was bad. A dissatisfied reader named Anderson had, upon one occasion, shot up both partners with so much popular approval (except for the fact that his bullets had not proved fatal), that no jury could be found to convict him.[1]

[1] For a vivid record of this precious pair, see *Timber Line*, by Gene Fowler.

A minor oil concessionaire named Stack owned a contract of doubtful validity in the Teapot Dome area. By turning over a share in his claim to Bonfils and Tammen, he enlisted their moral support. Observe the value of a newspaper unhampered by considerations of journalistic ethics. They knew something of what was going on between Sinclair and Fall and suspected more. A star reporter was assigned to examine into the matter. He visited the Three Rivers Ranch, and what he turned up there shocked the sensitive souls of the publishers. They had something to go on now. Fall's sudden prosperity would take a lot of explaining.

But how far dare they go? One does not rashly attack a powerful Cabinet official. The danger of libel is too great, and the editors had already suffered from carelessness in that field. Moreover, the New Mexican enjoyed the reputation of being Bad Medicine when aroused. It was said that he would shoot on provocation. Bonfils and Tammen had been shot enough.

So, at the outset they based their strictures on the allegation that the oil leases were contrary to the public interest. They mailed the series of articles from the *Post* to all Senators and Representatives. This brought results. Sinclair's lawyer, Colonel Zevely, advised his principal that this sort of publicity was harmful and he would better do something about it. A meeting was arranged. The partners were ready to listen to reason. But the oil man was stiff-necked. He had a distaste for blackmail. He balked.

The publishers returned home and resumed the attacks with enhanced virulence. Sinclair realized that he was too vulnerable to fight. He came down from his high horse and talked money, which interested Bonfils and Tammen more than peril to the public weal. His first proposition was a quarter of a million dollars cash and three hundred and twenty acres of the oil land for the newspaper coalition to exploit. Under further pressure he raised this to a million —

offered, but never paid. Thereupon there was a change of journalistic bias and another Bonfils-Tammen publication printed a very nice encomium of the big-hearted Mr. Sinclair.

They got less than a quarter of the million agreed upon, which doubtless accounts for a resumption of the *Post* attacks on the oil leases. Scruples or something of the sort began to trouble Sinclair's soul. Upon learning of the admission by Bonfils, covering his peculiar journalistic operations, the oil man plaintively inquired of a friend:

> I haven't yet paid those Denver people a million dollars, but if they, under oath, testified that they were blackmailing me, should I be allowed to pay it? [1]

Blackmail would not be, perhaps, a wholly accurate term to apply to the measures of another laborer in the vineyards of newsprint. John C. Shaffer was, by repute, more respectable than his competitors of the *Post*, and probably more powerful. He owned the *Chicago Evening Post*, the *Rocky Mountain News*, the *Denver Times*, and other dailies. Sturdy beggary was his line, and he pursued it with adroitness and determination.

Having dabbled in oil in the vicinity of Teapot Dome, he was familiar with the locality. Knowing that the Pioneer Oil Company held a putative title to three wells within the naval reserve, he called at their offices. When he left, he had in his pocket a contract allotting him a one-eighth interest in whatever leases the Pioneer might negotiate with the Government for the Teapot Dome wells.

For what consideration? Testimony differs as to this. Mr. Shaffer is on record to the effect that he performed no services, invested no money. One is left to surmise that they made him a gift for love of his *beaux yeux*, which has not been the usual practice of oil concerns then or since. With curious

[1] Pound and Moore: *They Told Barron.*

divergence from Mr. Shaffer's understanding of his relations with the company, the contract recites that he had expended moneys and performed services. The Pioneer secretary understood that Mr. Shaffer came to them 'representing himself as a man of nation-wide means and ability, who could be of service to us in representing us to get our lease.' Duly impressed, the directors felt that it would be 'desirable to grant a one-eighth interest.'

It is particularly to be noted that the resultant agreement specified only a share in whatever leases might be obtained. For all concerned it was a gamble, since the company had no leases. It never did obtain any. It sold out its claims, and the Shaffer contract was worth, as a legal commitment, just exactly nothing.

The sale was to Harry F. Sinclair's Mammoth Oil Company. Sinclair paid a million dollars. Straightway those applications for leases which Pioneer had fruitlessly pressed became effective under the magic touch of Secretary Fall's friend and benefactor. His visit to Three Rivers was bringing results. The Mammoth Oil Company got all it asked from the Department of the Interior. But where did that leave Mr. Shaffer?

He set about determining. Upon learning of the Mammoth-Pioneer transaction, he wrote to Judge E. C. Finney of the Department:

> As you know, I have a personal interest in this deal. Secretary Fall had arranged with Mr. Sinclair for some acreage for me personally.[1]

Judge Finney could not help. Undismayed, the journalist-oil man went back to the Pioneer Company with a request for the money to which he had no longer a vestige of a legal claim. What is more, he got it. The operation is outlined if not illumined by an inquiry which the oil company's Secre-

[1] *Oil Lease Hearings*, 1924 Report.

tary, Mr. Thomas underwent at the hands of the Senate Committee investigating the oil leases:

> You had not got any leases or contracts on the Teapot Dome?
> No, sir.
> And you had simply sold these claims of yours to Sinclair for a million dollars. And so Mr. Shaffer had no interest in anything?
> No, sir.
> But yet your company generously agreed to give him one-eighth of all the company got from Mr. Sinclair?
> I am forced to admit it, sir [replied the witness sadly].

Mr. Thomas begged off from analyzing the motives for this singularly charitable act, and the committee did not press him.

Mr. Shaffer not only resurrected the original contract, or its spirit, but he improved on it. Under the terms he would have received, up to the time of the superseding contract with Mammoth, about $28,000. Pioneer made him a 'loan' without interest of $62,500, 'on account.' This did not satisfy him.

'He came around a little later and said he would like some money,' Mr. Thomas testified.[1]

An additional $62,000 was the sum requested — if one may employ so gentle a term. The company cut it down to $30,000. Mr. Shaffer made further essays upon the treasury, but got no more. Still a clear profit of $92,500 for the mere trouble of asking is a tribute to Mr. Shaffer's persuasiveness with perhaps a hint of the power of the press in support. At this juncture any further publicity would have been disadvantageous both to Mr. Sinclair and to Secretary Fall.

While this transaction was in progress, Secretary Fall was assuring the press and the public through the *Denver Post*, now won over to friendliness, that no leases on Teapot Dome

[1] *Oil Lease Hearings*, 1924 Report.

had been allotted. Press and public accepted it as true. The unmasking of the Sinclair-Fall combination was a slow and arduous process.

It was the theory of the late Lincoln Steffens that the current of official corruption flowed from business to politics, and not the reverse as generally held; that corporate interests, seeking privilege, are the original promoters of bribery, and the office-holders their receptive agents. The thesis seems to apply in the case of Secretary Fall and the oil men.

★

XXVI. *Voyage of Under-*
standing

T HE term, 'voyage of understanding,' which President Harding had adopted as the slogan of his trip, was
double-edged. He hoped to persuade the nation to understand him, his purposes and policies, his plans to be furthered
in a second term. But also he desired for himself a better
comprehension of what the people thought and expected of
him. Throughout the journey he was sending up his trial
balloons.

International relations were still heavy on his mind. Although he had always been fearful of the anti-League of
Nation extremists, he was not at heart an isolationist. After
his inglorious retreat from the recommendations to the Senate that the United States participate in the World Court, [1]
he discussed this country's attitude toward Europe with
C. W. Barron:

'As to future helpfulness, I hope so, and that there will be
a time when we can help.' [2]

A year later he was still considering the project. However,

[1] The message of February 24, 1922.
[2] Pound and Moore: *They Told Barron.*

he decided not to make an active campaign for the World Court, but to await expressions of public opinion.[1] At St. Louis, he sounded out his hearers in a cautious and, if the truth be told, rather dull speech, which, nevertheless, was well received. He told the attentive thousands:

'My soul yearns for peace. My heart is anguished by the sufferings of war. My spirit is eager to serve. My passion is for justice over force. My hope is in the great court.'

But his ideas as to the nature of our possible participation were so confused, so hesitant and timorous, so hedged about with provisos of selfish nationalism that David Hunter Miller interpreted the speech as 'the first proposal for world super-government that any responsible American official has ever made.'[2]

'The possibility of American participation in the World Court during the present administration was ended by the speech of Mr. Harding in St. Louis,' he writes.

Caution was the keynote of the next address also, this one at Kansas City, dealing with railroad problems. It was one of those amiable efforts designed to please all and offend none. Being precisely what his admirers — and others — had come to expect from him, it was received and approved in the spirit of its offering. At Hutchinson, Kansas, the traveller was still on the trail of popularity. He delivered a long and harmless address on agriculture, after which, in the face of protests from the medical men and Mrs. Harding, he drove a binder around a wheatfield in the withering prairie heat. A gleam of brightness here was a surprise meeting with a boyhood sweetheart whom he had not seen for more than forty years. For a brief respite he was his happy, easy self again; 'W. G.,' plain as an old shoe.

A change had been working within him. Dimly and with struggle he had been groping toward a new conception of the

[1] *New York World*, May 2, 1923.

[2] *The World Court and Mr. Harding*.

social ethos. Some of his fellow voyagers got hints of it as the tour proceeded. Though still in principle the sound party man, committed to the sacredness of property rights, he was beginning to perceive other and broader national responsibilities. Speaking at the United States Army Hospital in Denver he took a position which illustrated this change. If there should be another war, he told his hearers, and he had anything to say about it, 'we are going to do more in this country than merely draft the boys; we are going to draft every dollar and every resource and every activity for the national defence.' At the outset of his term a thought so heretical would never have occurred to his mind.

It was no mere flash in the pan, to gratify the soldier boys. He expressed the same conviction a few days later and in the same address he announced:

'Nothing has been further from the purpose of the present Administration than any thought of destroying the right of either labor or capital to organize.' [1]

Taken by itself, this is conventional enough. But he went further and declared unequivocally his opposition to any 'deflation of labor,' impugning the policies of those who held that 'organized labor must be crushed.' An earlier Harding would not so far have committed himself. It is no injustice to say that he would have been afraid to, even had his mind so inclined.

That something new was stirring within him, he was himself aware. He told friends that he felt a 'conscious spiritual influence' [2] on his actions. Here he spoke without reservation for the faith that now inspired him. It was his fate that much of his sincerity was turned to cheapness in the minds of those with whom he had been associated in the public view. When the syndicate writer, David Lawrence, relayed his reference to spiritual influence to the newspapers, occult

[1] June 29, 1923, at Helena, Montana.
[2] Willis Fletcher Johnson: *The Life of Warren G. Harding*.

circles in Washington delightedly interpreted it to mean that
the President was acknowledging spirit control of the sort
which had so long guided Mrs. Harding. Gossip even went
so far as to identify a certain 'Mme. X' as his connecting link
with the occult powers. His secretary, George B. Christian,
Jr., positively affirms [1] that President Harding never visited
'Mme. X' nor any other medium, which must be accepted as
valid evidence. It does not wholly preclude the possibility
of the influence having at one time affected him, canalized
through the dominant personality of his wife. But if this
condition had ever existed, it was a thing of the past.

Mr. Lawrence sent out also an obviously inspired dispatch [2] to the effect that the President had formally abjured
the use of alcoholic stimulants. Former pronouncements to
this effect had been 'off the record.' This statement was accepted as being practically official. It had been foreshadowed
by the address in the Denver Auditorium, where President
Harding invoked the national conscience in support of the
prohibition law, attesting his belief that 'reverence and
obedience must spring from the influential and the leaders
among men,' which was generally regarded as tantamount to
a personal commitment. With a degree of optimism hardly
borne out by the facts, he believed that 'a gratifying, indeed
it may fairly be said, an amazing, progress has been made in
the last few years.'

'I am convinced,' he proclaimed, 'that they are a small
and a greatly mistaken minority who believe that the Eight-
eenth Amendment will ever be repealed.' (The crowd cheered
the prophet.) 'The country and the nation will not permit
the law of the land to be made a byword.'

Elsewhere it has been noted that the President, snubbed
and apparently defeated in his efforts to mitigate the mediæ-
val labor conditions in the steel industry, had not finished
with the subject. On May 25, Elbert H. Gary, head of the

[1] Statement to the writer.   [2] From Salt Lake City.

United States Steel Corporation and spokesman for steel in general, had flatly stated that 'abolition of the twelve-hour day in the steel industry is not now feasible.' In return, Harding wrote to Gary, expressing his disappointment at so unsatisfactory a decision on 'what must be manifestly accepted as a practice that should be obsolete in American industry.'

These are blunter words than Harding had been wont to use in his dealings with mighty industrialists. With them came an intimation that, in the course of his itinerary the writer of the letter would have something to say about the twelve-hour day.[1] It was as near a threat as his sense of the seemly and becoming would permit, and was quite probably interpreted in that sense by the steel man. Mr. Gary was too shrewd not to perceive that presidential utterances, if critical, might well develop a commitment which would later become a campaign issue. The steel industry was far too vulnerable to face such an indictment at the bar of public opinion.

With a delay of only nine days, the special committee of steel magnates which had promulgated that defiant report, produced a qualified letter of ifs and ands and whens and earliest-time-practicable non-promises. It was the first sign of weakening. Harding pushed his advantage. He put the industry on record by accepting the resolutions as issued in good faith. He read the letter as part of his address at Tacoma,[2] and used these hopeful words:

> It will heal a sore in American industrial life which has been the cause of infinite struggle and bitterness.... I should be proud, indeed, if my Administration were marked by the final passing of the twelve-hour working day in American life.[3]

[1] 'The President sent word to the Judge [Gary] that he was making a series of speeches on the... trip to Alaska; that one of them would be on the twelve-hour day in steel.' Paul Kellogg in the *Survey Graphic*, January, 1938.

[2] July 5.

[3] James W. Murphy (editor): *Last Speeches of President Warren G. Harding.*

Harding did not touch on the subject again. Presumptively he received word that it would not be necessary. Gary and the steelmasters, prodded from without and urged from within by Vice-President Dickson and a small but active group of humanitarians, reversed themselves. The President had supplied the final impetus to end the inhuman twelve-hour day. But he did not live to know it.[1]

The Hoovers joined the party at Tacoma. Secretary Hoover was specially welcome to the restless, diversion-seeking President, because he is an expert bridge-player. It was an ordeal for the new guest. Worry and irritated nerves exaggerated Harding's nocturnal propensities. It seemed to his worn companions that he had forgotten the uses of a pillow. Etiquette prohibits a participant in a presidential game from saying, 'What about making this the last rubber?' The other gamesters were hard put to it for sleep. Another factor added to their discomfort.

Persons whose childhood has been spent in straitened circumstances, under living conditions where heat is often a luxury, are prone to carry into their after-years a dislike of drafts, unconscious memory of nights when they could not get warm enough. Harding had this tendency. He liked to play cards with all the windows down. On the other hand, Hoover was a fresh-air addict. More than once, sympathetic but amused correspondents surprised the long-suffering Secretary of Commerce on the car platform, gaining a brief respite, while dummy, by inhaling deep gasping breaths in the effort to compensate his stifled lungs.

For the President there was no let-up in his grilling schedule. His prepared addresses were faithfully carried through without reference to difficulties. At Cheney,

---

[1] In dealing with the fight on the twelve-hour day, insufficient credit has been given to the Survey Associates of New York for their long and dogged fight against the evil for more than twenty years. A succinct outline may be found in the *Survey Graphic*, January, 1938.

Washington, where there was a delay, he made his appearance at 11.40 P.M. and talked until long after midnight. It was noted, however, that his impromptu orations were becoming briefer and less spirited.

Four days of sea travel, en route to Alaska, were counted upon to restore him. He was unable to avail himself of the opportunity of rest.

He played late and slept ill. In his devitalized state he wanted and doubtless needed a drink. But now — conclusive evidence of his fidelity to his new principles — there was nothing available. The presidential luggage carried no liquor. One of the secretaries borrowed some whiskey from a correspondent known to have brought along a small but choice stock.[1] On landing, Harding was in little better shape than when he embarked.

Alaska made many demands upon the worn man, too many for even his determination. He was obliged to abandon the excursion along the historic Richardson Trail. What Doctors Sawyer and Boone now wanted was to get their man back on shipboard with as little strain as possible. They were still prescribing rest for a man to whom it was a lost practice.

Another blow was awaiting him. From Washington a long message came to him by airplane. It was in code. After reading it, he suffered something like a collapse. For the remainder of the day he seemed half stunned. Nor did he emerge from this state with his normal power of recuperation. Several times he came out of fits of musing and muttering to ask whoever happened to be with him what a President was to do when his friends were false to him.[2] On the voyage back, when he should have been recuperating his forces, he

---

[1] Statement to the writer by the Good Samaritan who chooses to remain anonymous.

[2] William Allen White: *Masks in a Pageant.* It is noteworthy that this instance parallels both his perturbation and his utterance following the private talk with Secretary Fall's wife in Kansas City.

was absent-minded, distraught, obviously prey to an obsession which he could not shake off.

The transport *Henderson* landed its distinguished passenger in Vancouver on July 26. A roaring multitude had gathered. Since his efforts toward disarmament, Harding had been a great figure in British opinion. It was the kind of welcome which always inspired him to his best delivery. Now he seemed listless, effortful, without spontaneity or magnetism. Indeed, a feeling of strain and apprehension was beginning to pervade the entire company.

Cruel heat met the party at Seattle. Gamely the President stood forth in the sun-glare and went through with his stint. But he faltered more than once, once became confused and drooped as if he were going to give up the struggle, only to master his weakness by an effort of will, and finish. If a poll of the party had been taken then and there, every vote but Harding's own would have been for instant abandonment of the itinerary. It was put to him. He would not consider surrender. He would be all right after a night's sleep.

Sleep was not for him that night. In the early morning hours he suffered what was diagnosed as acute indigestion. Surgeon General Sawyer, officially in charge, made the diagnosis, which thus became authoritative. Unfortunately it was also erroneous, in detail as well as in general. Crab meat was identified as the cause of the upset. No crab meat was on the presidential menu. Furthermore, of those who had dined with the President on the same dishes, no other person was similarly disturbed. The solution to what was afterward made contributory, as evidence, to an ugly 'mystery' [1] is simple. Certain forms of heart disease, in their late stages, produce symptoms closely simulating acute indigestion. Harding's condition was in this category. Death is likely to follow after a few days' respite, a point to be noted.[2]

[1] The innuendo of deliberate poisoning.

[2] In its bearing on the poisoning theory.

Doctor Boone, finding the heart much enlarged, recognized the seizure as cardiac, not digestive, and confidentially advised Secretary Hoover and a few others of the gravity of the outlook. But Doctor Sawyer, in charge, gave out encouraging statements for publication. These were apparently justified by a rally on the part of the patient. Nevertheless, there was little optimism among the guests of the trip.

Speaking dates were cancelled. The train set out for San Francisco. As the various towns where he had been expected to show himself were threaded, the President, pillowed high in his stateroom, grieved over the people's disappointment which he was helpless to prevent.

After rallying from the Seattle attack, the patient believed that he was out of the woods. At least, he gave that impression to those about him. At the San Francisco Station where the special pulled in on Sunday, July 29, he rejected a wheeled chair. He had the physically strong man's impatience of decrepitude. Acceptance of artificial locomotion would be a sort of surrender, an admission from which he shrank. But his skin, grayish and flabby, his gait, torpid and lifeless, were testimony enough to the fact that only courage was sustaining him. The last pictures, taken as he went to the Palace Hotel, show a face beginning to sag, to lose its firm outlines as the muscular structure weakened. He was an old, drawn man, squinting into the sunlight with a painful, determined smile.

There was no yielding of spirit. He took to his bed because the physicians were peremptory on the point. They were not in accord. Cardiac dilatation and high blood pressure were indications which Doctor Boone and Secretary Work (an M.D.) interpreted in the gravest terms. They urged a consultation. Doctor Sawyer demurred. In this he was at first supported by the patient.

Harding did not now realize his condition. Having fought off, as he supposed, the 'digestive' complaint, he felt better.

But the innate protective power of the human machine to restore itself after derangement was gone. Unhappiness, worry, and apprehension had done their work; resistance was undermined. Pneumonia, that jackal among diseases, always lurking to spring in upon the undefended body, beset him.

It was not one of the more deadly types. Enough vitality was left in him to make a fight against it. But though he passed the crisis, it left him, as he told his wife, 'oh, so very tired.'

Up to this time he had clung to the hope of fulfilling his engagements. Appreciating that it would be impossible, he now consented to the consultation, for which two of the three physicians were still pressing. He was the more willing since, he thought, his incapacity to meet his appointments would be certified to the local populace by the word of experts with whose authority they were familiar. Doctor Ray Lyman Wilbur,[1] President of Stanford University, and afterward President of the American Medical Association, and Doctor Charles Minor Cooper, an eminent heart specialist, were called in.

First reports were encouraging. An X-ray of the chest showed that the lung area was clearing up satisfactorily. The patient rallied, both physically and in morale. He was confident that he was going to recover, in itself a potent factor in his favor. And, indeed, he would have won his gallant fight against the pneumonia had nothing else supervened. On Wednesday, August 1, Doctor Sawyer announced the passing of the crisis. Thursday's bulletins, with their record of slow and steady improvement, justified the opinion that immediate danger was passed. Pulse dropped to below 100, temperature had been normal for thirty-six hours. But the enlarged heart, the history of high arterial pressure, and the still labored breathing gave continued concern to the consultants.

[1] Later Secretary of the Interior in President Hoover's Cabinet.

Nevertheless, word went forth to the apprehensive entourage that they might go about their own affairs with confidence that any change would be for the better. The party scattered. George Christian went to Los Angeles to read the President's speech to the Knights Templar.

Harry Daugherty, who had crossed the continent to keep the appointment with his closest friend, came to the hotel, but did not go up to see the sick man, although Mrs. Harding urged him to. It was his last chance.

★

XXVII. Death—from Natural Causes

WARREN G. HARDING died at seven-thirty-five P.M., Friday, August 3. A small blood clot in the circulation struck to his brain. Death was instantaneous.

There was no forewarning. The President had felt successively better as the lung condition cleared up and his temperature dropped. He had made a game fight against the pneumonia, had beaten it out, and felt himself to be on the road to recovery. At half-past seven Mrs. Harding was reading to him an article in the *Saturday Evening Post*,[1] 'A Calm View of a Calm Man.' It was by Samuel G. Blythe, a well-known political commentator who, in his familiar manner of easy, humorous urbanity, gave a pen portrait of a President maintaining his poise and holding steadfastly to his course while partisans howled and factions battled around him. It was a pleasant picture. Harding liked it.

'That's good,' said he, as the reader looked up from the page to assure herself that he was not getting overtired. 'Go on. Read some more.'

As he spoke, a change passed over his face. His body

[1] July 28, 1923.

shuddered and shrunk. Dropping the magazine, Mrs. Harding ran into the corridor, shrieking:

'Doctor Boone! Doctor Boone!' [1]

Within a few seconds the two physicians, Sawyer and Boone, and the nurse who had been making up her records, were bending over the dead man. It had been a merciful passing; even a happy one. The dead man's face was placid, unharried.

The news passed swiftly through the city. Hushed, sorrowing crowds filled the streets.

Doctors Wilbur and Cooper were summoned. Together with Surgeon General Sawyer, Commander Boone, and Secretary Work they signed the death certificate.

No autopsy was held. The medical men urged it upon Mrs. Harding, but she could not be persuaded.[2] She would not even permit a death-mask to be cast.[3] Natural though her refusal to allow a *post mortem* was, it contributed negatively to the ultimate scandal.

Scandal, as it had clouded Warren G. Harding's life, haunted his death. Today there are many people in Ohio, contemporaries and in some cases friends of the Hardings, who are immovably convinced that Mrs. Harding made away with her husband by poison, a mercy killing to save him from impending disgrace.[4] They argue that she must have known how hopelessly he was compromised by the malfeasances of his friends and appointees. Because it does

[1] Another report has it that Mrs. Harding, as she ran from the apartment, cried, 'Call a doctor! Call a doctor!' Carter Field, who was the *New York Tribune* correspondent on the trip, states that, for the first two or three hours after the death, the information passed out was that no physician was present when the end came. Later this was altered to specify Doctor Sawyer's attendance. (Statement to the writer.)

[2] Letter from Doctor Wilbur to the writer.

[3] *New York World*, August 4, 1923.

[4] Not in Ohio alone. A jurist of eminent position, who knew both the Hardings well, expressed to the writer his conviction that Mrs. Harding compassed the President's death. This was before *The Strange Death of President Harding* had spread suspicion through the country.

not wholly lack presumptive and deductive plausibility, the theory calls for analysis and estimate. Let us first consider the data and hypotheses in support.

Harding himself was in a state of nervous dread, aggravated by portentous news which had reached him in the course of his itinerary. He could hardly have failed to foresee that the oil leases, if proven fraudulent (as they were proven), would react upon him with the probable result of his impeachment. Much if not all of this was known to Mrs. Harding. Add to her perturbation a jealousy which had so grown upon her as often to be an embarrassment to those about her, and additional motive is adducible. Presumably she now knew of the liaison with Nan Britton. Almost certainly she was cognizant of the earlier affair, his involvement with the Marion matron, and not improbably she had heard rumors of other escapades in Washington. Jealousy, combined with her dread of an impending catastrophe which might drive them both from the White House, would logically impel her to a solution natural to her strong-willed and violent temperament. Harding was 'mysteriously' ill in Seattle from supposed food-poisoning which affected nobody else in the party. Impetus was later given to the suspicion by the fact that Doctor Sawyer died in much the same manner in circumstances when he was accessible to Mrs. Harding, the imputation being that he was put out of the way because he knew too much.[1]

All the foregoing is adduced as the argument of the poison theorists. I have even heard the medium specified as arsenic.

Another widespread belief is that the President, heartsick over the defection of his friends and seeing only catastrophe ahead, killed himself. Still a third version goes to the lurid

[1] 'General Sawyer's death was almost identical with the manner of death of the late Warren G. Harding when General Sawyer was with the President in San Francisco. Mrs. Harding was at White Oaks Farm when General Sawyer was found dead. Members of his family had no intuition of the seriousness of the General's condition up to the moment he expired.' (*New York Times,* September 24, 1924.)

extreme of attributing his end to a plot hatched up between Mrs. Harding and Doctor Sawyer, conspiring to save the unsuspecting victim from his own black future.

It was a whispering campaign, curiously paralleling the negro-blood story in the manner of its spread. Little appeared in print until Gaston B. Means published his sensational and imaginative book, *The Strange Death of President Harding*, wherein, without making a direct accusation, he plainly implies that the wife poisoned the husband. Knowing that Means was a Department of Justice man, close to William J. Burns and to the Ohio Gang, and at one time in personal relations with the President, the reading public forgot or ignored the pertinent fact that he was a confessed perjurer, a convicted criminal, and a fantastic liar. The book, 'inside stuff,' was a shock and a thrill to a wide circle of sensation-eaters.

Historians were left in doubt. Frederick Lewis Allen, in his *Only Yesterday*, expresses the opinion that 'both the suicide theory and the Means story are very plausible.' In *Fighting Years*, Oswald Garrison Villard goes farther. 'I am of those who lean to the belief that there was foul play in his death,' he writes, and points out that Doctor Sawyer died 'just as unexpectedly and as suddenly as did the President, and under precisely similar conditions.' 'Without accepting the most sensational of the stories of his death,' writes James Truslow Adams in *The March of Democracy*, 'it must be admitted that the mystery of it has never been cleared up.'

That provocative term 'mystery' is ill-chosen. There was no mystery, other than that conjured up by excited minds, or concocted and commercialized by Gaston B. Means. Categorically it cannot be *proven* that Harding was not poisoned because no autopsy was performed. But giving all reasonable weight to the motives and opportunities cited above, there is absolutely no valid evidence for poison;

nothing more than suspicion and coincidence. On the contrary, to any who choose to take into consideration all available data, the indications that there was nothing abnormal about Harding's death, but that it was logical and even inevitable, seem to me hardly controvertible.

Take first what is definitely known of the patient's physical status. For a year he had been able to sleep only in a half-upright posture, a most significant symptom. His death had been forecast eight months earlier by a famous natural diagnostician, who had specified the cause correctly.[1] For several months he had known that he was in danger.[2] The sale of his paper and the drawing of his will may have been cautionary prevision. Finally, there was the warning attack in Seattle.

So much for internal evidence. Another factor to be carefully estimated is the character of the physicians in attendance upon the patient. Both professionally and personally the repute of Ray Lyman Wilbur is beyond criticism or suspicion. The same may be said of Charles Minor Cooper, called in because of his eminence as a diagnostician. Joel T. Boone, the Navy physician, had a war record of the highest distinction and is known for his professional attainments. Surgeon General Sawyer was the old and devoted friend of the Harding family. Doctor Hubert Work, while not in active practice, was a man of high repute.

All of these physicians united in a statement which was a pledge of their professional and personal honor. Not one of them doubted for an instant the nature of the fatal attack. To impute murder is either to assume that all of them were ignoramuses, or to indict them as accessories after the crime. Motive for concealment, is, of course, conceivable. There is always the hypothesis that a body of men in such a crisis

[1] Doctor Emmanuel Libman: see *The New Yorker*, April 8, 1939.
[2] *Saturday Evening Post*, October 13, 1923; Doctor Ray Lyman Wilbur's careful presentation of the facts.

might elect to cover up a scandal which, revealed, would shake a nation's morale. A body of men, *laymen* — but not a body of reputable physicians. He knows little of medical ethics and less of the moral standards of such a group, who believes that they would connive at the concealment of a capital crime. Assume, however, for argument the extravagant thesis that one or two out of five doctors, all holding important positions, would enter into a conspiracy of silence. Is it reasonable to believe that all five would join in a pact, not only profoundly immoral, but also potentially ruinous to their reputations and careers?

Doctor Wilbur's convincing *Saturday Evening Post* article should have sufficed to scotch the rumors. He has never found any reason for altering or qualifying the statements therein. 'Nothing could be more absurd than the poison theory' is still his considered opinion.[1] It must be remembered that, though the tragedy was a surprise to the nation, the attending physicians were not unprepared for it. For several days the heart symptoms had indicated if not a swiftly fatal, nevertheless a critical, condition.

Aside from the medical testimony, there are almost insuperable improbabilities in the poison theory. Examine into the accompanying circumstances of death, and the evidence fades into mist. Whatever killed President Harding struck instantly. Plenty of drugs act in this way. Few of them are in common use and of these few all leave palpable traces, traces which the first comer, be it nurse, physician, or layman, would be sure to notice. For example, carbolic acid or cyanide of potassium, to cite two of the commonest. For either murder or suicide there must have been secreted by one of the Hardings a rare and powerful drug. How could either of them have obtained it? Neither a President of the United States nor the wife of a President walks casually and unaccompanied into a drugstore and purchases a deadly dose

[1] Recent letter to the writer.

without being recognized or, for that matter, leaving a written record. Someone else might have procured it, as agent. True; but who? One of the secret service men? One of the secretaries? And without reporting so extraordinary a commission to a member of the medical staff, or mentioning it afterward? Probability is affronted by so extreme an assumption.

Again, if Mrs. Harding designed to kill her husband, there were many more favorable opportunities. She would hardly have chosen a time when he was surrounded by watchful care, when a nurse was at his elbow and several physicians within call. Mrs. Harding was not a fool, but — except for certain personal peculiarities and tendencies — a clear-thinking, logical woman. Finally, while we are on the track of absurdities, if Doctor Sawyer had, indeed, been her accomplice, would she not have called to him for help in the crisis, rather than for Doctor Boone or some other?

Intrinsically the case for suicide is more plausible, because better motivated than that for murder. Aside from the difficulty, noted above, of the President's obtaining a sure and swift agent of death, there is the matter of character. Warren G. Harding was definitely not of the suicidal type. As the unanimous opinion of those who knew him best, this fact cannot be discounted. He had planned his future, not his immediate future alone, but his candidacy for re-election. He put up a gallant and purposeful fight against pneumonia, without which effort he might well have succumbed, for, as every physician knows, the will to live is a potent factor in this type of disease. That, upon sudden impulse, he changed his mind, belied his normal character, and, in the presence of his wife, deliberately killed himself, is too extravagant for credence.

All these rumors, all this doubt and suspicion and scandal, could have been avoided by the simple and logical process of a *post-mortem* examination. Medical science could then have

said, 'These are the facts predicated from our findings.'
Based upon exterior evidence alone, medical opinion, never
dogmatic in its highest exemplification, could only say, 'We
believe.' But, backed by the overwhelming improbability of
any other cause, plus the unanimous opinion of the highest
authorities, the record must stand that Warren G. Harding
died a natural death which, in any case, could not have been
long postponed.

Looking forward to his inauguration, Harding had hoped
to be the best-loved President. Instead he is the most carefully forgotten. But in death, he was mourned with a more
heartfelt grief than any other modern Chief Executive. Since
McKinley was shot down by a madman, no President had
died in office. The earlier Ohioan's death had been more sensational; more of a shock to national sensibilities. But it did
not bring to the country such deep and wide sorrow as now
engrossed it.

The feeling of the man in the street was one of personal
loss. Harding himself was an ordinary man. He was one of
the people, a prototype of the average as no other President
within memory had been. His way of life, so far as it was
known to the public, was typically American. In him the
common man saw not only his type-representative, but, in a
sense, himself. He was 'just folks.' Not only did the nation
mourn him as a leader; the people mourned him as a comrade.
There were dirges for the President; there were tears for the
man.

Harding had done something to restore the pride of the
plain citizen in plain Americanism. None of the evil that
encompassed him was yet understood; none of his dreadful
errors in the choice of friends and lieutenants had yet come
to full exposure. The public saw in him one who, differing in
no respect from a score of men in their own environment, had
proved his competency in great things. Elevated to the

highest station, he had seemed to show that the sturdy, common stock could meet emergencies, could guide the national course, could stand in the sight of the world as exemplar of the courage, the purpose, the virtues of his race and kind; those qualities which every citizen felt innate within himself. Even his little weaknesses and foibles appealed to the masses; they were so human.

Two years later the sentiment would have been tragically different. But up to now, the President had been a reasonable success in his high office, a figure to command respect, loyalty, affection. The shortcomings of his régime were not counted against him; he was believed to be better than his party. None of the crimes, the betrayals, the corruptions which he had been too blind to see, too obstinately loyal to credit, or too inert to check, had reached the point of ferment where the stench poisoned the nostrils and shamed the pride of decent citizens. Warren G. Harding died in time.

'Our hearts are broken; we are sore stricken with the sense of loss,' prayed the Reverend James S. West in the simple ceremony at the Palace Hotel before the body was borne to the train for the return journey across the continent.

Someone had the kindly thought of setting the casket at the level of the car windows, so that it might be visible to the populace, gathered beside the tracks in city, town, and open countryside. Three millions are estimated to have participated in this last tribute of honor and grief. Advance notice of the schedule was published, and though adherence to it proved impracticable, everywhere the citizenry lined the tracks, an unsummoned, unofficial guard of honor to the dead.

Church and fire bells tolled as the catafalque passed through the cities. Country folk in the open threw flowers before the locomotive. Forty thousand people in Omaha stood silent and patient at three o'clock in the morning while the funeral car crawled between their ranks. When the train reached Ohio, the speed was reduced and the stops were frequent at Mrs. Harding's special request. Thousands of people slept in stations, in wagons and automobiles, on lawns, waiting for the long overdue arrival.

Washington was reached at half-past ten on the evening of August 7. An enormous crowd jammed the concourse. President Coolidge was waiting at the station. A military guard escorted the catafalque to the White House.

At ten o'clock the next morning the formal services were held. Three Presidents besides the dead man were there, a convocation not paralleled in our history; William H. Taft and Woodrow Wilson joined with Calvin Coolidge as mourners. Following the service, an artillery caisson under military escort carried the body back to the station for its last return to Marion. Once the cavalcade halted while massed children on Pennsylvania Avenue lifted their young voices in the hymn of comfort that had been sung at President McKinley's funeral, 'Nearer, my God, to Thee,' casting flowers in the path as they sang.

From the countryside around Marion the country folk flocked in. 'For miles around the city the throng stopped up the ways.' At four o'clock in the morning a crowd had already massed at the station. The funeral train did not arrive until noon, several hours behind schedule. The cortège moved slowly to the house of the President's father, Doctor George T. Harding, there to lie in state for a day.

'W. G.' had come back to his home town for the last time. The friends and neighbors who loved him passed in line before the bier. Men and women were in tears, open and unashamed. All the afternoon and evening the hushed crowds filed past. The body lay in state that night, a soldier and a sailor keeping vigil.

The burial followed next day. President and Mrs. Coolidge attended it, with Chief Justice Taft, Senator Cummings, President pro tem of the Senate, Speaker Gillett of the House of Representatives, and six members of the Cabinet. Will Hays and George Harvey came, but neither Charles R. Forbes nor Albert B. Fall was present.

The procession wound its slow way to the cemetery, through massed and hushed crowds, where waited the mausoleum, its iron gates ajar. There was a prayer. The Trinity Baptist Church choir sang 'Lead, Kindly Light.' The bearers with their burden mounted the single step to the tomb, entered and emerged. A bugle sounded taps. Mrs. Harding, her handkerchief pressed to her lips, walked into the small stone building, where for several minutes she remained beside her dead husband. Boyden Sparkes wrote in the *New York Tribune*: [1]

> The President of the United States, the Chief Justice, and all the others waited patiently. Then she reappeared. She walked firmly, her chin lifted, her eyes shining.

Throughout the nation the sorrow was unaffected and inclusive. A well-loved figure had passed.

Foreign sentiment, as it was presented through the press, was more than the formal expression of regret. Due to his efforts toward disarmament Harding had taken a place in world history. His death was regarded by nations still feverishly hopeful of a guaranty against future wars and a respite from the waste and panic of military expenditures, as an international loss. In London, Americans were stopped on the street with expressions of sympathy. With the British, Harding had not lost stature despite his vacillation on the League of Nations and eventual hostility to it. England felt that it had lost a friend. The London *Times* gave editorial expression to an estimate more balanced, less hampered by circumstance, but not less kindly than those of the American press: [2]

> President Harding was a happy man — happy in life, happy, we may believe, in death. He lived his life in a way that bore

[1] August 11, 1923.   [2] August 4, 1923.

him almost imperceptibly, almost unconsciously, and without overweening purpose, into a post of supreme responsibility and exceptional opportunity. He was not, himself, an exceptional President.... He was elected at a moment of reaction, when the American people were weary of trying to understand or to solve problems that seemed remote from their ordinary interests. He was a simple man from a little town in the Middle West, a man of no striking intellectual attainments, one who had fought his way to a competence from the backwoods.

It may be that his growing realization of the intimate relations between the outside world and his own expanding and still almost self-sufficing country lent a touch of bewildering tragedy to the closing years of his life....

President Harding was a thoroughly loyal party man and he wore himself out in an effort to express in rapidly changing conditions what he believed to be the average desire of his party. It may be that the task had already exceeded even his powers of conciliation, and that if he had lived he would have had to face successive disappointments.

President Warren G. Harding's body, in its tomb, had been interred with all official rites and honors. But it had not reached its last resting-place. Eight years were to elapse, the Harding tradition was to be shattered, the Harding reputation sullied, the Harding favorites scattered in suicide, in exile, in jail, before the President and the wife who had pressed so determinedly to make him President were to rest with those full formalities which national tradition prescribes.

Relegated to a place on the inner pages of the newspapers which carried the overshadowing headlines of the nation's mourning appeared a telegraphic dispatch reporting the action of the Iron and Steel Institute. That most reactionary of organizations had rescinded its resolutions on the twelve-hour day. It had reversed its refusal to consider any reform as inconsistent with the interests of the industry. Times had changed, and belatedly the steelmasters had changed with them, not that the leaders, as typified in Elbert H. Gary had wished to, but because a dead President had forced their hand. The twelve-hour day, last relic of the impregnable barbarism of the old-time corporations, was abandoned.

Thus, by a dramatic coincidence, the most salient advance of Harding's Presidency, the most positive achievement wrought by his own personal effort, coincides with his death. No other important measure of his furthering remains today, unless it be the budget system, which was probably more Mellon's brain-child than his. The nobly conceived disarmament project of which Borah was the true proponent, that rainbow hope of the nations, proved to be no more than the stuff of rainbows, and is today clouded in the smoke of war and smothered in the mass of monstrous, strangling debt for guns, ships, tanks, fortifications, submarines, aircraft, and poison gas. But the victory over Steel entrenched was real and has been lasting. That which the twelve-hour day represented in corporate arrogance and contempt for the decent rights of man has forever passed from the American scene. To Warren G. Harding is due the credit.

⭐

XXVIII. *Aftermath*

I

As IF a kingbolt had been removed by President Harding's death, the mechanism of the Administration which he had built, began to disintegrate. The first collapse was in the Department of the Interior.

The trap had been closing in on ex-Secretary Fall and his accomplices, and though most of them escaped, they left behind the rags and tatters of reputation. For a year Senator Thomas J. Walsh of Montana had been studying the complicated structure of the naval oil reserves, at first with no more than a general suspicion of wrongdoing, but, as the picture puzzle built itself up under his skilful adjustment of the pieces, with a conviction that the whole deal was rotten.

Walsh was a combination of sleuthhound and crusader. His reputation as a Senator was of the highest. Mark Sullivan says of him that 'he had an emotion of affection for integrity.' Yet that is not the complete picture. Perhaps no man in public life is quite invulnerable and in the midst of the investigation matter was adduced which showed another angle of his personality. While the investigation was in process, a telegram was accidentally (or perhaps not so accidentally) slipped into the sheaf of those which had been sub-

poenaed for the committee's examination, and (by no stretch
of imagination accidentally) allowed to leak to the newspapers. It forced into the record correspondence between
E. L. Doheny, the lessor of Elk Hills, and the counsel for the
investigation; correspondence which had been in the possession of the committee, but had been decided to be 'irrelevant
to the inquiry,' a suppression obviously for the purpose of
protecting Senator Walsh.[1]

The oil man, be it remarked, was already under suspicion.
Nevertheless, when an operator in Montana wrote to Walsh
about 'a great opening which there is in the oil business in the
Kelsey-Sunburst field,' adding pertinently and suggestively
that the 'investigation of Teapot Dome has, no doubt, led
you to analyze the national and world prospect of future oil
production,' Walsh forwarded a copy of the letter to Doheny,
with a personal letter expressing the hope that he had 'not
dismissed the idea of entering the Montana field.' This was
on the day before Doheny's first appearance as a witness
before the committee. Doheny replied suggesting that
Walsh or his brother participate in the suggested purchase,
to which the counsel for the committee replied by letter:[2]

> The suggestion you make to me is most alluring. . . . I should
> further appreciate very much the opportunity to be associated
> with you in some business enterprise. Were it not for the con-
> sideration to which I shall advert, I should gladly take a
> chance with you and Senator Hogan.

The consideration was that, in view of his official position,
he deemed it unwise to engage in any business dependent
upon Government favor. A very prudent consideration. But
the propriety of such an exchange between investigating
counsel and a witness already under suspicion of complicity
is less clear. Walsh himself was naturally perturbed and

[1] *Oil Lease Hearings*, Government Printing Office, 1924.
[2] December 24, 1923.

angry at what he denounced as a gross breach of confidence, the revelation of the telegram from Doheny which, though not called for by the Senate Committee's process, was gratuitously produced by the local telegraph officials. However, the committee did not permit it to hamper the progress of the inquiry, nor, so far as the record shows, did Walsh allow it to affect his attitude toward the witness. Certainly Doheny was subjected to a rigid course of questioning at the hands of the man who would like to have been associated with him.

Reporting to the Senate upon the oil leases in the spring of 1922, Fall had boldly assumed all responsibility, implying that the matter was one better left to the discretion of an expert (himself) without complications through extraneous interference (the Senate). Naval preparedness of the nation was involved; he had done his duty by the country to whose service he was sworn. Thus, wrapped in the folds of the flag he rested his case on patriotism. When the President of the United States came to his support, Fall had taken on the stature of a vigilant, loyal, and farsighted public servant.

Though the public, satisfied of his good faith, lost interest in oil, Fall was worried, as witness Mrs. Fall's private interview with Harding at Kansas City. He knew that he would have to account for his sudden prosperity to face the question, Where did he get it? He had no answer. So he set his ingenuity to providing one that would stand scrutiny.

The oil situation now summed up to this: Harry F. Sinclair was in undisputed possession of the Navy supply at Teapot Dome, on which he figured to make a profit of $1,000,000. E. L. Doheny was operating the Elk Hills leases in California, in the expectation of reaping an equally large return. Sinclair and other oil stocks had proved market bonanzas. No trouble was to be apprehended from the Department of Justice which, under Harry Daugherty, exhibited a reassuring lack of interest in petroleum.

The total receipts by the Secretary of the Interior from his oil deals are reckoned by the *New York Times* as follows: [1]

Liberty bonds from Harry F. Sinclair	$233,000
Two loans, Sinclair to Fall	71,000
Cash from E. L. Doheny in the black bag	100,000
Cash from Doheny for expenses	5,000
Total	$409,000

Thus, the late Jake Hamon's estimate, that the office should be worth $400,000 to the incumbent, seems to have been remarkably close to the mark.

To account for all of this would not be necessary, so far as Fall could now see. But he must invent some source for at least part of his opulence.

He was an apparently willing witness before the Senate Committee. The impression made by him was reassuring to his friends. He brought with him a touch of the Great Outdoors. His bronzed, controlled countenance suggested coolness and courage; his direct, blue gaze expressed self-confidence and frankness. His answers were sharp, responsive, competent. No question disturbed him, so long as the line held to the oil deals.

Why had he not called for bids on the leases?

> ... I regarded myself as the business agent of the Secretary of the Navy, acting in what I regarded as a military matter under the President of the United States. I did not purpose, so far as I am concerned, to call attention to the fact that contracts providing for enormous storages of oil for future use in a crisis were being made off the coast or in certain parts of the country.... If that information should be given out ... it must be by the parties who were more interested in it than I was.

Plausible and apparently conclusive. It convinced the audience, a friendly one, for Fall had been popular in the Senate and out. It convinced the newspapermen. The im-

[1] January 25, 1928.

pression which went forth to the country was that Walsh had found a mare's nest.

But that shrewd prosecutor did get into the record Fall's sworn statement that never at any time had he received compensation from Doheny or Sinclair or anyone connected with them for any service rendered. Thus, easy, emphatic, forthright, confident and inspiring confidence, did Albert B. Fall perjure himself.

Following him, Secretary of the Navy Edwin N. Denby was put on the stand to explain the transfer of the oil lands from his department to Fall's. He explained nothing. Comprehension is a necessary precursor to explanation. Denby knew nothing about anything. He had signed the papers; yes. Why? He did not know. Had he submitted the matter to the General Board? Not so far as he could remember. To the Council of Bureau Chiefs? He could not recall any such procedure. (Later he reversed this.) Was he familiar with the Act of Congress placing the reserves in the custody of the Secretary of the Navy? He really could not bring to mind whether he had read it or not. Did he know anything about the Navy's policy as to oil? Nothing. Could he state when the transfers were made? No.

Denby was answering honestly. It was not a case of evasion, quibbling, or concealment. It was sheer, blank, bottomless ignorance. Marcus Eli Ravage characterized him as

> ... a pitiable spectacle. He seemed a butterfly on the wheel. He was bewildered, helpless, pathetic, dumb. His ignorance, his weak memory, his irresponsibility, his feeble grasp of facts and their significance, his gullibility, and withal his cocky self-assurance would have discredited a junior clerk.[1]

The bedevilled witness was soon released. He had contributed nothing except a humiliating object lesson in the calibre of the men who sometimes attain important position in the political structure because there is nothing against

[1] Marcus Eli Ravage: *The Story of Teapot Dome.*

them. That he had sense enough to perceive his own proven unfitness is doubtful.[1] He was excused and went back to his job, but resigned after President Coolidge had resisted the Senate's attempt to force his resignation.

Though Fall had been released and all seemed to be going well, he had been forehandedly preparing his defence. The problem was to find some friend who would obligingly testify to having lent him the money for the rehabilitation of Three Rivers Ranch. As his first candidate he had selected Mr. Price McKinney of Cleveland, a rich mining and steel man, with whom he had travelled to the West Coast in 1921. He wrote a letter. Would McKinney be willing to state that he had lent Fall money for the purchase of land in New Mexico?

McKinney did not take the trouble to answer. So the anxious Fall sent his son-in-law, M. T. Everhart, to him.[2]

'I have not made him a loan and I could not say that I have,' was McKinney's decisive response to the son-in-law's plea.[3]

Fall next bethought himself of Edward B. McLean. Because Fall was masking his reluctance to resume the witness stand under a pretence of incapacitating illness, the obliging Ned came down to Atlantic City.

There Fall asked him if he would go to the front for an old friend. Moved by the plea of a man obviously broken in nerve, the millionaire, who was a good-natured if not quite bright person, said that he would do what he could. The story can best be told in his own words. He is answering Senator Walsh's question.

> ... Mr. Fall finally came in. He was in a sort of dark red wrapper or smoking gown and he had been asleep, and he was in a very nervous, bad physical condition. It didn't need a doctor to tell me that or anything. And he talked to me for a

[1] To the end of his life poor Denby maintained that in the same circumstances repeated, he would have followed the same course as to the leases.

[2] In November 1923.   [3] *Oil Lease Hearings*.

couple of minutes and he was awfully upset.... He said, 'Ned, you remember our check transactions of two or three years ago?' I said, 'I do.' He said, 'Will you say' — or 'Do you mind saying' — I don't know the exact phraseology used — 'that you loaned me that in cash?' And he said one thing, he said, 'It has nothing to do with Harry Sinclair or Teapot Dome.' And now these are his exact words: He said, 'They are barking up the wrong tree.' I remember that most distinctly because I hadn't heard that expression before. He said, 'They are barking up the wrong tree,' and he said, 'Will you do this? I am in an embarrassing position here. Some of my enemies are just trying to make it look as if it was something which it is not, and it has nothing to do with Harry Sinclair or Teapot Dome; not a cent of it came from them.'

Then the result of that was I said, 'Yes, I will, Senator.'

Pursuant to this agreement, and, of course, previous to his appearance before the committee, McLean wired his counsel a message for transmissal to them.

In 1921 I loaned Fall $100,000 on his personal note. I have never met Harry Sinclair nor have I ever met Doheny or any of the so-called oil crowd.... There is no stock of these oil companies pledged with the note. It is absolutely unsecured.

While the communication was deceptive and so intended, it was not technically mendacious. Checks for $100,000 were actually given by McLean to Fall. The loan was purely a paper transaction. The checks were not designed to be cashed; there was not money on deposit to cover them. McLean failed to state this salient fact in his long-distance assertions. And he did not propose to let the Senators elicit anything to that effect by direct questioning, for his plan was to keep as far away from Washington as Palm Beach and communicate from there. To this end he developed a severe and dangerous sinus affection which would necessitate an operation if he should be haled forth from his Florida retreat to the rigors of the Washington climate. For the first time in a protected and armored life, Mr. McLean was threatened by forces with which he felt himself incompetent to cope. He kept the wires hot with appeals for succor against those who might force him from his sanctuary, to lawyers, Senators, Congressmen, lobbyists, the executives of his newspapers, even to the President, who wired back:

> PRESCOTT IS AWAY   ADVISE SLEMP WITH WHOM
> I SHALL CONFER   ACKNOWLEDGE
>   CALVIN COOLIDGE

The 'Slemp' was C. Bascom Slemp, the President's secretary. He took a trip to Palm Beach and conferred with the 'stricken and beleaguered chieftain,' as one of his sympathizing henchmen termed McLean. But the fat was in the fire for Ned McLean. He was set for martyrdom to friendship.

He was not forced to endanger his nasal welfare by going to Washington. Washington came to him in the person of Senator Walsh. McLean was sworn as a witness. Now under oath, he dared not, or perhaps was unwilling to take further liberties with the facts. He stuck to his story about the checks, but admitted that they had never been cashed. The whole transaction was, as far as any transfer of money went, null. Within a month Fall had returned the unused checks to the maker.

So much was settled, then. But hardly to the satisfaction of Senator Walsh or the committee. Ned McLean was not Fall's personal angel; not the provider of the money for the ranch. Very well, then; who was? Where did Fall get it? Relying upon the impregnability of the McLean version, Fall had meantime fatally involved himself by covering the ground only too thoroughly in a Christmas Day letter which he wrote to the committee about the $100,000:

> The gentleman from whom I obtained it and who furnished me the cash was the Hon. Edward B. McLean of Washington, D.C. . . . I have never approached E. L. Doheny or anyone connected with him or any of his corporations, or Mr. H. F. Sinclair or anyone connected with him or any of his corpora-

tions; nor have I ever received from either of said parties one cent on account of any oil lease or upon any other account whatsoever.

His health, he explained, compelled him to keep to his bed; hence the method of the communication.

By this time one of those mysterious and medically unidentified epidemics which accompany official investigations was in full course. Ned McLean's sinus was holding him in the South. Albert B. Fall's general debility confined him to his bed. E. L. Doheny had gone to California on orders from his physician. Harry F. Sinclair, feeling far from well, took passage quietly for Europe. The Senate committee was in constant receipt of clinical reports which did nothing to forward their labors.

That element of the grotesque which is so often a concomitant of such procedure was injected into the inquiry when Walsh commandeered the file copies of the local telegraph companies and delved into the extensive wire operations of McLean and his correspondents. Such addenda to the gaiety of nations as the following were produced and decoded, in whole or in part:

> ZEV HOCUSING IMAGERY COMMENSAL ABAD
> OPAQUE HOSIER LECTIONARY CLOT PRATTLER
> LAMB JAGUAR ROVED TIMEPIECE NUDITY HOC
> USING LECTIONARY CHINCHILLA PETERNET BE
> DAZZLED RIP RALO OVERSHADE QUAKE ZEV
> PENTECOST SWINEHERD LAMB LAMBERT EULO
> GIES LEDGMENT REVELING HOSIER ENCAPSU
> LATES KETOSE LAMBERT KONITE REARS LEC
> TIONARY JAGUAR BAPTISTICAL FITFUL HUFF
> WAXWORK PAINLESS CASCADE WIFFEN
>
> W. O. D.

W. O. D. was McLean's private secretary, Duckstein, known in the code as 'the Duck.' 'Jaguar' was, with grim appropriateness, Walsh. Zev was Lawyer Zevely. In this ex-

cerpt the transmitter of the message was advising his principal that the investigation was going favorably and that
Walsh, who was not, in his opinion, impressive as a cross-
examiner, was leaving for Florida. There followed:

> HOXPW SENT OVERBUY BONKA AND HOUSE-
> HOLDER BONKA SULTRY TXVOUEP PROZOICS
> SEPIC BEFELT GOAL HOCUSING THIS POUTED
> PROPENENT   MARY

Both of these telegrams were in the Department of Justice
secret code supposed to be reserved for official business.
'Mary' was informing McLean that Burns (the unscrupulous
Chief of the Bureau of Investigation) had sent him a warning; inquiries were being made regarding McLean's connection with the Department of Justice.

These and many others of the sort made a considerable
impress upon the social life of Washington. Friends, meeting at a bar, instead of lifting their glasses with 'Banzai' or
'Tootle-loo,' would chant 'Rip ralo overshade quake,' or,
encountering on the street, would solicitously inquire, 'How
are your prozoics today?' It took the dignified Senator
Walsh quite a time to live down 'Baptistical Jaguar.'

E. L. Doheny's cipher, also injected into the hearings, was
both more open and more cryptic, as for example a telegram
from one of his vice-presidents advising him against offering
to give up the oil leases, and embodying such passages as this:

> CANNOT RESIST EYIXK YOU MY IZGUG THAT IT
> WOULD BE A IFGDU TO IVDYJ BACK GNYPY

Then there were the horticultural telegrams, as Walsh
termed them, to the bewilderment of McLean who had never
encountered that word and didn't know what it meant.

> JUST TALKED WITH APRICOT AND BELIEVE HE
> HAS THE THING WELL IN HAND HE ADVISES FOR
> YOUR INTEREST NOT TO TALK ABOUT PEACHES
> OR APPLES ETC

And this, of January 29, 1924, when the investigation was in full swing:

> SAW APPLES AND EVERYTHING FINE   ALSO SAW
> CHERRIES AND THEY WERE VERY GOOD   THE
> PEACHES WILL BE JUST WHAT YOU WANT AND I
> AM SURE THAT ANY CHANGE IN WEATHER WILL
> NOT AFFECT THEM

Apples meant Fall. Total interpretations are lacking, in spite of the best efforts of the decoding experts. Partial identification, however, was achieved in the matter of a Valentine Day message to McLean from 'The Count,' code for one of his editors:

> SAW WYFGE FOR NEARLY AN HOUR   HIS DIRECT
> MESSAGE TO YOU IS 'I AM AT WYCGO('S) ELBOW
> AND STANDING AT THE GUNS   ALL THAT IS POS-
> SIBLE TO DO WILL BE DONE BY US SO YOU
> SHOULD WORRY DELAY SELECTION PROSECUTOR
> GIVE WYHOL MY LOVE   I DON'T WANT WYHOL TO
> BE DISTURBED SO LONG AS I AM ON THE JOB
> YOU KNOW WHAT TO DEPEND UPON   THE FIGHT
> IS ON ME AND I AM READY FOR THEM AND FEEL-
> ING FINE'

Wyfge, it developed, was Attorney General Daugherty, otherwise and otherwhere known as Sonatone. Wyhol was Evalyn Walsh McLean, Ned's wife, but Wycgo remains a shadow of the unplumbed abyss. Why Daugherty should have believed that the fight was on him is inexplicable. Notwithstanding all efforts he had been connected up with the oil scandals only negatively, through failure to prosecute what had only recently seemed a valid case. His little defi suggests either prickings of conscience or delusions of prosecution.

McLean's switch to honesty left Fall in a highly insecure position. Even though his original story had been accepted,

the $100,000 loan would not fully account for the lavish
expenditures at Three Rivers Ranch. But it would have
been at least a foundation. Now that was removed. Fall
was under severe pressure. E. L. Doheny, outraged at the
aspersions upon the character of his old friend, as he insisted
upon reading into the record, was urging him to take the
stand, tell the truth, and clear his name. So was the Committee Chairman, Reed Smoot. Fall had no intention of telling
the truth; not while any alternative remained to him. Nor
had he any desire to face Walsh again. He still stuck to his
loan fiction, but abandoned the McLean version as no longer
tenable and endorsed the accuracy of the final McLean
testimony. Still too ill to see Walsh, he wrote him on January
11:

> I did not finally use the money from Mr. McLean, which he
> expressed himself willing to give me, because I found that I
> could readily obtain it from another source. I wish it thor-
> oughly understood that the source from which I obtained that
> money which I used was in no way connected with Mr. Sin-
> clair or in any way involved in any concession regarding the
> Teapot Dome or any other oil concession.

'Or any other oil concession.' Fall was still desperately lying
when the uselessness of it must have been borne in upon him.
What could he have hoped now to induce the Senators to believe? Search for another and a feasible lie was his only
recourse.

E. L. Doheny forestalled it. He was a singular apostle of
truth. Appearing earlier, he had flatly perjured himself.
This is the record:[1]

> *Sen. Lenroot* — Just one more question, Mr. Doheny. To
> your knowledge did Mr. Fall profit in any way, directly or in-
> directly, through the making of the contract with you?
> *Mr. Doheny* — Not yet. I want to say right here, though,
> that I would be very glad to take Mr. Fall in my employ if he
> ever wanted to come to us.

[1] *Oil Lease Hearings.*

At the former session he had endeavored, and pretty successfully, to produce an atmosphere of lily-white purity surrounding the oil lease transfers. All this was now to be changed. Doheny had one virtue of the buccaneer, boldness. He had probably never in his life been afraid of anything. It is doubtful whether he had ever before been in a situation more ticklish than this, in which he had decided to tell the truth, since Fall would not. Taking the stand, he reverted to his earlier testimony that Fall had not profited by the contract. Then, with consummate audacity, he continued:

> I wish first to inform the committee that on the 30th of November, 1921, I loaned to Albert B. Fall $100,000 upon his promissory note to enable him to purchase a ranch in New Mexico. This sum was loaned to Mr. Fall by me personally. It was my own money and did not belong in whole or in part to any oil company with which I am or have been connected. . . . This loan had no relation to any of the subsequent transactions.

Possibly, just possibly, his supplementary explanation that it was a casual personal loan to an old friend in straits might have been accepted, had it not been, first, for his concealment of the favor on his previous appearance, for which he now expressed 'regret'; second, for Fall's wrigglings and mendacity, and his efforts to induce Price McKinney and E. B. McLean to support his deceit. With these sinister concomitants, the transaction took on the aspect of a barefaced bribe. All the circumstances supported this appearance, the transfer of the cash in a satchel, the employment of Doheny's son as go-between, and finally the peculiar condition of the note when, after much delay, it was produced. The signature had been torn off. The explanation given by Doheny was some incredible nonsense about not being willing, in case of his untimely death, to have the borrower pressed for payment.

What the next step would be was now obvious. Fall took

the only course left. Facing prosecution on a criminal charge, he refused to answer the committee's questions on the ground that his testimony might tend to incriminate him. He was a pitiful spectacle as he shuffled out through the whispering audience, tap-tapping before him with the cane which formerly he had sported with such jauntiness.

Another melancholy exhibit was McLean. It had been assumed that Secretary Denby achieved an all-time low for intelligence as a witness. There were times when Ned McLean made him seem, in retrospect and by comparison, an intellectual giant. Confronted with his code correspondence, the playboy of Palm Beach could only throw up his hands. Wires were pouring in upon him, one hundred and fifty to three hundred per night, he pleaded (one wonders when he slept): how could he tell what they meant, by whom they were sent, to what they referred? He was unfailingly courteous, willing, amenable on the stand, but — he'd be darned if he knew; he'd be gol-darned if he could tell, Senator.

'I'm having trouble enough to think about my own things,' he set forth piteously. 'I don't know what the whole thing is about, in a way, about Mr. Fall.'

The one contention upon which he insisted, which he plaintively reiterated, which he implored the committee to believe, was that he intended no dishonesty; he had never deliberately done a dishonest act in his life. This may well have been true. The Senators inclined to believe him, even to feel sorry for him. But it was an illuminating and disconcerting social exhibit, this of a man without training, without education, with the mentality of a schoolboy and the standards of a country gawk, who, by the inheritance of millions, owned and directed the policy of two important papers, had a hand in forming public opinion, and was, in a measure, powerful behind the scenes of government.

Of the resonant scandals which later brought him into further and more unsavory publicity there is no need to speak here. He is now in a retreat for mental cases, another of the tragedies of the Harding régime.

2

Into the murk of suspicion, evasion, and perjury that enveloped the deal in oil, there blew a refreshing draft of decency and frankness. Assistant Secretary of the Navy Theodore Roosevelt (the younger), proceeding upon insufficient and sometimes garbled information as go-between for the totally uninformed Secretary of the Navy (Denby) in his transactions with the very thoroughly informed Secretary of the Interior (Fall), had been made to appear in an unfortunate, indeed a rather absurd light. It was no fault of his. As a subordinate, he could do no otherwise than carry out the directions of his superior. Nothing had yet transpired to arouse doubts of Fall's good faith. As soon as the dubious character of the Sinclair-Doheny-Fall operations became evident, Roosevelt acted with decision.

Archie Roosevelt, his younger brother, had entered the employment of Harry F. Sinclair two years before, as vice-president of the subsidiary handling the European business, and director 'of so many of them, of the subsidiaries, that I don't know just which ones.' He had followed with lively interest and growing apprehension the proceedings of the Senate investigating committee. The testimony of Ned McLean shook him. It also shook his employer, Harry Sinclair, who issued instructions to obtain a passage to Europe on the first liner, to keep his name off the passenger list and his plan from the knowledge of anyone in the office. On top of this, Sinclair's private secretary, G. D. Wahlberg, advised young Roosevelt, for the protection of his good name, to get out. Archie consulted his older brother. Ought he to resign? After hearing his story, Theodore said yes. But this was not enough. The older brother declared that it was Archie's duty to appear before the committee and tell what he knew. They decided that both would appear. The Assistant Secretary's testimony was a brief statement of the situation, introductory to Archie's statement. The latter was, if not legally conclusive, at least sensationally indicative. He had already resigned from all status in the Sinclair concerns, when, on January 21, 1924, he took the stand.[1]

His resignation he explained on the ground of the evidence adduced by the committee, plus the fact that 'two of the people most concerned with the naval leases had left the United States in a great hurry.' These matters 'convinced me that I was in the wrong place.' When Wahlberg advised his resignation, Roosevelt asked flatly whether Sinclair, in Wahlberg's opinion, had bribed Secretary Fall. Wahlberg hesitated before answering:

'Somebody might have lent Mr. Fall money.'

Wahlberg was unhappy, he told Archie Roosevelt, because he feared that he would be expected to lie about certain dealings, in particular a payment of sixty-eight thousand dollars to Fall's foreman, for which he had the cancelled check.

It took Archie's breath away. The fraternal conference followed.

'We concluded that this was the only thing that we could do — was to go before the committee on the matter.' [2]

But Wahlberg, called to the stand, had an explanation ready. In fact, he had two. The first was that the two Roosevelts (both had talked guardedly over the telephone with him) had misconstrued him. He had not sent sixty-eight thousand dollars to Fall's foreman. What he had said had reference to 'six or eight cows,' which, as the committee could readily perceive, sounded much like 'sixty-eight thous.' As to cancelled checks, he had made no reference of the sort.

---

[1] In the Oil Lease Hearings.

[2] *Oil Lease Hearings;* Archie Roosevelt's testimony.

Later he produced another and a more plausible version. On the day when he talked to Archie checks aggregating a little over sixty-eight thousand dollars were being sent out, not to Fall's manager, but to the manager of Sinclair's racing stable at Rancocas Farm in New Jersey.

'The sight of the checks brought to my mind a comparison between the horse-racing man's situation and mine, and that caused me to say to Mr. Roosevelt: "Now here are these salary checks for sixty-eight thousand dollars to the farm horse manager."'

More obviously fabricated testimony can hardly be conceived. The checks were dated January 14, mailed, according to Wahlberg, January 18, and not received until January 21. As the unfortunate man had lost his position with Sinclair, the committee was easy with him. Archie Roosevelt magnanimously admitted that he might conceivably have misunderstood. 'I cannot see how it is possible, and yet I suppose it must be so.'

Still concerned as to his proper course, in view of the testimony, Colonel Roosevelt went to see President Coolidge and asked his advice as to his subsequent course; presumably whether he should resign from the Navy Department. The President had no advice to offer. 'Alice [Roosevelt Longworth] tried, but Calvin flatly refused to have anything to do with the Senate investigation. Calvin was wise!' wrote Chief Justice Taft to his wife.[1]

Roosevelt remained. There was no reason for his doing otherwise. It was his misfortune to have been shuffled back and forth between a stupid and a corrupt official, Denby and Fall. His apparent errors of administration were those of an agent, not a principal.

Criminal prosecution in the oil cases was inevitable. Civil action preceded it. Suit was brought by the Government to

[1] William Allen White: *A Puritan in Babylon*, quoting from William H. Taft correspondence in the Library of Congress.

annul both the Elk Hills and the Teapot Dome leases. Teapot Dome came up first. The lease was adjudged to have been procured as a result of 'collusion and conspiracy' and invalidated by the United States Supreme Court.[1] The Elk Hills deal was also carried up to the highest court and abrogated on the ground of fraud and corruption.[2]

What followed over a period of years is a study in the illogicality of legal processes. Fall, Sinclair, and the Dohenys, father and son, were indicted, the charge against Fall and Sinclair being conspiracy, against Fall and Doheny conspiracy, against the two Dohenys bribery. Washington said cynically, 'You can't put a million dollars in jail,' and was pretty well borne out by the event. 'You can't keep a million dollars in jail' would have been one hundred per cent correct.

Fall and Doheny were acquitted on the charge of conspiracy.[3]

Fall and Sinclair were acquitted on the charge of conspiracy.[4]

Doheny was acquitted of bribery in the transfer of the cash-and-carry black satchel.[5] The younger Doheny had, meantime, died a violent death.

Fall was convicted of bribery in accepting the satchel cash.[6]

This, then, is the composite result: Fall was guilty of receiving a bribe from Doheny, but Doheny was innocent of giving a bribe to Fall. Sinclair and Fall were innocent of defrauding the Government through the Teapot Dome oil leases, but those same leases were secured by collusion and conspiracy on the part of Sinclair and Fall. Fall and Doheny were innocent of conspiracy in the deal for the Elk Hills oil,

---

[1] October 10, 1927. 'The Government hasn't a Chinaman's chance to cancel the Teapot Dome lease,' said Harry Sinclair to C. W. Barron in 1924. (Pound and Moore: *They Told Barron.*)

[2] December 28, 1927. [3] December, 1926. [4] April, 1928.
[5] November, 1930. [6] October, 1929.

but that deal was adjudged by the highest court of the land to be the product of fraud and corruption. It is a theme for opera bouffe.

When the verdict in the Fall trial was brought in, Doheny, who was present, turned purple with rage.

'That damn court!' he exploded, but was silenced by a friend before he got into trouble. On the way out, however, he further relieved his overburdened soul. 'That was not the verdict of the jury, but the verdict of the court,' he fumed.[1]

Nevertheless, when Judge Hitz, who sat in the Fall trial, was assigned to Doheny's case, no protest was made. Nor did the defendant have any cause for complaint. The judge's charge to the jury embodied this proviso:

'Evidence must show you beyond reasonable doubt that, when this money [the $100,000 in the satchel] passed, Mr. Doheny then and there intended to influence Mr. Fall, before he can be found guilty.'

Not being mind-readers, the jury acquitted on the first ballot.

Although he escaped conviction on the major count, Harry F. Sinclair did not get off scot-free. At the outset he answered fully the committee's questions, then took his hasty trip to Europe when the 'sixty-eight cows' episode came to light.

While he was away, Walsh was pursuing the trail of the Liberty bonds from the slush fund of the Continental Trading Company (subsequently branded by the United States Supreme Court as having been 'created for some illegitimate purpose') to the bank account of Fall. Thus the oil man found himself in the same peril as his fellow operator. Summoned again, to face the senatorial inquisition, he declined to answer questions, not on the ground that it would tend to incriminate him, 'because there is nothing in any of the facts or circumstances of the lease of Teapot Dome which does or

[1] *New York Times*, October 25, 1929.

can incriminate me,' but because he was reserving his evidence for the 'courts of proper jurisdiction,' by which he meant the criminal dock.

He was cited for contempt, sentenced to three months' imprisonment, and fined one thousand dollars. Nor was this the end of his troubles. When he was called to trial with Fall, he employed a detective agency to shadow the jurors. The agency selected was that of William J. Burns, of the Department of Justice. It is a question whether something more sinister than mere shadowing was not in process. The *New York Times* [1] declared it, 'The most sensational contempt of court case in the history of American administration of justice!' One juror was overheard to remark blithely that, in case of a hung jury, he expected to get something pretty good out of it. A mistrial was declared. Sinclair and several of his accomplices were found in contempt of court, and he was sentenced to a six-month term. Hence a million dollars — several millions, in fact — did get into jail, though not on the findings of twelve presumptively good men and true.

Oil was fountaining up like a foul geyser, tainting everyone it touched. The next victim was ex-Postmaster-General Will H. Hays, now czar of the motion-picture industry. In the course of the investigation into Teapot Dome, Sinclair's secretary had mentioned some Liberty bonds loaned to a 'Mr. Hayes' [*sic*]. These were more of the Continental Trading Company's stock-in-trade, and their purpose was to help pay off the campaign indebtedness of the Republican National Committee, of which Will Hays had been chairman and in which he maintained a fostering interest. Mr. Hays was recalled to the stand. On his first appearance he had been something less than frank. When questioned as to bonds of the Sinclair Company, alleged to have been delivered to him after the election of 1920, he put up a fine show of moral indignation. 'I cannot tell you about that, Senator, because it

[1] February 26, 1928.

is not true. That story is as false in content as it is libellous in purpose.' This was, of course, a quibble. The bonds in question were not Sinclair Company securities, but were other bonds juggled by Sinclair and his accomplices.

Nor was the witness more frank on his reappearance when Walsh tried to pin him down as to the amount contributed by Sinclair to make up the National Committee's deficit. This is a sample of his responses: [1]

> I do not know. I just do not know. I do not know.
> Do you know how much he did give? [insisted the examiner. Hays had already set a total of $75,000; he was quite sure it was not more than that.]
> That is my judgment, Senator.
> Seventy-five thousand dollars?
> Yes; sir. As a total. That is my judgment.

At that time there had passed from Sinclair to Hays, for the use of the committee, $185,000 in bonds from the slush fund, of which $25,000 was returned, leaving a balance of $160,000. Invited to resolve this discrepancy, the witness dodged, squirmed, quibbled, to such an extent that it moved Alice Longworth to pity for 'Mr. Will Hays whom Walsh practically tore to pieces on the stand so thoroughly that it was unpleasant to watch.' [2]

No suspicion attaches to Hays personally in respect to the oil bonds. There was no profit or advantage for him in the deal. Hays was no corruptionist. But he was the kind of politician who would come to the aid of the party by methods which he would never employ for his own financial advantage.

The oil men who participated in the Continental Trading Company trickery were, besides Sinclair, Colonel Robert W. Stewart, president of Standard Oil of Indiana; H. M. Blackmer, president of the Midwest Refining Company; and James

[1] *Oil Lease Hearings*, 1928.
[2] Alice Roosevelt Longworth: *Crowded Hours*.

E. O'Neil, president of the Prairie Oil Company. Upon all of them fell the blight of tainted oil.

The Continental Trading Company had quietly gone out of business. All its books, records, and papers were destroyed. The Liberty bonds, which were its medium of trade, had been divided up. But though the trail had been obscured as far as possible, there was danger in the air. Stewart, fearing investigation, discontinued cashing the bond coupons. Wanted as a witness at the Teapot Dome civil action, he disappeared; the Government stated that he had gone to Mexico and South America. Early in 1924, Blackmer and O'Neil fled to Europe and never returned.

At the 1928 Oil Reserve hearings, Stewart denied having received any of the Continental's bonds. Only when the coupons were traced to him, did he admit [1] having perjured himself. Under pressure, he turned over the bonds to the Sinclair Crude Oil Company. A movement was inaugurated by John D. Rockefeller, Jr., and Winthrop Aldrich which resulted in his being forced out of Standard Oil of Indiana.[2]

Harry F. Sinclair also admitted before the Senate committee his participation in the bond 'divvy.' This was after his acquittal on the criminal charge. He made restitution of the bonds.

Fall had profited handsomely by the dicker in oil. Sinclair and Doheny had been on the road to make $100,000,000 apiece. The partners in the Continental had shared a rich and easy rake-off. Back of these transactions loomed the figure of the dead President of the United States. By his own gratuitous statement he had assumed full responsibility for the leases which were the basis of the piratical deals. People began to ask what Warren G. Harding had got out of it.

[1] April 24, 1928.

[2] *New York Times*, February 11, 1929. The Rockefeller-Aldrich statement includes a valuable calendar of the various phases of the Continental Trading Company activities.

He had got nothing. That the leases might arouse criticism, he realized. But, had he believed that there was any financial crookedness involved, is it conceivable that he would have implicated himself by going on record officially in support of them? In this as in other matters he was a dupe. Harry Daugherty said of him that he was 'a man easily fooled by his enemies.' That was not the full measure of his tragic gullibility. He was a man easily fooled by his friends.

3

Of the bequests left by Harding to Coolidge, the most troublesome was Harry M. Daugherty. The new President did nothing about conditions in the Department of Justice at first. That policy of inertia, developing into slow motion only under extreme pressure, which had served Coolidge's political advantage so well in the Boston police strike, now guided his course. He accepted the Attorney General as a detriment, but he would make no direct move.

Characteristically he used a deputy. Chief Justice Taft, at White House instigation, strongly hinted that a change in the Attorney General's office would be advisable, but found the incumbent 'very sensitive' on the suggestion.[1] An official testimonial of disparagement and mistrust was forthcoming when the Attorney General was ignored in the prosecution of the oil frauds, and outside counsel, Atlee Pomerene from his own state and Owen J. Roberts were appointed to this important task. Still Daugherty stuck to his post.

In the Senate La Follette and Wheeler had been on Daugherty's trail. Wheeler introduced a resolution asking President Coolidge to demand the Attorney General's resignation. Coolidge ignored it. His attitude is expressed in his reply to Borah when the Idaho Senator advised him

[1] William Allen White: *A Puritan in Babylon.*

that Daugherty was a detriment to the Administration, and should be eliminated.

'Daugherty was Harding's friend. He stands high with the Republican organization. I do not see well how I can do it.' [1]

The Senate took a hand. It appointed a committee to investigate the alleged failure to prosecute Fall, Sinclair, Doheny, Forbes, and others, and to inquire into such activities of Daugherty and his associates as would tend to impair their efficiency as officers of the Government.[2]

Senator Burton K. Wheeler was selected as counsel. Wheeler was not of the calibre of his fellow Montanan, Walsh. He lacked Walsh's patient talent for accumulating and collating facts. He had not the same power of discrimination between the essential and non-essential, the relevant and irrelevant. Typically he was the prosecutor rather than the investigator. As for his judicial temperament, or lack of it, this excerpt from a speech by him in the Senate, ten days before the authorization of the committee for which he acted, is illustrative.

> Recently, when the oil scandal first developed, it appears that the Attorney General's name was mixed in it. It appeared, if you please, that he was a friend of Ned McLean's. Everybody knows that he is a friend of Sinclair. Everybody knows that he was a friend of Doheny. Everybody knows that those three men met in the apartment of the Attorney General from time to time.[3]

Though 'it appears' and what 'everybody knows' may come within senatorial privilege, they do not necessarily constitute fact. The allegations as to Doheny lack support. In a letter to the chairman of the committee then investigating the oil leases, Doheny requested that Wheeler be called and asked to produce evidence for his statements. The letter

[1] Claudius O. Johnson: *Borah of Idaho.*
[2] *Investigation of the Attorney General.*   [3] *Oil Lease Hearings.*

was incorporated into the record, but no action taken. Wheeler did not appear.

Again, as exemplifying the lengths to which Wheeler went as counsel; he is questioning Roxy Stinson about Jess Smith:[1]

> *Senator Wheeler* — Mr. Smith was one of Daugherty's partners, was he not?
>
> *Senator Moses of the Committee (interposing)* — Oh, no.
>
> *Senator Wheeler* — I say he was one of Mr. Daugherty's partners, was he not?
>
> *Miss Stinson* — In law?
>
> *Senator Wheeler* — No; in crime.

Wheeler employed the dragnet method. He brought in an enormous mass of undigested, ill-assorted testimony, some of which had the most tenuous connection with the subject. But as a build-up for public consumption, an incitement to public distrust and hostility, as a picture of Daugherty as an incompetent official, it was effectual. Daugherty's close association with the now notoriously corrupt suicide, Jess Smith, both domestic and financial, was made the most of. His unexplained affluence after entering upon office, the deposits in his brother's bank at Washington Court House, while not carried through to any definite conclusion, were suggestively presented. The 'government by blackmail' of his agency, the Bureau of Investigation under Burns, made a dark chapter. All these, if not wholly damning, at least presented the Attorney General in a dubious light, requiring explanation and justification. It was confidently expected by his friends that at the proper time he would face his detractors on the stand and confound them. Instead he took advantage of a timely technicality to avoid appearing.

An accountant for the committee investigating Daugherty had gone to Washington Court House to look through the books of Mally S. Daugherty's bank.[2] There he found sug-

[1] *Investigation of the Attorney General.*
[2] March 18, 1924.

gestive data: a certificate of deposit by Harry Daugherty for $74,000, a certificate of $63,000 in Liberty bonds for Jess Smith, other Liberty bonds aggregating $50,000 accredited to M. L. Daugherty, certificates for J. E. Grey for $2000 and $3000 respectively, bearing the mark of the New York State License Commission (liquor), four cancelled certificates of the same kind for $5000 each in the name of the same Grey. Nobody in Washington Court House had ever heard of a J. E. Grey, nor was he ever produced in person or by record. Expert Accountant Phelon testified as to the latter lot of certificates: [1]

'These were the ones, as I remember, that were endorsed by Mr. [H. M.] Daugherty.'

On the morning following these discoveries Mr. Phelon was barred from the bank. The records were abstracted. Cited for contempt of the Senate, Mally Daugherty appealed to the courts and obtained from an obliging federal judge [2] an opinion that the committee was not investigating but putting Attorney General Daugherty on trial, and upholding the Daugherty brother in his refusal of the books. Thereupon Harry Daugherty gratefully decided that the whole proceeding was illegal and it would be improper, in view of the court's decision, for him to appear before the committee. [3]

Unimpeachable as was his contention legally, it failed to commend itself to a public and a Senate now become critical, and even to President Coolidge, who was not naturally super-critical. When the Attorney General, basing his stand upon the same decision, refused to the committee certain official papers, his position became untenable. Coolidge asked for his resignation, assuring him that his personal integrity was not in question. So he was finally out, after a career more stormy than that of any predecessor.

[1] *Investigation of the Attorney General.*
[2] Judge A. N. J. Cochran of Kentucky, sitting in Southern District of Ohio.
[3] Letter of June 4, 1924.

Out of office, but not out of trouble. Criminal proceedings followed. The American Metal Company had been seized by the Alien Property Custodian as a German corporation, sold, and the proceeds invested in Liberty bonds. The deal whereby the original owners recovered nearly $7,000,000 through a judicious distribution of bonds to Jess Smith, John T. King, Alien Property Custodian Miller, and perhaps others, has already been detailed. Now the bonds were traced. Miller, Daugherty, and King were indicted.

Upon learning of the Government's intention to prosecute, King, who was in Paris, suffered a nervous collapse.[1] It is doubtful whether he ever recovered from it. He returned to this country and died a week after the indictment was handed down. There were rumors of suicide which, however, have no foundation.

The charge against Daugherty was conspiring to defraud the Government of his own services.[2] The direct charge of bribery was barred by the statute of limitations.[3] The prosecution sought to prove that part of the bribe money given by King to Jess Smith found its way to Daugherty's pocket.

The evidence, though largely circumstantial, was ugly; the defence testimony of Mally Daugherty as to Jess Smith's 'political' Account No. 3, unconvincing. The gist of it was that Jess had borrowed from the account which was actually a political fund established originally for the Harding campaign, and that his checks to it were restitution.

The first big sensation came with the testimony that in August, 1925, Harry Daugherty himself had burned the bank records. Why? The natural inference was that they would have indicated criminal transactions involving others besides Jess, now beyond the reach of the law.

---

[1] Statement to writer of Frederick C. Howe who was with King at the time.

[2] United States *vs.* Thomas W. Miller and Harry M. Daugherty, September and October, 1926.

[3] *New Republic*, October 24, 1926.

Aftermath

Harry Daugherty had a reason more startling than the act itself. It was generally believed, in view of the course which the trial had taken, that, to have any chance of acquittal, he must produce some valid explanation rebutting what Prosecutor Buckner had undertaken to show: that the proceeds of the sale of Liberty bonds traced from the American Metal Company to Mally Daugherty's bank had been deposited to the credit of Daugherty.

> Mr. Buckner said there were five such certificates [of deposit] for $10,000 each. Four of these he produced in evidence, each bearing Mr. Daugherty's name.[1]

Instead of going on the witness stand, the defendant wrote out a form of refusal to testify which profoundly shocked the nation.

> Having been personal attorney for Warren G. Harding before he was Senator from Ohio and while he was Senator, and thereafter until his death,
> And for Mrs. Harding for a period of several years, and before her husband was elected President and after his death,
> And having been attorney for the Midland National Bank of Washington Court House, Ohio, and for my brother, M. S. Daugherty,
> And having been Attorney General of the United States during the time that President Harding served as President,
> And also for a time after President Harding's death under President Coolidge,
> And with all of those named as attorney, personal friend, and Attorney General, my relations were of the most confidential character as well as professional,
> I refuse to testify and answer questions put to me, because: The answer I might give or make and the testimony I might give might tend to incriminate me.[2]

His counsel, Max D. Steuer, a criminal lawyer known for boldness of resource, went further. His client, he set forth,

[1] *New York Times*, February 9, 1927.
[2] *New Republic*, October 24, 1926.

feared that opposing counsel 'would cross-examine about matters of politics that would not involve Mr. Daugherty, concerning which he knew, and as to which he would never make disclosure.... If the jury knew the real reason for destroying the ledger sheets, they would commend rather than condemn Mr. Daugherty.'

One may take one's choice here of two solutions. Was Harry M. Daugherty drawing around him the protective sanctity of a shroud? Or would revelation of the banking figures actually have besmirched the dead President's name? Just how the latter dénouement could have been brought about under the rules of evidence is difficult to perceive. 'Matters of politics' not involving Daugherty would hardly be relevant to the inquiry. The most that could have been brought out was that there was a Harding account in the Daugherty bank, and that insinuation, too plain for any ambiguity, had already been put forth by the man on trial.

The device probably saved Daugherty. The jury convicted Miller, who served part of his term and was pardoned. His case seems to have been one of those inexplicable lapses into temporary criminality of a man otherwise and afterward honest. Daugherty got a disagreement, after a sixty-five-hour jury debate. He was retried. Again he declined to take the stand. Again the jury disagreed.[1] The ex-Attorney General thus stands justified in his boast:

'No charge against me was ever proven in any court.'[2]

The Daugherty-Steuer thesis, that the defendant was risking martyrdom to protect the name of his dead friend, did not lack for credence. Nor did the belief in his innocence of bribe-taking. Chief Justice Taft thought him personally honest.

His destruction of evidence, however, is damning. It was probably done for the purpose of concealing scandals con-

[1] March 4, 1927.
[2] Harry M. Daugherty: *The Inside Story of the Harding Tragedy.*

nected with the Harding Administration, for which he will have to suffer. I am very sorry.[1]

Mark Sullivan wrote:

> Of one thing I am sure; none of the money Jess Smith got to facilitate the American Metal case went into Daugherty's pocket.[2]

And David Lawrence, Daugherty's consistent defender and apologist, testifies to his faith that the Attorney General knew nothing of Smith's grafting operations, and ascribes the destruction of the bank records to the fact that they would have involved President Harding, 'though in no guilty way.' [3]

In what other conceivable way, then? For what innocent purpose should the President of the United States maintain an account under cover in Mal Daugherty's bank? And if, indeed, there were such an account, whence came the funds? Up to the sale of the *Marion Star*, shortly before his death, Harding's finances were in no flourishing state.

The federal court takes a less lenient view of Daugherty and his operations. Within the last two years suits have been brought by the present Department of Justice involving property wrongfully turned over by the joint action of the Alien Property Custodian and the Attorney General. More than fifty million dollars has been ordered restored to the Government, by court decisions. Practically all of these cases arose during the Daugherty-Miller incumbency, though not all of the claims were allowed with the connivance of those two.[4]

Of these, the American Metal Company case is one of the most important and perhaps the most significant. After the Government had won its original contention, that the

[1] Letter to William Allen White, quoted in *A Puritan in Babylon*.
[2] Mark Sullivan: *Our Times*, vol. VI.
[3] *Washington Court House Herald*, March 7, 1927.
[4] Letter to writer from Assistant Attorney General Brice Toole.

refund had been made through fraud, the company (now operating under a foreign name) appealed. The appeal was rejected. In presenting its case, the Government quotes from the decision of Federal Judge O'Donoghue:[1]

> The court cannot lose sight of the fact that this claim was presented to the Alien Property Custodian on September 20, 1921, and then was finally passed upon by the Alien Property Custodian on September 21, 1921, and was, two days later, upon the 23d of September, 1921, finally passed upon and approved by the Attorney General of the United States and orders immediately issued for the payment of the round sum of $7,000,000, or thereabouts.
>
> The court cannot overlook the remarkable thing that the Alien Property Custodian could go to New York and have a dinner with Merton, the representative of the plaintiff, and with King, employed by Merton to represent the plaintiff, and with Jess Smith, the intimate and confidential friend of the Attorney General of the United States. . . .
>
> Part of the claim allowed to the plaintiff, amounting to about $500,000, was paid by delivery of United States Government bonds. . . . It is again a very strange thing that about $40,000 of these bonds are traced, directly or indirectly, but with certainty, to the Attorney General, Harry Daugherty. . . .
>
> The court concludes that fraud has been shown in the claim made before the Alien Property Custodian, and that that fraud resulted in the Government of the United States turning over the sum of about $7,000,000 approximately, to the plaintiff. . . .

There remains to trace the other member of the family, Brother Mally. His bank crashed in a failure which all but ruined the once prosperous countryside about Washington Court House, owing $2,600,000. It had been for years conducted on the loosest principles, loaning money to the Daugherty family and friends on the flimsiest security,

---

[1] District Court of Appeals for District of Columbia, No. 6978; Société Suisse pour Valeurs de Métaux *vs.* Homer S. Cummings, Attorney General and William A. Julian, Treasurer of the United States.

making loans from other banks on pledge of its own worthless stock. Mally Daugherty, as president, was indicted on five counts, tried and convicted. He might have spent the rest of his life in prison had the case not been reversed on appeal — and dropped. Ohio immunity was still potent in 1930.

The Daugherty record, too, has its list of concomitant tragedies.

Thomas W. Miller, convicted and sent to jail.

Jess Smith, suicide.

The crash of the Daugherty bank, bringing disaster to a prosperous countryside.

Gaston B. Means died in federal penitentiary.

John T. King, died, a nervous wreck, while awaiting trial.

Thomas B. Felder, Daugherty's partner in the scandalous Morse pardon, convicted on another count, and disbarred.

Daugherty himself is no figure of tragedy. His head is bloodless and unbowed. He is living in something more than comfort, enjoying the companionship of a large circle of friends in Florida and Columbus, Ohio. Recently he announced his intention of writing another book.

If he tells half of what he knows, it will be a contribution to history.

4

No Ohio brand of justice dealt with Charles R. Forbes, whose conduct of the United States Veterans' Bureau equalled in boldness and surpassed in rapacity the most flagrant excesses of the Ohio Gang. The case of the United States *vs.* Charles R. Forbes and John W. Thompson was tried in the winter of 1924–25, before Judge Evan A. Evans in the United States District Court in Chicago. The assignment of Judge Evans was unfortunate for the defendants. Distinguished for scrupulous fairness, he was notoriously insusceptible to any political influence or considerations. His presence on the bench would be a guaranty against the whitewashing which was rumored widely before the case was set. An observer of eminent legal standing who was present wrote afterward:

'I have always believed and still believe that there were many more involved than Forbes and Thompson, particularly men of means.... In the case was a lawyer, John W. H. Crim [1] (an Assistant Attorney General from the Department of Justice staff). But for him there would never have been a conviction. The case was set for an acquittal. Nothing would have pleased the Government more than an acquittal. In a criminal case like this, the court properly holds the evidence to a narrow field, limited by its relevancy to the particular defendants before the court. In my opinion this rule was more strictly enforced than it should be. Consequently, the evidence did not show the things which, I believe, it could have shown had other defendants been present. But the story is a sordid one. The picture is one wherein grafters played the leading and the lesser rôles, where sex morality was as low as official integrity. Still, in the Federal Building at that time, all I heard was that the defendants were going to be acquitted. What prevented it was an honest jury and this man, Crim.' [2]

The monstrous graft of the medical supplies sales at Perryville, Maryland, had been exposed in the Senate Investigation of the Veterans' Bureau.[3] Because of the extent and intricacy of these transactions, the Government elected to base its case on the simpler charge of bribery and conspiracy in another phase of Forbes's activities. John W. Thompson of the Thompson-Black contracting firm was

---

[1] Crim had resigned from the Department of Justice. He was recalled on special assignment for this trial.

[2] Excerpt from a private letter.

[3] October, 1923.

indicted and tried with him.[1] Their agent and fixer, Elias H. Mortimer, turned state's evidence. Suspicion and a rabid jealousy of the young and pretty Mrs. Mortimer incited him to this course.

'I'm going to get that bastard if I go up for life,' he declared to Will Irwin, then preparing his series of syndicate articles on the Veterans' Bureau graft.[2]

Agreement was reached between counsel at the trial that certain reputations should be, as far as possible, protected. Hence reference to the late President Harding or any of his family was silenced as soon as it cropped up.

The evidence of collusion between Forbes and the contracting firm was direct and conclusive. Mortimer testified that in June, 1922, he and his wife and Forbes were on a cross-continental junket, ostensibly in the interests of the Veterans' Bureau. In Chicago they met John W. Thompson and had a protracted party with him. While the festivities were in progress, Forbes took Mortimer aside and mentioned a financial stringency. His wife, he explained, had taken all his bonds and gone to Europe. He needed $5000.

This was no surprise to Mortimer. He had expected some such hint. Thompson also was prepared to meet the emergency. From the Thompson-Black funds he turned over to Mortimer $15,000, of which the fixer gave $5000 to the needy Forbes, retaining the balance for travelling expenses.

Thereafter the journey continued at an increased tempo of festivity. Everywhere the party went there was entertainment, with Mortimer footing the bills. Business was not neglected. Charles F. Cramer, counsel to the Veterans' Bureau, hailed from San Francisco and maintained connections in California. Through his intercession the Director went from San Francisco up to Livermore to look at a site

[1] United States *vs.* Charles R. Forbes and John W. Thompson: for bribery and conspiracy: Northern District of Illinois.

[2] Statement to the writer by Mr. Irwin.

which Cramer thought suitable for one of the projected hospitals. Forbes agreed. The parcel of land, valued at $17,000, was sold to the Government, after some small and inexpensive improvements, for $105,000, with the Director's approval. There were other instances of profitable graft. At Excelsior Springs, Missouri, Forbes, acting for the Veterans' Bureau, agreed to pay $77,000 for property worth $35,000, and then obligingly increased the price to $90,000.

The big profits, however, were to be in the construction of the buildings. After the satisfactory conference at Chicago, a plan was agreed upon whereby in every hospital contract awarded to Thompson-Black, $150,000 was to be added arbitrarily to the normal cost and profit of the operation. Of this Forbes was to receive $50,000; the remainder was the contractors' cut. Sometimes the juggling was pretty barefaced, as in the Northampton, Massachusetts, hospital, where competitive bids were suppressed or distorted in favor of Thompson-Black.[1]

The Public Health and Marine Hospital Service had been erecting plants at a cost of $2972 per bed. Forbes's specially organized $100,000-per-year corps of architects raised the cost to $3957 per bed. There were minor scandals in the conduct of the institutions as well. One of them, the Speedway Hospital in Chicago, housed so many 'floaters' and so few genuine patients that it was closed after investigation.

Mortimer's story convinced the jury. Neither defendant took the stand. Both were convicted, fined $10,000 each, and sentenced to two years in Leavenworth Penitentiary, which they served. Thompson is dead. Forbes is living in the Northwest. Mortimer, whose wife — so he charged in court — betrayed him with Forbes, was divorced by her and killed himself. Cramer and Mortimer, suicides; Forbes and Thompson, convicts: the blight of the Harding tragedy was over the Veterans' Bureau also.

[1] For other details, see United States *vs*. Forbes and Thompson, *supra*.

★

XXIX. 'Débris of Decency'

HOLOGRAPH LETTERS of Warren G. Harding at one time commanded a higher price in the autograph market than any other presidential scripts. This is due to Mrs. Harding's campaign of destruction and suppression, undertaken with the worthiest motives and pathetically ineffective.

Surviving her husband by more than a year,[1] she used every endeavor to protect his memory. Officially the record of his administration was in process of being hopelessly tarnished, as she must have realized, although the full extent of the disgrace was not yet made known to the public. But Harding's personal repute was still untainted. Hoping to preserve it, she formulated her plan.

All the White House correspondence, official and unofficial, collected and packed at her command, was shipped to Marion. Added to it was what she could gather from the office files of the *Marion Star*. A secretarial corps was employed to examine and list the ana. Files of those to whom the dead man, no profuse correspondent at best, had written were compiled. With these people, wherever available, Mrs. Harding established communication. Appeals were sent out to each presumptive possessor of a Harding letter: would not

[1] She died, November 21, 1924, at Doctor Sawyer's sanitarium near Marion.

he (or she) send any such communication to the widow? Sentiment was the basis of the request. It had, in fact, quite another motivation. She had become almost morbidly concerned lest some unsavory or compromising missive might have been preserved.

Shortly after Harding's death, Doubleday, Page and Company asked permission to publish a volume of his letters. To this Mrs. Harding refused her consent. Several representatives of the publishing house, including the head of the firm, Frank N. Doubleday, called on her at her hotel in Washington. She said frankly that she had burned her husband's correspondence, as she feared that some of the letters would be misconstrued and would harm his memory. It became known later that she had overlooked a considerable number of letters stored in Marion by officers of the Harding Memorial Association.

After her death a representative of the Doubleday firm read many of them with the consent of a member of the Association, but others in that organization interposed and shut off further examination of the documents.[1]

Access to the correspondence is not now permitted.

Mementos less destructible than letters survived Mrs. Harding. A damaging financial exposure was narrowly averted. Ungerleider and Company, the Cleveland brokerage house which had established a successful Washington branch, were obliged to set against their legitimate profits a heavy loss from their most eminent Ohio customer. President Harding died, $180,000 in debt to the firm. He had been speculating under an 'account' name.

The question of what was to be done about the indebtedness was referred to Ungerleider's counsel, Newton D. Baker, Wilson's Secretary of War. He advised that an action would lie against the estate. Before deciding upon that step,

---

[1] Statement to the writer by Ralph H. Graves, one of the Doubleday, Page and Company representatives at the time.

Samuel Ungerleider, the head of the firm, came to Washington to consult a friend who was high in the inner councils of the Democratic Party. This man did not take a partisan but a patriotic view. He urged against any procedure which would bring the presidential speculations into the limelight.

'What you propose to do will create a scandal. It will show up a dead and honored President as having secretly played the market. Consider the effect on the country. You can't do this thing, Sam. If you do, you'll regret it all your life. Try to get the best settlement possible out of the estate, but don't bring it into the open.' [1]

Further, he urged Mr. Ungerleider, if he were called upon to testify before any investigation, to give testimony on this point only in executive (secret) session. This, however, did not develop. Had Harding lived, the matter might well have been brought up. Had he been impeached, it almost certainly would have been.

Mr. Ungerleider debated the problem and decided to take his loss. The compromise arranged with the estate was heavily to his disadvantage; he received approximately $30,000. His honorable patriotism cost him a net $150,000.

The protective mantle was effectively spread. No open publication revealed the President's speculations. The local Ungerleider manager, the ex-secret service man who had acted as Harding's messenger in the Nan Britton affair,[2] swore, when called before a Senate committee, that, to his knowledge, there was no account under a pseudonym or alias in the office.[3] Harding's name was not mentioned. Nevertheless, it was common gossip in financial circles that 'Sam Ungerleider got stuck good and plenty on the White

[1] The details of the arrangement with Ungerleider and Company came to the writer from a gentleman who was a consultant at several of the conferences.

[2] James Sloan, Jr. The nature of Mr. Sloan's activities reflects no discredit upon him. A secret service man, assigned to presidential duty, must obey orders and ask no questions.

[3] *Investigation of the Attorney General.*

House account.' This was coupled with the fact that the firm of Hibbs and Company maintained three admitted accounts under the name of W. W. Spaid. Accounts Nos. 2, 3, and 4 were Jess Smith and Harry Daugherty accounts. No testimony was adduced as to W. W. Spaid Account No. 1. It was the subject of much surmise.

Two exposures were in preparation which added to the 'débris of decency which was the Harding Administration.'[1] Government suppression had successfully dealt with the Chancellor book, attributing negro blood to Harding. But these later publications, far more damaging to his character, were to escape the ban of censorship. The first could have been shut off by legitimate methods.

Nan Britton, Harding's mistress from his Senate days, and mother of his child, applied to the Harding family after his death for help in supporting Elizabeth Ann. 'Daisy' Harding, for a time at least, believed Miss Britton's story. So did most of Harding's intimates. The man who, next to Harry Daugherty, was as close as anyone to the President, was sought out by the reporters when the book appeared in 1927. With an impassive face, he replied to their questions:

'I have no information, and I have no doubts.'

The Harding family rejected the young mother's representations and refused to help her. This is comprehensible. To aid openly would be to confirm Harding's responsibility and taint his memory. Nevertheless, it would seem to have been the part of policy, if not of humanity, to make a financial arrangement which would have precluded publication of the book. The mother made many attempts to obtain help from the Hardings. Only one of them responded and she failed to continue, owing probably to family pressure.

Daisy was the first member of the Harding family to learn the story of Elizabeth Ann's paternity from Nan Britton's

[1] William Allen White: *Masks in a Pageant.*

own lips. She was sympathetic and made many promises to help when she could get her own affairs in shape. During the fall of 1925 and the early part of 1926 she sent her checks for $110, $65, $70, $400, $125, $40, $40, and $40, totalling $890 in all. After hearing the story, Carolyn Harding (Mrs. Votaw) and her husband refused to see Nan and stated to Daisy Harding that they chose not to believe that Elizabeth Ann was Harding's child. In April of 1926, Daisy sent Nan a money order to cover expenses of a trip to Marion. While there, Daisy, Nan, and Doctor George Tryon Harding [1] had a conference in which Nan requested that they set up a $50,000 trust fund for Elizabeth Ann and give her $2500 cash. Doctor Harding questioned Nan for four hours and went over all her letters from Harding and assured her that she would hear from him in the near future. However, she was never able to get anything from him nor secure another interview with him. Daisy Harding also wrote her that she would be able to do nothing further for her, so Elizabeth Ann was sent back to California to be reared by Nan's sister, Elizabeth. [2]

Appearing in 1927, *The President's Daughter* had an instant *succès du scandale*. It titillated the prurient with the frankness of its carnal detail. It shocked the more scrupulous and nauseated the more sensitive of the reading public with its revelations of the White House being used as a love-nest. Though obviously authentic in the main, it exhibits lacunae which, from a legal viewpoint, are damaging to the main contention. This proved disastrous to Miss Britton's cause when she sued for a share in the Harding estate and the jury (Ohio) found no cause for action. [3] The plaintiff failed to produce letters of any significance, or other documents to support her claim. The ever unreliable Gaston B. Means asserts that he stole the letters from the Chicago apartment

[1] President Harding's younger brother.
[2] Nan Britton: *The President's Daughter.*   [3] November, 1931.

where Nan was visiting, under orders from Mrs. Harding.[1] Though few newspapers accepted the advertising — a censorship of good taste — the book's sale was large and immediate, mounting to nearly one hundred thousand copies.

If the dead man's memory had not already been made suspect by repeated exposures in the political field, the more intimate and personal scandal of the Britton narrative might not have been so generally accepted as truth. But by now the Harding reputation was so blown upon that the public was ready to believe anything. Other reflections upon him had been indirect; he was impugned by the sins of his friends; this was a direct and disastrous involvement. Stories of his relations with other women were immediately revived and passed into the common currency of gossip. One story was that the ledger sheets which Harry Daugherty destroyed with that fine, theatrical gesture of loyalty [2] would have betrayed his friend's contributions to Venus in more than one embodiment. From the common talk of club and bar it might have been inferred that Harding's lecheries ran up into the scores.

At first excited, then sickened by repeated revelations, the public by now, both Republicans and Democrats, wanted nothing better than to forget Harding, his friends, his women, his debts, and all his ways. Forgetfulness was not permitted them. Nan Britton kept cropping up in the headlines. There was a divorce action wherein she was innocently involved. There was a libel suit brought by her to clear her character. Her attempts to obtain a settlement from the Harding estate brought further publicity. Worse was to come.

One of the derelicts of the Harding régime was the notori-

---

[1] Miss Britton, who submitted the manuscript of *The President's Daughter* to Boni and Liveright, told the representative, Mr. T. R. Smith, that she had destroyed Harding's love-letters for fear of being charged with blackmail by the Harding family or others, a precaution whose logic Mr. Smith failed to understand. (Statement to writer by Mr. Smith.)

[2] United States *vs.* Daugherty and Miller.

ous Gaston B. Means. He had formed a temporary criminal partnership with Harry Daugherty's old associate in the Morse pardon case, Thomas B. Felder, which resulted in their indictment and Felder's disbarment. But the Department of Justice, which had a grudge case against him for his testimony against Daugherty and Burns, got him first. On a hold-over charge he was tried, convicted of bribery in connection with liquor release permits, and sentenced to Atlanta Penitentiary. He died last year in another federal prison where he was serving a term for defrauding Mrs. Edward B. McLean in connection with fake clues to the Lindbergh kidnapping.

Upon his release from Atlanta he produced an alleged contribution to history. *The Strange Death of President Harding*, which was issued in 1930 under the imprint of the Guild Publishing Company of New York City, is such a tissue of falsehoods as could have emanated only from the distorted brain of that modern Munchausen. Even his collaborator, a lady of pathetic gullibility, repudiated it on discovering that the documents which he promised in substantiation of his 'facts' were imaginary.

If the reader were to believe a small percentage of the statements, hints, innuendoes, and suggestions in Means's opus, it would appear that Jess Smith was murdered, Thomas B. Felder was done away with, John T. King committed suicide, Charles F. Cramer met with foul play, that Means himself, acting in a confidential capacity for Mrs. Harding, procured the evidence of Harding's liaison with Nan Britton and with it faced down the President in the White House, and finally that Mrs. Harding, embittered by her husband's faithlessness and influenced by a clairvoyant, poisoned him and perhaps Doctor Sawyer as well. He cites an alleged conversation between Mrs. Harding and himself. She asks:

'Can I prevent an autopsy?'
'Yes.'

'Can Doctor Harding (the President's brother) order an autopsy?'

'I think not.'

'Warren Harding died in honor.... Had he lived twenty-four hours longer he might have been impeached.... I have not betrayed my country or the party that my husband loved so much. They are saved — I have no regrets — I have fulfilled my destiny.... Mr. Means, there are some things that one tells nobody.... Mr. Means, I have no regrets.... But nothing, *nothing* can impede the carrying out of one's destiny — as that destiny has been decreed.' [1]

And so on, piling up the 'evidence' for a mercy killing; setting forth the theory that the wife killed the husband to save him from disgrace. The very wealth and exactitude of detail, to one who did not know the character of the author, would be convincing.

Here, then, was the composite picture as presented for the contemplation of the public; Warren G. Harding, President of the United States, for whom a whole nation had shed its tears, exposed as a lecher so heedless of the decencies as to use the White House for his assignations, as the associate of crooks, a faithless husband, a recreant lover and negligent father, a stock-market gambler whose debts his heirs in part repudiated, and finally the victim of a murder committed to save him from the logical consequences of his follies and misdeeds. The record seems like a transposition from some medieval history.

The 'folksy' Harding myth was dissipated; the Harding reputation was in tatters.

All this time loyal friends in Ohio and elsewhere were patiently at work on the plan to commit his body finally to a hero's tomb.

[1] Gaston B. Means: *The Strange Death of President Harding.*

★

XXX. *The Strange Burial of President Harding*

Ohio is famous for its clan loyalty. No sooner was its favorite son dead than a movement was initiated to build a suitable memorial in Marion where the body should lie in perpetuity. Money poured in, from large contributions by personal or political admirers to pennies gathered from school children who were taught that Warren G. Harding was an exemplar of the humble American virtues rewarded by a story-book success. Seven hundred thousand dollars accumulated in the treasury of the Harding Memorial Association. With it was erected a tomb, a model of simplicity, dignity, and beauty.

Those malign spirits which haunted Harding's career throughout his life took a final, sardonic fling at him after death. The special committee designated to select the design for the tomb were favorably considering the drawing submitted by the late John Russell Pope, when a belated member came in. He took one look at the model and threw up his hands.

'My God, gentlemen! You aren't going to take this!' he cried.

'Why not?' demanded the chairman.

The late comer set a finger upon the plan.

'Stick a handle on here,' said he, 'and what have you got? A teapot!'

They caught the idea. The Pope entry was dropped without debate. No one wished to perpetuate, no matter how vaguely, the suggestion of Teapot Dome.

Mrs. Harding died in November, 1924. It was decided that she should lie beside her husband. The cornerstone was laid in 1926. July 4, 1927, was selected as an appropriate date for the dedication.

Tradition prescribes that the final resting-place of a dead President be dedicated by the formal eulogy of the incumbent Chief Magistrate. Calvin Coolidge, then in the White House, was Honorary President of the Memorial Association.

Eminent names graced the roster. The active spirit was Hoke Donithen, a fellow townsman of Harding and his admiring friend. Encouraged by the ready response of the nation as represented by the stream of contributions, Mr. Donithen confidently expected that the regular procedure would be carried through without difficulty.

President Harding had died, if not precisely in the odor of sanctity, at least in the atmosphere of respectability and the incense of popularity. Slowly, cumulatively there arose a less fragrant emanation from the decomposition of the Ohio brand of politics, to gather about his memory. Such sinister memorials to his Administration as suicide (Jess Smith and Cramer), crime (Forbes, Miller, Fall), open corruption (Mannington, Means, the Ohio Gang), jury tampering (Sinclair), bribery (Doheny), maladministration (Daugherty and Denby), and the unholy alliance between big money and political expense accounts (Sinclair, Stewart, Blackmer, Hays) were thrusting up, impalpable but potent, to affront the public's sense of decency. Mark Sullivan commented that at the time of his death 'The country thought of Harding as a capable and deserving President who had died mid-term of a worthy administration.' Now he noted that the effect on the country's morale of the piled-up exposures 'was definite, visible, and most damaging.' [1]

None of the items noted above directly impugned the dead man. It could be claimed, and was generally believed in Ohio, that his worst sin was overtrustfulness in his friends. Charity could not thus palliate the liaison with Nan Britton. This was Harding's own misdeed, his individual, inexcusable breach of morals, his single, unshiftable responsibility. Denial of the book's allegations did not convince people; Harding's social repute in Washington, the discrediting of those whom he had chosen for his boon companions, combined to darken the record. A miasma of scandal rose to dim the austere beauty of the tomb.

Once started, a memorial of honor cannot be abandoned without implied dishonor to the dead. But there were times when Harding's best friends were near to despair. Newspapers became chary of the space once generously accorded the project. It was felt that perhaps the easiest and wisest way would be to bury not the body of Harding but his memory; to let it sink quietly into oblivion. The Memorial Association itself was content to wait for the noisome mists to subside. This was no time for a high and solemn canonization.

'It would have been unpleasant,' explained a member to the writer, 'to have Miss Nan Britton and her child turn up at the ceremony,' a view which cannot be impugned as exaggeration.

Between the Britton book and the Means volume, the muddied waters had time to settle. Tentative advances had been made to President Coolidge. That shrewd computer of political values perceived that here was a situation beset

[1] Mark Sullivan: *Our Times*, vol. VI.

with pitfalls. The oration which he was expected to deliver, if a painting in pure and candid white, would be hypocritical; if a critical or even lukewarm appraisal, would alienate votes in hero-worshipping and electorally important Ohio. He wrote a polite letter in which he stalled. In vain did Mr. Donithen use every persuasion which he could bring to bear; the President would not commit himself. He would be glad to talk it over; that is as far as he could be induced to go. There were too many hazards for his canny soul. He did not choose to run the risk.

Upon Hoover's election the committee resumed its hopeful activities. Perhaps he would prove less cautious than his predecessor. A journalistic feeler, bearing the earmarks of Washington inspiration, appeared in the *Columbus Dispatch*, indicating that President Hoover would be glad to attend the memorial services if invited, which, of course, meant that he would deliver the eulogy. Invitation was promptly sent. Thereupon it was discovered that the entire available schedule for the President's summer was made up. No date was open.

President Hoover was in a difficult position, but he was not alone in it. Four members of the Harding Cabinet were on the executive committee of the memorial, President Hoover, and Messrs. Hughes, Mellon, and Daugherty. Calvin Coolidge was practically another Cabinet man, since he had sat in at all meetings. Whether justly or unjustly, the country was now inclined to be critical of the Harding Cabinet on the ground that not one voice of the lot had been raised in criticism or condemnation of the processes of plunder, the accumulations of scandal with which everyone was now familiar. One of them, Daugherty, had been deeply involved. To gather them together now in memory of their dead chief would be to accentuate their past silence at a time when, many public-spirited citizens felt, there should have been frankness and plain speech. It is not surprising that Hoover liked the prospect as little as had his predecessor in office.

E. P. Mellon, himself a member, wrote to the head of the executive committee of the memorial:[1]

'I have just been advised by Secretary Mellon that it has been decided by the President and others interested, including yourself, that no dedication will take place in connection with the Harding Memorial.'

A neat and easy way out. No left-overs of the Harding régime, now in the Hoover Administration, would be required to go on record. No mordant memories would be stirred up. Nor would occasion be afforded for galling newspaper comment upon that long period of silence and inaction on the part of the Best Minds while the most flagrant graft in our national history was piling up its profits. Let the dead past bury its still living shame beside the body of its dead, in decent repression and without oratory or ceremonial.

Someone had slipped. Mr. E. P. Mellon's advices were erroneous. The executive committee had no idea of foregoing a dedication and thus, by implication casting obloquy, however hushed and negative, upon the dead President. The local air crackled with unpleasant attributions applied to people in high places, 'cowards,' 'crawfish,' 'skulkers,' 'renegades,' 'turncoats.' Two of Harding's closest friends, Harry Daugherty and ex-Senator Joseph Frelinghuysen, pressed for action. Frelinghuysen declared that it was the President's duty to assume the leading rôle in the services, but that if he failed to live up to it, he, Frelinghuysen, stood ready to substitute.

The Harding Memorial Association is a peculiarly private, and in some respects a peculiarly secretive body. A widening circle of Ohioans, aroused by official inertia in Washington, was demanding with increasing asperity why the re-

[1] October 7, 1929.

mains of their President still lacked final commitment to posterity, and what the Association was going to do about it. The explanation was to be found in the sheaf of correspondence in the committee's office. But Mr. Donithen felt that he lacked the authority to give this out.

Among the questioners was Robert S. Harper, a young editor on the staff of the *Ohio State Journal*. No particular admirer of Harding, he nevertheless felt, as a native Ohioan, that his state was being discredited in the withholding of the honor due its dead President. Something ought to be done about it. His own paper, never strongly sympathetic to the Harding brand of politics, did not care to stir up discussion. So, giving himself an assignment, Harper took train to Marion and called upon Mr. Hoke Donithen, to present his argument that it was time to remove the lid and explain the wherefore of the years of delay. To this end he desired access to the correspondence between the Association and Presidents Coolidge and Hoover and others. He found the chairman of the executive committee unresponsive.

'The first two or three times I saw him, he just sat and looked at me and said "No." He said, and I knew it to be true, that every great news service in the country and a dozen papers of the metropolitan press had sent men to see him.' [1]

Persistence and patience are the prime virtues of the newspaperman. Mr. Harper refused to be discouraged. Finally Mr. Donithen yielded, but it was in his own peculiar way. A large safe stood against the wall. On the occasion of the last interview, the committee chairman opened it and took out a letter which he handed to the caller. Why, Mr. Harper failed at first to understand, since the contents were quite insignificant. Comprehension dawned when the other consulted his watch and said:

'I find that I must go out for two hours, possibly more.

[1] Letter from Mr. Harper to the writer.

The door of this office locks automatically. No one will disturb you if you find it necessary to make notes of our conversation. Any further questions which are within my authority to answer, I shall be glad to consider if you are still here on my return.'

He went out, leaving the safe open. The caller did not find it necessary to await his return.

'He loved Warren Harding and turned upon the whole executive committee (then committed to the hush-hush policy) to hand over the facts of the stalling that prevented the dedication,' comments Mr. Harper.[1]

The Harper article appeared in the September, 1930, issue of a vigorous and now (unhappily) defunct magazine, *Plain Talk*. It was called 'Harding's Haunted Tomb.' Convincingly documented, it voiced the resentful sentiment of Ohio that until the nation, through its Chief Magistrate, should testify to its respect for the dead President, his uneasy spirit would, indeed, haunt them all, a wraith of appeal and protest.

To Ohio the article was a call to wrath. For official Washington it made unpleasant reading. Newspapers took it up widely. The issue could no longer be dodged. Action or stark repudiation were the alternatives now presented to the Administration. Refusal would be tantamount to disclaiming and disowning the man whom the party of the Administration had elected by an unprecedented majority. Messrs. Harper and Donithen had forced the official hand.

While the decision was still pending, Gaston B. Means contributed his calumnious half truths and whole lies to a situation already sufficiently complicated. But the movement for a national ceremony had gathered too much impetus to be checked. Perhaps, too, the country had become shockproof, anaesthetic to any more scandals.

Nearly eight years after President Harding's death, and

[1] Statement to the writer.

five years after the cornerstone-laying, on June 16, 1931, a convocation of the great again visited Marion to do him honor. Chief Justice Hughes spoke wisely and sympathetically, surprising his audience by telling them that, had Harding recovered, he would have been a doomed man and knew it, with idle invalidism as his best remaining hope of life. Ex-President Coolidge accepted the tomb, on behalf of the American people, in a speech more lifeless and perfunctory than most of its mechanical type.

What President Hoover would say was the subject of chief interest and speculation. In his place Harding would have flung high the banner and scattered riotously the roses of unstinted encomium. Coolidge would have been cautious, formal, conservative, apt at avoidance of the manifold difficulties inherent in overpraise of a career whereof the heritage was a profound national humiliation.

President Hoover's cue was to follow a like safe course. He did not adopt that method. Though he had evaded the event as best he could, when compelled to face it he did not dodge the issue which it presented. His oration was a shock. A Quaker, a man of peace, a practitioner of controlled speech, he chose what many regarded as an inopportune occasion for plain talk. Inappropriate or not, he lent the great and grave weight of presidential authority to a truth which needed expression, as a festering wound needs opening.

First he praised in kind, just, and measured terms what was good in the character and worthy in the achievements of the dead man.

> Those evil spirits, aroused by war, augmented by inestimable losses, deep animosities, the dislocation of industry, the vast unemployment in a world still armed and arming, confronted Warren G. Harding. . . . His was a mind and character fitted for a task where the one transcendent need was the healing quality of gentleness and friendliness.[1]

[1] *Columbus Dispatch*, June 16, 1931.

The Strange Burial of President Harding

Citing Harding's success in restoring prosperity, and his efforts for world adjustment through limitation of armament, he praised him as 'passionately patriotic.' Then he hit out:

> Here was a man whose soul was seared by a great disillusionment. We saw him gradually weaken, not only from physical exhaustion, but also from mental anxiety. Warren Harding had a dim realization that he had been betrayed by a few of the men whom he had believed were his devoted friends. That was the tragedy of the life of Warren Harding.

As he paused, the sibilation of indrawn breaths, the dim rustle which betokens involuntary movement when nerves are tensed, passed through the throng. Below the speaker, in the fourth row, sat and listened Harry M. Daugherty, poker-faced, grim-eyed. His soul was so seared by the presidential words that he went home and hired an ex-novelist [1] to write a book for him, in which he defied Mr. Hoover, taunted him with his endorsement of the criminal, Fall, and stood firm on his own record of never having had anything proved against him.

So turmoil, dissension, and recrimination followed that peace-loving, joy-seeking, and kindly soul, Warren G. Harding, to the last.

Few deaths are unmingled tragedies. Harding's was not. He died in time. Not only was he relieved of a burden at all times beyond his strength, but he escaped an ordeal of accusation and heaped-up blame which must have crushed a soul never too sturdy. Had he remained, as he wistfully desired, a small-city editor, a local magnate, a greeter and conciliator and adjuster by virtue of his amiable nature and talent for friendliness, he would have died, warmly loved

[1] The Reverend Thomas N. Dixon collaborated with Daugherty on *The Inside Story of the Harding Tragedy*. Incidentally, it was his sister, May Dixon Thacker, who wrote *The Strange Death of President Harding* for Gaston B. Means.

and sorely missed in his own environment. As President of the United States, he never wholly lost the public affection which he so craved, which was for him the reward most to be desired from life.

But it is the man, not the President, who is still loved and mourned.

THE END